Expanding the Self

The Intelligent Complex Adaptive Learning System

A New Theory of Adult Learning

by

David Bennet, Alex Bennet and Robert Turner
Mountain Quest Institute

MQIPress (2018)
Frost, West Virginia
ISBN 978-1-949829-22-8

The Knowledge Series

We exist in a new reality, a global world where the individuated power of the mind/brain offers possibilities beyond our imagination. The incompleteness of our knowledge draws us into the pursuit of learning and the exploration of new ideas.

Copyright © 2018 MQIPress. All rights reserved.
In the spirit of collaborative advantage, with attribution, any part of this book may be copied and distributed freely.
To keep MQIPress publishing, donations are welcome.

MQIPress
Frost, West Virginia
303 Mountain Quest Lane, Marlinton, WV 24954
United States of America
Telephone: 304-799-7267

eMail: alex@mountainquestinstitute.com
www.mountainquestinstitute.com
www.mountainquestinn.com
www.MQIPress.com
www.Myst-Art.com

ISBN 978-1-949829-22-8

Graphics by Fleur Flohil

Table of Contents

Table of Contents i
Tables and Figures iii
In Appreciation vi
Preface vii

Section I: CREATING A FOUNDATION 1
Chapter 1: Introduction 2
Chapter 2: Learning from the Inside Out 11
Chapter 3: Foundational Concepts 19

Section II: EXPERIENTIAL LEARNING MODELS 31
Chapter 4: Development of the Experiential Learning Model 32
Chapter 5: Introducing the ICALS Theory and Model 42

Section III: LEARNING AREAS FROM NEUROSCIENCE 51
Chapter 6: The Mind/Brain/Body 52
Chapter 7: The Learning Process 61
Chapter 8: Implementation of Learning (Part I) 68
Chapter 9: Implementation of Learning (Part II) 81
Chapter 10: The Environment 95

Section IV: NEUROSCIENCE FINDINGS 103
Chapter 11: The Concept Mapping Process 104
Chapter 12: (Group 1) The Unconscious, Memory, Emotion 109
Chapter 13: (Group 2) Stress, Creativity, Mirror Neurons, ... 121
         Anticipating the Future, Social Support
Chapter 14: (Group 3) **Lifelong Learning.** Social Interaction,
         Epigenetics, Plasticity, Exercise and Health, Aging 135
Chapter 15: Assessing the Findings 147

Section V: BUILDING THE ICALS THEORY AND MODEL 159
Chapter 16: The Intelligent Complex Adaptive Learning System 160
Chapter 17: The Five Modes of Learning 168

SECTION VI: DISCOVERING THE SELF 187
Chapter 18: The Self 188
Chapter 19: The Mind/Brain/Body Connection 201
Chapter 20: Co-Evolving with the Environment 213
Chapter 21: Self: Music in the Brain 225
Chapter 22: The Self as a Social Learner 239
Chapter 23: Self as the Locus of Change 253

Section VII: A CRESCENDO OF CAPACITY 265
Chapter 24: The Wisdom of Learning 266
Chapter 25: Knowledge and Knowing 281
Chapter 26: Living a New Frame of Reference 293

Glossary 296
Endnotes 305
References 307
Index 326
About Mountain Quest Institute 330
About the Authors 331

Tables and Figures

TABLES

Table 4-1. A brief comparison of pre-ICALS experiential learning models including Dewey, Lewin, Piaget and Kolb (1984).

Table 15-1. The four modes and their subelements and the characteristics of the four enhancement values.

Table 15-2. Potential influence of neuroscience items (Group 1). This table provides an example of the potential influences of the neuroscience items on the sub-elements of the adult experiential learning model. The table summarizes the connections discussed in Chapter 12.

Table 15-3. Potential influence of neuroscience items (Group 2). This table provides an example of the potential influences of the neuroscience items on the sub-elements of the adult experiential learning model. The table summarizes the connections discussed in Chapter 13.

Table 15-4. Potential influence of neuroscience items (Group 3). This table provides an example of the potential influences of the neuroscience items on the sub-elements of the adult experiential learning model. The table summarizes the connections discussed in Chapter 14.

Table 15-5. Items related to the environment.

Table 15-6. Items related to Self.

Table 15-7. Items related to continuous learning.

Table 15-8. Items related to health and exercise.

Table 19-1. My ICALS BrainKnow Toolkit.©

FIGURES

Figure 2-1. Neurons in the mind/brain. The picture above shows a typical neuron and its synaptic connections to the neuron. It has been estimated that the average brain contains 10 billion neuron cells with each neuron connected to about 10,000 other neurons through synapses or small gaps through which neurotransmitters may flow. The pattern of neuron connections, the flow of small electrical impulses through the neuron axons and dendrites, together with the flow of molecules through the synaptic junctions, creates the patterns within the mind/brain.

Figure 2-2. Learning as associative patterning

Figure 3-1. Knowledge (informing) and knowledge (proceeding)

Figure 3-2. The Learning-Knowledge Loop

Figure 5-1. The ICALS Model

Figure 8-1. A nominal graph displaying the relationship between learning capability and level of arousal or stress.

Figure 11-1. The concept map for neuroscience findings, Area 11, Plasticity.

Figure 11-2. A sample relationship concept map for neuroscience findings, Area 7, Anticipating the Future.

Figure 15-1. The expanded Kolb/Zull/Bennet experiential learning model. Built on the combination of Kolb's experiential learning model, Zull's physiological overlay, the environment, including social engagement, and the 13 areas of neuroscience that could enhance experiential learning. Note: This model serves as a stepping stone to the ICALS Model presented in Chapter 4, which brings in the concept of Self.

Figure 16-1. A concept diagram highlighting some interactions among the 13 neuroscience areas and the expanded Kolb/Zull/Bennet model. This highly simplified model illustrates the self-organization and complexity of the human mind/brain/body.

Figure 16-2. The Intelligent Complex Adaptive Learning System (ICALS) Model considering the five modes of learning (Active Experimentation, Concrete Experience, Social Engagement, Reflective Observation and Abstract Conceptualization), the environment, and the overlay of Self.

Figure 17-1. The relationships among the five learning modes with an emphasis on the knowledges that are facilitated.

Figure 18-1. External dimensions and internal knowledge dimensions of Self. Note that the model is counter-intuitive, bounding the external dimensions and putting no limits on internal knowledge dimensions.

Figure 18-2. Continuum of awareness of knowledge source/content.

Figure 18-3. The Seashore Use of Self Model.

Figure 19-1. The life-giving loop of learning and change.

Figure 19-2. Sample screens in ResearchKit-based apps. Open-source. (Pogue, 2015)

Figure 19-3. The optimal level of anxiety/stress facilitates learning.

Figure 20-1. Schematic Diagram for Direct Brain-to-Brain Interface (Rao et al, 2014, used with permission).

Figure 22-1. Social Learning, or the Social Creation of Knowledge.

Figure 23-1. The movement from a focus on value built on trust and respect of people to value built on the relationships of, respect for and resonance with ideas.

Figure 24-1. The growth of knowledge and sharing (a change model used in the US Department of Navy based on the seven levels of consciousness.

Figure 24-2. Conceptual model relating knowledge and consciousness.

Figure 25-1. The eternal loop of knowledge and knowing.

Figure 25-2. Spiritual characteristics and spiritual learning.

Figure 25-3. Developing the concept of knowing.

In Appreciation

There are so many wonderful people we meet along the way whose uniqueness of being in the world challenge our thoughts, and we are so grateful for this diversity. In 2013 we published an in-depth treatment on *Decision-Making in The New Reality: Complexity, Knowledge and Knowing*, which was dedicated to our mentor and friend, Dr. Charles N. Seashore of the Fielding University. This book flows from the continuous stream of sharing that was Charlie, as he was lovingly known to those who learned with him. As we moved through the process of expanding and enhancing Kolb's original Experiential Learning Model, it became clear as neuroscience findings surfaced that it was necessary to add a fifth mode of Social Engagement and that the Self—at the very core of experiential learning—required a larger presence in the model. The Seashore Use of Self Model, introduced in Chapter 17, provides a rich platform for exploring this larger presence. So, Charlie, we now share your wonderful work forward, as we continue to live in a state of grace for the knowing of you.

We would also like to give a very special thanks to our dear friend and co-author Bob Turner, who has spent hours exploring the ICALS Theory and Model, pushing David and Alex with questions that led to many discoveries. And we could not think the thoughts we think and act on them without the day-to-day support of Andrew Dean, our son and the Manager of Mountain Quest, our retreat center situated in the middle of the Allegheny Mountains of West Virginia. The three of us are also grateful to Bob's dear wife, Jane, for her continuous support in so many sustaining ways. A special thanks to our friend and graphic artist, Fleur Flohil, who designed the cover graphic. Finally, our deep appreciation for all those whose lives have touched us, and from whom we have learned as we moved through our professional careers in the government and private sectors and continue our learning from students in university settings around the world.

Consilience is said to broaden one's perspective—and so it may. But it also confuses, challenges, and creates more questions than answers. Meaning and knowledge are uphill, icy roads that strain every step, yet lead to a beautiful vision—and a wonderful journey of learning. We welcome those to come, and thank all past and present researchers who travel these slippery and exciting roads. Wherever we end up, we are the better for the effort.

Preface

Through the past 20 years we have engaged in extensive research—much of it experiential in nature—which has led us to break through life-long perceived limits and shift and expand our beliefs about Life and the world of which we are a part. The advent of self-publishing virtual books has opened the door to sharing this learning. To begin, we offer the following assumptions:

Assumption 1: The Quantum Field, which has many names such as Noosphere or God Field, refers to an unlimited field of possibilities. When things within this field are heading in the same direction, they group together and create a subfield; uniquely different from the infinite field, pursuing a probability, yet pulling along related elements outside that probability. So it is with consciousness; and in this subfield, uniquely different, we become the co-creators of our Self and our life.

Assumption 2: Learning is the creation and application of knowledge, with knowledge considered to be *the capacity (potential or actual) to take effective action in varied and uncertain situations* (Bennet and Bennet, 2004). Knowledge consists of understanding, insights, meaning, intuition, creativity, judgment, and the ability to anticipate the outcome of our actions. A brief treatment of knowledge is included in Chapter 3. (For a more in-depth treatment, see Bennet et al., 2015a).

Assumption 3: Experience is the primary realm for human learning. Learning and knowledge are two aspects of a continuous cycle as we move through life, with learning enabling the creation of knowledge and applied knowledge (effective action) creating the feedback for continuous learning.

Assumption 4: As technology and the complex systems it produces increase at an exponential rate, the magnitude and transfer rate of information is exploding. This information explosion sets the stage for the following hypothesis: World complexity is increasing and, because of this, the continuous creation and application of knowledge and learning is essential for the future welfare of the planet. Complex systems can rarely be understood by analytical thinking or deductive reasoning alone. Therefore, deep knowledge created from effortful practice, the development of intuition and tacit knowledge through experience and continuous learning, and the recognition of and sensitivity to our inner knowing is required. See Chapter 25 on Knowledge and Knowing.

Assumption 5: Human beings and the organizations we create are complex adaptive systems.

A complex adaptive system (CAS) contains many parts that interact with each other. Complex adaptive systems are partially ordered systems that unfold and evolve over time. They are largely self-organizing, learning and adaptive—thus their name.

To survive and thrive, they foster and create new ideas, scan the environment, try new approaches, observe the outcomes, and change the way they operate. To continuously adapt, they must operate in perpetual disequilibrium, which can result in unpredictable behavior. Having nonlinear relationships, the CAS creates global properties that are called emergent because they seem to emerge from the multitude of elements within the system and the relationships among these elements. Examples are life, ecosystems, economies, organizations and cultures.

Assumption 6: The human mind is an associative patterner that is continuously re-creating knowledge for the situation at hand. Knowledge exists in the human brain in the form of stored or expressed neural patterns that may be selected, activated, mixed and/or reflected upon through thought. Incoming information is associated with stored information. From this mixing process, new patterns are created that may represent understanding, meaning and the capacity to anticipate, to various degrees, the outcomes of potential actions. Thus knowledge is context sensitive and situation dependent, with the mind continuously growing, restructuring and creating increased organization (information) and knowledge for the moment at hand.

Assumption 7: We are social creatures who live in an entangled world; our brains are linked together. We are in continuous interaction with those around us, and the brain is continuously changing in response. Over the course of evolution, mechanisms have developed in our brains to enable us to learn through social interactions. Neuroscience findings supporting this assumption are presented in Chapter 14.

Assumption 8: The unconscious mind is multidimensional and has a vast store of tacit knowledge available to us. It has only been in the past few decades that cognitive psychology and neuroscience have begun to seriously explore unconscious mental life. Polanyi felt that tacit knowledge consists of *a range* of conceptual and sensory information and images that could be used to make sense of a situation or event (Hodgkin, 1991; Smith, 2003). We agree. The unconscious mind is incredibly powerful, on the order of more than half a million times more processing speed than the conscious stream of thought. The challenge is to make better use of our tacit knowledge through creating greater connections with the unconscious, building and expanding the resources stored in the unconscious, deepening areas of resonance, and sharing tacit resources.

Assumption 9: There are still vast workings of the human mind and its connections to higher-order energies that we do not understand. The limitations we as humans place on our capacities and capabilities are created from past reference points that have been developed primarily through the rational and logical workings of the mechanical functioning of our mind/brain, an understanding that has come through extensive intellectual effort. Yet, we now recognize that knowledge is a living form of information, tailored by our minds specifically for situations at hand (see *Assumption 4* above). The totality of knowledge can no easier be codified and stored than can our feelings, nor would it be highly beneficial to do so in a changing and uncertain environment. Thus, in this book, given the limitations of our own perceptions and understanding, we consider and explore areas and phenomena that move beyond our paradigms and beliefs regarding learning and knowledge to the larger area of knowing beyond the basic activities of our cognitive functions to consider the energy patterns within which humanity is immersed.

Building on these assumptions, the focus of this book is learning.

Section I, Creating a Foundation, lays the groundwork for understanding the in-depth material in the following sections. We begin with an Introduction, identifying three underlying issues that provide the incentive for this work. In Chapter 2 we introduce an overarching concept that appears throughout this book: learning from the inside out. Chapter 3 provides foundational concepts and their definitions for purposes of this book.

Section II, Experiential Learning Models, is short, but important, laying the groundwork for the expanded experiential learning model that is ICALS. First, we briefly discuss the primary experiential learning models that the ICALS is built upon. Then, taking a systems approach, we introduce the Intelligent Complex Adaptive Learning System (ICALS) Model. The model is detailed later in the book following a literature review of neuroscience findings and the coalescing and weighting of these findings.

Section III, Learning Areas from Neuroscience, is a literature review of a number of areas of neuroscience that have the potential to enhance learning. This section addresses the following areas: The Mind/Brain/Body (Chapter 6), The Learning Process (Chapter 7), Implementation of Learning (Part I) (Chapter 8), Implementation of Learning (Part II) (Chapter 9), and The Environment (Chapter 10).

Section IV, Neuroscience Findings, begins with a short description of the concept mapping process (Chapter 11). Thirteen areas of neuroscience findings are divided into three groups, which are detailed in Chapter 12, Chapter 13 and Chapter 14. This section ends with assessing the findings. Taking to heart neuroscience finding Item 2-J—repetition improves memory recall—each area begins with a brief description of the findings based on the discussion in Chapters 6-10, repeating critical findings, then ends with a breakdown of specific concepts (or items) that relate to the subelements of the four modes of the adult experiential learning model.

Section V, Building the ICALS Theory and Model, delves into the new experiential learning theory and model and the five modes of learning in detail. The three new elements of the expanded theory are Self, the external environment, and a fifth mode (social engagement).

Section VI, Discovering the Self, expands our understanding of Self in terms of its usage in the ICALS theory and model. Chapter 18 builds on the introduction of Self in Chapter 2; Chapter 19 looks at the mind/brain/body connection; Chapter 20 focuses on the co-evolving of Self and the external environment; Chapter 21 presents music and sound as an in-depth example of the impact of the environment on Self; Chapter 22 explores the Self as a social learner; and Chapter 23 provides examples of Self as the focus of change in a social setting.

Section VII, A Crescendo of Capacity, expands our capacity for learning by first exploring the wisdom of learning (Chapter 24), then addressing more fully the concept of knowledge and knowing (Chapter 25), tying this to experiential learning, and Chapter 26 briefly looks towards the future. We do not even begin to suggest that this book provides the answers for the future, for that future is emerging even as we complete the writing of this preface. As we go through life, we run into a wide range of experiences and situations that challenge us with respect to understanding and taking action. What we do propose is that **increasing our appreciation of the power of learning and knowledge** will help us recognize and engage more fully the amazing shifts that are occurring as humanity moves into *a new time of Lightenment*.

Yours in learning, David Bennet, Alex Bennet and Robert Turner

The Drs. Bennet live at the Mountain Quest Institute, situated on a 450-acre farm in the Allegheny Mountains of West Virginia. See www.mountainquestinstitute.com and www.mountainquestinstitute.com Alex and David Bennet may be reached at alex@mountainquestinstitute.com Robert Turner is a long-time friend and colleague who has been involved in developing this theory and model from the onset. He may be reached at turnerrg@hotmail.com

Section I
Creating a Foundation

Experiential learning has been around as long as man ... it is one of the hallmarks of the Earth's action-oriented culture. Thus knowledge—at the very core of what it is to be human—expanded even as civilization emerged. Today global connectedness and collaborative entanglement offer new learning situations in experiential settings, bringing social engagement and the environment into the experiential learning model of Self. It is within this framework that we offer this work.

This section lays the groundwork for understanding the in-depth material in the following sections. We begin with an Introduction, identifying three underlying issues that provide the incentive for this work. In Chapter 2 we introduce an overarching concept that appears throughout this book: learning from the inside out. The three areas of focus are the associative patterning process of the mind/brain, Self in the subject/object relationship, and the power of intent. Chapter 3 provides foundational concepts and definitions for purposes of this book (information, knowledge, learning, the learning-knowledge loop, systems and complexity, and theory).

We invite you to join us in this exciting excursion into the mind/brain of the human, exploring adult learning through the potential offered by neuroscience findings.

Chapter 1
Introduction

We do live in unprecedented times; indeed, turbulent times that can arguably be defined as ushering humanity into a new Golden Age—a new time of "Lightenment"—transcending the limitations of the past and offering the opportunity to embrace new ways of living and learning in a globally and collaboratively entangled connectedness (Bennet & Bennet, 2007a). In this shifting and dynamic environment, life demands accelerated cycles of learning experiences.

Fortunately, we as a humanity are looking more deeply within ourselves to better understand the way our mind/brain operates, the amazing qualities of the body that power our thoughts and feelings, and the reciprocal loops as those thoughts and feelings change our physical structure. This emerging knowledge begs us to relook and rethink what we know about learning, providing a new starting point to expand toward the future. As Bloom (2007, p. 70) describes, "Because of its broad implications for individual and social well-being, there is now a general consensus in the scientific community that the biology of the mind will be to the 21st Century what the biology of the gene has been to the 20th Century."

While various forms of "teaching and education" have been around for centuries, until recently, the state-of-the-art of adult learning was primarily based on cognitive psychology and educational theories developed from the behaviorist approach of observation and experiments. This approach measures behavior, inferring that learning outcomes from behavior (Anderson, 2004; Johnson, 2006). While this has yielded considerable knowledge about learning, it is an outside in, black box approach that provides little understanding of the what, why, and how that goes on inside the mind/brain. This is understandable, since prior to the 1980s there was not much information and knowledge available about how the mind/brain works, much less learns.

> Until recently, the state-of-the-art of adult learning was primarily based on cognitive psychology and educational theories developed from the behaviorist approach of observation and experiments.

Advances in brain measurement techniques at the turn of the century accelerated research in, interest about, and public awareness of, the importance and potential of neuroscience and related fields. All this provides a new science-based understanding of how the individual mind/brain/body learns (Ward, 2006). The result of this new technology has been a significant increase in our understanding of the internal workings of the mind/brain. Although there is still very much that is not known, some of the emerging findings have the potential to significantly enhance adult experiential learning. In addition, there are indications that related fields of inquiry, such as biology and evolutionary psychology, need to be integrated with cognitive psychology and education to advance the art and practice of learning (Blakemore & Frith, 2005; Bloom, 2007; Plotkin, 1994; Zull, 2002).

We increasingly recognize that we are holistic beings, and that the mind is an integrated, biological and complex part of our human system. Accordingly, exploring the intersection of neuroscience and adult learning will contribute significantly to our understanding and implementation of experiential learning. In this regard, it is easy to resonate with E. O. Wilson's work on consilience, the bringing together of two or more disciplines or when two or more inductions drawn from different disciplines come into agreement (Wilson, 1998). It is humans that separate knowledge into different domains, not nature. Observing from a systems perspective, limitations and challenging problems often derive from our inability to rise above the tendency to categorize and specialize in separate disciplines. While disciplines are convenient artificial constructs that may be effective within their boundaries, they may also be limited by their own frames of reference and accepted procedures and practices.

As we move into a quantum frame of reference, recognizing that energy and matter are indefinite and that thought affects energy (Heisenberg, 1949; Planck, 2015), more and more individuals are recognizing that the limitations and boundaries we create close us off from fields of possibilities. This can happen within a discipline as well as across disciplines. An example of such a limitation within a discipline was the dominance of behaviorism on learning research in the 20th century. As David Kolb (1984, p. 2) posits, "In the overeager embrace of the rational, scientific, and technological, our concept of the learning process itself was distorted first by rationalism and later by behaviorism."

By looking across fields, it may be possible to see interactions and possibilities that are not obvious within individual disciplines. Examples in this research are past beliefs regarding adult learning that have been shown to be false through neuroscience findings. In this work we look across fields to enhance understanding and find new ways of achieving objectives. Howard Gardner calls this synthesis, what he considers the ability to knit together information from disparate sources into a coherent whole. Gardner (2006) notes that the Nobel prize-winning physicist Murray Gell-Mann believes that the mind most at a premium in the 21st century will be the mind that can synthesize well. Gardner further states that,

> By looking across fields, it may be possible to see interactions and possibilities that are not obvious within individual disciplines.

> The ability to knit together information from disparate sources into a coherent whole is vital today. The amount of accumulated knowledge is reportedly doubling every two or three years (wisdom presumably accrues more slowly!). Sources of information are vast and disparate, and individuals crave coherence and integration. (Gardner, 2006, p. 46)

REFLECT:
What new ways of learning am I experiencing?
Do I reach out to other disciplines to learn?

Since adults learn primarily through experience after their formal education, the focus of this work is on adult experiential learning, although at the end of this book we expand into the deeper sense of "knowing". The widespread use of experiential learning, particularly outside formal educational systems, and the breadth of experiential learning applications make it an ideal candidate for study.

We use David Kolb's (1984) experiential learning model as a baseline. Kolb's Model is one of the most widely used adult experiential learning theories. As Pickles offers, Kolb's ideas "have had a dramatic impact on the design and development of lifelong learning models" (Pickles, 2007, p. 1). In his introduction to the *Handbook of Experiential Learning*, the editor, Mel Silberman, notes that "David Kolb [1984], the author of the classic text, *Experiential Learning*, summed this concept up with his well-chosen words: *Learning is the process whereby knowledge is created through the transformation of experience*" (Silberman, 2007, p. 3). We agree.

Three underlying issues provide the incentive for this work: first, the increasing demands on knowledge and learning in dealing with uncertainty and complexity in a turbulent world; second, the limits of current adult learning as exemplified by Kolb's experiential model, and third, the recent opportunities offered through neuroscience to enhance current approaches to learning. As an introduction to this rather hefty book, we briefly consider each of these issues below.

Increasing Demands on Knowledge and Learning in a Turbulent World

The increase in world and local dynamics, uncertainty, and complexity is impacting citizens across the globe. As we have moved through the age of information into the age of knowledge, everything moves faster, farther, and gets entangled with other people, societies, and technology. Companies collaborate instantly around the world, people work at home, Internet traffic gets heavier, money moves faster among nations, and organizations move from control oriented to empowered workforces. To operate successfully, individuals and organizations must deal with the increasing speed, unpredictability, and the complexity of the environment. To be effective it is necessary to continuously observe, think about, and develop an intuitive comprehension (knowledge) of the current situation and where it is likely to go.

While some levels of complexity have undoubtedly existed throughout history, the explosion of information, communication speed, and networking has moved the world toward an increasingly complex state. The saying *complexity begets complexity* (Battram, 1996) has proven itself over the past few decades in such examples as the Internet, utility power grids, international finance and market flows (Bennet & Bennet,

2004; Friedman, 2005; Kurzweil, 2005). Complexity builds on complexity because of the competitive nature of the world. As the futurist Peter Schwartz (2003) frames it: "Since the scientific discoveries of the seventeenth century, complexity and turbulence in the world at large have been facts of life, looming larger and larger in people's concerns until today there is hardly anyone unaffected by them" (p. 2). This global trend can be characterized as CUCA, that is, increasing **C**hange, rising **U**ncertainty, growing **C**omplexity, and ubiquitous **A**nxiety (Bennet & Bennet, 2013; 2004).

As an example of the reality of growing anxiety, *Scientific American* reported that 40 million adults in America (13 percent of the population) suffered from some form of anxiety disorder with 26 percent of American adults suffering from some form of mental disorder in any given year. The data were taken from a 2005 survey by the National Institute of Mental Health using guidelines from the official handbook for mental illness, the DSM-IV (*Mental Illness*, 2008).

Ray Kurzweil (2005) proposes that the computational power of supercomputers will equal that of the human brain around 2020, what he calls the *point of singularity*:

> Biological evolution for animals as complex as humans takes tens of thousands of years to make noticeable, albeit small, differences. The entire history of human culture and technological evolution has taken place on that timescale. Yet we are now poised to ascend beyond the fragile and slow creations of biological evolution in a mere several decades. Current progress is on a scale that is a thousand to a million times faster than biological evolution. (p. 94)

Kurzweil (2005) also argued that the computational power (10^{16} computations per second) "required for human brain functional simulation" would be achieved in 2013 (p. 71). While his projection was premature, we are certainly knocking at the door of that power, and this indicates just how fast *the future is accelerating toward us*. It also emphasizes the need for maximizing our learning capacity to deal with CUCA.

Peter Schwartz (2003), a widely published and internationally recognized futurist, suggests ten ways to prepare for this future, two of which are particularly relevant: "Be aware of the competence of your judgment and the level of judgment that new situations require" (p. 232), and, "Place a very high premium on learning. Most failures to adapt are, in effect, failures to learn enough in time about the changing circumstances" (p. 232-233). We interpret Schwartz to mean learning, knowledge and the consequent actions needed to deal with change, uncertainty, and complexity. As things change, old knowledge often becomes outdated.

We will discuss knowledge a great deal in this book because it is not commonly understood in a way that can be applied and studied. We have been researching, studying and writing about knowledge over the past 20 years and have come to believe that the capacity to create, apply and learn from knowledge is one of the most important capacities needed for survival and success in our current and future environment.

REFLECT:
How does increasing environmental complexity affect me?
Do I place a high enough premium on learning?

When uncertainty increases, problem solutions take on a different character. One example would be getting to work in the morning in a large metropolitan area. As traffic increases over the years, traffic jams, accidents, road repairs, and so on can significantly impact time to get to work. Solutions would include leaving home earlier, no meetings scheduled first thing in the morning, identifying alternate routes to work, listening to the radio for information on traffic status, and/or checking your traffic app on your smart phone. In other words, flexibility, adaptability, and a larger systems perspective may be needed, all due to increasing uncertainty.

> As situations become more complex, the nature of learning, knowledge, and action shift.

What today and tomorrow's knowledge workers need to know is very different from the workers in a control-oriented organization within a stable, predictable environment. Employees must increasingly think for themselves and collaborate, and carefully study their environment and its co-evolution, so they can develop an intuitive knowledge to make effective decisions and take the right actions. They use experience, networks of colleagues, and continuous analysis of their environment and organizational objectives to help meet their responsibilities. As situations become more complex, the nature of learning, knowledge, and action shift. In other words, the art and science of learning (creating and applying knowledge) plays a more critical role in successfully maneuvering through an increasingly challenging environment.

Taken together, this knowledge-based world—fueled by a widespread information explosion and accessibility, rapid growth of technology, financial and economic globalization, and the need for expanded capacity and new competencies—creates demands for the continuous creation and acquisition of knowledge, both individual and social (Tan, 2004). CUCA comes down to increased risk and opportunity throughout society and the world. As this risk of rapid change, high uncertainty, and confusing complexity continues to grow, the capacity to learn, understand, decide, and implement effective actions plays a large role in growth and survival (Wilson & Hayes, 2000). This increasing pressure to learn and create knowledge suggests it is time to review current approaches to learning and identify and coalesce neuroscience findings that enhance adult learning and hence adult personal and professional capacities.

Limits of Adult Learning Theory

While a number of theories and models of adult learning have been developed, these theories and models typically emphasize only one aspect of learning: the learner, the process, or the context. For example, Merriam et al. in their chapter on traditional learning theories, provide a summary table that describes the major aspects of each of five theories: behaviorist, humanist, cognitivist, social cognitive, and constructivist. Taken together, these cover the major ideas, assumptions, and applications in the field.

In Kolb's book, after outlining the history of experiential learning and the traditions of the founding giants Dewey, Lewin, and Piaget, Kolb (1984) offered, "Common to all three traditions of experiential learning is the emphasis on development toward a life of purpose and self-direction as the organizing principle for education" (p. 18). This emphasizes the importance of lifelong learning and the need for continuous personal development.

A number of other approaches use experience as a basis for adult learning and in a sense build off of Kolb's work. One example is Mezirow's (2000) transformation theory of learning. Merriam, Caffarella and Baumgartner (2007) note that "Mezirow's theory concerns how adults make sense of their life experiences" (p. 132). Another example is Reg Revans' (1980) action learning which is also experientially related as Marquardt describes, "Action learning builds on the education principles of knowledge; Dewey, Kolb and Mezirow and their emphasis on adult learning, utilitarianism and practicality; learning styles; and transformative learning " (Marquardt, 1999, p. 20). Further, Marsick and Watkins (2001) note that Kolb's theory was related to their study of informal and incidental learning.

> The nature of learning—a complex process—needs to be studied not only through information, memory, and logic, but also through emotions, intuition, judgment, patterning, better use of the unconscious, and creative thinking.

Merriam et al. (2007) also identify a number of specific models that have been developed to aid adults in their learning process. Examples include Andragogy and Self-Directed Learning as well as Transformational Learning, Action Learning, and Experiential Learning. Note that none of these theories or models takes an integrated approach that considers the full learning system, that is, the learner, the learning process, and the context (Merriam et al., 2007). The roles of the unconscious, emotions, memory, epigenetics, health, and exercise are generally ignored.

Since complexity is intractable to causal analysis (Battram, 1996), the nature of learning—a complex process—needs to be studied not only through information, memory, and logic, but also through emotions, intuition, judgment, patterning, better use of the unconscious, and creative thinking (Bennet, 2006; Stacy et al., 2000).

> The emphasis of teaching is often on surface learning, that is, learning that relies primarily on short term memorization—cramming facts, data, concepts and information to pass quizzes and exams…deep learning asks that we create and re-create our own personal understanding. (Chickering et al., 2005, pp. 132-133)

Chickering and his colleagues discovered that in Scotland, Canada, and Australia 90 percent of student learning was surface learning and felt this figure was similar to that in the United States. From a cognitive viewpoint, this suggests that future adults may not have sufficient learning experiences to address problems requiring shallow or deep knowledge (Bennet & Bennet, 2015a).

Other studies support the general shortcomings of adult learning. In a *Business Week* article on the future of work, Mandel (2007) says that the percentage of young people (25 to 29-year-olds) in the U. S. with at least a bachelor's degree has fallen over the past decade, indicating a possible growing gap between what the workforce needs and what the workers can do (Mandel, 2007). Another concern is the current falling behind of the United States in terms of research and development and student learning in science. As the National Research Council (2000) noted

> The sheer magnitude of human knowledge renders its coverage by education an impossibility; rather the goal of education is better conceived as helping students develop the intellectual tools and learning strategies needed to acquire the knowledge that allows people to think productively about history, science and technology, social phenomena, mathematics, and the arts. (p. 5)

There are efforts to mitigate these shortcomings. For example, action research was used by physics teachers in the San Francisco Bay area in a form of collaborative action research called enhanced normal practice (Feldman, 1996). The broad challenge is to improve the learning capacity of all citizens.

As we explore the larger capacities and capabilities of the mind/brain, these shortcomings push us to look beyond our learning paradigms and cognitive approaches to consider the human sense to "know", which will be explored in the final chapters of this book.

Using Neuroscience to Rethink Current Approaches to Learning

While humans have studied the brain since ancient Greece and perhaps before that, neuroscience is a very young field. Although an association of professional scientists known as The Society for Neuroscience was formed in 1970 (Bear et al., 2001), it wasn't until the early 1990s that the field of neuroscience was able to provide much support to adult learning. As introduced in our opening paragraphs, this changed with the development and application of measurement and excitation technology (George, 2007; Ward, 2006). This is detailed below. During the 1990s, the pace of neuroscience was so fast that the U. S. Congress designated it the *Decade of the Brain*.

Spreading beyond traditional academic journals into the popular media, articles concerning new discoveries about how the mind/brain works began regularly weaving their way into such popular publications as *Time, Newsweek,* and *National Geographic.* This was driven by two factors: the increase in discoveries from neuroscience related to findings that could impact individuals, and the rising interest in the public of such discoveries. For example *Scientific American* began a new quarterly publication called *Scientific American MIND: Thought-Ideas-Brain Science.* Topics ranged from nutritional health to aging to mirror neurons to unconscious pattern recognition. This expanding interest sparked dialogues between neuroscientists, educators, and psychologists, even though each discipline—with its own culture, language, and frames of reference—may have some level of difficulty communicating with other fields (Byrnes, 2001).

This intense interest in neuroscience research was reinforced by the creation and sophistication of brain measurement instrumentation such as functional magnetic resonance imaging (fMRI), the electroencephalograph (EEG), and transcranial magnetic stimulation (TMS) (George, 2007; Kurzweil, 2005; Ward, 2006). The fMRI is used for neuroimaging to produce precise measurements of brain structures (Hyman, 2007). EEG is another noninvasive technique that measures the average electrical activity of large populations of neurons (Nicolelis & Chapin, 2007). TMS uses head-mounted wire coils that send very short but strong magnetic pulses directly into specific brain regions that induce low-level electric currents into the brain's neural circuits. This technology is young but appears to be able to "turn on and off particular parts of the human brain" (George, 2007, p. 21).

REFLECT:
How am I expanding my learning capacity?
What resources can I tap to learn more about the mind/brain?

Identifying, mapping, and analyzing the human brain has been raised to a new national priority by the White House. On April 2, 2013, the United States President announced a large-scale innovative initiative to *gain greater insight on how we think, learn and remember and to better understand and treat diseases ranging from autism to schizophrenia.* The President went on to characterize core research which would "...accelerate the development and application of new technologies that will enable researchers to produce dynamic pictures of the brain that show how individual brain cells and complex neural circuits interact at the speed of thought." (National Institutes of Health, 2014, p. 5)

Six scientists had proposed the exploration earlier and, under the White House direction, a set of federal agencies were given the charge to provide initial financing and long-term planning for the program with the aim of promoting a public-private partnership. The ten-year strategic vision was created with the input of a diverse national community of experts, with projects program funding requirements at $400 to $500 million per year. This sort of investment in researching the most complex organism in our known universe is understandable when one considers that in the United States alone Medicare and Medicaid costs of Alzheimer's and other dementias are currently in excess of $150 billion per year.

Below is a brief introduction to The BRAIN Initiative from the program's website at the National Institutes of Health.

The Brain Research through Advancing Innovative Neurotechnologies (BRAIN) Initiative is part of a Presidential focus aimed at revolutionizing our understanding of the human brain. By accelerating the development and application of innovative technologies, researchers will be able to produce a revolutionary new dynamic picture of the brain that, for the first time, shows how individual cells and complex neural circuits interact in both time and space. Long desired by researchers seeking new ways to treat, cure, and even prevent brain disorders, this picture will fill major gaps in our current knowledge and provide unprecedented opportunities for exploring exactly how the brain enables the human body to record, process, utilize, store, and retrieve vast quantities of information, all at the speed of thought. (National Institutes of Health, 2015)

At the same time in Europe, the European Commission launched their own $1.6 billion brain research endeavor. The Human Brain Project (HBR) involves hundreds of researchers from 135 partner institutions in 26 countries. HBR "…aims to build an IT infrastructure to integrate research data from neuroscience and medicine in an effort to understand the human brain by simulation and ultimately to emulate its cognitive capabilities by computational technologies" (HBR, 2015, p. 2). HBR initially has received criticism from the European neuroscience communities that it needs to be more specifically oriented to the neuroscience side of the research. Ironically, from the viewpoint of the learning function of the human brain, Geoffrey Everest Hinton, a British-born cognitive psychologist and a computer scientist noted for his contributions on artificial neural networks, has said "The real problem with that project is they have no clue how to get a large system like that to learn." (Brean, 2014, p. 1)

In brief, the term "mind/brain" connotes the combination of the physiological brain and the patterns of neuron firings and synaptic connections (the mind) that exist in the brain. Knowledge provided by neuroscience, appropriately combined with adult education models or theories, can move our understanding of adult learning beyond "learning from the outside in" to "learning from the inside out", thereby expanding our knowledge about, and implementation of, adult learning. The results of this additional perspective and understanding will provide the guidance and deeper knowledge of learning to adults who desire to increase their capacity for lifelong learning.

With continual research and more powerful technology, neuroscience will be able to significantly contribute to our understanding of the mind/brain/body learning complex. *The sooner we bring neuroscience into the major challenges throughout society—adult learning as an example—the sooner we will understand these challenges and embrace them.* This work takes a well-needed step in that direction.

We begin.

Chapter 2
Learning from the Inside Out

Each and every human being is unique, whether considered from the frame of reference of DNA, experience, culture, family, thought patterns, beliefs, values, or emotions and feelings. At the core of all this difference is the *Self*, with a subjective mind, exploring the world from the inside out, a protagonist ready for action. The mind is the seat of consciousness, enabling awareness of our Self as a knower, as an observer and learner, and as one who takes action. But knowing, observing, learning and taking action are not static, nor is the Self. The perception of Self is a *learned pattern*, beginning early in the journey of individuation and shored up by the subject and object relationship. **We are a verb, not a noun**, continuously associating incoming information with stored patterns, creating and recreating a continuous series of Nows that become our source of thoughts and actions.

> Each and every human being is unique. At the core of all this difference is the Self, with a subjective mind, exploring the world from the inside out, a protagonist ready for action.

The reference to mind inevitably pulls up a vision of the brain. For purposes of this conversation, the **brain** consists of a molecular structure and the fluids that flow within and through this structure. The **mind** is the totality of the *patterns in the brain and throughout the body*, created by neurons and their firings and connections. These patterns encompass all of our thoughts. As used in this book, the term **mind/brain** refers to both the structure and the patterns emerging within the structure (Bennet & Bennet, 2010) *and* throughout the nervous system.

While historically the brain has been presented as the seat of control—and it certainly plays a continuous role in the process of thought—the body-mind acts as an information network with no fixed hierarchy (Pert, 1997). As we interact with life, our neuronal circuitry rewires itself in response to stimulation. Neurons are not bound to each other physically and have the flexibility to repeatedly create, break and recreate relationships with other neurons, the process of plasticity (Figure 2-1).

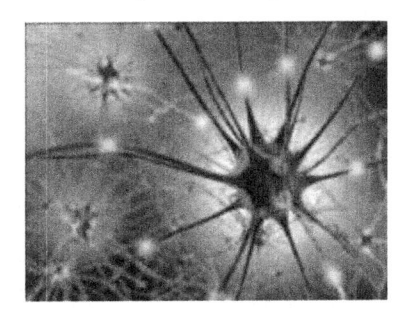

Figure 2-1. *Neurons in the mind/brain.*

The picture above shows a typical neuron and its synaptic connections to the neuron. It has been estimated that the average brain contains 10 billion neuron cells with each neuron connected to about 10,000 other neurons through synapses or small gaps through which neurotransmitters may flow. The pattern of neuron connections, the flow of small electrical impulses through the neuron axons and dendrites, together with the flow of molecules through the synaptic junctions, creates the patterns within the mind/brain.

Neurons exist throughout the body! For example, there are neurons in the spinal cord, the heart, the peripheral nervous system and the gut. While these neurons are largely focused on autonomic functions, that is, automatic activity not under voluntary control of the individual such as the heartbeat, all of these neurons provide sensory feedback to the brain, which affects emotions.

With the understanding that the mind-brain-body are all part of our experiential learning system, we focus below on the concepts of associative patterning, the subject/object relationship, and the power of intent.

Associative Patterning

Very different than a computer, the human mind is uniquely prepared to address and respond to an environment that is continuously shifting and changing, and to context-rich situations and opportunities. Our mind is an associative patterner, engaged in a continuous learning process. Incoming external information (new information) is mixed, or semantically complexed, with internal information, creating new neuronal patterns in the brain that may represent understanding, meaning, and/or the anticipation of the consequences of actions; in other words, information or knowledge that is unconsciously tailored to the situation at hand.

> The human mind is uniquely prepared to address and respond to an environment that is continuously shifting and changing, and to context-rich situations and opportunities.

Let's take a closer look at this process from the inside out. Imagine a 3D snapshot that lasts a tenth of a second. This picture, or pattern, is a part of the sequence of coordinated patterns and an understanding of their relationships that we call consciousness, supported by an associated set of non-conscious coordinated patterns. For example, in this picture I'm simultaneously gardening with one hand, swatting a buzzing fly away from my eye with another, and feeling the warmth of the day and the freshness of the air, while visually catching a glimpse of the blue haze of distant mountains and mentally reflecting on the potential value of a knowledge state. In the truest sense, the mind, considered to be the set of three-dimensional neuronal patterns within the brain, as introduced above, is multidimensional, and we live every moment of our lives multi-tasking.

During that tenth of a second, visual, aural, olfactory, and kinesthetic sensory inputs combine with mental thoughts, emotional feelings and internal patterns to create an internal perception and feeling of external awareness. The firing of networks of neurons creates the internal patterns of the mind that express our awareness of the external world. As a general rule, the human brain processes at a rate of approximately 10^{15} cycles per second. (Kurzweil, 2005, pp. 123-124). While this certainly represents incredible processing power in any terms, there is an even higher number of signals continuously bombarding us, but many of these come in without being recognized. For example, light waves and sound waves outside the range of our sensors.

Aspects of these incoming patterns may cause random firings, form uninteresting patterns, or create a pattern that has historical significance. In the brain, everything is relative, that is, *every individual has their own internal sets of patterns and their associations that enable them to make sense of the world*. Relationships between two patterns are quasi-unique to each individual because (1) the patterns are different in each brain and (2) each of us has built our personal frame of reference from different pattern relationships.

> Every individual has their own internal sets of patterns and their associations that enable them to make sense of the world.

The patterns in the brain are a result of our physiology and differing representations of, and relationships with, the world, some of which are consistent with the external world and others that are only consistent and integrative within the individual. For example, my sense of the color red is consistent with the color related to red when I was a child, but it is not necessarily the same color that another individual related to red as a child. However, if I was inclined toward the study of art, I might learn to discern many variations of red, expanding my previous associations of the term and color. While still associated with red, each variation would be represented in the mind as a unique pattern. So, while over the long-term, thinking/perception may agree with physical reality much of the time, since pattern relationships are built on different sets of experiences and observations, each set is context sensitive and situation dependent. This is why the creation of knowledge is unique to each individual, such that if I try to communicate understanding of a phenomenon it doesn't necessarily mean it will make sense to someone who has a different set of patterns and pattern relationships that represent that understanding.

As we gain experience, we create neurons as well as new synaptic connections. Thus, "Experience creates new synaptic connections among neurons and also alters existing patterns of connections." (Byrnes, 2001, p. 179). For example, if you bring in a new concept, such as the pattern created when you think about the Intelligent Complex Adaptive System Model of organizations (Bennet and Bennet, 2004), it is first associated with other related patterns you have in your mind, experiences and the patterns associated with those experiences. The new pattern focused on the situation at hand is built on these associations, that is, relationships with other patterns already in your mind that provide meaning. If the process of learning and understanding

14 | Expanding the Self

creates sets of patterns (larger patterns made out of smaller patterns), it exists in the mind in relationship to patterns already there and in relationship to new patterns coming in from the external world. See Figure 2-2.

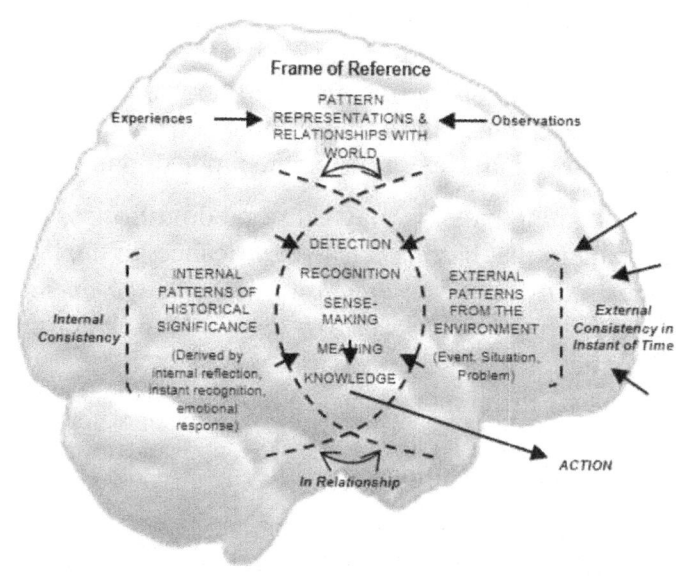

Figure 2-2. *Learning as associative patterning.*

The interpretation and meaning of incoming patterns, then, are very much a function of preexisting patterns in the brain. As Stonier explains, "Meaning ... involves the integration of a message into the internal information environment of the recipient. Such a process creates a new information unit: the combination of the external information, complexed with the information provided by the internal information environment" (Stonier, 1997, p. 157). Knowledge is created by recursive interactions between external information and internal patterns of historical significance. The intermixing of the external patterns with the internal patterns may create recognition, sense-making, meaning, and ultimately knowledge. Figure 2-2 lays out the major aspects of these processes.

The discussion above conjures up a very different perspective of mental health in terms of the physical brain (nutrition), neuron-firing (use it or lose it), and the patterns and pattern of patterns coming in that form the basis of our frame of reference to the world. In regards to these patterns, what does this tell us about reading daily headlines focused on death and destruction, or watching the dearth of horror movies emerging in the market place? Recall that the patterns we take in combine with internal patterns of personal historical significance to form the framework for the way we view the world and interpret future incoming patterns. Thought (in terms of patterns) *does* create our reality, and what we learn is heavily influenced by what we know.

REFLECT:
What significant patterns repeatedly surface in my thinking?
What new patterns would I like to create in my life?

Subject and Object

At the highest level of Self is the perception of separation, with boundaries of Self encompassing a set of physical, mental, emotional and spiritual characteristics and beliefs. (See Chapter 18 on The Self.) A learned pattern, this perception of separation expanded as humankind focused first primarily on the physical strength of the body, then primarily on mental strength, with physical strength still retaining a place of honor. This mental focus flourished in the bedrock of bureaucracy, where knowledge was held close since position and remuneration were highly dependent on that knowledge, i.e., knowledge as power. The Self that was valued, then, was determined in a dualistic fashion, that is, the capabilities of this physical body versus the capabilities of others; the knowledge of this manager versus the illiteracy of others. Intelligence was determined by an IQ test, and competition moved to the fore, determining success in sports, education and business and creating winners and losers.

It wasn't until the latter part of the 20th century that it was generally recognized that emotional intelligence had a great deal to do with success. As was previously believed, emotions could not be left at the door when entering the workplace. Then, it was discovered that emotions have a great deal to do with judgment and decision-making. A few years later the concept of spiritual intelligence emerged, that is, the recognition that our values, beliefs and connections to the larger humanity and the planet are always with us, affecting our day-to-day lives. So today, in our educational and work systems, we have reached a point of recognition of—and focus on—*the holistic and individuated human, each with unique physical, mental, emotional and spiritual characteristics.*

> We have reached a point of recognition of—and focus on—the holistic and individuated human, each with unique physical, mental, emotional and spiritual characteristics.

While the understanding of Self in the "Self-world" distinction has shifted, nonetheless there has been considerable development through the years of the "I-as-subject" concept, with considerable debate around immunity to error as an essential ingredient of being self-conscious in terms of thought and experience (Eilan et al., 1995). For example, the substantive self-consciousness thesis considers the Self as a persisting object with self-consciousness, the recognition of Self, as an object. Gibson (1979) forwarded that the Self and the environment are co-perceived, that is, our perception of Self co-evolves with the perception of the environment as we move from infancy into adulthood.

This awareness of Self as a persisting object (the substantive self-consciousness thesis) supports connecting the Self to the physical body and the perceived boundaries of the body as separate from our environment and other "Self's" within that environment. (Note that the substantive-consciousness thesis does not explain whether the Self as an object is a mental or physical Self.) For the next two paragraphs we will adopt this stance, looking from the viewpoint of the physical Self as an object, which has—and projects—characteristics of mind, emotion and spirit.

As one object in a world of perceived objects, we can now consider the relationship between subject and object (bringing in the "I-as-Subject" Thesis, with "I" as the self-conscious subject of thought (me), which includes experiences producing knowledge that helps build the idea of Self). From the viewpoint of associative patterning, we would say that interactions in the environment have provided incoming information that, when complexed with internal information, produced *new patterns of thoughts and feelings*. These patterns—part of a continuous information stream—produce our ever-changing internal map of Self and the world within which we live. In the brain a network of neurons mimics the structure of the body parts to which they belong and *literally map the body*, creating a virtual surrogate of it, what Damasio (2010) refers to as a neural double.

In brief, neurons are about the body, and this "aboutness," this relentless pointing to the body, is the defining trait of neurons, neuronal circuits, and brains. When the body interacts with its environment, changes occur in the body's sensory organs, such as the eyes, ears, and skin; the brain maps those changes, and thus the world outside the body indirectly acquires some form of representation within the brain.

There is considerable precedence for considering the information processing system of Self as subject. The subject of experiences is linked to the point of view of the Self, that is, a specific way of looking at a field of consciousness. Taking a reductionist approach, this would mean that "perceptual states are conscious just when they are representations from the subject's point of view" (Eilan, et al., 1995).

In literature, as in life, the awareness of events from a specific point of view is in their associations by comparison or contrast. This question of association is a basic and indispensable principle in the description of any system. The process of selection depends on comparison and contrast, similarities and differences. When the "I" as subject perceives the "things" around the "I" as objects, it is through the unconscious lens of association and in comparison to other objects in the environment. The illusion of Self as separate, with boundaries, is what enables this process, with the Self being the observer and the objects outside the Self being that which is observed.

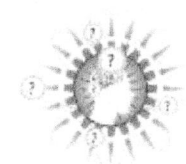

REFLECT:
What learning characteristics are unique to me?
How do my reactions change in different environments?

Damasio forwards that conscious minds begin when Self comes to mind. He describes three distinct steps to achieving Self, starting with the *protoself*, that is, the generation of primordial feelings. The *core Self*, all about action, is the next step, which "unfolds in a sequence of images that describe an object engaging the protoself and modifying that protoself, including its primordial feelings" (Damasio, 2010, p. 24.). The protoself (and its primordial feelings) and the core Self are what constitute the *material me*, the physical me.

The *autobiographical Self* is the final step and includes biographical knowledge that pertains to the past, as well as anticipation of the future. The higher reaches of the autobiographical Self embrace "all aspects of one's social persona ... a 'social me' and a 'spiritual me'" (Damasio, 2010, p. 24). (The autobiographical Self is further detailed in Chapter 9 and Chapter 18.) Note the emphasis on the holistic Self introduced earlier. In addition, the combination of the core and autobiographical selves construct a *knower*, another variety of subjectivity. As will be detailed in Chapter 25 on the relationship of knowing and knowledge, Mulvihill (2003) notes that during the initial processing and linking of information from the different senses, "it becomes clear that there is no thought, memory, or knowledge which is 'objective,' or 'detached' from the personal experience of knowing" (p. 322). While we agree, conscious awareness of the autobiographical Self moves the Self into the position of both the observed and the observer, an expansion of self-conscious awareness, enabling the living of life more fully and increasing our engagement with choice.

In quantum physics there is an Observer Effect, recognition that the act of observing or measuring some parameter changes that parameter, that is, the observer affects the observed reality. This description emerged out of research by the Weizmann Institute of Science noting that, when observed, particles can also behave as waves (Buks et al., 1998). The import of this phenomenon shifts the focal point of the subject/object relationship back to the observer (as subject). This leads us to explore the power of intent.

While this quick treatment is far too thin to do justice to these concepts—and the many related concepts—the intent [pun intended] is to set the stage for looking at the experiential learning process in terms of Self and the social interactions occurring in, and social support coming from, the environment.

The Power of Intention

As early as the hunter-gatherer, we see the beginnings of structure and dedicated efforts to meet objectives through intention, planned action, and individual roles (Bennet & Bennet, 2004). Intention is the source with which we are doing something, the act or instance of mentally and emotionally setting a specific course of action or result, a determination to act in some specific way. Intention includes the purpose and attitude toward the *effect* of one's action, the outcome, with purpose implying having a goal in mind or the determination to achieve something and attitude encompassing loyalty and dedication to achieving that goal.

Intent focuses energy and knowledge; knowledge is the "know how" and intent is the power to focus the knowledge and maintain direction toward a sense of the anticipated future. It may take the form of a declaration (often in the form of action), an assertion, a prayer, a cry for help, a wish, a visualization, a thought or an affirmation.

Perhaps the most in-depth and focused experimentation on the effects of human intention on the properties of materials and what we describe as physical reality has been that pursued for the past 40 years by Dr. William Tiller of Stanford University. Tiller (2007) has demonstrated through repeated experimentation that it is possible to significantly change the properties of physical substance by holding a clear intention to do so. His mind-shifting and potentially world-changing results began with using intent to change the acid/alkaline balance in purified water. The ramifications of this experiment have the potential to impact every aspect of human life.[1]

> Intent may take the form of a declaration, an assertion, a prayer, a cry for help, a wish, a visualization, a thought or an affirmation.

Bennet and Bennet (2004) identify intent as one of the four forces that directly influence an organization's success. This also applies to individuals. These four forces are the force of direction, the force of intent, the force of knowledge and the force of knowing. These forces are aligned when: Direction is set and understood. Intent moves the organization or individual in the desired direction. Knowledge ensures effective actions follow intent and direction. Knowing improves knowledge, bolsters intent, and signals the organization or individual whether the actions and directions are on track. Indeed, these same four forces are at play in the Self, as you will see when we explore the Seashore Use of Self Model in Chapter 18.

It is with the intent of learning that we now move into a focus on, and expansion of, the concept of experiential learning.

Chapter 3
Foundational Concepts

The assumptions, concepts and definitions introduced in the first few chapters of this book help provide a common language to develop, understand and share the expanded experiential learning model that represents our Intelligent Complex Adaptive Learning System. We now consider the relationships between information, knowledge and learning; then take a high-level look at systems and complexity; and briefly discuss the role of theory.

Information

Information and knowledge are concepts that have long histories and multiple interpretations, making it difficult to communicate their meaning, even within a given context. Theoretical biologist Tom Stonier (1997) defined information in the following way:

> Specifically, a system may be said to contain information if such a system exhibits organization. That is, just as mass is a reflection of a system containing matter, and heat is a reflection of a system containing energy, so organization is a reflection of a system containing information. (p. 14)

By organization, Stonier means the *existence of non-random patterns*. From Stonier's perspective, information is a fundamental property of the universe and takes equal status with energy and matter (Stonier, 1990; 1997). Embracing Stonier's work, *we take information to be a measure of the degree of organization expressed by any non-random pattern or set of patterns*. The order within a system is a reflection of the information content of the system. Data, a subset of information, is factual information organized for analyses. In computer science, it is used to describe numerical or other information

> Information is the measure of the degree of organization expressed by any non-random pattern or set of patterns.

represented in a form suitable for processing by computers. The term "data" is also used to represent values derived from scientific experiments (*American Heritage Dictionary*, 2006). While data and information are both patterns, they have no meaning until some organism recognizes and interprets the patterns (Stonier, 1997; Bennet & Bennet, 2008C). Thus information exists in the human brain in the form of stored or expressed neuronal patterns that may be activated and reflected upon through conscious thought.

This interpretation of information offers three advantages. First, it recognizes the foundational nature of the concept and, as such, information becomes a part of all life and the physical world, as we understand it at this time. Second, information is precisely defined such that the definition circumvents the confusion of multiple interpretations. Third, this definition should be applicable to both the natural sciences and the humanities, at least to the extent that where interpretations contradict each other they can be recognized and acknowledged as personal opinion.

Knowledge

Knowledge has an interesting history beginning with Plato and Aristotle up to the present. The early definition forwarded by Plato, which is still used by many people today, is knowledge as justified true belief. In other words if someone believed X, and could justify their belief and demonstrate that X was true, then that person had knowledge of X. For example, if we said that Austin was the capital of Texas and showed it to you on a map to justify the statement, and you went to Austin, Texas, and validated that truly there was an Austin, Texas, then we would both agree we had knowledge of the existence of Austin, Texas. While we do not take issue with the justified true belief approach, and certainly it served humanity well in beginning the conversation around knowledge, we define knowledge in a different manner, such that it represents a more relevant and significantly important concept for the modern age.

As a functional definition, *knowledge is considered the capacity (potential or actual) to take effective action in varied and uncertain situations* (Bennet & Bennet, 2004), a human capacity that may consist of understanding, insights, meaning, intuition, creativity, judgment, and the ability to anticipate the outcome of our actions.

> Knowledge is the capacity (potential or actual) to take effective action in varied and uncertain situations.

Understanding includes the description of the situation and its information content that provides the *who, what, where* and *when*. It involves the frame of reference of the observer, including assumptions and presuppositions. This can be referred to as surface knowledge (Moon, 2004; Bennet & Bennet, 2008c; 2015a). Insight can be described as, "The capacity to discern the true nature of a situation; penetration. The act or outcome of grasping the inward or hidden nature of things or of perceiving in an intuitive manner" (*American Heritage Dictionary*, 2006, p. 906). Meaning is the significance created in the mind/brain of the knower by relating the incoming information of a perceived situation to the current cognitive structures of the learner. Thus meaning can be determined only by the learner and can result from the situation, its history, and/or the implications of the situation as affecting the future (Edelman & Tononi, 2000; Sousa, 2006; Stonier, 1997).

REFLECT:
What are my best sources of insights?
How do I differentiate information and knowledge?

Intuition is the act or faculty of knowing or sensing without the use of rational processes; immediate cognition (*American Heritage Dictionary*, 2006, p. 919). From another perspective, insight is also the result of searching for new relationships between concepts in one domain with those in another domain (Crandall et al., 2006). It creates a recognition and understanding of a problem within the situation, including the how and why of the past and current behavior of the situation. It is often the result of intuition, competence, and the identification of patterns, themes and cue sets (Crandall et al., 2006). Insight may also provide patterns and relationships that will anticipate the future behavior of the situation. Creativity is the emergence of new or original patterns (ideas, concepts, or actions) that "typically have three components: originality, utility and some kind of product" (Andreasen, 2005, p. 17). For clarity, that product would be considered innovation.

As used here, prediction is the anticipation or expectation of solutions to, and the outcomes of, proposed actions on some situation. Prediction does not imply certainty, rather it is the best estimate, expectation, or probability that an individual has for anticipating the outcome of his or her actions. For a complicated situation it may come from identifying and understanding the causal relationships within the situation and their influence in the future. For a complex system it may come from intuition, pattern recognition, creative exploration, or an awareness of approaches to influencing such systems. It could also include past experience with, and an understanding of, complex systems theory and practice (Bennet & Bennet, 2004; 2008a; 2013). An advantage of these definitions of information and knowledge is that their meaning can be applied in terms of the mind/brain and in social communication.

While knowledge has an information component called knowledge (informing), it also has a process component called knowledge (proceeding) that consists of the capacity to put information together in different ways by recalling, selecting, combining, and integrating internal and external information to create and implement effective actions (Bennet & Bennet, 2008e).

> Knowledge has an information (content) component and a process (action) component.

Knowledge (informing) is the *information (or content)* part of knowledge. While this information part of knowledge is still generically information (organized patterns), it is special because of its structure and relationships with other information. Knowledge (informing) consists of information that may represent understanding, meaning, insights, expectations, intuition, theories and principles that support or lead to effective action. When viewed separately this is information even though it *may* lead to effective action. It is considered knowledge when used as *part of the knowledge process*. In this context, the same thought may be information in one situation and knowledge in another situation.

Knowledge (proceeding), represents the *process* and *action* part of knowledge. It is the process of selecting and associating or applying the relevant information, or knowledge (informing), from which specific actions can be identified and implemented, that is, actions that result in some level of anticipated outcome. There is considerable precedent for considering knowledge as a process versus an outcome of some action. For example, Kolb (1984) forwards in his theory of experiential learning that knowledge retrieval, creation and application requires engaging knowledge as a process, *not* a product. Bohm reminds us that "the actuality of knowledge is a living process that is taking place right now" and that we are taking part in this process (Bohm, 1992, p. 64). Note that the process our minds use to find, create and semantically mix the information needed to take effective action is often unconscious and difficult to communicate to someone else; therefore, by definition, the resultant knowledge is tacit.

In Figure 3-1 below, "Justified True Belief" represents the theories, values and beliefs that are generally developed over time and are often tacit. "Justified True Belief" is the definition of knowledge credited to Plato and his dialogues (Fine, 2003). The concept is based on the belief that in order to know a given proposition is true you must not only believe it, but must also have justification for believing it.

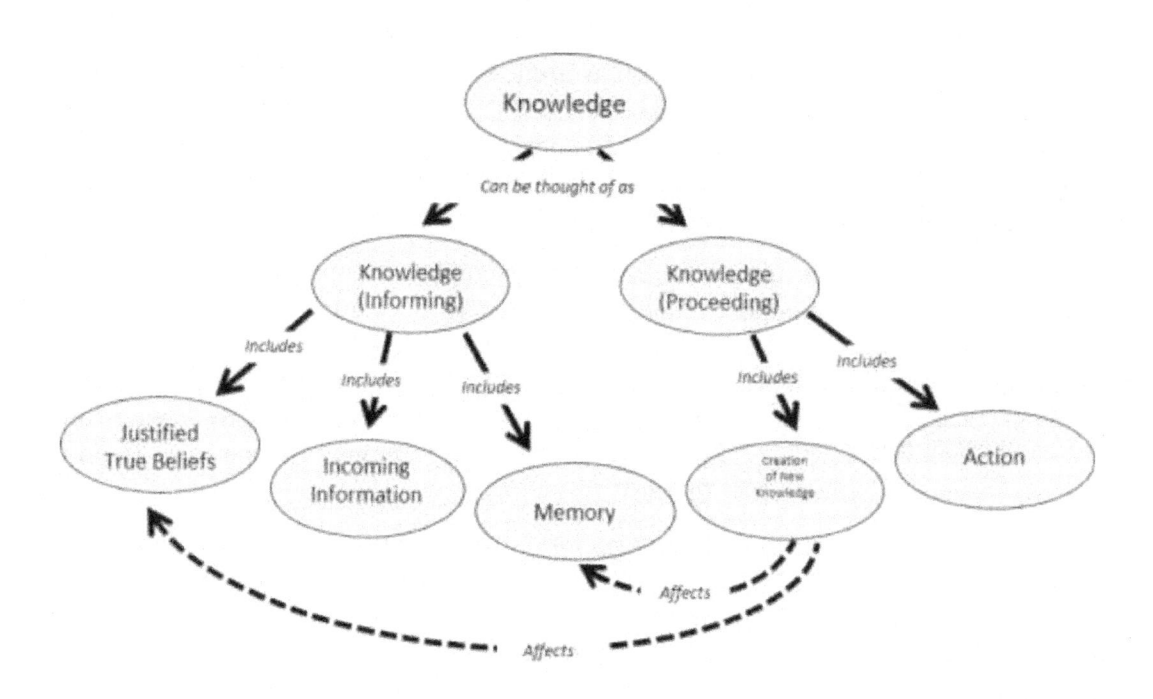

Figure 3-1. *Knowledge (informing) and knowledge (proceeding)*

Note that justified true belief represents an *individual's* truth, that is, whether judging my personal experience or judging the experience of others, the beliefs and values that make up our personal theories, all developed and reinforced by personal life experiences, impact that judgment. Therefore, it is acknowledged that an individual's justified true belief may be based on a falsehood (Gettier, 1963). However, if it is used to take effective action in terms of the user's expectations of outcomes, then *it would be considered knowledge from that individual's viewpoint*. Note that this is only one part of knowledge (informing), and that our beliefs and theories are part of the living process described above (Bohm, 1980). The term "memory" is used as a singular collective and implies all the patterns and connections accessible by the mind occurring before the instant at hand.

As a foundational concept, knowledge (informing) and knowledge (proceeding) will be used throughout this book as a tool for understanding ever-expanding concepts of knowledge about knowledge. Building on the definitions of knowledge (informing) and knowledge (proceeding) introduced above, it is also useful to think about knowledge in terms of three levels: surface, shallow and deep. Recognizing any model is an artificial construct, the focus on three levels (as a continuum) is consistent with a focus on simple, complicated and complex systems (Bennet & Bennet, 2013; 2008a) and appropriate in the context of its initial use with the U.S Department of the Navy (DoN), the first government organization to be named as a Most Admired Knowledge Enterprise for their extensive work in Knowledge Management and organizational learning.

> It is convenient to think about knowledge as having three levels: surface, shallow and deep.

Surface knowledge is predominantly, but not exclusively, simple information (used to take effective action). Answering the question of what, when, where and who, it is primarily explicit, and represents visible choices that require minimum understanding. Surface knowledge in the form of information can be stored in books and computers. Because it has little meaning to improve recall, and few connections to other stored memories, surface knowledge is frequently difficult to remember and easy to forget (Sousa, 2006).

Shallow knowledge includes information that has some depth of understanding, meaning and sense-making. To make meaning requires context, which the individual creates from mixing incoming information with their own internally-stored information, a process of creating knowledge (proceeding). Meaning can be created via logic, analysis, observation, reflection, and even—to some extent—prediction. Shallow knowledge is the realm of social knowledge, and as such this focus on knowledge overlaps with social learning theory (Bennet & Bennet, 2010; 2007a). For example, organizations that embrace the use of teams and communities facilitate the mobilization of both surface and shallow knowledge (context rich) and the creation of new ideas as individuals interact, learn and create new ideas in these groups.

For **deep knowledge,** the decision-maker has developed and integrated many if not all of the following seven components: understanding, meaning, intuition, insight, creativity, judgment, and the ability to anticipate the outcome of our actions. Deep knowledge within a knowledge domain represents the ability to shift our frame of reference as the context and situation shift. Since knowledge (proceeding) must be created in order to know when and how to take effective action, the unconscious plays a large role, with much of deep knowledge being tacit. This is the realm of the expert who has learned to detect patterns and evaluate their importance in anticipating the behavior of situations that are too complex for the conscious mind to understand. During the lengthy period of practice (lived experience) needed to develop deep knowledge in the domain of focus, *experts have developed internal patterns, models, and theories* that guide their knowledge (proceeding) (Bennet & Bennet, 2008c).

Note that all knowledge is both imperfect and incomplete, and context sensitive and situation dependent. The environment within which we live and learn is continuously shifting and changing, what we often describe as CUCA, that is, increasing change, uncertainty, complexity and anxiety. As we co-evolve with this environment, we also are continuously changing, and our knowledge needs are shifting and changing. Further, with the advent of the Internet and global connectivity, information is available to a larger segment of the population, with the result of an exponential rise in new ideas. Thus, it is increasingly difficult to discover and access information that may have a significant impact on an individual's decisions and actions. (See Bennet et al., 2015a). The incompleteness of knowledge that is never perfect serves as an incentive for the continuous human journey of learning and the exploration of new ideas.

Learning

Building on the definition of knowledge, *learning is considered the creation of the capacity (potential or actual) to take effective action, that is, knowledge*. From a neuroscience perspective, this means that learning is the identification, selection and mixing of the relevant neural patterns (information) within the learner's mind with the information from an external situation and its environment to create understanding, meaning and anticipation of the outcomes of selected actions (Bennet & Bennet, 2008e). Each learning experience builds on its predecessor by broadening the sources of knowledge creation and the capacity to create knowledge in different ways. When an individual has deep knowledge, more and more of their learning will continuously build up in the unconscious. In other words, in an area of focus, knowledge begets knowledge. The more that is understood, the more that can be created and understood, relegating more to the unconscious to free the conscious mind to address the instant at hand. The wider the scope of application and feedback, the greater the potential to identify second order patterns, which in the largest aggregate leads to the phenomena of Big Data (Mayer-Schönberger & Cukier, 2013).

> Each learning experience builds on its predecessor by broadening the sources of knowledge creation and the capacity to create knowledge in different ways.

Experiential learning is the process of acquiring new skills, expertise, attitudes and ways of thinking by doing. We can learn from activities, mistakes, consequences and achievements. Action strengthens retention, the motivation to learn and apply what you learn, *and creativity*. **Experience** consists of the "total response of the learner to a situation or event: what the learner thinks, feels, does or concludes at the time or immediately thereafter" (Boud et al., 1994, p. 18). *Experiential learning is the creation and application of information and knowledge through experience*, that is, exposure to people and activities and/or active participation in events over time. (Experience is defined at the beginning of Chapter 4.) The experience may be either primary (through sense experiences) or secondary (mediated experiences) (Jarvis, 2004). We will also consider internal experiences in which an individual reflects on or has an internal dialogue with him/herself that leads to deeper knowledge or creative ideas.

REFLECT:
How do I bring information together to make decisions?
In what areas do I need more deep knowledge?

The Learning-Knowledge Loop

As introduced in the Preface, an underlying assumption for this work is that experience is the primary realm of human learning (*Assumption 2*). We also understand that learning does not occur in isolation, that is, we are social creatures who live in an entangled world (*Assumption 6*). Thus, the Learning-Knowledge loop focuses on the learning environment and begins with experience directly impacting learning while acknowledging that social interaction (social engagement) and thinking (cognitive processes) also directly impact the learning experience, all combining to create knowledge, the capacity to take effective action. Social Engagement and, consistent with Kolb's (1984) model, the modes of Concrete Experience, Reflective Observation, Abstract Conceptualization and Active Experimentation that are part of the experiential learning model, are detailed in Chapter 17.

> The Learning-Knowledge loop focuses on the learning environment and begins with experience directly impacting learning.

Figure 3-2 can be viewed from the framework of the individual Self or an organization. From the viewpoint of Self, we start with the question: What do you think completely determines the performance of an individual on any given day? We propose that the answer is: The actions taken by an individual on any given day determine the performance of that individual on that day. We then ask: What determines the actions an individual takes? This is where knowledge and feelings come into play, both the knowledge and feelings emerging from within the individual (conscious and unconscious cognitive processes) and the knowledge and feelings triggered by the external environment (social interaction and social support). It is knowledge and feelings that influence the perception and effectiveness of the actions that are taken.

Think about all of the relationships and activities that occur on a given day. While these activities often seem minimal in the course of life, over time they completely determine our individuation, the development of Self. From this viewpoint, we can see that daily actions taken may become extremely important for sustainability and the achievement of long-term goals.

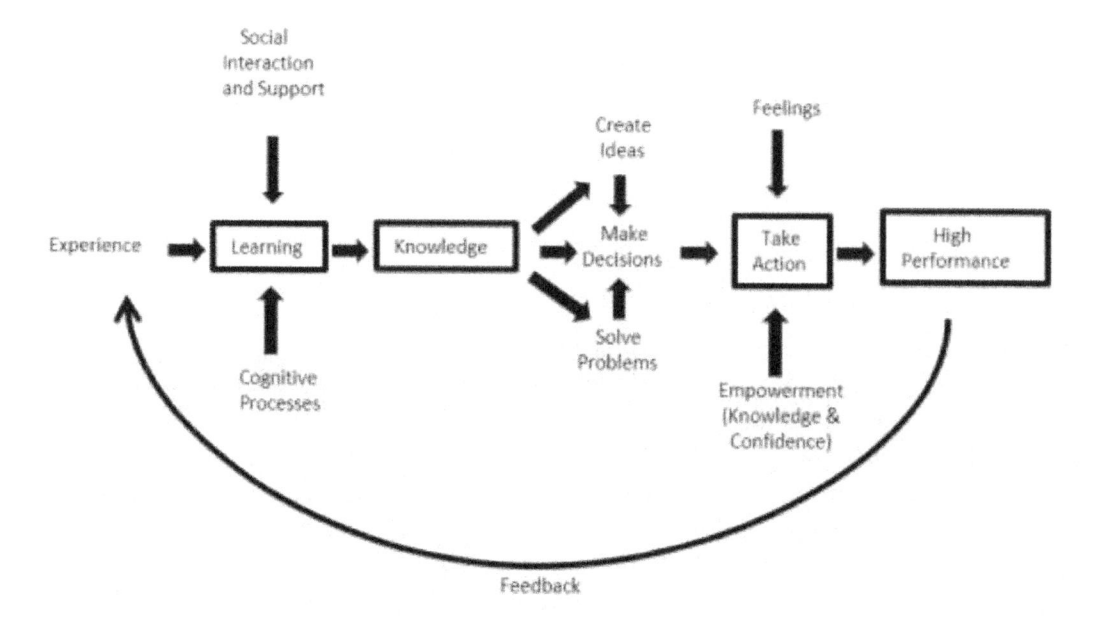

Figure 3-2. *The Learning-Knowledge Loop*

Systems and Complexity

A **system** is a group of elements or objects, the relationships among them, their attributes, and some boundary that allows one to distinguish whether an element is inside or outside the system. **Systems thinking** is a conceptual framework, or body of knowledge and tools, that has been developed over the past 50 years to explore the structure and functions of systems and their patterns of change to enable a better understanding of their behavior and to solve problems more effectively. Miller's work in the late 1970s provided an extensive analysis of living systems in terms of the overall systems perspective, hierarchies, interfaces, and structures (Miller, 1978). In 1991, MIT's Peter Senge published his seminal book *The Fifth Discipline: The Art & Practice of the Learning Organization* that introduced systems thinking to visually and qualitatively understand how system elements interact and affect each other, and how that insight can serve as leverage for change and development (Senge, 1990).

In 1984 the Santa Fe Institute was created to better understand complex systems (or complexity) and, specifically, complex adaptive systems (CAS). The Santa Fe Institute initiated a consilience approach to their study of CAS, developing a consortium of leading researchers in such diverse fields as biology, physics, economics, and management. The Institute defined complexity as,

> ... the condition of the universe which is integrated and yet too rich and varied for us to understand in simple, common mechanistic or linear ways. We can understand many parts of the universe in these ways but the larger and more intricately related phenomena can only be understood by principles and patterns—not in detail. Complexity deals with emergence, innovation, learning and adaptation. (Santa Fe Institute in Battram, 1996, p. 12)

Building on this definition, *we consider complexity as the condition of a system, situation, or organization that is integrated with some degree of order, but has too many elements and relationships to understand in simple analytic or logical ways.* Complex adaptive systems, that is, partially ordered systems that unfold and evolve through time, contain many agents (people) that interact with each other. They are mostly self-organizing, learning, and adaptive (Bennet & Bennet, 2004). Stacy (1996) considers complex adaptive systems as having a large number of people with multiple, non-linear relations that allow the system to learn and adapt. Morowitz and Singer (1995) see complex adaptive systems as involving numerous interesting agents, "where aggregate behaviors are to be understood. Such aggregate behavior is non-linear; hence it cannot simply be derived from summation of individual components behavior" (Morowitz & Singer, 1995, p. 2). As used in this book, *a complex adaptive system is a system composed of a large number of self-organizing components that seek to maximize their own goals, but operate according to rules and in the context of relationships with other components and with the deterministic and inherently unpredictable external world.*

As complex adaptive systems continuously interact with their environment and adapt, they operate at some level of perpetual disequilibrium, which contributes to their unpredictable behavior (Bennet & Bennet, 2004). Having nonlinear relationships, complex adaptive systems create global properties that are called emergent because they emerge from the multitude of elements and their relationships and actions. Axelrod and Cohen (1999) define emergence as a property of a system that its separate parts do not have. The example they point out has to do with consciousness, "no single neuron has consciousness, but the human brain does have consciousness as an emergent property" (Axelrod and Cohen, 1999, p.15). These emergent properties cannot typically be understood through analysis and logic because of the large number of elements and relationships. As Johnson points out, "it wouldn't truly be considered *emergent* until those local interactions resulted in some kind of discernible macro-

> Complex adaptive systems operate at some level of perpetual disequilibrium, which contributes to their unpredictable behavior.

behavior" (Johnson, 2001, p. 19). Examples are Life, ecosystems, economies, organizations, and cultures (Axelrod & Cohen, 1999).

Other potential properties of a complex adaptive system include nonlinearities, feedback loops, time delays, tipping points, power laws, correlations, unpredictability, and butterfly effects (Battram, 1996; Buchanan, 2004; Gell-Mann, 1994; Gladwell, 2000). Simultaneously, the system has multiple connections, relationships, and is often surprise prone. While an in-depth treatment of complexity is beyond the scope of this book, there are ways to influence complex adaptive systems. These include boundary management, absorption, optimum complexity, simplification, sense and respond, amplification, and seeding (Bennet & Bennet, 2008a; 2013). Variety is one measure of complexity and represents the number of possible states that a complex system can have. Variety also represents the number of options or possible actions that an organization has when interacting with its environment.

REFLECT:
What feedback loops help me learn from my experiences?
How can understanding systems help me in my work?

Ashby's law of requisite variety says that for a complex system to survive in a complex environment, it must have a greater variety than its environment in areas that are relevant to the organization's health. "Optimum complexity is that level of variety needed to manage the complexity of the present and deal with the anticipated future level" (Bennet & Bennet, 2004, p. 303). To simplify a complex system is to look at its characteristics and behavior and to separate the unimportant from the critical information, events, or signals. This is where teams, networking, contingency planning, experience, and deep knowledge become essential. The Nobel physicist Murray Gell-Mann proposes that we look at the whole system and then allow potential simplifications to emerge (Gell-Mann, 1994).

> To simplify a complex system is to look at its characteristics and behavior and to separate the unimportant from the critical information, events, or signals.

Boundary management influences what comes in or goes out through the boundary of the system, where it interacts with its environment. Absorption is bringing the complex system into a larger complex system so that the two can intermix, thereby resolving the original issue by dissolving the problem system. Optimum complexity is building the optimum amount of complexity into the implementation strategy to deal with the complexity of the situation.

Simplification reduces uncertainty, but may miss core issues and often creates system backlash, resulting in counterintuitive behavior. Sense and respond is a testing approach where a situation is first observed, then perturbed in some manner, and the response to that perturbation studied to provide a learning process to understand the complex system's behavior. Amplification is an evolutionary approach where a variety of actions are tried to determine which ones succeed, then building upon (amplifying) those that are successful. Seeding is the process of nurturing a complex system through a set of simultaneous actions that move the system in a desired direction.

Theory

A theory, as forwarded by Merriam et al., (2007) is "a set of interrelated concepts that explain some aspect of the field in a parsimonious manner" (p. 79). Knowles gives another perspective of a *theory* as a "comprehensive, coherent, and internally consistent system of ideas about a set of phenomenon" (Knowles et al., 1998, p. 10). Kolb (1984) refers to his work on adult learning both as a theory and as a model. He refers to his diagram as a model of experiential learning, consistent with the definition of model as, "A schematic description of a system, theory, or phenomenon that accounts for its known or inferred properties and may be used for further study on its characteristics" (*American Heritage Dictionary,* 2006, p. 1130). We use the term "model" when referencing Kolb's experiential learning cycle.

Reflecting on the assumptions, concepts and definitions in these early chapters, we begin to recognize the relationships among information, knowledge and learning; complex adaptive systems; and the human mind/brain. We now begin our journey, using new discoveries in neuroscience to expand the experiential model of learning.

Section II
Experiential Learning Models

With the foundation laid, including a few initial concepts that pushed the edges of our thinking (very much in preparation for what is to come), we now briefly take a look at history, focusing on the primary experiential learning models that the Intelligent Complex Adaptive Learning System (ICALS) Model is built upon.

Then, taking a systems approach, we introduce the ICALS Model right here in the front of the book, noting that the justification for this model has not yet been presented, and the detail of this model will not be provided until Section V, following exploration of neuroscience findings. Nonetheless, we share this model now so that as we build it theoretically throughout the book (the *why*) you will have a perspective (the *what*) of where we are going.

Chapter 4
Development of the
Experiential Learning Model

The *American Heritage Dictionary* (2006) defines experience as an apprehension (ability to understand) of an object, thought, or emotion through the senses or mind; an event, or series of events, participated in or lived through. In describing the relationship between *reflective observation* and *experiential learning*, Boud et al. forwards that "experience consists of the total response of a person to a situation or event: what he or she thinks, feels, does and concludes at the time and immediately thereafter" (Boud et al., 1994, p. 18).

Experience is the fundamental way people learn. The term covers much territory, from living in a certain environment to a direct interaction with another person, to a frightening event, to the internal experience of dreaming, meditation, reading or reflecting on action. All of these are ways that information can come to the attention of the mind and thereby interact and influence its thoughts and perceptions of the world. Oakshott (1933) offers that *experience*, "of all the words in the philosophic vocabulary, is the most difficult to manage" (p. 9). Individuals may make sense of their experience in many ways, including discussions with friends, collaboration with colleagues, or through communities of practice (Merriam et al., 2007).

> Experience is the fundamental way people learn.

Lindeman (1961) offers that "the resource of highest value in adult education is the learner's experience" (p. 6). Knowles argues that the role of experience in adult learning is becoming increasingly important, particularly in the professional development arena. He suggests four ways that an adult's experiences affect learning. These are through (a) creating a wider range of individual differences, (b) providing a rich resource for learning, (c) creating biases that can inhibit or shape learning, and (d) providing grounding for the self-identity of adults (Knowles et al., 1998).

Kolb chose to call his model *experiential* learning to tie its intellectual origins to the work of Dewey, Lewin, and Piaget (discussed in detail below) and to emphasize the strong role of experience in the learning process. Putting experience in terms of creating knowledge, Kolb (1984) says that, "Knowledge is continuously derived from and tested out in the experiences of the learner" (p. 21). While Kolb differentiates his model from the rationalists, behaviorists, and other cognitive theories of learning, he posits that experiential learning complements both cognitive and behavioral theories of learning. Cognitive theories give heavy emphasis to abstract symbols and their manipulations and behavioral theories ignore consciousness and subjective experiences in the learning process. In his use of the expression *concrete experience*,

Kolb intends his approach to be a holistic integrating perspective on learning and tends to consider the combination of experience, perception, cognition, and behavior (Kolb, 1984).

Jarvis considers two general situations of experience: mediated and practical. Mediated experience includes conversations, listening to the media or instructor, lectures, debates, group or team discussions, or reading. Information is communicated primarily through words or pictures and, although there is a direct sense experience between the contributors, it is not a direct experience with the phenomenon itself. Practical experience, on the other hand, occurs when there is a direct, undiluted relationship with the phenomenon and the learner. The signals, patterns, and information from the environment come directly into the learner's embodied senses, thereby initiating internal bodily sensations that may be perceived and apprehended by the learner (Jarvis, 2004). Jarvis posits that,

> Many writers have focused on experience as a basis for human learning over the years but it has been Kolb's work that has become its popular focus, although one of his main aims was building a theory based on the thinking of those who preceded him. (2004, p. 92)

Considering that we all live in and through time, Jarvis also suggests that experience is irrevocably related to learning because learning is the process through which people grow and develop. When adults are actively involved with thinking or action, they are typically unconscious of time (Jarvis, 2004, p. 92). This unawareness of time comes very close to Csikszentmihalyi's detailed research on autotelic work experience, what he refers to as a flow state (Csikszentmihalyi, 1990).

REFLECT:
What kind of experiences help me learn?
What is the relationship between experiencing and time?

Historical Beginnings

As introduced above, three individuals played a significant role in laying the foundation upon which Kolb built his model of experiential learning. Kolb (1984) felt strongly about the magnitude of their contribution and while not saying it directly, implied that he, like Isaac Newton, accomplished his work by standing on the shoulders of giants. The three major traditions of experiential learning that provided an intellectual base and practices that shaped and guided the development of his new theory each had their own proponent: John Dewey, Kurt Lewin, and Jean Piaget (Kolb, 1984).

John Dewey. In 1938 Dewey wrote *Experience and Education* to clarify and help resolve the growing separation between his progressive approach and the traditional education of the times. In a nutshell, Dewey (1938/1997) expressed his belief when he said, "I take it that the fundamental unity of the newer philosophy is found in the idea that there is an intimate and necessary relation between the processes of actual experience and education" (1938/1997, pp. 19-20). Dewey's ideas centered on free activity, expression, and the cultivation of individuality, the acquisition of skills through goal attainment, and making the most of present opportunities. Dewey's ideas were meant to meet the changes of the times and needs of lifelong learning (Kolb, 1984). Since then his ideas have found greater acceptance as more adults continue to learn and desire to combine work and study, theory and practice.

Chickering (1977) notes that experiential learning affects higher education. Chickering wrote, "There is no question that issues raised by experiential learning go to the heart of the academic enterprise. Experiential learning leads us to question the assumptions and conventions underlying many of our practices" (pp. 86-87). Thus Dewey's progressive ideas made a significant contribution to the changing educational (and learning) environment and set the stage in the 1980s for a new appreciation of experiential learning (Kolb, 1984).

Kurt Lewin. Lewin's contributions to experiential learning were in the areas of training and organizational development. Lewin, the founder of American social psychology, focused his research on group dynamics, social psychology, and organizational development (Marrow, 1969). By bringing together immediate experience and conceptual models (theory), Lewin realized that learning was best within an environment where there was a dialectic tension and conflict between direct experience and analytic detachment. The concern with theory versus experience continued to exist for decades after Lewin's death in 1947 and was to become a significant part of Kolb's Model (Kolb, 1984). The debate included values and personal experience on one side and behaviorist theories and science-based logical analysis on the other; in one sense it was subjectivism against objectivism, or feelings against thoughts.

Out of this dialectic came the recognition that humanistic values coupled with responsibility and authentic relationships could improve human relationships and the management of organizations. With the help of the research of people like Schein, Schon, Argyris and Bennis, management styles were moved from control (theory X) to theory Y to theory Z (Bennet & Bennet, 2004). Kolb (1984) referred to Lewin's work as having "far-reaching practical significance" (p. 8).

Jean Piaget. The third tradition behind Kolb's research was created by the French psychologist and epistemologist Jean Piaget. Piaget's work centered on the cognitive development processes of children. His focus was on the nature of intelligence and how it evolved during the maturation from young childhood to adolescence. His theory informed how intelligence was shaped by experience. This brought to light the importance of the interaction between the individual and the environment. He also showed that children learn to reason in different stages as they mature from concrete actions tied directly to experience to an iconic stage where understanding is separated from their experiences to where their knowledge is represented in symbols that may be independent of external reality (Kolb, 1984).

A significant result of Piaget's work was a movement for the design of experienced-based educational programs that followed the cognitive development theory from his research. When successfully accomplished, the child took on the role of the discoverer, creating his or her own knowledge and understanding. This was significantly different from surface learning through memorization (what we defined earlier as surface knowledge). The child often started with little understanding; it was the direct experience of the child in the interactive process of learning that created the self-discovery of understanding (Kolb, 1984). Referring to Piaget, Kolb (1984) says that,

> His distinctive contributions to experiential learning are his description of the learning process as a dialectic between assimilating experience into concepts and accommodating concepts to experience, and his work on epistemology—the relationship between the structure of knowledge and how it is learned. (p. 18)

Table 4-1 is a comparison of the primary elements of the models forwarded by Dewey, Lewin, Piaget and Kolb. It also includes the primary elements of Kolb (1984), as well as the Kolb/Zull Model (discussed below).

To summarize, Dewey changed the thinking about education from classical to progressive by bringing the ideas of experience, individuality, and goal attainment into education. Lewin, through his T-groups and group dynamics, highlighted the role of tension between experience and abstract thinking. Piaget discovered the stages of maturation of thinking and the efficacy of tying experience to learning—helping to move learning from information memorization to surface or deep knowledge. While each of these giants in their field had detractors, the combination of their contributions set the stage for Kolb's detailed analysis of the learning process and the important role of experience within that process. This is not to imply that others did not contribute to the intellectual resource that Kolb drew upon for his work. Kolb specifically mentions such men as Carl Rogers, Carl Jung, Fritz Perls, and Abraham Maslow as having created streams of thought (particularly their socio-emotional, therapeutic, and adaptation aspects) that contributed significantly to his research (Kolb, 1984).

> Dewey, Lewin and Piaget set the stage for Kolb's detailed analysis of the learning process and the important role of experience within that process.

Two other individuals helped clarify the dialectic between theory and practice. Paulo Freire and Ivan Illich—with their beliefs that the educational system was primarily one of control—emphasized the distinction between abstract concepts and subjective experience in the educational and political conflicts between maintenance of social order on the one hand and the value of individual freedom and expression on the other (Kolb, 1984). Kolb also saw experiential learning as not being a set of techniques for learning, but rather a way to significantly recreate personal lives and social systems. Torbert (1972) summed up Kolb's viewpoint when he said,

> We must recognize too that the art of organizing through living inquiry—the art of continually exploring beyond pre-constituted universes and continually constructing and enacting universes in concert with others is as yet a publicly undiscovered art. To treat the dilemma of organizing experiential learning on any lesser scale is to doom ourselves to frustration, isolation or failure. (p. 42)

Table 4-1. *A brief comparison of pre-ICALS experiential learning models including Dewey, Lewin, Piaget and Kolb (1984).*

MODEL	PHASES OF MODEL				FOCUS OF MODEL
Dewey's Model of Learning (1938)	Impulse	Observation	Knowledge	Judgment (Repetition of process as an upward spiral, each cycle building on previous cycle	•Brings the ideas of experience, individuality and goal attainment into education •Learning as a dialectic and integrating process •Impulse provides force and ideas give direction to impulse
Lewinian Experiential Learning Model	Concrete experience	Observations and reflections	Formation of abstract concepts and generalizations	Testing implications of concepts in new situations	•Highlights the role of tension between experience and abstract thinking; emphasis on concrete experience to validate and test abstract concepts •Based on feedback processes
Piaget's Model of Learning and Cognitive Development (1970)	Concrete Phenomenalism	Internalized Reflection	Abstract Constructionism	Active Egocentricism	•Intelligent adaptation from a balanced tension between accommodation to experience and assimilation from experience •Stages of maturation of thinking; steps of Learning Cycle AND Life Cycle
Kolb's Model of Experiential Learning (1984)	Concrete Experience (Apprehension)	Reflective Observation (Reflection)	Abstract Conceptualization (Comprehension)	Active Experimentation (Action)	•Builds on and expands models forwarded by Lewin, Dewey and Piaget; detailed analysis of the learning cycle. •Suggests a holistic integrative perspective on learning that combines experience, perception, cognition, and behavior.
Kolb/Zull Model of Experiential Learning	Concrete Experience (sensory and post-sensory part of the brain)	Reflective Observation (temporal integrative cortex)	Abstract Hypothesis (frontal integrative cortex)	Active Experimentation (premotor and motor physiology)	•First formal treatment using learning from neuroscience to expand experiential learning model •Demonstrated the relationships between the modes of thinking and the physiological sections of the human brain.

Kolb's Model of Experiential Learning

In 1984 David Kolb published his foundational book on experiential learning: *Experiential Learning: Experience as the Source of Learning and Development.* In the preface, Kolb (1984) says,

> My purpose in writing this book is to share these rewards through a systematic statement of the theory of experiential learning and its applications to education, work and adult development. (p. xi)

From this we can infer that Kolb's intention was to address learning from experience in all of its forms and situations. It is also significant that Kolb considered his work to be a *theory*, not just a *model*, although he does provide a model as part of the theory and seems to use the two words interchangeably.

Kolb's working definition of learning is "*the process whereby knowledge is created through the transformation of experience*" [Emphasis added] (1984, p. 38). He also proposed that "knowledge results from the combination of grasping experience and transforming it" (p. 41). Thus, learning becomes a fundamental characteristic of complex adaptive systems. Kolb's experiential learning model is similar to the models proposed by Lewin, Dewey, and Piaget. While their terminology is somewhat different and their diagrams differ in style, their functional processes are closely related (Kolb, 1984).

> Kolb's working definition of learning is "the process whereby knowledge is created through the transformation of experience."

Each has its own specific variations but essentially cover the same four modes of the learning process. These are characterized by Kolb as a cycle involving four adaptive modes, namely concrete experience, reflective observation, abstract conceptualization, and active experimentation. The model also contains two distinctive dimensions made up of concrete experience/abstract conceptualization along the vertical axis and active experimentation/reflective observation along the horizontal axis. The learning process derives from the transactions among these four modes and the resolution of the adaptive dialectics between them. Dialectics plays an important role in Kolb's (1984) Model because each pair of opposite modes is considered to be dialectically related. See Chapter 17 for a deeper discussion of the five modes of the Intelligent Complex Adaptive Learning System (ICALS) Model, which builds on the four modes emerging from the work of Dewey, Lewin, Piaget, Kolb and Zull.

REFLECT:
Recall a recent learning experience.
How do these theories help me understand that experience?

Limitations of Kolb's Model

The amount of criticism that has been generated since Kolb's Model was published in 1984 is indicative of its prominence in learning theory. The intent of this section is to provide a representation of this criticism to understand the limitations of the model and potentially how findings in neuroscience enhance areas of learning that were not extensively addressed in Kolb's Model.

In addition to general criticisms of grandiosity, critics of Kolb's experiential learning model include those who have empirical issues and those having theoretical issues. A subset of both groups would be linguistic and conceptual criticisms regarding Kolb's definition of experience.

Atherton (2005), after noting that Kolb provides one of the most useful descriptive models of the adult learning process, goes on to point out that Kolb has a tendency to elevate his model to grandiose theories of life, the universe, and everything. Race (2005), finds Kolb's Model unrealistic, prescriptive and needlessly academic. Hopkins (1993) criticizes Kolb's structural reductionism and failure to account for the process nature of experience.

Another criticism is that the relationship between learning and knowledge is weak and questionable. For example, Jarvis (1987) says that although in his book Kolb discusses the structure of knowledge, he does not explore it in terms of the historical debate within philosophical and social theory. Another critique says that Kolb's Model is a misreading of Lewin, Dewey, and Piaget (Miettinen, 1998). Jarvis (1987) and Tennant (1997) note that empirical support for the model is weak.

> The amount of criticism Kolb's experiential learning model generated is indicative of its prominence in learning theory.

Theoretical criticism focuses on the lack of context in Kolb's learning theory. For example, Anderson (1988) points out that the model takes very little account of various cultural experiences and conditions. Another concern is that there is too much emphasis on the individual and too little on the social and institutional aspects (Holman et al., 1997; Reynolds, 1999). Specifically, Reynolds (1999) argues that the experiential learning theory promotes a primarily individualized perspective at the expense of social and political influences. Holman et al. (1997) draw on Vygotsky's (1978) social learning theory which views individual learning as a process that is inseparable from the social and historical aspects of the learner. They state that this emphasis "decontextualizes" the learning process (Vygotsky, 1978).

Vince notes its lack of consideration for the psychodynamics of learning. Vince has identified a number of drawbacks such as not considering the impact of power relationships like social status, gender, and cultural influence. He says that the theory does not adequately account for the effect of these power relationships on learning, does not take into account the role of the unconscious, and does not consider meta-learning processes such as critical thinking, and so on. Further, Vince (1998) also says that the theory emphasizes reflection on the past too much and does not pay enough attention to the "now" of experience. Similarly, Reynolds (1999) advocates a greater emphasis on reflexivity, emphasizing the role of critical reflection beyond reflective observation. As a point of contrast, Boud et al. (1994) say that Kolb's Model pays insufficient attention to the reflection process.

Another criticism is that the idea of stages or steps does not fit well with how people think (Dewey, 1938/1997; Illeris, 2002; Schon, 1983). Specifically, Illeris (2002) notes that Kolb's learning cycle is an oversimplification of the way people actually think and solve problems. Rather, it is "more that one starts off with what one knows and regards as important or striking, ...and from there one attempts to make progress in a combined acquisition and clarification process" (p. 40). Schon (1983) suggests that people cope by thinking about the elements they think are important in a parallel and somewhat random fashion. From another perspective, one study found that the learning cycle was useful and effective when implemented in a research and development group and that the most effective teams cycled through the four stages several times (Carlsson et al., 1976).

In summary, these criticisms suggest some limitations of Kolb's Model in terms of reductionism, not taking into account the process nature of experience, and social and environmental impacts on experiential learning.

In a **critique of the critics of experiential learning**, Reynolds (1999) says that many of the criticisms are based on what he calls "simplistic reductions of Kolb's work" (p. 539). Kayes (2002) agrees: "Much of the criticism of ELT [experiential learning theory] seems preoccupied with the learning cycle and the concept of learning styles ... such reductionism leads to revisiting old theoretical territory" (p. 141). Further, Kayes (2002) believes that critiques,

> ... fail to preserve the fundamental assumptions of ELT by first, relaxing assumptions about the inherent potential of human beings to learn (i.e., humanism) and second, abandoning the belief that improving human potential lies in problem solving (i.e., pragmatism) ... Much of the current criticisms of ELT are rooted in critical theory and social criticism (e.g., Habermas, Marx). Such theoretical influences are generally in opposition to the pragmatic-humanism suggested by the likes of Dewey and Maslow. Thus, much of the criticism of ELT arises from fundamentally different assumptions. (p. 142)

In spite of all of the criticisms of Kolb's theory, as Tennant (1997, p. 92) states, "... the model provides an excellent framework for planning, teaching, and learning activities and it can be usefully employed as a guide for understanding learning difficulties, vocational counseling, and academic advising and so on."

Considering the focus of this research and the concerns from Vince (1998) that Kolb's Model does not take into account the role of the unconscious and does not consider meta-learning processes, this book includes topics such as the unconscious, memory, stress, exercise, aging, mirror neurons, and anticipating the outcome of actions. Additionally, the criticism that Kolb's Model is an oversimplification of the way people think (Illeris, 2002) and that it does not fit with the way people think (Dewey, 1938/1997; Illeris, 2002; Schon, 1983); this book includes discussions of topics such as creativity and Stonier's concept of information (see Chapter 3).

Some learning researchers have taken the position that "all learning is experiential learning" (Moon, 2004, p. 1). While all learning may involve some type of experience, Kolb's concrete experience is only one type of experience. Note that the dictionary definition of concrete is "an actual or specific thing or instance, something that exists in reality and is perceptible by the senses" (*American Heritage Dictionary*, 2006, p. 485).

The Kolb/Zull Experiential Learning Model

As our technology advanced and a deeper exploration of the mind/brain became a reality, there have been expressed concerns related to experiential learning and the role of neuroscience in learning. For example, Merriam et al. (2007) offer that, "Connecting what we know about the brain and related systems to learning in adulthood is at best a set of working hypotheses" (p. 416).

The first formal treatment using learning from neuroscience to expand on Kolb's experiential learning model was forwarded by biologist Dr. Michael Kull who suggests a related view of the human brain. The learning cycle arises naturally from the structure of the brain. The superposition of Zull's Model demonstrates the relationships between the modes of thinking from Kolb and the physiological sections of the human brain from Zull. The sensory, and post-sensory part of the brain relate directly to the incoming information from concrete experience. This would include all methods of sensing the external world. Reflective observation, or reflection occurs in the temporal integrating cortex or what is often called the back cortex. Although it does not lie physically in the back of the brain, it is the back of the cortex. This is because the cortex folds in on itself as the adolescent develops. The temporal integrating cortex is where incoming experience is reflected upon and the various incoming signals are combined to form an integrated representation of external reality. Reflection on this re-presentation begins the process of understanding and meaning.

> The learning cycle arises naturally from the structure of the brain.

The frontal integrative cortex relates to what Zull calls abstract hypothesis and Kolb calls abstract conceptualization or comprehension. The frontal integrative cortex is also referred to as the prefrontal cortex. It is here that the mind creates a deeper knowledge or understanding and additional insights related to the incoming concrete experience. This prefrontal cortex also looks for ways of influencing the external situation as a guide to what action will have the most effective outcomes. This area is what Goldberg (2001) calls the executive part of the brain. Zull also points out the relationship between active experimentation and the premotor and motor physiology.

Here is where the body initiates the execution of actions determined by the prefrontal cortex through comprehension and higher-level thinking.

In summary and as Zull explains, "Concrete experience comes through the sensory cortex, reflective observation involves the integrative cortex at the back, creating new abstract concepts occurs in the frontal integrative cortex, and active testing involves the motor brain" (Zull, 2002, pp. 18-19).

The Kolb Model of experiential learning—built on the work of Dewey, Lewin and Piaget—and the Zull overlay provided the baseline for development of the **Intelligent Complex Adaptive Learning System** Model, which is the subject of this book.

Chapter 5
Introducing the ICALS Theory and Model

To date Kolb's theory of adult learning, first published in 1984, is still arguably the major experiential learning theory and model broadly available. However, its approach is primarily that of cognitive psychology, and as such it does not directly address the environment, social engagement (social support and interactions), or the role of the unconscious, emotions, and plasticity. What is needed is an updated theory of learning that integrates neuroscience findings with many aspects of Kolb's theory, including the four modes of learning, while providing insights and guidance to learners desiring to understand meta-learning to make their learning more efficient, effective, and sustainable.

It would seem likely that such a theory would be guided by a conceptual framework. Huberman and Mile's propose that a conceptual framework "explains, either graphically or in narrative form, the main things to be studied—the key factors, concepts, or variables—and the presumed relationships among them" (Miles & Huberman, 1994, p. 18). We propose that the conceptual framework underpinning the ICALS Theory take into account the following: *consilience, epistemology (a grounded definition of information and knowledge), constructivism, and learning as a complex adaptive system.*

Consilience represents the issues and advantages of bringing several fields of study together to create a deeper understanding and more effective application; in this instance, the intersection of neuroscience and experiential learning. *By building clear definitions of information and knowledge we can see how information and knowledge relate to each other, and how they relate to neuroscience and experiential learning.* The purpose of this theory is to improve adult experiential learning, that is, the acquisition of information and the creation and application of knowledge: the capacity to take effective action in varied and uncertain situations. Constructivism provides the grounding for the ICALS theoretical

> The conceptual framework underpinning the ICALS theory is built on four foundational constructs: consilience, epistemology, constructivism and complex adaptive systems.

approach to experiential learning. Constructivists take the position that meaning is constructed by the mind and not through procedures (activities). Adults learn from a whole range of approaches such as listening, concrete experience, dialogue, intuition, feelings, and insights (Mezirow, 2000).

By taking a systems perspective and considering both the learner and the learning process as a self-organizing Intelligent Complex Adaptive Learning Systems (ICALS) embedded within a complex adaptive environment, we can include both the interactions between the individual and his or her environment and the internal interactions within the individual's mind/brain/body. However, this begs the question:

What is the appropriate level of inquiry to best address this system? To take a top-down approach would mean studying the entire mind/brain/body of the learner from a high-level perspective such as behavior and thinking processes to infer what is happening within the brain. This is the area of cognitive psychology and serves well as the framework for Kolb's experiential learning modes. However, from the neuroscience perspective, such an approach would not work because one cannot deduce what is happening within the mind/brain by using only outside observations. On the other hand, observing an individual neuron's behavior, including the behavior of groups of neurons, does not explain how such behavior leads to understanding or meaning. Thus we take a mid-level approach and look at the major physiological subsystems that may impact the learning process, identifying their relevant holistic characteristics and considering them in regard to their potential ability to enhance experiential learning at the individual level. Keep in mind that the brain is primarily driven from the inside. Buzsaki (2006), in his book *Rhythms of the Brain* takes a strong stand when he posits that,

> The brain is perpetually active, even in the absence of environmental and body-derived stimuli. In fact, a main argument put forward in this book is that most of the brains activity is generated from within, and perturbation of this default pattern by external inputs at any given time often causes only a minor departure from its robust internally controlled program. (pp. 10-11)

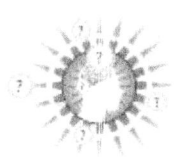

REFLECT:
How does "how I think" inform "what I think"?
What is the connection between neuroscience and learning?

The ICALS Model

As introduced in Chapter 2 and further detailed in Chapter 18, the elements of Self offer potential contribution to the experiential learning process. Additionally, Self cannot be separated from any of the five modes in the ICALS Model, which suggests that the idea of Self be inserted at the very center of the model. See Figure 5-1 below.

The four boxes circled around Self represent Kolb's original four modes of learning, built on the work of Dewey, Lewin and Piaget. Kolb's learning cycle starts with concrete experience, passing through reflective observation, then abstract conceptualization, and finally active experimentation. Although the sequence appears clean, it was recognized by Kolb that as learning occurs a learner experiences many direct connections between and among all of these modes. The larger circle moves from Active Experimentation to Social Engagement to Reflective Observation, with a direct interactive link with Concrete Experience. This brings the importance of social

44 | Expanding the Self

learning into the experiential learning model. See Chapter 17 for a detailed treatment of the five modes in the ICALS Model.

Further, while Kolb recognized the influence of the environment on internal learning, as will be seen in our learning from neuroscience, the environment is actively engaged in the learning process. At the top level of the model, the addition of Self as an underlying foundation and acknowledgement of the role of the environment in the learning process—and adding Social Engagement (including both social interaction and social support) as a fifth mode of learning—fully reflects the findings from neuroscience.

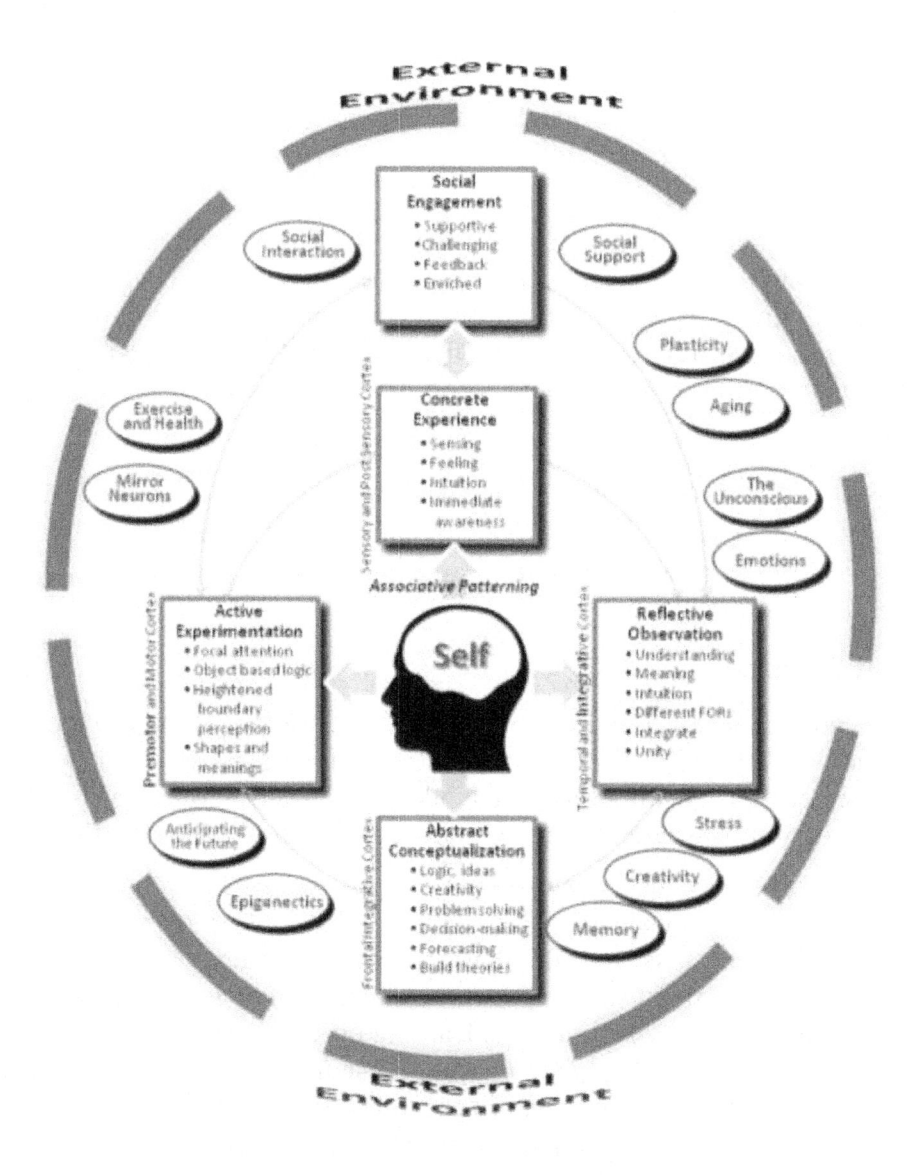

Figure 5.1. *The ICALS Model.*

Characteristics of the ICALS Model

Kolb forwarded five major characteristics that were essential to the Kolb Experiential Learning Model (Kolb, 1984): (1) Learning is best conceived as a process, not in terms of outcomes; (2) Learning is a continuous process grounded in experience; (3) The process of learning requires the resolution of conflicts between dialectically opposed modes of adaptation to the world; (4) Learning is a holistic process of adaptation to the world; and (5) Learning invokes transactions between the person and the environment.

The ICALS Model is consistent with Kolb's characteristics (1) and (4). Characteristics (2) and (5) have been expanded to include the human capacity to dialogue with one's Self. See the descriptions below. Kolb's characteristic (3), asserting that the process of learning requires the resolution of conflicts between dialectically opposed modes of adaptation to the world, is neither supported nor unsupported by the ICALS approach. Although there are different ways of viewing the world and different philosophies relative to modes of adaptation to the world, looking from a neuroscience perspective, we find nothing that would support Kolb's belief that the modes of thought were dialectically opposed, although they certainly *may* be different ways of thinking. For example, considering the past-present timeframe of the reflection mode and the present-future perspective of the comprehension mode, these two modes would appear to be more complementary than dialectically opposed.

> The ICALS Model includes a fifth mode, that of *social engagement*, and brings in the process of associative patterning, which supports all five modes from the viewpoint of Self.

Further, the ICALS Model includes a fifth mode, that of *social engagement*, and brings in the process of associative patterning, which supports all five modes from the viewpoint of Self. These processes certainly work in tandem with the original four modes and, since all knowledge is context sensitive and situation dependent (Bennet & Bennet, 2007a), may or may not affirm Kolb's belief that learning requires the resolution of conflicts between dialectically opposed modes of adaptation to the world. Accordingly, Kolb's characteristic (3) is not considered a characteristic of the ICALS Model.

An additional characteristic essential to the ICALS Model is: Learning is a self-organizing system. This is included as characteristic (5) below. Considering all of these changes, here are five major characteristics essential to the ICALS Theory and Model:

1. Learning is Best Conceived as a Process, not in Terms of Outcomes. That learning is a *process* is emphasized in Kolb's Model to differentiate it from the behavioral theory of learning and the idealist approach to education, both of which consider learning to be a product or outcome, not a process. Their epistemology derives from the concept that there are "mental atoms" or simple ideas that are constant and their combinations create patterns of thought (Kolb, 1984). Kolb's Model takes learning to be the result of a potentially complex process made up of the interactions of four modes, two that represent knowledge and two that create knowledge through transformation.

This is consistent with the ICALS Theory as seen from a neuroscientific view of the mind/brain and the associative patterning process (Chapter 2), that is, recognition that knowledge, context sensitive and situation dependent, is being recreated for the instant at hand, thus continuously shifting and changing in response to new associations and influences of the environment. Recall that learning is the process of creating knowledge, that is, the process of creating the capacity (potential or actual) to take effective action (Chapter 3), part of a continuing journey toward intelligent activity (Bennet et al., 2015a).

2. Learning is a Continuous Process that is either Grounded in Experience or an Emergent Property of Consciousness. This builds on characteristics 1 above. Knowledge is continuously developed from and tested in the experiences of the learner (the associative patterning process introduced in Chapter 2). New ideas emerge from this combining/associating of incoming information from the environment with internally stored information (Bennet & Bennet, 2008e).

Consciousness is a process, a sequential set of ideas, thoughts, images, feelings and perceptions and an understanding of the connections and relationships among them (Bennet, 2001). It is the sum total of who we are, what we believe, how we act and the things we do, so it's all of our actions, thoughts and words (Dunning, 2014). William James (1890/1980) was amazed at the continuity of human consciousness. Dewey noted that, "the principle of continuity of experience means that every experience both takes up something from those which have gone before and modifies in some way the quality of those which come after" (Dewey, 1938/1979, pp. 35-44 in Kolb, 1984, p. 27).

We agree that a significant contribution to learning occurs through concrete experience. However, another way of learning is through internal dialogue with oneself. As will be detailed in Chapter 12, important parts of the mind/brain such as the unconscious, the emotions and the memory systems play a strong role in creating knowledge. There are useful techniques for the conscious mind to interact and communicate with the unconscious, the emotions, and memory without immediate input from concrete experience. For example, artists, writers, and theoretical scientists do not necessarily require continuous concrete experience to enhance their learning. Gedanken experiments can create new ideas and knowledge.

While having a dialogue with one's Self might be characterized as an "experience", this is not the intent of the descriptor of concrete experience. Therefore, we have expanded Kolb's original characteristic to include the learning occurring through self-dialogue, an emergent property of consciousness.

3. Learning is a Holistic Process of Adaptation to the World (formerly Kolb's fourth characteristic). Experiential learning is a holistic concept that represents the major process of human adaptation to the social and physical world. Kolb's learning model is holistic in the sense that learning and the knowledge it creates emerge from the interplay and interaction of the four modes. Experiential learning also includes such adaptive concepts as creativity, problem solving, decision-making, and attitude change (Kolb, 1984). Learning is also holistic in that it exists in all individual and social environments and encompasses all ages of life.

By holistic Kolb means that learning "seeks to describe the emergence of basic life orientations as a function of dialectic tensions between modes of relating to the world" (Kolb, 1984, p. 31). This seems to be partially correct, but it neglects the actions that the learner can implement that can influence the world. Modern complexity theory considers co-evolution and autopoietic interactions as normal evolutionary processes of interacting complex systems.

While the underlying neuroscience findings on which the ICALS Model is built reinforces Kolb's acceptance of learning as a holistic process relative to basic life orientation, we take the position that this is due to the *complementarity* of the reflective observation and abstract conceptualization modes instead of their dialectic tension. Further, this work broadens the system to include the learner (Self), the external environment, and a fifth learning mode of social engagement, collectively viewed as a complex adaptive learning system.

4. Learning Invokes Transactions Between the Person and Internal and External Environments. This is an expansion of the former characteristic (5) forwarded by Kolb. As Kolb (1984) says, "The casual observer of the traditional educational process would undoubtedly conclude that learning was primarily a personal, internal process requiring only the limited environment of books, teacher, and classroom" (p. 34). In his experiential learning model Kolb emphasizes that experience is both personal and internal, and social and externally driven. Kolb's use of the word *transaction* has a special denotation; he means a fluid, interpenetrating relationship between the person and the environment such that when they become related, both are changed (Kolb, 1984). This is very similar to the autopoiesis concept proposed by Maturana and Varela (1987) in their theory of coevolving complex adaptive systems. The grasping or creating of figurative representations of that experience through apprehension and comprehension, coupled with the transformation of those representations through reflection and active experimentation, create understanding, meaning, insight, creativity, intuition, and the ability to anticipate the outcome of one's actions, that is, knowledge (the capacity to take effective action).

As in characteristic (2) above, we agree with Kolb as far as concrete experience and action are concerned. However, this is not so clear when one considers learning being generated between the conscious and unconscious mind. For example, recall Poincare's statement relative to the volleyball effect during the creative process in which thoughts and concepts are continually passed between the conscious and the unconscious mind resulting in new ideas, that is, learning (cited in Andreasen, 2005). Further, there is a sense of knowing that emerges from the unconscious that may or may not be linked to the external environment, although it certainly emerges from the internal environment of Self. See Chapter 25 for a deeper treatment of knowing.

5. Learning is a Self-Organizing System. Envision a situation where the individual learner and the environment are mutually interacting and adapting to each other. Adaptive implies that the system is capable of studying and analyzing the environment and taking actions that internally adjust the system and externally influence the environment in a manner that allows the system to fulfill local and higher-level goals. This is the process of co-evolving with our environment such that an individual moves in a desired direction or towards a desired goal. A complex adaptive system that is self-producing (or self-preserving) is referred to as an autopoietic system (Maturana & Varela, 1987; Battram, 1996; von Krogh & Roos, 1995).

In the context of a learning system, self-producing means that as learners create and adjust their internal patterns (thoughts, concepts, beliefs) in response to incoming information, they will maintain, modify, or enhance their concepts of Self and individuality. In the process of reflecting and comprehending in response to the external world, the learner undergoes changes in both brain patterns and neural architecture, what is called neuroplasticity. The creation of these new patterns (learning) represents an emergent phenomenon (information and knowledge) that results from numerous internal pattern associations. There are many interactions and a high level of communication among the various patterns, neurons, and chemicals of the mind/brain/body of the learner. For example, mind patterns are continuously associated with one another, the emotional system tags all incoming information at some level, and thoughts and ideas bounce back and forth between the prefrontal cortex and the integrated cortex (Zull, 2002).

This attribute of learning will be further explored in Chapter 12.

REFLECT:
What role does social networking play in my life?
Do I consciously self-organize my learning experiences?

In Summary ...

The Intelligent Complex Adaptive Learning System takes into account the following aspects of the mind/brain/body: the self-organizing complex adaptive behavior; the fundamental neuroscientific subsystems as identified in this study; the key cognitive parameters such as those identified in the work of Kolb, Dewey, Lewin and Piaget; the environmental influences (both human and physical); and the power of the self-conscious mind to achieve a high capacity to learn through developing a knowledge of meta-learning. Chapters 6 through 15 of this book detail the road to development of the ICALS Model. Chapter 16 offers a quick overview assessment of the learning and moves through an expanded Experiential Learning Model to the ICALS Model. Chapter 17 discusses the five modes of the model and the specific neuroscience findings supporting each of these modes.

In support of the new theory and model, Chapter 18 focuses on the idea of Self; Chapter 19 looks at the mind/brain/body connection; Chapter 20 focuses on learning and the environment, Chapter 21 provides a detailed treatment of music and sound as an example of the impact of the environment on the learner, Chapter 22 considers social learning, and Chapter 23 provides several examples of Self as an agent of change. Chapter 24 introduces the wisdom of learning, including guidelines emerging from the ICALS research. Building on the theory, learning in terms of knowledge and knowing is explored in Chapter 25, and in Chapter 26 we glimpse what it might mean to live in this new frame of reference.

Section III
Learning Areas from Neuroscience

This section is basically a literature review, long on words and short on pictures, of which there are none. Nonetheless, for those wishing to dig deeply into neuroscience findings that offer the potential to enhance learning, here is the place to begin. Don't worry if you can't capture all the concepts the first time around. The findings will be presented more succinctly in Section IV.

This section addresses the following areas: The Mind/Brain/Body (Chapter 6), The Learning Process (Chapter 7), Implementation of Learning Part I (Chapter 8), Implementation of Learning Part II (Chapter 9), and The Environment (Chapter 10). To begin our exploration of the learnings from neuroscience, we first look through the framework of the mind/brain/body.

Chapter 6
Learning from Neuroscience:
The Mind/Brain/Body

The fascination for how the mind/brain works expressed by Christos (2003), a mathematician from Australia who studies neural networks, memory, learning, and adaptive systems, is a good way to start this chapter:

> It is fascinating to consider how a simple process of integrating and firing neurons can account for not only memory but a diverse range of brain functions such as language, conscious awareness, creativity, the ability to understand the world mathematically, and emotions like joy, sorrow, and anger, to mention just a few. (Christos, 2003, p. 4).

Knowledge of how the mind/brain learns will undoubtedly have a great impact on education and learning. Understanding the brain mechanisms that underlie learning and memory, and the effects of genetics, the environment, emotion, and age on learning could transform educational strategies and enable us to design programs that optimize learning for people of all ages and of all needs (Blakemore & Frith, 2005). *It is an axiom of this research that knowledge of how the mind/brain learns applies to adult experiential learning.*

James Zull, a biologist and an educator, suggests that biology deepens our understanding of what learning is all about. In his view, understanding the biology of the brain and how it learns shows the essential entanglement of learning with life. This perspective makes clear the importance of intrinsic motivation and suggests a fundamental weakness of extrinsic rewards. Learning can also be viewed as a natural outcome of experience (Zull, 2002). Even though learning is natural, studying and understanding the learning process can significantly enhance the efficacy of that learning process. As an example, consider the value to a learner who understands how the process of learning occurs within the mind/brain when that learner is informed that *learners create their understanding by building on what they already know*. Recalling Stonier's semantic mixing previously discussed, this statement can lead the learner to recognize and expand their own frames of reference, beliefs, and assumptions. Conversely, without understanding the learning process within the brain, this statement has an entirely different context, and may not be taken seriously. As Zull (2002) sums up,

> The human mind ... wants to know how things work. We need reasons. It is giving us the chance to move beyond dependence on authority and authorities. Understanding the concepts of neuronal networks and synapse change gives

> Learners create their understanding by building on what they already know.

> credence to constructivist theories of learning and of educating. It helps to know why, and we are richer for it! (p. 248)

Knowing how and why allows each person to face new challenges in personal learning with the ability to select, modify, and adapt their personal learning approach to maximize the outcome.

It is perhaps a coincidence that both neuroscience and experiential learning have become major interests over recent decades. For example, Miller (2000) in *The Handbook of Adult and Continuing Education* argues that there has been a major growth in interest in learning from experience during the previous ten years. He suggests that the reason is because of rising uncertainty, technological advances, and rapid social change. From the field of neuroscience, the Nobel laureate Eric Kandel (2006)—in his book *In Search of Memory*—offers the following,

> My central premise of this book is that neuroscientific evidence is clearly relevant to the extent that it (1) corroborates (or refutes) contemporary models of cognition and learning, and (2) generates surprising findings that would not have been anticipated if one were to rely solely on contemporary psychological theories that lack a neuroscientific emphasis. (p. 9)

Emerging in the early 1900s, the field of neuroscience is relatively young. While progress was slow in those early years, significant gains in understanding the mind, the brain, and the body have been made since then. Today neuroscience is one of the most rapidly growing areas of science, what is sometimes referred to as the last frontier of biology (Bloom et al., 1999). At the first Annual Meeting of the Society for Neuroscience in 1971 there were 1,100 scientists participating. By the 27th Annual Meeting in 1997, there were 27,685 scientists participating with more than 14,000 research presentations made (Bloom et al., 1999).

New technologies such as functional magnetic resonance imaging (fMRI), transcranial magnetic stimulation (TMI), and others have significantly aided research in determining where physiologically the brain has been most active or what happens when you send strong signals composed of very short magnetic pulses directly into specific brain regions, thereby inducing painless tiny electrical currents in an individual's neural circuitry (George, 2007; Gusnard & Rauhle, 2004; Ward, 2006). By observing patient's behavior, listening to their narratives, and then comparing them with the physical location of the activity in the brain, researchers have been able to make significant advances in understanding how the brain operates.

We now look at findings from neuroscience that relate to adult experiential learning with a focus on the nature and health of the mind/brain/body. The area of Health is broken down into five subelements: good health, physical and mental exercise, issues of age, and the plasticity of the brain. Along the way, certain myths related to adult learning will be noted.

The Nature of the Mind/Brain/Body

One major objective of neuroscience has been to understand the nature and operation of the human mind and brain. Given this, however, it is now being expanded to include the body as researchers are finding more and more that the mind/brain/body operates as a complex, interwoven, and interdependent system (Church, 2006; Jensen, 2006; Lipton, 2005; Pert, 1997). As the Nobel laureate Gerald Edelman (1992, p. 148) stated, "the brain giving rise to the mind is a prototypical complex system, one more akin in its style of construction to a jungle than a computer. Another aspect of the mind/brain/body is the apparent dichotomy of possessing both unity and individuality. Since the brains of living organisms are basically made up of the same atoms, molecules, and cell types, there is a unity and consistency of species.

> The mind/brain/body operates as a complex, interwoven, and interdependent system.

At the same time, considering the specificity of the genetic structure, the phenomenon of epigenetics and the variability and impact of the environment coupled with the plasticity of the brain, it has been demonstrated that thoughts (patterns of neuron connections and synapse strengths) in the mind can change the physical structure of the brain. Conversely, changes in the neural physiology of the brain can change thoughts or patterns of the mind. Thus, individual variety and uniqueness are major characteristics of the human species. It is just such variability, plasticity, and uniqueness that challenges black box approaches to understanding adult learning. Our knowledge will be improved in this area as neuroscience, working closer to the unitary characteristics of the individual—cells, chemicals, and networks—develops a knowledge base of how and why things work the way they do within the mind/brain (Edelman, 1992). William James, introducing the term plasticity in his 1890 *Principles of Psychology,* noted that the mind is cumulative, and not recurrent, and that "no state once gone can recur and be identical with what was before" (Gediman, 2005, p. 286).

REFLECT:
How does my brain work?
What am I learning from my everyday thoughts?

Health of the Mind/Brain/Body

While this section primarily focuses on the effect of health on the mind/brain, it is also true that the mind/brain/body affects health. Specifically, the brain can significantly influence the behavior of the body's cells. This came about through evolution. As Lipton (2005) explains,

> As more complex animals evolved, specialized cells took over the job of monitoring and organizing the flow of the behavior regulating signal molecules. These cells provided a distributed nerve network and central information processor, a brain. The brain's function is to coordinate the dialogue of signal

molecules within the community. Consequently, in a community of cells, each cell must acquiesce control to the informed decisions of its awareness authority the *brain*. The brain *controls* the behavior of the body's cells. (p. 131)

Lipton stresses that this is a very important point to consider when we blame our cells for the health issues we experience. In brief, his point is that beliefs control biology. We can experience, interpret, and anticipate our responses to external events and decide on our response as we choose. Our thoughts can change our brains. Our brains can change our body (Lipton, 2005).

Good Health Increases Learning

Cozolino sees the direct relationship between optimal health and functioning and increasingly advanced levels of growth and integration as a basic assumption of neuroscience. As Cozolino (2006) explains,

> On a neurological level, this equates to the integration and communication of neural networks dedicated to emotion, cognition, sensation, and behavior. On a psychological level, integration is the ability to experience important aspects of life while employing a minimum of defensiveness. (p. 26)

Mezirow (1991) says that people who do not learn have "rigid and highly defended thought patterns" (p. 156). As Taylor (2006) forwards, "This suggests that what constitutes optimal health and functioning from the perspective of brain function and psychotherapy is among the goals of adult education" (p. 79).

Physical and Mental Exercise

John Medina is a developmental molecular biologist and Director of the Brain Center for Flight Learning Research at Seattle Pacific University. In his book called *Brain Rules,* Medina (2008) has offered several principles relative to neuroscience and the age of learning. His first rule recognizes that exercise boosts brainpower. According to Medina, our brains were built for walking about 12 miles a day or the equivalent exercise. Exercise gets more blood to your brain, bringing glucose for energy and oxygen to soak up the toxic electrons that are left over. Exercise also stimulates the proteins that keep neurons connected (Medina, 2008).

Richard Wrangham, Professor of Biology and Anthropology at Harvard University, believes that during early evolution man walked on the average between 10 and 20 kilometers per day, and women walked about half that distance (Bobe, 2002). Thus, the brain of Homo sapiens was created with exercise being a necessity for life. The connection between exercise and brain effectiveness is direct: Exercise increases the blood flow and provides additional oxygen to the brain. As Medina (2008) states, "a lifetime of exercise can result in a sometimes astonishing elevation of cognitive performance, compared to those more sedentary" (p. 14). Exercise also has an immediate, positive effect on the brain capability, although Medina notes that "Short-term memory skills ... and certain types of reaction times appear to be unrelated to physical activity" (p. 14) and that the degree of benefit can vary quite a bit among individuals.

Exercise stimulates neurogenesis, the ability of the brain to generate new neurons, and exerts a protective effect on hippocampal neurons that lasts about 3 days, thus heightening brain activity (Amen, 2005). Recognizing this value, Amen quips, "People who only work out at the gym are not as smart as people who work out and then go to the library" (2005, p. 123). The hippocampus is part of the limbic system and plays a significant role in consolidating learning and moving information from working memory to long-tem memory. "It constantly checks information relayed to working memory and compares it to stored experiences. This process is essential for meaning" (Sousa, 2006, p. 19).

Begley (2007) suggests that voluntary physical activity alone can generate new brain cells. The key word here is "voluntary." Begley says that it appears the effects of running on neurogenesis and learning is highly dependent on volition. In other words, the running must be a voluntary act.

> Forced exercise, it seems, does not promote neurogenesis ... voluntary exercise is marked not only by the absence of stress. It is also characterized by the presence of brain rhythms called theta waves. These waves, which have a frequency of six to twelve cycles per second, are also present when you pay close attention to something but not when you eat or drink or are otherwise on automatic pilot. (Begley, 2007, p. 68)

Referring to Henry Ford, Lipton (2005) points out those positive and negative beliefs not only impact our health, but every aspect of our life:

> Henry Ford was right about the efficiency of assembly lines and he was right about the power of the mind ... Your beliefs act like filters on a camera, changing how you see the world. And your biology adapts to those beliefs. When we truly recognize that our beliefs are that powerful, we hold the key to freedom ... we can change our minds. (p. 143)

Begley (2007) agrees: "By meditative exertion and other mental exercises, you can actively change your feelings, your attitudes, and your mind-set" (p. 14). Indeed, Buddhism, for example, avows that the mind has a formidable power of self-transformation. The impact of emotions on the mind/brain is more fully discussed later in this book.

Goldberg (2005) points out that if mental exercise can stimulate neuronal growth, then this might be a pattern for growth in other parts of the brain. Specifically,

> The brain is a diverse, heterogeneous organ. Different parts of the brain are in charge of different mental functions, and different mental activities call upon different parts of the brain. If mental exercise, the use of one's brain, stimulates

the growth of new neurons, then it is quite plausible that different forms of mental activity will stimulate such growth in different parts of the brain. (p. 251)

In terms of aging, there are two specific ways that exercise improves brain performance. As introduced earlier, the first is through increased blood flow that allows more brain cells easier access to the blood glucose for energy, and oxygen for toxic material removal. The second is that exercise stimulates a growth factor called BDNG (Brain Derived Neurotrophic Factor), which, much like fertilizer, aids in developing healthy tissue (Medina, 2008). This brings us to a discussion of the aging brain.

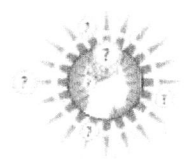

REFLECT:
How much physical exercise do I give my brain?
Do I have a balance of physical and mental health?

Issues of Age

Over the last few decades extensive research has been aimed at understanding the changes in the mind/brain that occur during aging. As a result, today there is a relatively comprehensive picture of those changes occurring in the aging brain, both in a healthy brain or one encumbered by neurological illness or dementia (Goldberg, 2001).

MYTH: A damaging idea was that as individuals grow older, their mental powers decrease due to the continuing loss of neurons. In fact, it has been shown that so long as individuals use their brain and continue to actively think, barring age-related diseases, their brain capacity will maintain a good capability. For example, Carl Jung did some of his best work between the ages of 73 and 83. While it is true that neurons continue to die as one ages, it is also true that in several areas of the brain, neurons continue to be created so long as the brain is active. For example, the hippocampus produces new neurons after birth, and continues to do so well into old age (Sapolsky, 1999). In reality, there is no reason to assume elderly people should be unable to use their brain and their minds (Amen, 2005; Goldberg, 2005; Sapolsky, 1999).

Amen (2005) points out that regardless of age; any set of circuits that does not get used grows weaker. "New learning causes new connections to form in the brain. No learning causes the brain to start disconnecting itself. No matter what your age, mental exercise has a global, positive effect on your brain" (p. 113). Using middle-aged people returning to college as an example, when they start classes they often feel slow

> Regardless of age, any set of circuits that does not get used grows weaker.

and stupid, but after becoming engaged in mental exercise over a couple of semesters, learning becomes easier (Amen, 2005). While the level of activity of the enzymes in one's cells starts to decline with age, becoming less efficient and agile, Amen goes on to say that in some respects, a 50 year old will do better than an 18 year old in academic studies because the frontal lobes, which include the prefrontal cortex, are better developed. It is the frontal lobes that help an individual pay attention and ask good questions.

> A more developed frontal lobe allows you to take better advantage of new knowledge, to know what to focus on, and to relate it to life experiences so that it has more useful value to you. The eighteen-year-old may be able to memorize facts more easily, but his frontal lobe isn't as good at selecting which facts to memorize. (Amen, 2005, p. 115)

Goldberg (2005) points out that the aging brain can accomplish remarkable mental feats and that there are triumphs that only age can bring. As he explains,

> Frequently, when I am faced with what would appear from the outside to be a challenging problem, the grinding mental computation is somehow circumvented, rendered, as if by magic, unnecessary. The solution comes effortlessly, seamlessly, seemingly by itself. What I have lost with age in my capacity for hard mental work, I seem to have gained in my capacity for instantaneous, almost unfairly easy insight. (Goldberg, 2005, p. 9)

As do other researchers in the field, Amen (2005) says that the best mental exercise is new learning, acquiring new knowledge, and doing things you've never done before. For example, the Nuns Study conducted by a research team from the Rush University Medical Center in Chicago, studied how often 801 older nuns, priests, and other clergy engaged in mentally stimulating activities such as reading a newspaper. The researchers discovered that,

> The best mental exercise is new learning, acquiring new knowledge, and doing things you've never done before.

> Those who increased their mental activity over the five years reduced their chance of developing Alzheimer's disease by one-third. These more mentally active individuals also reduced their age-related decline in overall mental abilities by 50 percent, in concentration and attention span by 60 percent, and in mental processing speed by 30 percent. (Amen, 2005, p. 114)

Physical exercise is also needed. In a 1991-92 Canadian Study of Health and Aging, 9,008 randomly selected men and women 65 or older were used to study the relationship between physical activity and the risk of cognitive impairment and dementia. Each was extensively interviewed and 6,434 were deemed cognitively normal during the baseline study. Of this number, 4,615 were available for follow-up after five years. After screenings and clinical evaluation, 3,894 had no cognitive impairment, 436 had some cognitive impairment, and 285 were diagnosed with dementia. This data associated physical activity with lower risks of cognitive impairment. The conclusion was that, "regular physical activity could represent an important and potent protective factor against cognitive decline and dementia in elderly people" (Amen, 2005, p. 124). Specific suggestions for mitigating the risk of dementia were cardio-vascular exercise (for the heart) and resistive exercise (for strengthening muscles).

Plasticity of the Brain

Andreasen (2005) clarifies, "When we neuroscientists say that the brain is 'plastic,' we are not talking about polymers. We mean that the brain is marvelously responsive, adaptable, and eternally changing" (p. 146).

The concept of neuroplasticity can be found not only in the history of the evolution of man, but also in the current maturation of the individual. The brain maintains a high degree of plasticity, changing in response to experience and learning. As Buonomano and Merzenich explain, "The brain has been shaped by evolution to adapt and readapt to an ever-changing world. The ability to learn is dependent on modification of the brain's chemistry and architecture" (Buonomano & Merzenich, 1998, pp. 11-12). This is the process of neural plasticity, the ability of neurons to change their structure and relationships according to environmental demands or personal decisions and actions.

Learning depends on the level of arousal of the learner. Too little arousal and there is no motivation, too much and stress takes over and reduces learning. Maximum learning occurs when there is a moderate level of arousal. This initiates neural plasticity by increasing the production of neurotransmitters and neural growth hormones, which in turn facilitate neural connections and cortical organization (Cowan & Kandel, 2001; Cozolino & Sprokay, 2006; Zhu & Waite, 1998).

REFLECT:

How will I build new neurons as I age?
Am I excited when I learn something new?

As we are exposed to more diverse and varying conditions, the brain creates new patterns and strengths of connections and thereby changes its physiological structure (Kandel, 2006). It is also true that the structure of the brain—containing a huge number of networks of neurons—significantly influences how incoming signals representing new thoughts (that is, patterns composed of networks of neurons) are formed. These new patterns entering the brain associate or connect with patterns already in the brain.

In 2000 Eric Kandel won the Nobel Prize for showing that when individuals learn, the wiring in their brain changes. He showed that when even simple information entered the brain it created a physical alteration of the structure of neurons that participate in the process. Thus, we all are continuously altering the patterns and structure of neuronal connections in our brains. The conclusion is significant; thoughts change the

> Thoughts are continuously altering the patterns and structure of neuronal connections in our brains.

physiological structure of our brains. This plasticity results from the connection between the mind (neuronal patterns) and the physical brain. The implications are significant: What and how we think and believe impacts our physical bodies (Medina, 2008; Kandel, 2006).

Merzenich and his team have shown through animal studies that, "under optimal environmental conditions, almost every physical aspect of the brain can recover from age-related losses" (Wang et al., 1995, pp. 71-75). Kempermann et al. (1997) discovered that there was a significant increase in neurons in young adult mice, which spent 45 days in an enriched environment. The environment was created to resemble the complex surrounding of the wild, including such things as wheels, toys, and tunnels. After the 45 days, the animals had undergone a dramatic spurt of neurogenesis. Begley describes the results of their experiment by noting that,

> The formation and survival of new neurons increased 15 percent in a part of the hippocampus called the dentate gyrus, which is involved in learning and memory. The standard 270,000 neurons in the hippocampus had increased to some 317,000. (Begley, 2007, p. 58)

As Fred Gage (a member of Merzenich's team) described this finding to the Dalai Lama, "It's not a small number: 15 percent of the total volume can be changed just by switching experience" (Begley, 2007, p. 58). Indeed, Begley (2007) describes this as one of the most striking findings in neuroplasticity that "exposure to an enriched environment leads to a striking increase in new neurons, along with a substantial improvement in behavioral performance" (p. 58).

In addressing evolution, brain organization, and neuroplasticity, MacGregor (2006) concluded the following:

> Neural plasticity is vulnerable to vagaries of early conditioning experiences and training much of which can be limited, misleading, wrong, or debilitating. On balance, however, neural plasticity introduces vast amounts of incalculably useful immediately life-relevant learning, the ability to create constructive responses to new situations, and the life-long ability to modify and self-correct established action patterns. It also produces a rich personal internal reflective world of imagination and creativity which provides the center stage of individual human existence. These qualities of neural plasticity open up the human potential to vistas far surpassing those based on genetic-prescription only. (p. 48)

Chapter 7
Learning from Neuroscience: The Learning Process

Calaprice quotes Einstein as saying, "The significant problems we face cannot be solved at the same level of thinking we were at when we created them" (Calaprice, 2000, p. 317). From this perspective, thinking goes as learning goes: Adults need to learn, take action, and adapt at least as fast as their environments evolve.

The brain stores information in the form of patterns of neurons, their connections (synapses), and the strength of those connections. These patterns represent thoughts, images, beliefs, theories, emotions, and so on. Although the patterns themselves are nonphysical, their existence as represented by cells and their connections are physical, that is, composed of atoms and molecules. If we consider the mind as a totality of neuronal patterns, then we can consider the mind and the brain to be connected in the sense that the patterns cannot exist without the brain (atoms and molecules), yet the brain would have no mind if it had no patterns. It may be helpful to consider the following metaphor: The mind is to the brain as waves of the ocean are to the water in the ocean, that is, particles bumping against each other creating wave patterns rather than the perceived movement of the water (Bennet & Bennet, 2008c).

> The mind is to the brain as waves of the ocean are to the water in the ocean, that is, particles bumping against each other creating wave patterns rather than the perceived movement of the water.

Even this is simplified because surrounding the neurons are continuous flows of blood, hormones, and other chemicals that have complex interactions within the brain (Pert, 1997; Church, 2006). The power of the metaphor derives from the relationship between the neuronal network patterns used to represent the external (and internal) world of concepts, thoughts, objects, and relationships and the physical neurons and other material in the brain.

To get some idea of the density and intricacies of the brain, consider the following: "A piece of brain tissue the size of a grain of sand contains a hundred thousand neurons and one billion synapses, all talking to one another" (Amen, 2005, p. 20). As another example, consider the following description of how the brain creates patterns of the mind. In this quote, Antonio Damasio is using the term "movie" as a metaphor for the diverse sensory images and signals that create a show and flow we call mind. The quote also brings out a few of the large number of semi-independent systems in the brain that work together to make sense of our external environment.

> Further remarkable progress involving aspects of the movie-in-the-brain has led to increased insights related to mechanisms for learning and memory. In rapid succession, research has revealed that the brain uses discrete systems for different types of learning. The basal ganglia and cerebellum are critical for the acquisition of skills—for example, learning to ride a bicycle or play a musical instrument. The hippocampus is integral to the learning of facts pertaining to such entities as people, places or events. And once facts are learned, the long-term memory of those facts relies on multi-component brain systems, whose key parts are located in the vast brain expanses known as cerebral cortices. (Damasio, 2007, pp. 63-64)

We learn by changing incoming signals (images, sounds, smells, sensations of the body) into patterns (of the mind and within the brain) that we identify with specific external concepts or objects. These incoming neuronal patterns have internal associations with other internal patterns that represent (to varying degrees of fidelity) the corresponding associations in the external world. Thus we re-present external reality through the creation and association of internal patterns of neuron firings and connections. This is done by what Stonier (1997) refers to as semantic mixing or complexing (the associative patterning introduced in Chapter 2). During reflection, the mind/brain is thinking about the incoming concepts, ideas, objects, and their relationships by associating them with various internal neuron patterns.

The discussion below focuses on how the brain stores information and anticipates the future.

How the Brain Stores Information

In Chapter 4 we discussed adult experiential learning as seen from the psychological/educational perspective. In this section we address the process of adult learning from the inside out, that is, from a neuroscientific/biological perspective.

One of the goals of neuroscience is to determine and understand what is happening in the mind/brain that relates directly to the learning process. In terms of neuroscience as a field, learning falls under the segment known as Behavioral and Cognitive Neuroscience (Zigmond et al., 1999). In a chapter entitled "Learning and Memory: Basic Mechanisms," Beggs et al. note that "during the last quarter century, we have witnessed remarkable progress in understanding how the nervous system encodes and retrieves information" (Beggs et al., 2007, p. 1411). Further, they cite several general principles that have emerged from current research which indicate the ties between neuroscience and learning:

> Multiple memory systems are present in the brain; short-term forms of learning and memory require changes in existing neural circuits; these changes may involve multiple cellular mechanisms within individual neurons; and finally, changes in the properties of membrane channels are often correlated with learning and memory. (Beggs et al., 1999, p. 1411)

Additionally, Beggs et al. note that, "long-term memory requires new protein synthesis and growth, whereas short-term memory need not" (Beggs et al., 2007, p. 1411).

In a chapter in *Best of the Brain from Scientific American,* Nobel laureate Eric Kandel (2006) says "understanding the human mind in biological terms has emerged as the central challenge for science in the 21st century" (p. 68). He suggests that this new science, building on the power of molecular biology, is based upon the following five principles:

> (a) The mind and brain are inseparable, the mind is a set of operations carried out by the brain; (b) each mental function of the brain is carried out by special neural circuits in different regions of the brain; (c) all of the neural circuits are composed of the same basic signaling units, nerve cells, or neurons; (d) these neural circuits use specific molecules to generate signals within and between neurons; and (e) these specific molecules have been conserved throughout evolution. (Kandel, 2006, p. 69)

In 1949 the Canadian psychologist Donald Hebb explained learning and memory as a result of the strengthening of synapses (connections) between neurons in the brain. In other words, when neurons fire simultaneously, their synaptic connections become stronger (Begley, 2007). This has become known as Hebb's rule: Learning takes place when pairs of neurons fire concurrently. Although an oversimplification, the colloquial version is that *neurons that fire together wire together*. Another result of Hebb's rule is the ease with which we can remember sequences of information.

Begley (2007) describes this process as "traveling the same dirt road over and over leaves ruts that make it easier to stay in the track on subsequent trips" (p. 30). This is why we remember songs or stories much better than isolated or disconnected facts. This is also why memory of information can be improved by repeating the information over and over. In other words, the more often we recall what we have learned the better we will remember it. From the opposite perspective, the rule is, "*use it, or lose it*" (Christos, 2003, p. 95). While the pattern may stay in memory, it may be very difficult to retrieve. Freud suggested that there are separate sets of neurons for perception and for memory. The neural networks concerned with perception create fixed synaptic connections and by doing so ensure the accuracy of our perceptual capability. On the other hand, neuronal networks concerned with memory make connections that change in strength as we learn. This is the basis of memory and of higher cognitive functioning (Kandel, 2006, p. 198).

REFLECT:
How often do I engage in conscious reflection?
Do I address issues from the inside out or outside in?

Anticipating the Future

A significant aspect of the mind/brain is its capability to continually make sense of its environment and anticipate what's coming next. As Buzsaki (2006) states,

> Brains are foretelling devices and their predictive powers emerge from the various rhythms they perpetually generate ... The specific physiological functions of brain rhythms vary from the obvious to the utterly impenetrable. (p. vii)

In other words, our behavior is closely related to our capacity to form accurate predictions. This perspective is reinforced by the neuroscientist Rudolfo Llinas (2001), who considered predicting the outcome of future events as the most important and common of all global brain functions. The sense of movement of the body provides a simple demonstration of the need—and power—of anticipating the future. Imagine walking down a staircase and accidentally missing a step, recognizing the surprise one has when beginning to fall (Hawkins, 2004). Since for thousands of years survival has depended upon humans being capable of anticipating their environment and taking the right actions to survive, perhaps it should be no surprise that that capability has come through the evolution of the brain. As Damasio (1999) explains,

> Survival in a complex environment, that is, efficient management of life regulation, depends on taking the right action, and that, in turn, can be greatly improved by purposeful preview and manipulation of images in mind and optimal planning. Consciousness allowed the connection of the two disparate aspects of the process—inner life regulation and image making. (p. 24)

Jeff Hawkins, a computer scientist who is the originator of the Palm Five and creator of the Redwood Neuroscience Institute that promotes research on memory and cognition, wrote a book called *On Intelligence* that investigates how the mind predicts the future. This is not about long-term forecasting, rather it is about how the brain anticipates the outcomes of its actions. Recall above where we defined knowledge as the capacity to take effective action. This definition clearly requires some anticipation of the outcome. Hawkins believes that the brain constantly predicts and that what we perceive is not coming only from our senses. Our perceptions are the result of a combination of what we sense, our brain's memory, and our capacity to anticipate the outcome of our actions. As he explains, "your brain makes low-level sensory predictions about what it expects to see, hear, and feel at every given moment, and it does so in parallel. All regions of your neocortex are simultaneously trying to predict what their next experience will be" (Hawkins, 2004, p. 88).

> Every decision we make and every action we take is based—either consciously or unconsciously—on the anticipated outcome.

According to these sources, then, prediction is a primary function of the neocortex and is also the basis for intelligence. Hawkins (2004) says that intelligence is "measured by the capacity to remember and predict patterns in the world, including language, mathematics, physical properties of objects, and social situations" (p. 97). This conclusion ties in nicely with Kolb's experiential learning concept of comprehension (or abstract conceptualization) as previously described and with the definition of knowledge as the capacity to take effective action.

One way the brain anticipates the future is through the process of storing sequences of patterns. Recall the ease of remembering songs and stories described earlier. Since we never see the same world twice, the brain (as distinct from a computer) does not store exact replicas of past events or memories. Rather, it stores invariant representations. These forms represent the basic source of recognition and understanding of the broader patterns (Hawkins, 2004).

According to Hawkins (2004), "the problem of understanding how your cortex forms invariant representations remains one of the biggest mysteries in all of science" (p. 78). It is so much so that "no one, not even using the most powerful computers in the world, is able to solve it. And it isn't for a lack of trying" (p.78). As Kandel (2006) explains,

> By storing memories in invariant forms, individuals are able to apply memories to situations that are similar but not identical to previous experiences. Cognitive psychologists would describe this as developing an internal representation of the external world, a cognitive map that generates a meaningful image or interpretation of our experience. (p. 298)

The brain stores patterns in a hierarchical and nested fashion. Thoughts are represented by patterns of neuronal firings, their synaptic connections, and the strengths between the synaptic spaces. For example, a single thought could be represented in the brain by a network of a million neurons, with each neuron connecting to anywhere from 1 to 10,000 other neurons (Ratey, 2001). Incoming external information (new information) is mixed, or associated, with internal information, creating new neuronal patterns that may represent understanding, meaning, and/or the anticipation of the consequences of actions, in other words, knowledge (Stonier, 1997). Recall that the term *associative patterning* describes this continuous process of learning by creating new patterns in the mind and stored in the brain (Bennet & Bennet, 2008e). From the viewpoint of the mind/brain, any knowledge that is being "re-used" is actually being "re-created" and, in an area of continuing interest, most likely complexed over and over again as incoming information is associated with internal information (Stonier, 1997).

> A single thought could be represented in the brain by a network of a million neurons, with each neuron connecting to anywhere from 1 to 10,000 other neurons.

Further, if knowledge (informing) is different, there is a good chance that knowledge (proceeding) will be different. Recall that knowledge (proceeding) is the *process* of pulling up and sequencing associated knowledge (informing) and semantically complexing it with incoming information to make it comprehensible. In essence, every time we apply knowledge (Informing and Proceeding) it is to some extent new knowledge because the human mind—unlike an information management system—*unconsciously tailors what is emerging as knowledge to the situation at hand* (Edelman & Tononi, 2000).

REFLECT:
How well am I able to anticipate the outcomes of my actions?
Are there any specific tunes that repeatedly trigger memories?

Another characteristic of this process is that, as Marchese (1998) points out, when you see a picture, only about 20 percent of what you are seeing is brought into your brain; the other 80 percent of that image comes from information, ideas, and feelings *already in your brain*. The point is that the mind/brain doesn't store memories like a computer, that is, storing everything that comes in. It stores the *core* of the picture, what was referred to above as an invariant (Hawkins, 2004).

This particular phenomenon of relating external and internal forms of experience is called "appresentation" (Marton & Booth, 1997). As Moon (2004) explains, "Appresentation is the manner in which a part of something that is perceived as an external experience can stimulate a much more complete or richer internal experience of the 'whole' of that thing to be conjured up" (p. 23).

For example, if you see your friend from the side or back you can usually recognize who they are since your mind has stored a core basic memory that includes major features of that person (Begley, 2007; Hawkins, 2004). When you see your friend, your mind is filling in the blanks and you recognize the incoming image as your friend. There is also robustness in the way the brain *stores* core memories. Assume that it takes a million neurons to create a specific pattern (the core part of incoming information), the brain may set aside 1.4 million neurons with their connections as space for that pattern, providing a looseness to account for future associative changes, or dying cells (Hawkins, 2004). Thus for this particular pattern you could lose tens of thousands of brain cells and still have significant aspects of the core memory available for future retrieval via re-creation.

Further complicating the situation, at the same time you catch sight of your friend and are smiling, getting ready to call out and wave, you may be swatting gnats away from your eyes, shivering from a soft breeze, registering the dark clouds moving in from the west, feeling hunger pains in your stomach, and sensing a soreness in your little toe from tight shoes, and so on. The brain is multidimensional, simultaneously processing visual, aural, olfactory, and kinesthetic sensory inputs and, as discussed above, combining them with mental thoughts and emotional feelings to create an internal perception and feeling of external awareness (Bennet, 2006).

As discussed above, the brain is simultaneously identifying and storing core patterns from incoming information; in other words, there is a hierarchy of information where hierarchy represents "an order of some complexity, in which the elements are distributed along the gradient of importance" (Kuntz, 1968, p. 162). A hierarchy of knowledge is analogous to the physical design of the neocortex, "a sheet of cells the size of a dinner napkin as thick as six business cards, where the connections between various regions give the whole thing a hierarchical structure" (Hawkins, 2004, p. 109).

In a hierarchy the dominant structural element may be a central point such as in a circular structure, or have an axial symmetry. Wherever the central point (dominant structure) is located, each part is determined by where it is located in relation to that central point. While it is true that in a radial version of hierarchy the entire pattern may depend directly on the open center, most hierarchies consist of groups of subordinate hierarchies who in turn have groups of subordinate hierarchies, with each group having its own particular relation to the dominant center point (Kuntz, 1968). The higher-level pattern stored in the brain could be described as a pattern of patterns with possibly both hierarchical and associative relationships to other patterns.

Considering the brain as a semi-independent subcomponent of the body that contains a hierarchy of patterns associated with other patterns, the higher-level (core) patterns would retain their associations (in terms of meaning, understanding, and anticipation of the future of Kolb's abstract conceptualization mode) even as the lower level patterns (internal information that is situation dependent) are re-created in response to new incoming information from Kolb's concrete experience or perhaps his reflective observation mode. A study of chess players showed that experts examined the chessboard patterns (not the pieces) over and over again, looking at nuances, generally "playing with" and studying these *patterns*. P.E. Ross (2006) noted that their ability to chunk patterns for ease of memory and retrieval was a significant part of their success.

The above discussion brings home the fact that the mind/brain develops robustness and deep understanding derived from its capacity to use past learning and memories to complete incoming information and instead of storing all the details, it stores only meaningful information. This provides the ability to create and store higher-level patterns while simultaneously semantically complexing incoming information with internal memories, adapting those memories to the situation at hand. Through these processes the brain supports survival and sustainability in a complex and unpredictable world.

As a brief summary, our brain receives patterns from the outside world, stores them as memories, and makes predictions by combining what it has seen before and what is happening now. In particular, the cortex is large and has a large memory capacity. It is constantly predicting what we will see, hear, and feel. This usually occurs in our unconscious. The reason we can do this is because our cortex has built a model of the world around us. Hawkins (2004) briefly described the hierarchical and nested structure of the cortex and believes that this structure "stores a model of the hierarchical structure of the real world" (p. 125).

Chapter 8
Learning from Neuroscience: Implementation of Learning (Part I)

This chapter addresses recent neuroscience findings that will help adult learners to understand key areas of the mind/brain/body and **their effect on the learning process** and be able to adjust their individual behavior to specific situations and goals. Focus areas in Part I include emotions and stress.

As Kurt Lewin has said, "There is nothing so practical as a good theory" (cited in Kolb, 1984, p. 4). This knowledge not only allows the adult learner to apply the process of learning, but also offers the opportunity to adjust that learning process to specific applications. An example is our understanding of attention. One part of the brain that may keep individuals from paying attention is the amygdala, the part of the brain where incoming sensory input is continuously screened for potentially dangerous situations. If a threat is sensed, the amygdala immediately sends a signal that sets in motion a quick action such as the fight or flight response before the cortex is even aware of what has happened. As Zull (2002) details, when a threat is sensed, "our actions will not be controlled by our sensory cortex that breaks things down into details, but by our survival shortcut through the amygdala, which is fast but misses details" (p. 141). Conversely, Begley (2007) notes that attention, one of the parameters of successful learning, also pumps up neuronal activity. She says that, "Attention is real, in the sense that it takes a physical form capable of affecting the physical activity [and therefore the structure] of the brain" (p. 158).

> Attention, one of the parameters of successful learning, pumps up neuronal activity.

Another example is our understanding of perception. The brain does not have a system dedicated to perception. Rather, perception "describes in a general way what goes on in a number of specific neural systems—we see, hear and smell the world with our visual, auditory and olfactory systems" (LeDoux, 1996, p. 16). Each system evolved to solve different problems that animals face. Emotions play a role in perception. LeDoux (1996) further describes,

> The perception in oneself of an attitude (disguised as fact) about a racial group can seem to be as valid as the perception of the color of their skin. When one is aware of biases and possesses values against having these, he or she can exercise control over them. However, the ability to do this depends on being aware of the unconscious influences, which is quite another matter. (p. 63)

We further address the role of emotions from the mind/brain/body perspective below. While the role of the unconscious is included in this discussion in terms of its relationship with emotions (or more specifically, feelings), this area is further explored in Chapter 9.

Emotions

Edelman and Tononi (2000) say that moving to a biologically based epistemology would,

> ... create a much broader base for thinking about thinking and feeling. Moreover, it would not limit our descriptions to the boundary between our skin and the rest of our world. Most important, it would open our inquiry to include feelings and emotions in terms of bodily mechanisms that go far beyond computation. (p. 217)

This chapter explores what that might mean.

We start with descriptions of emotion as offered by several primary resources and then provide an operational definition. While none of the below descriptions of emotion contradict each other, they each add different features around the concept. One exception is LeDoux's separation of feelings and emotions whereas many authors take feelings and emotions to be the same. From the neuroscience perspective, a clean definition of the meaning of emotion may not be possible since it describes a phenomenon that includes many physiological parts of the brain, a complex network of neuronal connections throughout the brain, the hormones that spread information throughout the body, and connections with the conscious and unconscious aspects of the body.

From Pert's (1997) viewpoint:

> When I use the term emotion, I am speaking in the broadest terms, to include not only the familiar human experiences of anger, fear, and sadness, as well as joy, contentment, and courage, but also basic sensations such as pleasure and pain, as well as the "drive states" studied by the experimental psychologists, such as hunger and thirst. (p. 131)

Pert's research has focused on the biochemical substrate of emotion. As she forwards, "Neuropeptides and their receptors thus join the brain, glands, and immune system in a network of communication between brain and body, probably representing the biochemical substrate of emotion" (p. 179).

LeDoux (1996) says that, "Bodily changes follow directly the PERCEPTION of the exciting fact, and that our feeling of the same changes as they occur IS the emotion" (p. 43). He further notes that, "emotions are things that happen to us rather than things that we will to occur…once emotions occur they become powerful indicators of future behavior" (p. 19).

Separating emotions and feelings, Damasio (1999) proposes the following:

The term feeling should be reserved for the private, mental experience of an emotion, while the term emotion should be used to designate the collection of responses, many of which are publicly observable (p. 42).

He further states that, "In short, emotional states are defined by myriad changes in the body's profile, by changes in the state of viscera; and by changes in the degree of contraction of varied striated muscles of the face, trunk, and limbs" (Damasio, 1999, p. 282).

While none of the other authors cited below provide definitions of emotion, they often refer to common characteristics of emotion such as sadness, fear, happiness, and anger.

As an operational definition of emotion, we take the dictionary definition, with the caveat that the various peripheral characteristics of emotion noted in this section may also apply depending upon the author, context, and content of application. Emotion is "a mental state that arises spontaneously rather than through conscious effort and is often accompanied by physiological changes; a feeling" (*American Heritage Dictionary*, 2006, p. 585).

There is solid agreement on the link between emotions and learning. Zull (2002) considers emotions the foundation of learning, with the chemicals of emotion modifying the strength and contribution of each part of the learning cycle, directly impacting the signaling systems in each affected neuron. Similarly, Blackmore (2004) reminds us that reason cannot operate without emotions.

> Emotions are the foundation of learning, with the chemicals of emotion modifying the strength and contribution of each part of the learning cycle.

Further, Greenfield (2000) is convinced that emotions are the building block of consciousness. As she points out, they are with us all the time to a greater or lesser degree, "depending on how much you are using, or losing, your mind at any one moment (p. 21). Plotkin (1994) says that emotional content is almost always present in verbal and non-verbal communication. If it wasn't, that would be a sign of pathology. "Normal human life is lived within a sea of experienced and expressed emotions" (Plotkin, 1994, p. 211). Plotkin (1994) also asserts that emotional knowledge is every bit as important as other forms of knowledge.

REFLECT:

Am I aware of—and can I exercise control over—my biases?
How do my personal perspectives affect my perceptions?

Zull never defines emotions, but refers to LeDoux several times, and looks at emotion as asking ourselves what we want and what we do not want. From a teacher-learner perspective Zull (2002) suggests that, "Our emotions still seem very important and if we want to help people learn, we must expect to encounter emotion, and we must take it seriously" (p. 52). Further, he says that emotions are almost always present. "The fear and pleasure machinery in our brains are at work all the time" (p. 52). Zull also notes that, in basic ways they run our lives, as they have for millions of years. They are still important,

> ... and if we want to help people to learn, we must expect to encounter emotion, and we must take it seriously. We cannot dismiss the learner's emotions, even when they seem trivial or unjustified to us. (Zull, 2002, p. 52)

Thus, there is clearly value in studying the way emotions work in the brain. As LeDoux (1996) notes, "there are many possible solutions to the puzzle of how emotions might work, but the only one we really care about is the one that evolution hit upon and put into the brain" (p. 13).

The term "emotion" is a label for what LeDoux (1996) sees as a "convenient way of talking about aspects of the brain and its mind" (p. 16) and that we experience as "coordinated responses spreading through the whole body frequently linked to a social context" (Bownds, 1999, p. 229). Damasio (1994) sees the essence of emotions as a collection of changes in the body state such as skin color, body posture and facial expressions. These changes are induced by nerve cell terminals "under the control of a dedicated brain system, which is responding to the content of thoughts relative to a particular entity or event" (p. 139). Damasio's dedicated brain system that is associated with the processing of emotionally significant information is the limbic system. The limbic system operates behind the scenes, in the unconscious (Tallis, 2002). As Lipton (2005) explains,

> The evolution of the limbic system provided a unique mechanism that converted the chemical communication signals into sensations that could be experienced by all of the cells in the community. (p. 131)

Damasio (1994) calls these internal signals experienced by the conscious mind feelings and their external expression emotions. The physiological responses that return to the brain in the form of bodily sensations are the observable aspects of emotion. Pert's (1997) study of information-processing receptors on nerve cell membranes led her to discover the presence of the same neural receptors on most of the body's cells. As Lipton (2005) sums up,

> Damasio calls the internal signals experienced by the conscious mind feelings and their external expression emotions. This is a useful differentiation.

Pert's "elegant experiments established that the 'mind' was not focused in the head, but was distributed via signal molecules to the whole body" (p. 132). Pert has studied how the mind, spirit, and emotions are unified with the physical body in a single intelligent system.

The above discussion demonstrates the complexity and holistic aspects of the mind/brain/body and therefore its self-organizing and autopoietic properties. While Pert (1997) understands that molecules are the building blocks of thoughts and emotions, she also recognizes a two-way system of communication where, for example, endorphins can be released into the body to cause pain relief but they can also be released within the body through a state of mind.

Each emotion has a unique quality resulting from a pattern of sensory feedback from separate neural systems that have evolved for different reasons. As LeDoux (1996) explains,

> Fear feels different from anger or love because it has a different physiological signature. The mental aspect of emotion, the feeling, is a slave to its physiology, not vice versa: we do not tremble because we are afraid or cry because we feel sad; we are afraid because we tremble and sad because we cry. (pp. 44-45)

LeDoux ties his conclusion all the way back to Henry James' premise that emotions are often accompanied by bodily responses such as racing heart, a tight stomach, sweaty palms, or tense muscles. James (1890) said that emotions feel different from other states of mind since they give rise to internal sensations. Further, different emotions feel different from each other because they are accompanied by different sensations and bodily responses. Thus, "the physiological responses return to the brain in the form of bodily sensations and the unique pattern of sensory feedback gives each emotion its unique quality" (LeDoux, 1996, p. 44). In the 1920s a prominent psychologist, Walter Cannon (1929), discovered through studying bodily responses to hunger and intense emotion that when an "emergency reaction" (the fight or flight response) occurred, a specific physiological response accompanied any state in which physical energy was required. This was an adaptive response occurring in anticipation of energy expenditure.

Integrating findings from neuroscience, LeDoux (1996) says that "emotion and cognition are best thought of as separate but interacting mental functions mediated by separate but interacting brain systems" (p. 69). He supports this belief through the following concepts:

*Animals or humans lose the ability to emotionally appraise stimuli (without loss in the capacity to perceive the same stimuli as objects) when a certain region of the brain is damaged.

*Emotional meaning can begin prior to perceptual processing of a stimulus, making it possible for the brain to know whether something is good or bad *before* it understands exactly what the stimulus is.

*The brain mechanisms that register, store, and retrieve emotional significance are different than those through which related cognitive memories are processed.

*Emotional appraisal systems and emotional response systems are directly connected.

The net result "is that bodily sensations often accompany appraisals" and become "part of the conscious experience of emotions" (LeDoux, 1996, p. 70).

A considerable amount of study has been done on the asymmetry in prefrontal activity that underlies differences in mood. In 1992, Davidson and colleagues at Harvard reported that activity detected by EEG in the brain's prefrontal cortex was a reflection of a person's emotional state.

> When activity in the left prefrontal cortex is markedly and chronically higher than in the right, people report feeling alert, energized, enthusiastic, and joyous, enjoying life more and having a greater sense of well-being. Put simply, they tend to be happier. When there is greater activity in the right prefrontal cortex, people report feeling negative emotions, including worry, anxiety, and sadness. (in Begley, 2007, p. 225)

Since emotional processing can—and regularly does—take place outside of conscious awareness, we may not be aware of what is driving our decisions and actions. As LeDoux (1996) details, "The emotional meaning of a stimulus can begin to be appraised by the brain before the perceptual systems have fully processed the stimulus" (p. 69). This means that it is possible for the brain to know that something is good or bad before the individual consciously recognizes what that something is. For example, LeDoux (1996) describes one patient where emotional significance of a stimulus had leaked across the brain, even though the identity of the stimulus had not. "The left hemisphere, in other words, was making emotional judgments without knowing what was being judged. The left hemisphere knew the emotional outcome, but it did not have access to the processes that led up to that outcome" (p. 15). Further, LeDoux notes that "emotion involves action tendencies and bodily responses, as well as conscious experiences" (p. 52).

> Since emotional processing can—and regularly does—take place outside of conscious awareness, we may not be aware of what is driving our decisions and actions.

REFLECT:
How does my body feel when I experience strong emotions?
What is the impact of strong emotions on my thinking and actions?

The idea of consciousness has always been a difficult concept to pin down. As an operational definition we consider consciousness to be a state of awareness and a private, selective and continuously changing process; A process, a sequential set of ideas, thoughts, images, feelings and perceptions and an understanding of the connections and relationships among them and our Self. We also use Edelman and Tononi's (2000) focus on the properties of consciousness, namely unity—each conscious state is experienced as a whole, and informativeness, which means that "within a fraction of a second each conscious state is selected from a repertoire of billions and billions of possible conscious states, each with different consequences"

(p. 18). As an operational definition of unconscious, we use LeDoux's (2002) interpretation as "the many things that the brain does that are not available to consciousness" (p. 11).

Some studies have shown that our emotions (in the form of internal feelings) are more easily influenced when we are not aware that the influence is occurring. However, by understanding that emotions are things that happen to us rather than things we order to occur, we can set up situations where external events provide stimuli to trigger desired feelings (LeDoux, 1996). We do this regularly when we go to the movies or visit an amusement park, or even when we consume alcohol or stimulate our palate with a gourmet meal.

From a neuroscience perspective, in addition to Kolb's (1984) four-mode learning model of sensing, reflecting, comprehending, and acting (represented as four regions of the cortex), we need to consider the emotional systems of cells that can be thought of as chemical-delivery neurons. As Zull (2002) describes, neurotransmitters "are ancient, evolutionarily speaking, and their modern-day function is often associated with emotion: adrenaline, dopamine, and serotonin are examples" (p. 4).

Information coming into the body first moves through the amygdala, that part of the limbic system that is important for both the acquisition and on-line processing of emotional stimuli. This processing encompasses "both the elicitation of emotional responses in the body and changes in other cognitive processes, such as attention and memory" (Adolphs, 2004, p. 1026). Thus, the neurotransmitters described above are linked with information. As Mulvihill (2003) explains,

> Because the neurotransmitters which carry messages of emotion, are integrally linked with the [incoming] information, during both the initial processing and the linking with information from the different senses, it becomes clear that there is no thought, memory, or knowledge which is "objective," or "detached" from the personal experience of knowing. (p. 322)

LeDoux (1996) points out that emotions just happen to us. Emotions, attitudes, and the like are activated automatically without any conscious effort. As part of our evolving learning system, memories and the emotional tags that gauge the importance of those memories become part of an individual's everyday life. "Tags" is a term indicating that the amygdala "tags" or puts some level of danger or importance on the incoming signal indicated by release of hormones throughout the body. Christos (2003) agrees that emotions and mood play a prominent role in learning, or what he calls the laying down of memories. However, he adds that consciousness also plays an important role in the learning experience. "We seem to have to become conscious of something before we can learn it properly" (p. 40). The *stronger the emotional tag* (from the amygdala), the greater the strength of the memory connections and the easier to recall (LeDoux, 1996). Memory is

> Emotions, attitudes, and the like are activated automatically without any conscious effort.

enhanced when emotions (such as fear or joy) are heightened (Christos, 2003). As Kluwe et al. (2003) details,

> Often we experience that emotionally arousing events result in better recollection of memories. It appears to us that we will not forget certain events in our life whenever they are accompanied by very pleasant or fearful emotions. (p. 51)

This is true because emotions have priority in our stream of consciousness and our memory. Consciousness is comprised of a single, linear stream of thought patterns (Edelman & Tononi, 2000). Through evolution (based on survival of the fittest) our brain has been wired such that the neuronal connections from the emotional systems to the cognitive systems are much stronger than the connections from the cognitive systems to the emotional systems (LeDoux, 1996). Further, LeDoux observes that,

> Emotions have priority in our stream of consciousness and our memory.

> There is but one mechanism of consciousness and it can be occupied by mundane facts or highly charged emotions. Emotions easily bump mundane events out of awareness, but nonemotional events (like thoughts) do not so easily displace emotions from the mental spotlight—wishing that anxiety or depression would go away is usually not enough. (p. 9)

As Zull (2002) confirms, "emotions influence our thinking more than thinking influences our emotion" (p. 75).

This brings us to a further discussion of cognition and emotions. LeDoux (1996) offers that cognition is not as logical as it was once thought and emotions are not always so illogical. Damasio (1999) sees emotions as the undercurrent of cognition, in that our feelings tell us what we need to know about a current situation.

Both cognition and emotion seem to operate unconsciously, "with only the outcome of cognitive or emotional processing entering awareness and occupying our conscious minds, and only in some instances" (LeDoux, 1996, p. 21). Further, another aspect of influence (and learning) deals with unconscious exposure. LeDoux (2002) suggests that the emotional mind appears to be more susceptible to stimuli of which the conscious mind is unaware:

> The mere exposure effect is much stronger when the stimuli are subliminally presented than when the stimuli are freely available for conscious inspection ... our emotions are more easily influenced when we are not aware that the influence is occurring. (p. 61)

As an example, demonstrating that emotional processing can occur without conscious awareness, LeDoux offers research by Zajonc and his associates. The emotional unconscious has been investigated using a procedure called *subliminal emotional priming*. A priming stimulus such as a picture of a smiling or frowning face is very briefly presented (about 5 milliseconds) followed by a masking stimulus to prevent the subject from being able to consciously recall the priming stimulus. Following a delay, a target stimulus pattern is presented long enough for the subject to consciously recall.

After seeing many patterns this way, it was found that the subjects liked or disliked the target stimulus depending upon whether the prime was a positive or negative stimulus, that is, a smiling or frowning face. Further, it was found that the emotional priming was more effective when unconscious presentations were used than when the subjects were consciously aware of the stimulus (LeDoux, 1996). LeDoux finds the prospect that emotional learning bypasses the neocortex intriguing, "for it suggests that emotional responses can occur without the involvement of the higher processing systems of the brain, systems believed to be involved in thinking, reasoning, and consciousness (1996, p. 161).

REFLECT:
Do I use of my emotional guidance system effectively?
How can I embed emotions in my learning experiences?

Understanding and harnessing the power of emotion can improve an individual's ability to learn. Recall the old adage: *Follow your passion*. Passion is considered those desires, behaviors, and thoughts that suggest urges with considerable force (Frijda, 2000). Specifically, Polanyi's (1958) assertion that positive passions affirm that something is precious, and that passion can be used as a determinant of what is great and of higher interest. A passion to learn or a deep passion related to the content of learning embeds strong emotional feelings with what is being learned, directly impacting the number of synapse connections created and the strength of those connections (Bennet & Bennet, 2008e).

> Passion for learning or the content of learning embeds strong emotional feelings with what is being learned, strengthening the synapse connections.

Another aspect of learning involves the conscious intent to learn. In a study of information-processing receptors on nerve cell membranes, Pert (1997) discovered that emotions were not simply derived through a feedback of the body's environmental information, but that through self-consciousness the mind can use the brain to generate "molecules of emotion" and override the system.

Pert (1997) ran a research laboratory at the National Institute of Mental Health (NIMH) focused on researching and demonstrating how internal chemicals in the body, neuropeptides and their receptors, "run every system in our body's and how this communication system is in effect a demonstration of the body and mind's intelligence..." (p. 19). Pert's research, along with other scientists, resulted in some surprising conclusions. For example, Pert (1997) proposes that,

If we accept the idea that peptides and other informational substances are the biochemicals of emotion, their distribution in the body's nerves has all kinds of significance...the body is the unconscious mind! Repressed traumas caused by overwhelming emotion can be stored in a body part, thereafter affecting our ability to feel that part or even move it. The new work suggests there are almost infinite pathways for the conscious mind to access – and modify – the unconscious mind and the body, and also provides an explanation for the number of phenomena that the emotional theorists have been considering. (p. 141)

As introduced in Chapter 6, this self-conscious mind processing occurs in the prefrontal cortex that is, on the scale of evolution, the newly evolved organ that observes our behaviors and emotions (Lipton, 2005, p. 133). This portion of the brain has access to most of the data stored in our long-term memory bank and as discussed earlier is the executive part of the brain that solves problems, creates ideas, makes decisions, and initiates actions (Goldberg, 2001). What this means is that *our minds can choose to embed stronger emotional tags with specific incoming information*. For example, this occurs when we engage new ideas and become excited about the potential offered by these new ideas. LeDoux (1996) believes that this struggle between thought and emotion may ultimately be resolved, by "a more harmonious integration of reason and passion in the brain, a development that will allow future humans to better know their true feelings and to use them more effectively in daily life" (p. 21).

Although LeDoux does not address the issue of what he means by "true feelings," we would interpret the statement to mean that an individual may cognitively be sensitive to, and aware of, his or her emotions. This does not mean that emotions will go away. Indeed, LeDoux (1996) says that "many emotions are products of evolutionary wisdom, which probably has more intelligence than all human minds together" (p. 36). Evolutionary wisdom describes the concept that a species' past contributes to explaining the individual's current emotional state (Tooby & Cosmides, 1990). This means that through selection and survival, evolution would keep those emotions that aid the survival of the individual.

Stress

Stress plays a strong role in arousal and attention, both of which significantly impact the motivational and cognitive aspects of learning. From a neurological perspective, "the stress system is an active monitoring system that constantly compares current events to past experience, [and] interprets the relevance (salience) of the events to the survival of the organism" (Akil et al., 1999, p. 1146). The human distress system is primarily an emotional system. Akil et al. (1999) say that, "much of our learning is emotional as opposed to the more intellectual learning of less emotionally laden material such as calculus. We can conceive of stress mechanisms as fundamental to such emotional learning" (p. 1146).

It has been confirmed that stress is not solely a physical trauma. For example, four hours after a Harvard boat race the crew had a decline in cosinophil count (a stress blood measure). While the physical stress of the race might have caused this in the rowers, a similar decline was noted in the coxswains and coaches, whose stress was psychological (Thompson, 2000). A second example is the study by Seymour Levine of Stanford University and Holger Ursin of the University of Olso, Norway. They examined the hormonal and behavioral responses of Norwegian paratroop trainees following repeated jumps off a 10-meter tower. There was a dramatic elevation of cortisol in the blood following the first jump, but in subsequent jumps the cortisol level in the blood was at basal levels. In addition, Levine and Ursin noted that fear levels as expressed by the participants were similarly significantly reduced after the initial jump (Levine & Ursin, 1991).

> Stress is not solely a physical trauma. It has a psychological component.

Thompson (2000) agrees with these examples, explaining that stress is not just created by a physical phenomenon:

> The extent to which situations are stressful is determined by how the individual understands, interprets, sees, and feels about a situation. It is fundamentally a "cognitive" phenomenon depending more on how the individual construes the situations than on the nature of the situation itself. The key aspects are uncertainty and control: the less knowledge the individual has about a potentially harmful situation, the less control he or she feels can be exerted, the more stressful the situation is. Conversely, the more understanding and certainty the individual has about a situation the more he or she feels in control and the less stressful it is. (Thompson, 2000, p. 210).

As Thompson (2000) summarizes, it appears that, "We and other mammals appear to be driven by nature toward certainty" (p. 210). Further, he forwards that this may be the basis for the existence of various belief systems, since even if a person's understanding is wrong, "A person firmly committed to a belief system does in fact 'understand' the world and the nature of the controls that operate" (p. 210). Thompson describes several studies that support his belief that stress is not created only by a physical phenomenon.

REFLECT:
Do I follow my passion?
What is my optimal level of stress?

There are a number of physical characteristics to the stress response. Adrenaline is released, the heart rate increases, blood pressure goes up, and blood-clotting elements increase in the bloodstream. As the body readies for movement (flight or fight), the senses are more alert, muscles tense, and palms become sweaty. Simultaneously, "cortical memory systems retrieve any knowledge relevant to the emergency at hand, taking precedence over other strands of thought" (LeDoux, 1996, p. 39).

Stonier (1992) cites an example as the recall of the details of an accident. As he explains,

> In recounting the event later you are struck by the way your mind goes over and over your impressions of that scene just prior to the crash. Nature meant it to be that way. The physiological stress associated with the accident made certain that the lightly weighted connection—the "commonplace" sensory inputs describing the scene above—became heavily weighted. Somewhere in all these "commonplace" sensory inputs lie hidden environmental clues to an impending disaster. The neural network does not discriminate specifics. (Stonier, 1992, p. 145)

However, there appears to be an optimal level of stress for this to occur. Low stress can be good and is often termed arousal (see Figure 8-1). If stress relates to fear, this does not allow learning. "The reason is that if fear becomes too strong the amygdala takes control and tends to miss details" (Zull, 2002, p. 141). As noted above in the discussion of emotion, in an emergency, the faster information is processed the more likely an organism will survive. But this quick response simultaneously constricts the blood vessels in the forebrain, reducing its ability to function effectively (Lipton, 2005). As Lipton (2005) states,

> The simple truth is, when you're frightened, you're dumber. Teachers see it all the time among students who "don't test well." Exam stress paralyzes these students who, with trembling hands, mark wrong answers because in their panic, they can't access cerebrally stored information they have carefully acquired all semester. (p. 151)

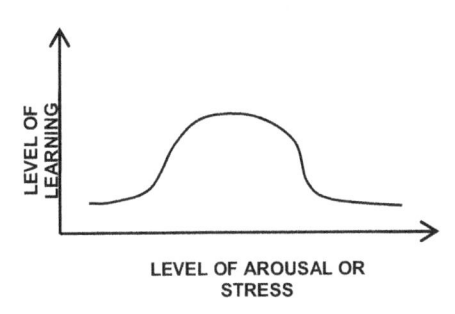

Figure 8-1. *A nominal graph displaying the relationship between learning capability and level of arousal or stress.*

Further, that same fear that causes a fight or flight response—specifically, the excessive levels of cortisol accompanying that response—can bring about negative long-term results for learning. As Byrnes (2001) observes,

Excessive levels of cortisol (a substance secreted by the adrenal glands during stress reactions) causes permanent damage to several regions of the brain, including the hippocampus (important for memory) and the locus ceruleus (important for selective attention). (p. 181)

By measuring activity in the amygdala using the fMRI—an area active during times of distress, fear, anger, and anxiety—Davidson discovered that some people were able to consciously change their level of response. He discovered that, "individuals with greater activation in this area are better able, when they have the aspiration to relieve suffering, to change their brain and reduce the activation in the amygdala" (Begley, 2007, p. 233). As recorded by Begley, the Dalai Lama's response to Davidson's discovery provides a good summary of Davidson's findings. "What seems to be very clear is that a purely mental process—for example, deliberately cultivating this aspiration—can have an effect that is observable in the brain level" (Begley, 2007, p. 233).

Chapter 9
Learning from Neuroscience: Implementation of Learning (Part II)

This chapter is the second part of the Implementation of Learning (beginning in Chapter 9), which addresses neuroscience findings that will help adult learners to understand key areas of the mind/brain/body and **their effect on the learning process** and be able to adjust their individual behavior to specific situations and goals. Focus areas in Part II include memory, mirror neurons, creativity, and the unconscious.

Memory

As Tennessee Williams wrote in *The Milk Train Doesn't Stop Here Anymore*, "Has it ever struck you ... that life is all memory, except for the one present moment that goes by you so quickly you hardly catch it going?" (cited in Kandel, 2006, p. 281). Memory is everywhere, stored throughout neurons in the brain and other parts of the body: approximately 100 billion neurons in the brain, 20,000 in the heart, and 6,000 in the gut. Parts of the brain act as central control systems and operating posts to connect incoming and outgoing signals to the many different regions of the central nervous system, and no two patterns of this creative process are the same (Kandel, 2006).

As represented by the multiple references cited below, it is generally accepted that there are at least two basic types of long-term memory. The first type is declarative (explicit) memory, that is, the recollection of those memories that in principle can be consciously retrieved and reported (Kluwe et al., 2003; Markowitsch, 1999, 2000; Schacter, 1996; Squire & Knowlton, 1995).

> It is generally accepted that there are at least two basic types of long-term memory: declarative and procedural.

The second type is "procedural (or implicit) memory, which includes skills and habits, priming, classical and operant conditioning and non-associative learning, i.e., habituation and sensitization" (Kluwe et al., 2003, p. 53).

The storage and retrieval of memories lie in the structure, association, and activities of neurons and their synaptic connection strengths. Ascoli (2002), head of the Computational Neuroanatomy Group at the Krasnow Institute for Advance Study, says,

> The principal axiom of modern neuroscience: the key substrate for all the functions performed by nervous systems, from regulation of vital states, reflexes,

and motor control, to the storage and retrieval of memories and appreciation of artistic beauty, lies not in some "magic" ingredient, but rather in the structure and assembly of neurons. (2002, p. 3).

Both learning and memory are expressed physiologically in the formation of new synapses, the connections between neurons, and the strengthening of existing synapses (Begley, 2007).

"Brains have complex rules of guessing that allow them to extract information from incoming signals and create meaning and understanding without storing the full incoming signal" (Hawkins, 2004, p. 75). Memory storage, recall and recognition all occur at the level of invariant forms, what Hawkins (2004) describes as "a form that captures the essence of relationships, not the details of the moment" (p. 82). Recall the example provided earlier of the memory of your friend's face, which is stored in a form such that it is independent of any particular view. The face can be recognized because of its relative dimensions, colors, and proportions. As Hawkins describes, there are spatial intervals between the features of the face just as there are pitch intervals between the notes of a song. Further, Hawkins sees the entire cortex as a memory system, storing sequences of patterns, recalling patterns auto-associatively, and storing patterns in a hierarchy (Hawkins, 2004). The significance of hierarchy was discussed earlier. As a working definition, memory systems refer to the full set of memory patterns stored throughout the mind/brain/body.

> Memory storage, recall and recognition all occur at the level of invariant forms.

There is no equivalent concept in computers for invariant forms, yet using invariant forms a human can perform significant tasks reliably in half a second or less. As Hawkins (2004) describes regarding a simple thought experiment,

> This task is difficult or impossible for a computer to perform today, yet a human can do it reliably in half a second or less. But neurons are slow, so in that half a second, the information entering your brain can only traverse a chain one hundred neurons long. That is, the brain "computes" solutions to problems like this in one hundred steps or fewer, regardless of how many total neurons might be involved. (p. 66)

Of course, the brain is not computing the answers to problems at all. The entire cortex is a memory system (Hawkins, 2004), associating new incoming information with stored patterns (associative patterning); (Bennet & Bennet, 2004). Hawkins (2004) says of this process,

> All memories are like this. You have to walk through the temporal sequence of how you do things. One pattern (approach the door) evokes the next pattern (go through the door), which evokes the next pattern (either go down the hall or ascend the stairs). ... Truly random thought doesn't exist. Memory recall almost always follows a pathway of association. (Hawkins, 2004, p. 71)

As he describes this process, you need to finish one part of the story before moving on to the next. Hawkins (2004) likens it to a story in which—whether written, oral or visual—the narrative is conveyed in a serial fashion. Recall the earlier discussion on consciousness as a single stream of thought. Thus one part of the story is associated with the next part of the story in a linear telling: "it's almost impossible to think of anything complex that isn't a series of events or thoughts" (p. 70).

Bloom (2007) points out that progress in neuroscience involving aspects of the "movie-in-the-brain" is leading to increasing insights related to the mechanisms of learning and memory.

> In rapid succession, research has revealed that the brain uses discrete systems for different types of learning. The basal ganglia and cerebellum are critical for the acquisition of skills—for example, learning to ride a bicycle or play a musical instrument. The hippocampus is integral to the learning of facts pertaining to such entities as people, places or events. And once facts are learned, the long-term memory of those facts relies on multicomponent brain systems, whose key parts are located in the vast brain expanses known as cerebral cortices. (pp. 63-64).

REFLECT:
What memories do I wish I had more of?
How do I combine ideas to make them more memorable?

This brings us to a discussion of what is generally known as the binding problem. To form a complete memory, fragments of associated patterns need to be in some way combined. As Christos (2003) describes,

> Fragments of attractors need to be combined in some way (called the "binding problem") to form a complete memory. The hippocampus may be involved in this function. Another particularly interesting candidate is the thalamus, which is the gateway to all sensory information entering the neocortex and for some reason also receives reciprocal information from each of the areas in the neocortex that it sends information to. It is also known that neurotransmitters like norepinephrine are implicated with learning and are thought to be released from the locus coeruleus when something is to be learned. This needs to be coordinated with the task of observation. (p. 51)

A second issue has to do with memory traces, which do not necessarily involve pathways identical to incoming information. The greater the differences from the original incoming thought, the fuzzier the memory (Stonier, 1997). This is where Edelman's neural Darwinism comes in, the fact that pathways are continuously being corrupted or weakened. The less the pathways are used the faster they become corrupted (Rosenfield, 1988). There is a competition of thoughts (neural Darwinism) coming into consciousness. There are, however, exceptions. As Stonier (1997) describes,

> The evolution of the brain has created special categories of nerve traces which become relatively incorruptible. For example, those created during the developing embryo relating to vital functions are probably stable during our entire lifetime. Those involving imprinting phenomena in juveniles, likewise, are less prone to decay. The same thing may be said for those which become habits and those learned during emotional stress. (p. 154)

This brings us back to a focus on the relationship of emotions and memory. As mentioned above, memory seems to be enhanced if our emotions (such as fear or joy) are heightened. From a neuroscience perspective, "The amygdala sends signals to the locus coeruleus and other related brain structures to release more neurotransmitters, "which help the brain to cement the learning experience" (Christos, 2003, 51). Gladwell (2005) calls memory the embodiment of emotion tied to experience—not just "what happened" but "how my body reacted to what happened" (Taylor, 2006, p. 81). As Kluwe et al. (2003) state,

> The fact that memory and emotions are closely connected is a part of our daily life. Often we experience that emotionally arousing events result in better recollection of memories. It appears to us that we will not forget certain events in our life whenever they are accompanied by very pleasant or fearful emotions. (p. 51)

Christos says that some memories are stored with great intensity, "say if they mean something to us (if they heighten our conscious awareness or involve our emotions in some way)" and other memories are stored very weakly (Christos, 2003, p. 85). The greater the power of the emotion that is associated with an experience, the more lasting the memory (Johnson, 2006). An example is what is called the "flashbulb memory" involving a very vivid memory for extremely emotional events such as the death of a close friend or a catastrophe like that experienced in New York on September 11 (Kluwe et al., 2003). However, this same event can cause the opposite response. As Taylor points out, "The exception is when the initial experience is so traumatic that dissociation occurs; under these circumstances, memories may be deeply buried or completely inaccessible to recall" (Taylor, 2006, p. 81).

Educators use this power of emotion to promote learning and memory through role-playing and other experiential activities. Wolf says that the probability that important data will be stored in rich, permanent networks can be influenced by educators. "By intensifying the student's emotional state, they [educators] may enhance both meaning and memory" (Wolfe, 2006, p. 39).

Mirror Neurons

An athlete training to become a pole-vaulter may make a video of his perfect pole vault and by repeatedly reviewing that movie increase his athletic capability. The patterns going through his brain while executing the vault are *the same* as the patterns in his brain when he is watching a video of that same vault. As Blakemore and Frith (2005) describe,

> Simply observing someone moving activates similar brain areas to those activated by producing movements oneself. The brain's *motor regions* become active by the mere observation of movements even if the observer remains completely still. (pp. 160-161)

Neuroscientific research has identified this phenomenon and refers to it as mirror neurons. As Dobb's (2007) explains,

> These neurons are scattered throughout key parts of the brain—the premotor cortex and centers for language, empathy and pain—and fire not only as we perform a certain action, but also when we watch someone else perform that action. (p. 22)

Zull (2002) suggests that mirror neurons are a form of cognitive mimicry that transfers actions, behaviors and most likely other cultural norms. Thus, when we *see* something being enacted, our mind creates the same patterns that we would use to enact that "something" ourselves. While mirror neurons are a subject of current research, it would appear that they represent a neuroscientific mechanism for the transfer of tacit knowledge between individuals, or throughout a culture. Siegel suggests that mirror neurons are the way in which our social brain processes and precedes the intentional or goal-directed action of others. Thus, mirror neurons link our perception to the priming of the motor systems that engage the same action. In other words, "what we see, we become ready to do, to mirror other's actions and our own behaviors" (Siegel, 2007, p. 347).

> Mirror neurons facilitate the direct and immediate comprehension of another's behavior without going through complex cognitive processes.

Nelson et al. (2006) suggest that the research has contributed to a simulation theory of mentalizing "which argues that we understand other people's behavior by mentally simulating it" (p. 141). He also suggests that this neural resonance between observed actions and executing actions may be behind the imitation of facial gestures observed in human babies (Meltzoff & Decety, 2002; Nelson et al., 2006). In an article entitled *The Neurobiology of the Self*, Zimmer suggests that the sense of Self may be fragile because the mind is continually trying to get inside the minds of other people. This would occur because mirror neurons tend to mimic the experiences of others (Zimmer, 2007).

REFLECT:
Am I able to imitate behaviors that I admire?
What does understanding mirror neurons say to us about the importance of the activities in which we participate and the movies we watch?

Creativity

As a working definition, creativity means the ability to conceive new ideas, concepts or capabilities that have not been created before. Hobson (1999) says that creativity is inherent in the basic operation of the nervous system. Andreasen (2005) sees the brain as a "self-organizing system that can create novel linkages on a millisecond time scale" (p. 64). Christos (2003) says that it stands to reason from a scientific perspective that individual creativity is a function of the brain (and what is stored in it), but the question is how this occurs.

> I believe the answer is related to the fact that memory is stored distributively in wide areas of the brain in such a way that different memories overlap each other or use common neurons and synapses for their storage and representation. This overlapping store of memory in common areas naturally gives rise ... to new states or memories that were not intentionally stored in the network. (Christos, 2003, p. 74)

For the most part, these are new associations of patterns, or in other words connections that represent other ideas and knowledge. As Christos (2003) explains,

> We often imagine that creativity is totally new and original, but in most cases it is not. It generally possesses features of known facts (or stored memories). Ideas are built on other ideas and knowledge, and no person is truly and absolutely original. Creative ideas are copied, borrowed, and manipulated versions of what we know and acquire. Human creativity and imitation (or memes) play complementary roles in the evolution of ideas. (p. 87)

Christos draws on Blackmore (1999) to describe a meme as,

> ... taken to be something, like a skill, technique or useful idea that we have copied from someone else, such as how to make a fire, how to use tools, how to grow crops, ...or just a piece of information or knowledge generally. (cited in Christos, 2003, p. 73)

Christos (2003) also says that the human brain has a natural capacity to be creative, the ability to generate something entirely new—its own information or memory-like states—not formally acquired from the overlapping storage of memory. This overlapping storage of memory in common areas gives rise to what Christos calls "spurious memories," new states or memories

> The human brain has a natural capacity to be creative, the ability to generate something entirely new.

not intentionally stored in the network. While spurious memories may possess some subtle combinations of stored memories, they,

> ... have the capacity to generate new ideas that combine different bits of information ... [and] may be extremely useful (and possibly essential), not just for creativity but also so that a neural network can learn something new, adapt, generalize, classify, think, and make new associations. (Christos, 2003, pp. 74-75)

These spurious states made up of an endless variety of combinations of features of stored memories may be what we call creativity.

> They may correspond to what we commonly identify as creativity, or the ability to do something new or different. Spurious states clearly give the brain added flexibility to adapt and to develop nonbiological abilities. (Christos, 2003, p. 36)

Andreasen (2005) talks about ordinary and extra-ordinary creativity. Referring to behavioral aspects of highly creative people, she calls out specific personality and cognitive traits such as openness to experience, curiosity, and a tolerance of ambiguity. She also describes creative people as often receiving their ideas as flashes of insights "through moments of inspiration, or by going into a state at the edge of chaos, where ideas float, soar, collide, and connect" (p. 159). Further,

> We have learned that this creative state arises from a mind and brain that are rich in associative links that encourage new combinations to occur freely. And we have learned that the brain is plastic—that we can change, and hopefully improve, our brains by exercising them. We have also learned that all of us possess, at a minimum, something I have called ordinary creativity. To call it ordinary is not to diminish it. The fact that we can generate novel speech "on the fly" is a testament to the "extraordinary ordinary creativity of our glorious human brains." (Andreasen, 2005, p. 159)

On the other hand, extraordinary creativity, she concludes, is at least sometimes based on a "qualitatively different neural process than ordinary creativity" and at least sometimes arises from that "over the precipice component of human thought that we call the unconscious" (p. 77). She also feels that unconscious mental life may be highly relevant to extraordinary creativity (p. 77).

REFLECT:
When am I the most creative?
How do I nurture and honor my imagination?

Tallis (2002) agrees that creativity works more efficiently when consciousness has been—at least temporarily—dissolved. This is not a new idea. In Poincare's discussion about his own experiences with creativity (1908/1982), he forwards a volleying back and forth between the conscious mind and the unconscious mind (Andreasen, 2005). As Christos (2003) describes this process:

> [Poincare] asserts that new ideas are often generated through a process whereby a problem reverts from the conscious mind (required to initiate the "search") to the unconscious mind (required to generate new ideas) and back to the conscious mind (required to ascertain the usefulness of the ideas generated by the unconscious mind). (p. 90)

Andreasen 2005) offers that "there is a resonance between an inspired nonrational state and a more rational state in which the details were elaborated" (p. 43). While Amen does not address this "volleying," he does say that creative people slip into a state of intense concentration and focus that is similar to an unconscious state, where a person is no longer in touch with reality. But he adds,

> In a subjective sense ... the creative individual is moving into another reality that is actually more real ... a place where words, thoughts, and ideas float freely, collide, and ultimately coalesce. (Amen, 2005, p. 37)

Finally, Begley states that,

> It has become a truism that the better connected a brain is, the better it is, period, enabling the mind it runs to connect new facts with old, to retrieve memories, and even to see links among seemingly disparate facts, the foundation for creativity. (Begley, 2007, p. 69)

While Begley (2007) refers to the strength of the associative patterning process (through various methods discussed above), it is now recognized that strengthening connections can change the physiology of the brain. Andreasen (2005) forwards Davidson's work with Buddhist monks to suggest that meditation, in this study non-referential meditation, created high levels of gamma synchrony. Further, she says that this "gamma power" was the greatest "in the association cortices that are the reservoir of creativity—frontal, temporal, and parietal association regions," concluding that,

> People can change their brains by training them in the practice of meditation, so that they improve the quality of their moment-to-moment awareness not only during meditation but also during the routine of everyday life. (Andreasen, 2005, p. 164)

Andreasen says there are other ways to "open the brain" that are quite different from meditation. These methodologies focus on achieving an intentional focus on an object (referential) or on a state (nonreferential) through "just thinking." Andreasen (2005, p. 165) says that an example is the state of "random episodic silent thought" (REST), which is a way of "achieving a more creative state of mind."

Sound can also play a role in opening the brain, specifically, in opening the connection between the conscious and the unconscious mind. Pinker (2007) notes that neuroscience has slowly begun to recognize the capability of internal thoughts and external information such as sound to affect the physical structure of the brain—its synaptic connection strengths, its neuronal connections, and the growth of additional neurons. Hemispheric synchronization is the use of sound coupled with a binaural beat to bring both hemispheres of the brain into unison (Bennet & Bennet, 2007).

H.W. Dove, a German experimenter, identified binaural beats in 1839. In the human mind, binaural beats are detected with carrier tones (audio tones of slightly different frequencies, one tone to each ear) below approximately 1500 Hz (Oster, 1973). The mind perceives the frequency differences of the sound coming into each ear, integrating the two sounds as a fluctuating rhythm and thereby creating a beat or difference frequency. This perceived rhythm originates in the brainstem (Oster, 1973), is neurologically routed to the reticular activating formation, also in the brainstem (Swann et al., 1982) and then to the cortex where it can be measured as a frequency-following response (Hink et al., 1980; Marsh et al., 1975; Smith et al., 1978). This inter-hemispheric communication is the setting for brain-wave coherence, which facilitates whole-brain cognition, assuming an elevated status in subject experience (Ritchey, 2003).

What can occur during hemispheric synchronization is a physiologically reduced state of arousal while maintaining conscious awareness (Atwater, 2004; Delmonte, 1984; Fischer, 1971), and the capacity to reach the unconscious creative state described above through the window of consciousness. An in-depth treatment of hemispheric synchronization is included in Chapter 21 where music and sound are used as an example of the impact of the environment on learning.

REFLECT:
How can meditation practices serve me?
How do I create a resonance between the rational and non-rational?

The Unconscious Brain

While the existence and nature of the unconscious mind/brain has been a challenge for many years—from Freud to modern neuroscience—there is increasing evidence of the existence and importance of the role of our unconscious minds/brains in affecting our lives and behaviors. The following paragraphs address aspects of the unconscious mind that relate to adult experiences of learning.

We start with a dictionary definition, and then briefly consider comments by researchers in the field. Unconscious is not conscious or occurring in the absence of conscious awareness or thought, without conscious control; involuntary or unintended (*American Heritage Dictionary*, 2006, p. 1873). The definition offered by James Uleman (2005) in his introduction to *The New Unconscious* is, "we define the unconscious as internal qualities of mind that affect conscious thought and behavior, without being conscious themselves" (p. 3). In addressing the new unconscious, Uleman (2005) says that,

> The new unconscious is much more concerned with affect, motivation, and even control and metacognition than was the old cognitive unconscious. Goals, motives and self-regulation are prominent without the conflict and drama of the psychoanalytic unconscious. (p. 6)

At the beginning of the introduction to their book *Philosophy in the Flesh*, Lakoff and Johnson (1999) offer the following: "The mind is inherently embodied. Thought is mostly unconscious. Abstract concepts are largely metaphorical. And these are three major findings of cognitive science." (p. 3) Further, they say that, "All of our knowledge and beliefs are framed in terms of a conceptual system that resides mostly in the cognitive unconscious" (Lakoff & Johnson, 1999, p. 13). While they have a chapter on the cognitive unconscious and give it high importance in their book, no definition of "unconscious" could be found. However, similar to Uleman's definition, the implication from their use of the term "cognitive unconscious" is that the unconscious is that which is not conscious.

Agreeing with the above definitions, LeDoux (2002) says, "What I mean by the term is the many things that the brain does that are not available to consciousness" (p. 11). Addressing the unconscious processes, LeDoux (2002) offers that,

> They include almost everything the brain does, from standard body maintenance like regulating heart rate, breathing rhythms, stomach contractions, and posture to controlling many aspects of seeing, smelling, behaving, feeling, speaking, thinking, evaluating, judging, believing and imagining. (p. 11)

These processes also include emotions. As LeDoux (1996) says, "It now seems undeniable that the emotional meanings of stimuli can be processed unconsciously. The emotional unconscious is where much of the emotional action is in the brain" (p. 64). Thus, people take many actions the reason of which they are unaware.

> We concluded people normally do all sorts of things for reasons they are not consciously aware of (because the behavior is produced by brain systems that operate unconsciously) and that one of the main jobs of consciousness is to keep our life tied together into a coherent story, a self-concept. (LeDoux, 1996, p. 33)

Other authors publishing in neuroscience or related fields express similar perspectives of the unconscious. Taken together, these thoughts contribute to a new way of thinking about the unconscious, one far removed from the classical Freudian psychoanalysis. For example, Tallis (2002), in his book *Hidden Minds: A History of the Unconscious* forwards that, "We feel the presence of our unconscious minds like a ghost, invisible but nevertheless somehow there" (p. ix). He further states that, "It is now almost impossible to construct a credible model of the mind without assuming that important functions will be performed outside of awareness" (p. xi). While never defining unconscious, Tallis clearly considers it to be that part of the mind/brain that is beyond awareness of the individual.

Below are several brief descriptions of how other neuroscientists working in this area perceive the unconscious. "The intelligence of the unconscious is in knowing, without thinking, which rule is likely to work in which situation." (Gigerenzer, 2007, p. 19) Similar to Tallis, Gigerenzer does not define the unconscious but uses it in a way that denotes it is beyond awareness. Hawkins, (2004) forwards that, "Our brains never turn off, and we should neither devalue our unconscious states nor overvalue our conscious ones." (p. 68)

Hawkins does not explain his use of the concept of unconscious although the implication would be that unconscious states are those states that the individual is not aware of. "From this perspective, to which most neural scientists now subscribe, most of our mental life is unconscious; it becomes conscious only as words and images." (Kandel, 2006, p. 424) And Kandel (2006) goes on to say, "As I was to learn later, in reading Freud's Psychopathology of Everyday Life a fundamental principle of dynamic psychology is that the unconscious never lies. (p. 25)

From the example surrounding Kandel's latter statement, his meaning is that the unconscious mind, being part of the individual's mind/brain/body system, exists to aid in its growth and survival. As such, it collects and stores information, experiences, feelings, and knowledge gained throughout life. But it is not separate from the individual and, while it may be wrong in its thoughts and conclusions, it is not independent of the individual and its output is the results of its history. This builds on Freud's (1901/1989) thought forwarded in the *Psychopathology of Everyday Life* that an individual's truth is based on what has been experienced and learned by the individual.

> While the unconscious may be wrong in its thoughts and conclusions, it is not independent of the individual and its output is the results of its history.

Though William James (1890/1980) characterized unconscious thought as a contradiction in terms, evidence for implicit thought is mounting (Dorfman et al., 1996; Eich et al., 2000; Kihlstrom et al., 1996). We are always aware of our own conscious thoughts; however, we frequently forget about the large amount of thinking that is occurring throughout our brain via the unconscious. The cognitive processes that give rise to intuitive or unconscious knowledge cannot be examined directly because they are not conscious, so we don't know what they are or even what information they draw upon (Carter, 2002). Note that although intuition is a subset of the unconscious, the unconscious does not imply intuition. Klein (2003) proposes that intuition is

> ... the way we translate our experiences into judgments and decisions. It is the ability to make decisions by using patterns to recognize what's going on in a situation and to recognize the typical action script with which to react. (p. 13)

As Tallis (2002) forwards,

Virtually every aspect of mental life is connected in some way with mental events and processes that occur below the threshold of awareness…the profound importance of unconscious procedures, memories, beliefs, perceptions, knowledge, and emotions is recognized universally. (p. 182)

Our unconscious processes many incoming signals such as recognizing patterns or creating a general sense or feeling before our conscious attention may be directed to these signals. We often develop feelings and perspectives about others through our unconscious processing and reactions. This is the phenomenon of implicit learning, or acquiring new patterns of behavior without being aware of the patterns themselves (Adams, 1957; Neal & Hesketh, 1997; Reber, 1993).

Experiments on influencing complex systems indicate that subjects can learn to manipulate inputs to control outputs without being able to describe the relationships between those inputs and outputs. For example, in one of a series of many experiments, Paul Lewicki and his colleagues at the University of Tulsa sat subjects in front of a computer screen divided into quadrants with arrays of "random" digits appearing in all four quadrants. The subjects were asked to search for a particular digit and press one of four buttons depending on which quadrant the particular digit appeared in. They repeated this many times during blocks of seven trials. Unbeknown to the subjects, the position of the particular digit was determined by a complex algorithm such that the pattern developed through the first, third, fourth, and sixth trials showed where that digit would be on the last (seventh) trial. Responses on the seventh trial became progressively faster than responses on the other six, showing that the subjects could *unconsciously* make use of this information. When subjects were asked whether they were aware of their improved performance, they responded negatively. Further, they had no idea of the information they were using. Subjects were then given six more trials and asked to *consciously* predict the position for the seventh trial. Their results reflected no difference from the first six trials (Lewicki et al., 1992).

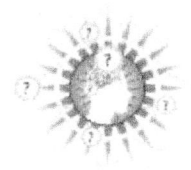

REFLECT:
Do I give my unconscious mind quiet time to process?
How do I listen to my unconscious?

In a different experiment, subjects who performed well were given unlimited time to study the arrays and offered financial rewards for explaining how it was done. They were still unable to find the hidden pattern (algorithm). In a variation of this experiment, preschool children age 4 to 5 also showed faster responses on the final trial (Lewicki et al., 1992).

During other experiments, subjects acquired the ability to predict forthcoming events although they could not specify the underlying sequential structure they had obviously learned. For example, in an experiment at Oxford University in 1984, subjects were asked to stabilize the output of sugar on a simulated production line by controlling input variables. Although they were not told the fairly complex equations that would determine the effect of their decisions, their performance improved over several days. They did not know why (Lewicki et al., 1988).

These examples indicate the existence of an unconscious mind that is capable of thinking and recognizing patterns; in other words, the unconscious ability to learn and know what to do without conscious awareness (Berry & Broadbent, 1984). This is also one source of tacit knowledge, when the individual intuitively understands and knows something yet is unable to articulate the reasons or evidence for knowing (Polanyi, 1958; Bennet and Bennet, 2008c). There is considerable uncertainty in terms of how much processing is done in the unconscious. However, it appears that a large proportion of brain processing occurs *outside* of consciousness (Taylor, 2006; Jensen, 2006). Daniel Schacter, a neuroscientist and expert on memory, believes that as we sleep our brains are probably working very hard to save the experiences that we all carry around with us for much of our lives. This memory consolidation during sleep is for the purpose of remembering the important aspects that happened the previous day while discarding the junk. Schacter (1996) offers that,

> Memory consolidation during sleep is likely influenced by what we think about and talk about while awake. The important events in our lives that we often review during waking may be frequently replayed during sleep. (p. 88)

Another perspective on the unconscious relates to what neurologist Antonio Damasio calls the autobiographical Self (introduced in Chapter 2). This is the idea of *who* we are, the image we build up of ourselves and where we fit socially. This *Self* is built up over years of experience, and is constantly being remodeled. Damasio (1999) believes that much of this model is created by the unconscious. The autobiographical Self is discussed in more detail in Chapter 18.

While generally discussed earlier, creativity is another area where the unconscious plays a significant role. Amen offers that extraordinary creativity, at least sometimes, comes from a qualitatively different neural process than ordinary creativity, and that it may arise from that component of human thought called the unconscious (Amen, 2005). As introduced earlier, Christos (2003), in discussing creativity and creative ideas, refers to Poincare talking about his own creativity. Poincare asserts that new ideas are often generated when a problem reverts from the conscious mind to begin the search to the unconscious mind to generate new ideas and then back to the conscious mind to evaluate the usefulness of the ideas generated by the unconscious mind (cited in Christos, 2003).

As we become more proficient in performing a task, the number of cortical signals needed to perform the task becomes smaller. As Nobel Laureate Edelman states, "With further practice, new and specialized circuits may augment those already present in the specialized areas that are involved, and performance becomes fast, accurate, and largely unconscious" (Edelman & Tononi, 2000, p. 61).

John Kihlstrom (1987) published a brief article in the journal *Science* entitled 'The Cognitive Unconscious." Kihlstrom accepts the evidence that, in specific circumstances (as demonstrated in laboratory studies), meanings and the implications of those meanings can be understood in the absence of awareness. Consequently, individuals can make a judgment (for example, whether they like someone), and then act on it, without any knowledge of how that judgment was reached. This,

> ...means that the process of judgment or inference has become automated, and hence unavailable for introspection. Although the unconscious might seem dumb, it is after all very smart. In many respects, it is re-formatted intelligence. (Tallis, 2002, pp. 107-108)

From the above information it seems the unconscious represents a very important aspect of the brain/mind and of learning. Addressing the importance of understanding and appreciating the influence of the unconscious, LeDoux (1996) forwards that,

> The fact that emotions, attitudes, goals, and the like are activated automatically (without any conscious effort) means that their presence in the mind and their influence on thoughts and behavior are not questioned. They are trusted the way we would trust any other kind of perception. When one is aware of biases and possesses values against having these, he or she can exercise control over them. However, the ability to do this depends on being aware of the unconscious influences, which is quite another matter. (p. 63)

Chapter 10
Learning from Neuroscience: The Environment

The way the brain operates—and in particular the process of associative patterning—was introduced in Chapter 2 and is brought up as appropriate throughout this book, each time in relationship to a different area of focus. In this chapter, the focus is on the mind/brain relationship with its environment, specifically, the complexing of incoming information (extrinsic signals) with internally stored patterns (intrinsic signals). Using Edelman and Tononi's words,

> Extrinsic signals convey information not so much in themselves, but by virtue of how they modulate the intrinsic signals exchanged within a previously experienced neural system. In other words, a stimulus acts not so much by adding large amounts of extrinsic information that need to be processed as it does by amplifying the intrinsic information resulting from neural interactions selected and stabilized by memory through previous encounters with the environment. The brain is a selectional system, and matching occurs within enormously varied and complex repertoires. (Edelman & Tononi, 2000, p. 137)

Begley (2007) likens this amazing co-evolution of the human mind/brain with its environment to "wise parents who teach their children to respond to each situation that presents itself, adapting their behavior to the challenges they meet" (p. 130). She then goes on to say that nature has equipped the human brain similarly,

> ... endowing it with the flexibility to adapt to the environment it encounters, the experiences it has, the damage it suffers, the demands its owner makes of it. The brain is neither immutable nor static but is instead continuously remodeled by the lives we lead. (Begley, 2007, p. 130)

The areas of focus in this section are the influences of the internal environment (Epigenetics) and the influences of the external environment. The external environment is also explored in terms of social interaction and social support.

Epigenetics (The Influences of the Internal Environment)

The internal environment discussed here is within the individual. What has been discovered is that the genes cannot be expressed without influence from the immediate environment of the cell. Gene expression means that the DNA information within a gene is released and influences its surrounding environment. Epigenetics—literally meaning control above genetics—is profoundly changing our beliefs and knowledge of how life is controlled. The implication is that humans can no longer assume their

> Destiny is not in the genes, but rather in the way those genes are expressed.

destiny is in their genes. The myth that genes are destiny is false. Instead, nature, nurture, and individual choices all play a significant role in our learning and development.

Bruce Lipton, a cell biologist, offered this description of the effect of epigenetics:

> We are living in exciting times, for science is in the process of shattering old myths and rewriting a fundamental *belief* of human civilization. The belief that we are frail bio-chemical machines controlled by genes is giving way to an understanding that we are powerful creators of our lives and the world in which we live. (Lipton, 2005, p. 17)

Jensen (2006) takes another strong stand:

> It is now established that contrasting, persistent, or traumatic environments can and do change the actions of genes....in another study, researchers showed that the actual genes do not even have to change, but instead, heritable changes in gene expression can occur without a change in DNA sequence. (p. 10)

Although DNA was once thought to be destiny, this idea is changing as neuroscience and biology expand their frontiers of understanding. Epigenetics—one of the active areas of scientific research—is the study of the molecular mechanisms by which the environment influences gene activity (Lipton, 2005). C. A. Ross (2006) proposes that,

> Biology is no longer inevitable gene expression driven unidirectionally by the DNA. Rather, genes for brain growth and development are turned on and off by the environment in a complex, rich set of feedback loops. Causality in brain development involves a dance between two partners, DNA and the environment. (p. 32)

The way the environment influences the genes is through the process of covering. As Lipton (2005) describes,

> In the chromosome, the DNA forms the core, and the proteins cover the DNA like a sleeve. When the genes are covered, their information cannot be read. As a result, the activity of the gene is "controlled" by the presence or absence of the ensleeving proteins, which are in turn controlled by environmental signals. (pp. 67-68)

Lipton, himself, expressed feelings of surprise at this discovery. As he says,

> While I was reviewing research on the mechanisms by which cells control their physiology and behavior, I suddenly realized that a cell's life is controlled by the physical and energetic environment and not by its genes. Genes are simply molecular blueprints used in the construction of cells, tissues and organs. The environment serves as a "contractor" who reads and engages those genetic blueprints and is ultimately responsible for the character of a cell's life. It is a single cell's "awareness" of the environment, not its genes, that sets into motion the mechanisms of life. (Lipton, 2005, p. 15)

Lipton is not alone in his recognition of the role of the environment and influencing genes. In recent years, research in biology has shown that the genome is more fluid and responsive to the environment than was previously thought (Zull, 2002). It is also clear that information can be transmitted to descendants in ways other than through the base sequence of DNA (Jablonka & Lamb, 1995). After identifying several factors that determine the brain's initial and later architecture, Byrnes (2001) posits that the effect of extrinsic factors,

> ... suggests that neural organization of an adult brain is not set in stone at birth. In addition, it suggests that there are many ways to explain a structural difference that might emerge over time between the brains of two individuals (e.g., genetics, experience, prenatal nutrition, etc.). As such, it would be unwise to retroactively reason back from an observed brain difference to one particular factor (with corroborative evidence). For example, if genes, experience, and nutrition could all cause a structural difference that might someday be observed in postmortem studies of men and women (e.g., a higher density of neurons in the right parietal lobe), it would be inappropriate to assume that this difference must have been caused by genes (because it could have also been caused by experience or nutrition). (p. 171)

REFLECT:
What are my thoughts, feelings and life-style expressing?
How might I influence my genes toward improved health?

Regarding studies involving how maternal care alters the activity of the gene in the brains of their offspring, Begley (2007) noted that this plasticity didn't involve connections between neurons. Rather, "The modifications occur at the level of the gene itself ... That means we can talk about creating an environment that will affect the DNA and thus the way the animal responds to stress." (p. 173)

From another perspective, it has been discovered that DNA blueprints are not set in concrete at the birth of the cell as they were once thought to be (Church, 2006). Environmental influences such as nutrition, stress, and emotions can modify those genes without changing their basic blueprint. And those modifications can be passed on to future generations (Reik & Walter, 2001; Surani, 2001). Also, what we believe leads to what we think, which leads to our knowledge, which leads to what actions we take. Redundant →Thus what we believe and how we think determine what we do. It is our actions that determine our success, not our genes (Bownds, 1999; Lipton, 2005; Rose, 2005; Begley, 2007).

We now move to a discussion of external environmental influences.

The Influences of the External Environment

We are social creatures. While this concept has been around for centuries, Cozolino believes that we are just waking up to this fact from a biological perspective. As he describes,

> As a species, we are just waking up to the complexity of our own brains, to say nothing of how brains are linked together. We are just beginning to understand that we have evolved as social creatures and that all of our biologies are interwoven. (Cozolino, 2006, p. 3)

The advent of brain imaging allows us to watch the neurophysiology of learning unfold. "Not only can we trace the pathways of the brain involved in various learning tasks, but we can also infer which learning environments are most likely to be effective (Johnson & Taylor, 2006, p. 1). The literature suggests that there are specific changes within the brain that occur through enriched environments. Specifically, thicker cortices are created, there are larger cell bodies, and dendritic branching in the brain is more extensive. These changes have been directly connected to higher levels of intelligence and performance (Begley, 2007; Byrnes, 2001; Jensen, 1998). Byrnes sees the results of research on the effects of enriched environments on brain structure as both credible and well established (Byrnes, 2001).

> There are specific changes within the brain that occur through enriched environments.

For example, Skoyles and Sagan presented the results of research on adolescent monkeys that suggested prefrontal cortices respond better than other parts of the brain to an enriched learning environment. After a month of exposure to enriched environments, the monkey's "prefrontal cortices had increased their activity by some 35 percent, while those of animals not exposed to an enriched environment had slightly decreased their activity" (Skoyles & Sagan, 2002, p. 76). These authors go on to say that, "As the most neurally plastic species, we can choose to put ourselves in stimulus-rich environments that will increase our intelligence" (Skoyles & Sagan, 2002, p. 76). Social forces clearly affect every aspect of our lives. As Rose (2005) describes,

> The ways in which we conduct our observations and experiments on the world outside, the basis for what we regard as proof, the theoretical frameworks within which we embed these observations, experiments and proofs, have been shaped by the history of our subject, by the power and limits of available technology, and by the social forces that have formed and continue to form that history. (p. 9)

The effects of social forces, of course, are often not in conscious awareness. The role of the conscious is to connect it all together. LeDoux (1996) says that the present social situation and physical environment are part of what is connected. Following extensive research, LeDoux (1996) concluded that,

> People normally do all sorts of things for reasons they are not consciously aware of (because the behavior is produced by brain systems that operate unconsciously) and that one of the main jobs of consciousness is to keep our life tied together into

a coherent story, a self-concept. It does this by generating explanations of behavior on the basis of our self-image, memories of the past, expectations of the future, the present social situation and the physical environment in which the behavior is produced. (LeDoux, 1996, p. 33).

Stonier agrees that when people are engaging in heavy duty thinking "it is not generally in terms of unlabeled images, sounds, smells, tastes or tactile experiences" (Stonier, 1997, p. 151). Stonier posits that thinking is actually talking to oneself, and that,

> This ability to talk to oneself is so basic a part of our human internal information environment that it tends to shape all our thought processes. It is this fact that allows us to be so influenced by our social and cultural surroundings. (Stonier, 1997, p. 151)

REFLECT:
What can I do today to help my children learn tomorrow?
How do my social and cultural surroundings influence me or my children?

Social Interaction

Amen (2005) says that physical exercise, mental exercise and social bonding are the best sources of stimulation of the brain. Social neuroscience is the aspect of neuroscience dealing with the brain mechanisms of social interaction. Studies in social neuroscience have affirmed that over the course of evolution, physical mechanisms have developed in our brains to enable us to learn through social interactions. Johnson says that "these physical mechanisms have evolved to enable us to get the knowledge we need in order to keep emotionally and physically safe" (Johnson, 2006, p. 65). She also suggests that these mechanisms enable us to: (1) engage in affective attunement or empathic interaction and language, (2) consider the intentions of the other, (3) try to understand what another mind is thinking, and (4) think about how we want to interact (Johnson, 2006, p. 65).

> People are in continuous two-way interaction with those around them, and the brain is continuously changing in response.

People are in continuous, two-way interaction with those around them, and the brain is continuously changing in response. As Cozolino and Sprokay (2006) explain,

> It is becoming more evident that through emotional facial expressions, physical contact, and eye gaze—even through pupil dilation and blushing—people are in constant, if often unconscious, two-way communication with those around them.

It is in the matrix of this contact that brains are sculpted, balanced and made healthy. (p. 13)

Through these interactions, the genes are operating options "that are tested as an environment provides input that results in behavior" (Bownds, 1999, p. 169). Which supporting neuronal pathways become permanent depend on the usefulness of the behavior in enhancing survival and reproduction (Bownds, 1999). During this process, social preferences are also being developed. Tallis (2002) says that unconscious learning most likely influences people's day-to-day social preferences. As he describes,

Human beings are constantly forming positive or negative opinions of others, and often after minimal social contact. If challenged, opinions can be justified, but such justifications frequently take the form of post-hoc rationalization. Some, of course, are laughably transparent. (Tallis, 2002, p. 129)

Social Support

From a neuroscience perspective, trust in a relationship is very important in enhancing learning. When a secure, bonding relationship in which trust has been established occurs, Schore says that there is "a cascade of biochemical processes, stimulating and enhancing the growth and connectivity of neural networks throughout the brain" (Schore, 1994, as cited in Cozolino, 2002, p. 191). Thus, a caring, affirming relationship promotes neural growth and learning.

Cozolino (2002) says that language and significant social relationships build and shape the brain. Further, he offers that the two powerful processes of social interaction and affective attunement, when involving a trusted other, contribute to "both the evolution and sculpting of the brain ... [since they] stimulate the brain to grow, organize and integrate" (Cozolino, 2002, p. 213). Andreasen cites mentoring as one of the elements that helps create a cultural environment to nurture creativity. The five circumstances she believes that create what she calls a "cradle of creativity" include an atmosphere of intellectual freedom and excitement; a critical mass of creative minds; free and fair competition, mentors, and patrons, and at least some economic prosperity. As she concludes, "If we seek to find social and cultural environmental factors that help to create the creative brain, these must be considered to be important ones" (Andreasen, 2005, p. 131).

Following a study of unconscious communications which supported the fact that people are in constant interaction with those around them, often unconsciously, Cozolino and Sprokay say that one possible implication of this finding of specific interest to the adult educational environment is the fact that "the attention of a caring, aware mentor may support the plasticity that leads to better, more meaningful learning" (Cozolino & Sprokay, 2006, p. 13). Further, Cozolino (2002) says that the efficacy of the mentoring relationship—a balance of support and challenge—is supported by the literature on brain function. "We appear to experience optimal development and integration in a context of a balance of nurturance and optimal stress" (p. 62). (See the areas on "stress" and "neuroplasticity".)

The notion of affective attunement is connected to Dewey's observations that an educator needs to "have that sympathetic understanding of individuals as individuals which gives him an idea of what is actually going on in the minds of those who are learning" (Dewey, [1938] 1997, p. 39). As Johnson (2006) explains, "According to social cognitive neuroscience, the brain actually needs to seek out an affectively attuned other if it is to learn. Affective attunement alleviates fear" (p. 65).

Fear has been identified as an impediment to learning throughout the field of adult learning (Brookfield, 1987; Daloz, 1986, 1999; Mezirow, 1991; Perry, 1970/1988). The limbic system, the primitive part of the human brain, and in particular its amygdala, is the origin of survival and fear responses.

The literature is extensive on the need for a safe and empathic relationship to facilitate learning. Cozolino says that for complex levels of self-awareness, that is those that involve higher brain functions and potential changes in neural networks, learning cannot be accomplished when an individual feels anxious and defensive (Cozolino, 2002). Specifically, he says that a safe and empathic relationship can establish an emotional and neurobiological context that is conducive to neural reorganization. "It serves as a buffer and scaffolding within which [an adult] can better tolerate the stress required for neural reorganization" (Cozolino, 2002, p. 291). Taylor (2006) explains that,

> Safe and empathic relationships facilitate learning.

> Adults who would create (or recreate) neural networks associated with development of a more complex epistemology need emotional support for the discomfort that will also certainly be part of that process. (p. 82)

Johnson (2006) agrees. Referring to discoveries in cognitive neuroscience and social cognitive neuroscience, she says that educators and mentors of adults recognize "the neurological effects and importance of creating a trusting relationship, a holding environment, and an intersubjective space" (p. 68) where such things as reflection and abstract thinking can occur. As LeDoux (2002) notes, "The amygdala is part of the brain system that controls freezing behavior and other defensive responses in threatening situations" (p. 7). Phelps offers that the left amygdala mediates the expression of fears learned from verbal communication (Phelps et al., 2001). This was demonstrated by using fMRI.

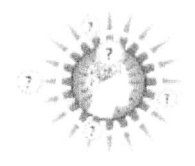

REFLECT:
Do I engage in mentoring experiences?
What significant social relationships do I have?

The amygdala synapses are wired by nature to release hormones and create fear that responds to dangers that are learned through vision or verbal communication. The procedure was to tell subjects that when they saw a blue square a weak electrical shock would follow and when they saw a yellow square no shock would follow. The fMRI indicated that the subjects showed greater physiological arousal during the blue squares than during the (safe) yellow squares, indicating amygdala involvement in the processing of instructed fear. Instructed fear is created when a subject is verbally instructed about the aversive nature of some phenomenon. None of the subjects ever received a shock (Phelps et al., 2001).

Cozolino and Sprokay say that it is essential to strengthen the orbitofrontal-limbic connections in both therapy and mentoring. The orbitofrontal cortex is a major component of the prefrontal cortex, which is considered the executive part of the brain (Goldberg, 2001). Strengthening is done through "activation of both affective and cognitive circuits" which allows "executive brain systems to reassociate and better regulate them" (Cozolino & Sprokay, 2006, p. 15). The approach here is for teachers or mentors who are relaying factual information and encouraging critical thinking to help students "acknowledge and integrate intellectual challenges with emotional and physiological experiences" (p. 15). (See the discussion below on emotions.)

One example of affective attunement that stimulates the orbitofrontal cortex is eye contact because "specific cells are particularly responsive to facial expression and eye gaze" (Schore, 1994, p. 67). As Johnson explains, literally "looking into the eyes of the affectively attuned other is another significant form of social interaction that can assist in promoting development" (Johnson, 2006, p. 67). Similarly, Frith and Wolpert (2003) forward that an infant and caregiver enter into an intersubjective space. This space may be created around the infant and caregiver through the process of emotional resonance or affective attunement (Johnson, 2006).

While the roles of a mentor and intersubjective space are emphasized above, Caine and Caine (2006) bring us back to the role of the individual in this relationship.

> In order to adequately understand any concept, or acquire any mastery of a skill or domain, a person has to make sense of things for himself or herself, irrespective of how much others know and how much a coach, mentor or teacher tries to help. We have also argued that although there is an indispensable social aspect to the construction of meaning, there is also an irreducible individual element. (p. 54)

Section IV
Neuroscience Findings

Now that we have explored some of the findings coming out of neuroscience, how do we make sense of this in terms of experiential learning? We first group these findings into areas and further explore those areas that have the potential to influence experiential learning. The next step is concept mapping, a process used to organize and structure knowledge. This process is briefly explained in Chapter 11.

Looking at the 13 areas of neuroscience findings we conveniently divide them into three groups:

Group 1 is made up of the unconscious (1), memory (2), and emotion (3), and represents a foundational group that is always involved in learning (Chapter 12)

Group 2 represents findings that influence learning in specific situations. It includes stress (4), creativity (5), mirror neurons (6), anticipating the future (7), and social support (9) (Chapter 13)

Group 3 supports the capacity for, and enhancement of, lifelong learning. This group is made up of social interaction (8), epigenetics (10), plasticity (11), exercise and health (12), and aging (13) (Chapter 14)

Taking to heart neuroscience finding Item 2-J—repetition improves memory recall—each area begins with a brief description of the findings based on the discussion in Chapters 6-10, repeating critical findings, then ends with a breakdown of specific concepts (or items) that relate to the subelements of the four modes of the adult experiential learning model. By now you have enough exposure to these concepts to reflect more deeply.

In Chapter 15 we assess the findings as a group and further explore those items that appear to enhance experiential learning but do not specifically affect one of the four modes of the historical experiential learning model.

Chapter 11
The Concept Mapping Process

In Chapters 6 through 10 we reviewed a number of areas of neuroscience that appeared to have the potential to improve the historic experiential learning theory and model. While there is an ever-expanding scope of neuroscience research available, from this material, 13 areas were identified that clearly offered the potential to enhance the practice of experiential learning. The 13 areas are: (1) the unconscious, (2) memory, (3) emotion, (4) stress, (5) creativity, (6) mirror neurons, (7) anticipating the future, (8) social interaction, (9) social support, (10) epigenetics, (11) plasticity, (12) exercise and (13) aging.

First, it is necessary to further understand what is meant by *enhance* in terms of experiential learning. At the top level, enhance means to (a) increase efficiency, (b) increase effectiveness, (c) improve understanding of the learning process (meta-learning), and/or (d) improve the sustainability of learning. However, to further understand these four areas of enhancement, it is useful to identify indicators that can guide our thinking as we explore the influence of neuroscience findings on experiential learning. The identified indicators that reflect the four elements of enhancement are:

Efficiency (speed and effort): addresses the speed of learning; the flexibility of learning or different ways of learning; and the minimum use of time and energy.

Effectiveness (scope and quality): addresses the understanding of incoming information; the meaning or significance of incoming information; insight or the recognition of relationships, patterns, possibilities, and probabilities; creativity or the conceptions of ideas, processes, and capabilities; or anticipation and the taking of effective action.

Meta-Learning (understanding the learning process): addresses the understanding of the learning process; the understand phases of the phases of learning; the ability to adapt the learning process; the understanding of the context of learning; and the understanding of personal learning characteristics.

Sustainable Learning (long-term learning capacity): addresses the adaptability or the capability to adapt the learning process; the robustness or capability to handle a broad range of learning situations; the healthy mind or long-term learning capacity; and resilience or self-efficacy and inner strength.

With this understanding as guidance, each of the 13 neuroscience areas is individually assessed as to how they can contribute to one or more of these enhancements. Additionally, within each area specific neuroscience findings are identified and for purposes of this work are labeled as *items*.

Concept Mapping

We now explain the concept mapping process to explore the connections of the neuroscience findings or items in the 13 areas to the four modes of the historic experiential learning model. Concept mapping—a process to explore relationships between concepts—is used to organize and structure knowledge. Developed by Cornell University in the 1970's (Novak, 1996; 1998), concept mapping is based on the cognitive theories of Ausubel (1968) that stressed that new knowledge was built on prior knowledge. This theory is, of course, consistent with the way the mind/brain works in terms of associative patterning, although it was promulgated long before we were able to map the workings of the mind/brain.

To increase the effectiveness of this process, it was necessary to develop subelements of the four modes, that is, **characteristics that described what was occurring when this mode is engaged**. To surface these characteristics, referred to as subelements, we look to the work of Kolb (1984) and Zull (2002) as well as other educators and theorists who have explored the experiential learning model. Building on the descriptions of the four modes in this body of work, the subelements of the four modes are identified as follows:

For the mode **Concrete Experience** (grasping through apprehension), the identified characteristics or subelements are: *sensing; feeling; awareness; attention; and intuition*.

For the mode **Reflective Observation** (transformation via intention), the identified characteristics or subelements are: *understanding; meaning; truth and how things happen; intuition; integrate; and look for unity*.

For the mode **Abstract Conceptualization** (grasping via comprehension), the identified characteristics or subelements are: *concepts, ideas, logic; problem solving; creativity; build models and theories; anticipation of outcome of action; control, rigor, and discipline*.

For the mode **Active Experimentation** (transformation via extension), the identified characteristics or subelements are: *act on the environment; focus attention; object-based logic; heightened boundary perception; and sensory feedback to brain*.

Next, the process of *concept mapping* is used to explore and display the connections between each of the 13 neuroscience areas and their respective items and the subelements of each of the four modes of the Kolb (1984) adult experiential learning model. In the *concept mapping process*, the items or specific neuroscience findings in each area are listed to the left, the subelements of the experiential learning model are grouped to the right, and the relationships are shown by connecting lines.

Take, as an example, the neuroscience findings or items for area 11, plasticity. Item 11-A in Figure 11-1 indicates that plasticity is the result of the connection between neural patterns in the mind and the physical world—what we think and believe impacts

106 | Expanding the Self

our physical bodies. This is what is called neural plasticity, the ability of neurons to change their structure and relationships, depending on environmental demands and personal decisions and actions. Relative to concrete experience, such plasticity can broaden the scope of sensing as well as feelings.

While Item 11-B does not appear to have a direct relationship with any of the subelements of the four modes, knowledge of this finding can help learners recognize their potential for building knowledge, influencing their own brain, and developing in whatever direction they choose. Thus, from this perspective it has the potential to enhance any or all of the subelements. The full set of findings or items for area 11, plasticity, are detailed in Chapter 14.

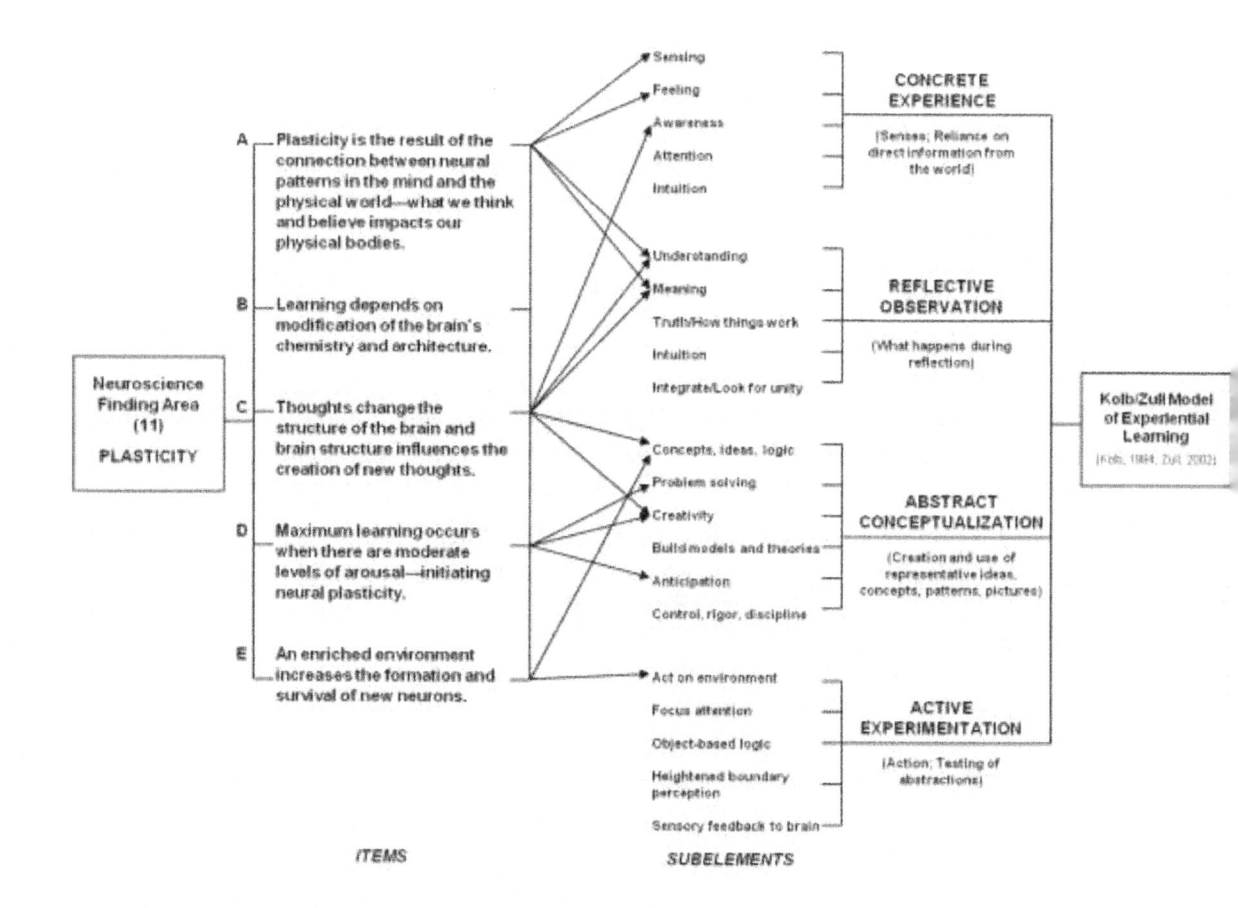

Figure 11-1. *A sample relationship concept map for neuroscience findings, Area 11, Plasticity.*

As a second example, Figure 11-2 below is a sample concept map for neuroscience findings or items for area 7, anticipating the future. As will be detailed in Chapter 13, Item 7-A is "The neocortex constantly tries to predict the next experience". As reflected in the concept map, this aspect of anticipating the future is part of understanding and meaning in reflective observation and of anticipating in the abstract conceptualization mode. This concept of prediction can become a valuable learning tool. Item 7-D is "the mind uses past learning and memories to complete incoming information." The capacity to complete incoming information from past experience enhances both efficiency and the effectiveness of learning. It impacts the ability to create meaning during reflective observation as well as problem solving and anticipating the outcomes of actions during abstract conceptualization. Further detail is provided in Chapter 13.

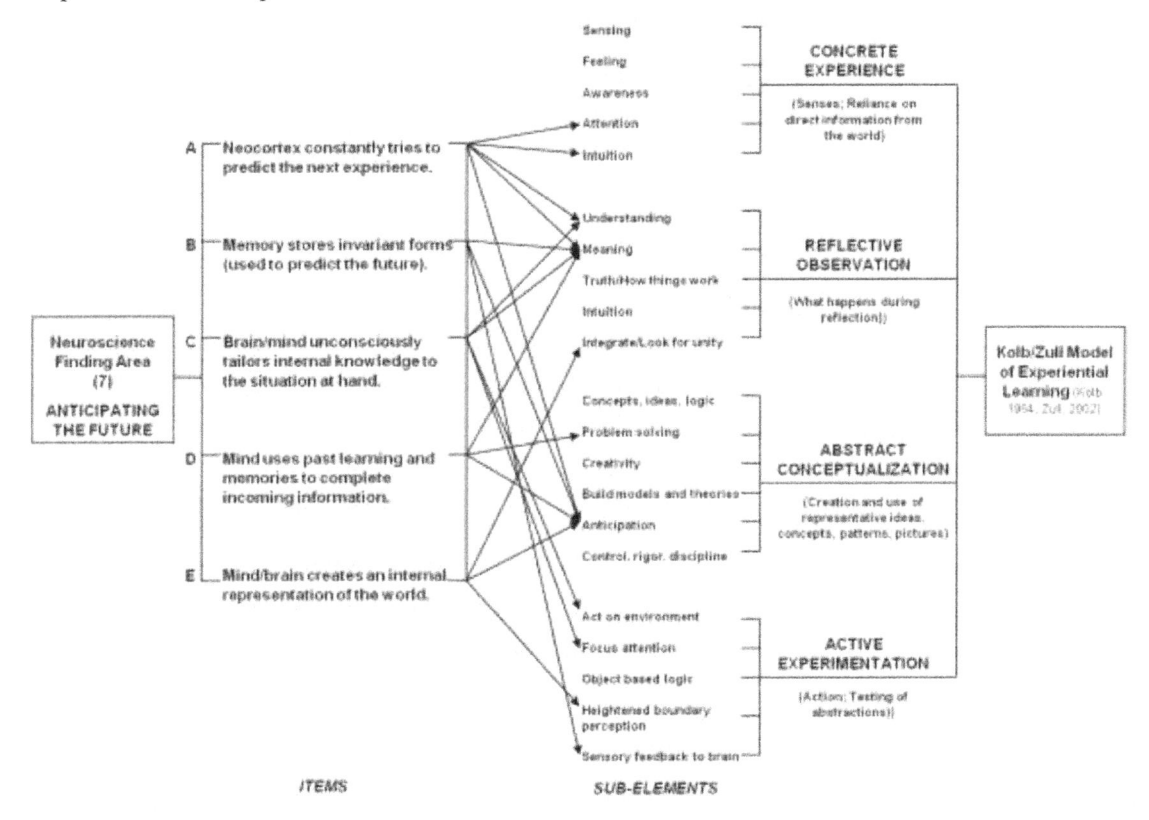

Figure 11-2. *A sample relationship concept map for neuroscience findings, Area 7, Anticipating the Future.*

While concept mapping is certainly not an exact science, it is helpful in discovering relationships, and in our example, the relationships between specific neuroscience findings (items) and the modes of experiential learning, provides a sampling of possible connections between the items and subelements. For each neuroscience finding area we indicate a sampling of potential ways that each of the neuroscience finding items could influence—and thereby enhance—experiential learning. This process helped provide insights into how these findings impact adult experiential learning. We encourage those who are interested to explore this process further—and enhance their own learning—by creating their own concept maps.

Note that in a learning experience, each potential neuroscience finding's impact on learning would be context sensitive and situation dependent, and therefore all possible influences cannot be shown. However, whether a potential finding enhances learning or not will depend heavily upon whether the learner is aware of, and chooses to use, a particular neuroscience finding area item as part of his or her learning process. As presented in Section III and addressed in Chapter 14 of this section, *what we think and believe impacts our physical bodies*. Quite literally, thoughts change the structure of the brain, and brain structure influences the creation of new thoughts.

During this study a number of neuroscience findings were identified outside the scope of the historic experiential learning model. As a set, these findings offered considerable potential to expand the experiential learning process and led to the creation of the ICALS Theory and Model with a fifth mode of social engagement (social interaction and social support), a clear representation of Self, and a larger account of the influence of the environment.

In Chapters 11 through 14 each neuroscience area is addressed. Each area begins with a brief description of the findings in that area based on the in-depth discussions in Chapters 6 through 10, and ends with a breakdown of the area into specific concepts, that is, items.

Chapter 12
(Group 1)
The Unconscious, Memory, Emotion

Looking at the 13 areas of neuroscience findings we conveniently divide them into three groups:

Group 1 is made up of the unconscious (1), memory (2), and emotion (3), and represents a foundational group that is always involved in learning.

Group 2 represents findings that influence learning in specific situations. It includes stress (4), creativity (5), mirror neurons (6), anticipating the future (7), and social support (9).

Group 3 supports the capacity for, and enhancement of, lifelong learning. This group is made up of social interaction (8), epigenetics (10), plasticity (11), exercise and health (12), and aging (13).

Each area begins with a brief description of the findings based on the discussion in Chapters 6-10, then ends with a breakdown of specific concepts (or items) that relate to the subelements of the four modes of the adult experiential learning model.

Area 1: The Unconscious

As noted in Chapter 9, the unconscious part of the brain plays a significant role in our thinking and feeling. Most of our thinking is unconscious (Jensen, 2006; Kandel, 2006; Taylor, 2006), as is most of the processing of the emotional meaning of stimuli (LeDoux, 1996). The brain is always processing information (Hawkins, 2004), and we as individuals often act for reasons of which we are unaware (LeDoux, 1996). This is the unconscious at work. For the purpose of this research, it is assumed that there is a distinction between the conscious and the unconscious. While the unconscious exists throughout the brain, Edelman and Tononi note the serial nature of conscious experience in that "its temporal evolution must follow a single trajectory" (Edelman & Tononi, 2000, p. 151).

Kandel (2006, p. 39) forwards that a fundamental principle of the unconscious is that it never lies, but it could be wrong! It is part of the individual and has a role in its survival. The unconscious part of the mind can detect patterns without the individual's conscious awareness, and individuals may act upon those patterns without being aware they are doing so. As Bargh (2005) notes, "an individual's behavior can be directly caused by the current environment, without the necessity of an act of conscious choice." Such implicit behavior, and learning, is widespread. From a learning perspective the key is realizing that *a great deal of learning occurs in the unconscious part of the mind*. As a result, our unconscious can influence our thoughts and emotions without our knowing it.

There is also a great deal of activity in the unconscious mind during sleep. Such activity may include dreaming, problem solving, or creating new ideas. Several researchers have concluded that during sleep the unconscious mind is evaluating and filtering the previous day's incoming information, keeping what is important and discarding what is not important (Rock, 2004; Schacter, 1996). As described in the literature review, there are several techniques for getting in touch with one's unconscious (Andreasen, 2005; Begley, 2007; Bennet & Bennet, 2007a; Pinker, 2007). An example is included in Chapter 21. From a learning perspective, it is recognized that a great deal of past learning resides in long-term memory and the unconscious (Jensen, 2006; Taylor, 2006). The challenge for learners is to build up this knowledge base over time, recognize its value, and be able to retrieve what they know when it is needed. This may take the form of intuition, heuristics, judgment, or inference (Tallis, 2002). One useful technique is to learn to ask yourself the right questions, and carefully listen to your answers. Dialogue with a trusted colleague is another way to bring out information and knowledge that individuals may not know they have (Bohm, 1992).

The unconscious part of the mind/brain plays a significant role in experiential learning. Since the unconscious receives information from the environment of which the conscious mind may not be aware, an enhanced awareness of the unconscious may show itself through a sense that something is right or wrong (sensing), or a good or bad feeling about a situation (feeling), or perhaps through intuition. These represent efficient ways of learning and are in addition to, rather than in place of, conscious reflection and comprehension. Also, the unconscious may enhance learning effectiveness by developing understanding and insight over time.

For example, we often take action based on our intuition that comes from associating previous experiences in our unconscious. Recognizing the power of the unconscious, and understanding to some degree how it works, can help learners build and more fully engage their unconscious capability. As reviewed above, part of our memory is unconscious, that is, we do not have direct access to it upon conscious request. Nevertheless, a large amount of what we have learned in the past still resides in memory. Recognizing this enables a learner to build knowledge that may not be immediately apparent or consciously beneficial but may pay dividends later as individuals learn to more effectively access their unconscious. This is a contribution to long-term sustainable learning.

Items of the unconscious neuroscience finding area that could potentially enhance experiential learning are as follows: (A) the unconscious brain is always processing, (B) the unconscious never lies, (C) the unconscious can influence our thoughts and emotions without our awareness, (D) the unconscious processes emotional meanings of stimuli, (E) thinking is mostly unconscious, (F) the unconscious plays a big role in creativity, (G) we may act for reasons we are not aware of, and (H) our model of Self comes from the unconscious.

Item 1-A: The unconscious brain is always processing. Because of this sub-item, it could be said that the unconscious affects all modes of the adult experiential learning model. However, we consider several subelements in the learning model to provide an indication of the unconscious brain's potential impact on learning. Note that the brain uses 80 percent as much energy when sleeping as it does when awake (Schacter, 1996). This is consistent with the finding that the high rate of energy usage by the human brain is not changed much by mental activity (Laughlin, 2004). It is also known that when under deep anesthesia 50 percent of the brain's energy consumption is used for maintenance. Specifically,

> Deep anesthesia abolishes electrical activity and reduces the metabolic rate of the whole brain by 50 percent, suggesting that, on average, energy consumption is equally divided between neural signaling and maintenance. (Laughlin, 2004, p. 188)

Building on these findings, it appears that in terms of the subelements of concrete experience (sensing, feeling, awareness, attention, and intuition) that our unconscious mind uses about 30 percent of the brain's energy for processing during sleep, that is,

If, 50% of the brain's energy consumption is used for maintenance;

And, 80% of the brain's energy is being used when we sleep;

Then, 30% of the brain's energy is used by the unconscious mind during sleep.

This would be much higher if the individual were awake. The unconscious would then be processing a great deal of information from the external environment. These incoming signals often show themselves as feelings or intuitions and guide our reactions to future experiences. As Pert (1997) has noted, the emotional system works through the generation and transmission of chemicals throughout the body, which in turn impact neuron activity. These chemical changes represent the emotional tag of the amygdala.

Item 1-B: The unconscious never lies. This sub-item taken from Kandel, may seem odd, but when it is realized that the unconscious is a part of the overall living individual, "lying" to self would not make sense (Kandel, 2006). This idea relates to the truth and how things work under reflective observation. Although the intuition coming from our unconscious may not be right, it is still what our unconscious *perceives as truth*. The same phenomenon would occur with problem solving in the abstract conceptualization mode. Being aware of, and listening to, our unconscious can improve our learning scope and rate.

Item 1-C: The unconscious can influence our thoughts and emotions without our awareness. This affects our understanding of the making of meaning and a desire to find the truth and how things work as described under the reflective observation mode.

Item 1-D: The unconscious processes emotional meanings of stimuli. As LeDoux notes, the unconscious is where much of the emotional action is in the brain (LeDoux, 1996). Since a great deal of thinking has emotional tags attached to it, this item would likely apply to most subelements of the adult experiential learning model. This item also emphasizes the role of "meaning" relative to unconscious processes vice memorizing or simple understanding. As stated earlier, the mind/brain is a meaning-making system.

Item 1-E: Thinking is mostly unconscious. Unconscious thinking may lead to abstract conceptualization, the role that the unconscious plays when it comes to creating concepts dealing with ideas and logic, or building models and theories. As Lakoff and Johnson (1999) have noted, "All of our knowledge and beliefs are framed in terms of a conceptual system that resides mostly in the cognitive unconscious" (p. 13).

Item 1-F: The unconscious plays a big role in creativity. This idea has been emphasized by researchers in the area of creativity, in particular in the work of Andreasen (2005) and Christos (2003). During the process of creating new ideas and approaches to solving problems or making decisions—as occurs in the abstract conceptualization mode—the unconscious can be taken into account and utilized to its fullest. Techniques such as daydreaming, visualization exercises, meditation, and lucid dreaming have been mentioned in the literature review.

Item 1-G: We may act for reasons we are not aware of. This aspect of the unconscious clearly influences many subelements of active experimentation. Because of the dual roles of the conscious Self with its stream of consciousness and the large and continuously operating unconscious, our conscious mind cannot and does not control all aspects of our actions. It is important to recognize that the unconscious significantly *affects our thinking and actions, and therefore our learning process*.

Item 1-H: A model of the Self comes mostly from the unconscious. Damasio believes that much of the model of the Self comes from the unconscious mind. This model creates the idea of *who* we are and the image we build up of ourselves. During active experimentation the Self interacts with objects and the external world, and hence is typically very aware of the boundaries between the individual and that external world.

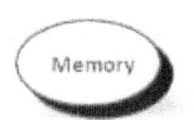

Area 2: Memory

Memory is involved in all phases of the learning cycle. For example, in grasping experience through apprehension an individual may use sensing, feeling, awareness, attention, and intuition. If the current experience is similar to a past experience (either good or bad) memory will influence the level and nature of the incoming information as it relates to the reflection and comprehension processes. This influence may significantly change the nature and interpretation of the experience.

Reflection creates understanding and meaning by associating and integrating incoming information with information stored within memory. Abstract conceptualization or comprehension works with concepts and solves problems by recalling ideas and past experiences from memory and creating new ideas and solutions to problems. Here both working memory and long-term memory will likely be actively involved. Working memory refers to representations of information currently in active use, such as when a person tries to remember a telephone number. If not rehearsed, the information will be forgotten within a few seconds (Haberlandt, 1998). As Schacter forwards,

> As working memory, it [the mind] holds on to small amounts of information for short periods of time—usually a few seconds—while people engage in such ongoing cognitive activities as reading, listening, problem solving. (Schacter, 2001, p. 28)

Short-term memory can easily be overloaded, and unless the learner chunks the incoming information, overloading is likely to occur. Long-term memory has no fixed limits on how long the information can be stored and retrieved (Haberlandt, 1998). Factors that influence an individual's length of memory recall are repetition during learning, frequency of recall, and the emotional level when first experienced.

Most action is an implementation of tacit knowledge residing in memory (Kluwe et al., 2003; Markowitsch, 1999, 2000; Schacter, 1996). As action is implemented, rapid feedback information is combined with past memories to offer a quick reaction guide to new actions (Bennet & Bennet, 2004; Hawkins, 2004). Again, both working memory and long-term memory become involved.

A good, accurate memory that can be recalled when needed is clearly an important aspect of experiential learning. We consider the following findings from neuroscience that relate to memory.

Memory is represented in the brain as an extremely large number of patterns, each composed of a large number of neurons with many synaptic junction connections and with many different junction strengths. These patterns exist throughout the brain and a single pattern (concept, object, thought) may be spread out over many regions of the brain (Christos, 2003). When memory is recalled, the temporal sequence of patterns representing the memory is brought into consciousness by assimilating the multiple parts of the memory that were stored in different areas of the brain. There are several factors that influence the integrity of the memory as it is recalled.

One of these is the overall health of the brain. Both nutrition and exercise can significantly influence the biological health of the neurons, their chemicals, and their patterns (Amen, 2005; Begley, 2007; Lipton, 2005; Medina, 2008). A second effect is whether the pattern has been recalled recently. Repetition of use strengthens neuronal memory patterns, thereby making them more easily recalled. A third factor is the emotional tag of the memory. If there was a strong emotional context when the memory was first created its recall will be much easier (Christos, 2003). There is an exception to this that occurs when the emotional impact is extremely negative and the memory is buried within the unconscious mind and is not available to consciousness. A fourth factor is the rate at which neurons are dying, or perhaps being born within the regions that contain the memory patterns (Hawkins, 2004; Ratey, 2001).

As discussed in Chapter 9, one of the somewhat surprising results from neuroscience is that typically an individual retains only a part of the incoming information, for example, from an image. To create the whole concept (in the image example, a whole picture), the rest of the incoming information is filled in by the individual when they describe or try to remember the image (Hawkins, 2004). Edelman calls this reconstructing memory (Edelman & Tononi, 2000). What this means is that the mind does not store memories in the same sense that a computer does. Rather, the mind stores the most important part of incoming information, that is, its meaning or *invariant* form, and fills in the missing parts during recollection (Hawkins, 2004). Understanding this helps the learner to be aware of the imprecision and possible irregularities in their memories, and to treat them carefully during the learning process.

What this says to experiential learners is to be cautious of their own and others' memories in terms of accuracy of recall. There is still much that is unknown, or perhaps misinterpreted, and one should be cautious in one's interpretations of specific research findings. This is not to impugn the research so much as to recognize the complexity and interrelationships among the subsystems of the brain. This suggests the value of keeping an open mind, both during conversations as well as internal reflection and comprehension as the conscious mind communicates with its memory. As mentioned earlier, memories are stored as temporal sequences of associated patterns. Information is much more easily remembered and recalled if put in a story-like form. Memory patterns are also very resilient to neuron death. For example, as many as 40 percent of neurons composing a memory pattern may be lost and the pattern still be recalled (Begley, 2007; Hawkins, 2004). From an evolutionary view, this takes into account the continual death of neurons in the brain.

The items of the memory area that could potentially influence experiential learning are as follows: (A) the brain stores only a part of the incoming sensory information and the gaps are filled in (recreated) when the memory is recalled; (B) emotional tags impact memory; (C) less than seven hours of sleep may impair memory; (D) memories are re-created each time they are recalled and therefore may not be the same (the environment influences the re-creating process); (E) memory recall is improved through temporal sequences of associative patterns, that is, stories and songs; (F) memory is scattered throughout the entire cortex (it is not stored locally); (G) working memory is limited; (H) memory patterns cannot be erased at will; (I) memory patterns may decay slowly with time; and (J) repetition increases memory recall.

Item 2-A: The brain stores only a part of the meaningful incoming sensory information. The gaps are filled in (re-created) when the memory is recalled. This item primarily relates to the sensing aspect of concrete experience in the adult experiential learning model. It makes the point that when we sense or feel our environment not all of the incoming information goes into memory. In fact, at best only things that are meaningful to us are usually remembered. Memory storage, recall, and recognition all occur at the level of the invariant forms, what Hawkins (2004) describes as "a form that captures the essence of relationships, not the details of the moment" (p. 82). This means that individuals cannot fully trust the details of their memory.

Further, an individual's reaction to an experience may be based on past, misinterpreted information that in turn may color the individual's immediate experience and therefore impact learning. This could also impact the quality or validity of an individual's intuition.

Item 2-B: Emotional tags impact memory. Since the amygdala checks all incoming information for danger and places a tag on it relative to the emotional impact, some level of emotion from zero to high is attached to our thoughts and memories. Damasio (1994) separates feelings and emotions by asserting that, "Although some feelings relate to emotions, there are many that do not: all emotions generate feelings if you are awake and alert, but not all feelings relate to emotions" (p.139).

It is through feelings (which are inwardly directed and private) that emotions (which are outwardly directed and public) begin their impact on the mind (Damasio, 1999). Thus the feeling we get when we sense an external experience is an important part of our evaluation of that experience, and thereby affects our learning.

Item 2-C: Less than seven hours of sleep may impair memory. This item is shown as affecting attention and awareness in terms of concrete experience. It emphasizes the importance of adequate sleep in keeping the brain performing well enough to ensure an effective memory.

Item 2-D: Memories are re-created each time they are recalled and therefore never the same. The environment influences the re-creating process. This item is shown as impacting attention, understanding, truth/how things work, and integrate/look for unity. All of these factors in the adult experiential learning model would be very sensitive to the accuracy of memories. For example, if a specific memory was recalled as an inaccurate representation, it could significantly change the interpretation (and therefore the meaning) of the original event.

Item 2-E: Memory recall is improved through temporal sequences of associated patterns, that is, stories and songs. This item would affect attention, understanding, and meaning in that if the information were difficult to recall it could distort any of these aspects of learning. On the other hand, if the memory had been stored in story form it would be easier to recall and have less chance of recall errors. For example, compare recalling a story to recalling a random sequence of numbers. Hawkins (2004) states that,

> Written, oral, and visual storytelling all convey a narrative in a serial fashion and can only be recalled in the same sequence...You can't remember the entire story at once. Your memory for songs is a great example of temporal sequences in memory...You cannot imagine an entire song at once, only in sequence. (pp. 71-72)

Item 2-F: Memory is scattered throughout the entire cortex; it is not stored locally. This phenomenon primarily impacts unity and creativity. Because memory is scattered physically throughout the cortex there may be errors in its reconstruction. On the other hand, from a creativity viewpoint, such errors—which build on the ability to assimilate memory from many sources—may create new ideas and concepts.

Item 2-G: Working memory is limited. This item could impact learning in the aspects of concepts, ideas, and logic as well as problem solving and building models and theories. Working memory is essential for having a conversation and comprehending what we are reading. However, it can get overloaded, and when it does it may cause confusion and mistakes (Christos, 2003). Because working memory is limited to roughly 7 plus or minus 2 bits, it is very helpful to chunk patterns to improve recall (Miller, 1956). Working memory impacts concepts, ideas, and creativity as well as conceptual thinking.

Item 2-H: Memory patterns cannot be erased at will. This item is significant because in problem solving, building models, and using theories we frequently rely on past knowledge and memory. However, as new knowledge is created, we do not forget what was learned before and therefore must be careful not to use outdated knowledge to solve new, different problems. In addition to solving problems, the brain also operates by storing solutions to problems, and while often very efficient it can fail when new challenges present themselves and the old solutions no longer apply (Hawkins, 2004).

Item 2-I: Memory patterns decay slowly with time. This depends upon the emotional and cognitive importance of the memory. When coupled with the potential errors during memory recall, it suggests that learning may be enhanced by evaluating specific material or experience for its relevance and importance to the learner. One example is to underline important passages while reading and "judge" the value (to the reader) of these passages, marking them with one to three stars in the margin. This presses the reader to *consider how important* the specific information is to his or hers own interests and goals. Repeatedly focusing attention on critical knowledge also helps solidify past knowledge.

Item 2-J: Repetition increases memory recall. This item would impact control, rigor, and discipline in abstract conceptualization and focus attention in active experimentation. This is a well-known phenomenon and goes back to Hebb's rule that *neurons that fire together wire together*. Thus, the more a given pattern is repeated the stronger the neuronal connections are and the easier a specific memory can be recalled.

Area 3: Emotions

Emotions play a strong role in experiential learning. All incoming signals and information are immediately passed to the amygdala, where they are assessed for potential harm to the individual. The amygdala places a tag on the signal that gives it a level of emotional importance (Adolphs, 2004; Zull, 2002). If the incoming information is considered dangerous to the individual, the amygdala immediately starts the body's response, such as pulling a hand away from a hot stove. In parallel but slower than the amygdala's quick response, the incoming information is processed and cognitively interpreted as usual. Another aspect of the emotional system is the role it plays in individual memory. Situations that have a high emotional impact are much easier to recall, sometimes remembered throughout life. From a learning perspective, this means that (consciously or unconsciously) the learner is always evaluating the importance of incoming information and this process helps the individual to remember the information (Christos, 2003).

One aspect of the emotional system is that it is not concerned with the details of the information. Its primary concern is with the meaning and impact of the information (Plotkin, 1994). Since the emotional system is always operating, it continuously impacts all modes of the learning process. For example, research has shown that if the amygdala is damaged the individual is unable to make decisions. There is no basis to consider one choice better or worse than another (Damasio, 1994). A high emotional event or situation can easily distract an individual's attention or focus it (Christos,

2003; Kluwe, et al., 2003;). For these reasons, it is important that learners recognize and understand the role and significance of their emotions. With practice an individual can learn to sense, and to some degree manage, internal feelings (Begley, 2007). This capability becomes useful during stressful situations such as learning or taking tests.

Our unconscious mind is continually interpreting situations and these interpretations influence our emotional response. Since our emotional state affects learning and feelings about the information learned, recognition and control of feelings related to some learning situation may significantly enhance our learning capacity (Christos, 2003; Kluwe et al., 2003). For example, if we voluntarily desire to learn, our emotions create less stress and better support, and focus the learning process. On the other hand, if learning is involuntary, the emotional system may create more stress and thereby decrease learning. Creating a positive attitude and an environment that is positive, exciting, and stress-free enhances the learning outcome (Lipton, 2005; Zull, 2002). As noted above, all of this is driven internally, within the learner, by chemicals generated by the perceptions and feelings of the situation and the material to be learned (Pert, 1997). While the external environment and the material to be learned may have a significant role in the learning outcome, the perception and interpretation by the learner can significantly impact the result.

As described above, from a long-term learning perspective, learning can be enhanced by asking questions and deliberately assigning importance levels to the material. By developing a positive attitude toward learning, individuals can improve their learning rate and their recall. Because emotions operate through chemical generation and flows, their impact may include the entire body (LeDoux, 1996). How we feel about a situation or a goal is an overall state of the body rather than a specific set of patterns in the mind.

In summary, emotions are always part of learning processes and can significantly modulate the learning process and its results. For example, during the concrete experience mode of the adult experiential learning model high positive emotions increase an individual's sensing, feeling, and awareness as well as support focused attention. Positive emotions not only excite an individual to learn, but also encourage exploration and flexibility in learning. When we are excited about something, our minds are more open and we look to building ideas and improving our understanding. On the other hand, negative emotions tend toward the opposite result. With strong negative emotions ruling a situation, the learner may start to close in and become more cautious and fearful, with the result of paying less attention to learning.

As Pert (1997) details,

> Emotional states or moods are produced by the various molecules known as neuropeptide ligands, [molecules] and what we experience as an emotion or a feeling is also a mechanism for activating a particular neuronal circuit -- simultaneously throughout the brain and body -- which generates a behavior involving the whole creature, with all the necessary physiological changes that behavior would require. (Pert, 1997, p. 145)

Although the amygdala may be the source of our emotions, these emotions quickly spread throughout the body.

The items in the emotional area that could potentially influence experiential learning are as follows: (A) the brain can generate molecules of emotion to reinforce what is learned; (B) emotional tags influence memory recall; (C) emotions miss details but are sensitive to meaning; (D) unconscious interpretation of a situation can influence the emotional experience; (E) the entire body is involved in emotions and the body drives the emotions; (F) emotions can increase or decrease neuronal activity; and (G) emotions influence all incoming information.

Item 3-A: The brain can generate molecules of emotion to reinforce what is learned. Pert (1997) offers that through self-consciousness the mind can use the brain to generate molecules of emotion and override the cognitive system. If positive, this phenomenon could provide control over attention during the concrete experience. It can also improve understanding and meaning, and seek truth/how things work. This could influence activities in both concrete experience and reflective observation of the adult experiential learning model.

Item 3-B: Emotional tags influence memory recall. We remember things that are emotionally significant. This helps our understanding and the creation of meaning, as well as our ability to anticipate the outcomes of actions. Thus this item supports both reflective observation and abstract conceptualization. The mind solves many complex problems by recalling the core (or meaning) of past solutions. The most significant past problems have emotional tags that aid in recall.

Item 3-C: Emotions miss details but are sensitive to meaning. Emotions exist to alert and protect individuals from harm and to energize them to action when they have strong feelings or passions. However, emotions are concerned with the meaning of the information and not the details. Thus, this phenomenon may influence a number of aspects of the adult experiential learning model either positively or negatively, depending on circumstances. Specifically, feeling, awareness, intuition, understanding, and meaning can all be influenced by the emotional state of the individual. Where learners can control their emotions by taking a positive attitude they can enhance their learning.

Item 3-D: Unconscious interpretation of a situation can influence the emotional experience. As stated earlier, the unconscious mind is always working and, through the release of neurotransmitters it may create bodily emotional experiences. This process can impact the understanding and meaning aspects of an external experience during a learner's reflective observation.

Item 3-E: The entire body is involved in emotions and the body drives the emotions. LeDoux (1996, 2002) offers that emotions are a slave to physiology, not vice versa. This aspect of the emotions may singularly impact how we act on the environment and how much control, rigor, and/or discipline we can exert. It would also impact on how well we can focus attention and maintain awareness.

Item 3-F: Emotions can increase or decrease neuronal activity. The level of emotion that an individual experiences can influence not only awareness but also how well he or she can focus attention. Because of the presence and significance of emotions throughout the mind and the body, this item could well impact any of the sub-elements that are part of the adult experiential learning model. Here we point out several of the most likely aspects.

Item 3-G: Emotions influence all incoming information. This is another finding that could potentially influence all aspects in the adult experiential learning model. However, there are three specific aspects that will most likely be subjected to emotional influence: understanding, meaning and truth/how things work. As Mulvihill (2003) notes,

> During both the initial processing and the linking with information from the different senses, it becomes clear that there is no thought, memory, or knowledge which is "objective," or "detached" from the personal experience of knowing. (p. 322)

Chapter 13
(Group 2)
Stress, Creativity, Mirror Neurons, Anticipating the Future, Social Support

Recall that the 13 areas of neuroscience findings are conveniently divided into three groups:

Group 1 is made up of the unconscious (1), memory (2), and emotion (3), and represents a foundational group that is always involved in learning.

Group 2 represents findings that influence learning in specific situations. It includes stress (4), creativity (5), mirror neurons (6), anticipating the future (7), and social support (9).

Group 3 supports the capacity for, and enhancement of, lifelong learning. This group is made up of social interaction (8), epigenetics (10), plasticity (11), exercise and health (12), and aging (13).

Each area below begins with a brief description of the findings based on the discussion in Chapters 6-10, then ends with a breakdown of specific concepts (or items) that relate to the subelements of the four modes of the adult experiential learning model.

Area 4: Stress

As described earlier, all signals of information coming into experience are tagged with an emotional factor. As Akil et al., (1999) state,

> The stress system is an active monitoring system that constantly compares current events to past experience, interprets the relevance (salience) of the events to the survival of the organism's ability to cope (p. 1146).

If the emotional content of incoming information is one of strong fear or uncertainty to the individual, stress is created and may significantly limit any learning involved. However, if there is too little arousal/stress involved then there may be no desire for learning. Thus, for each individual there exists some optimal level of arousal/stress (Zull, 2002). Note that low levels of stress are often referred to as arousal.

It is possible for individuals to control their perception of stress by recognizing its existence and understanding that stress is created inside the body and can therefore be understood and managed (Begley, 2007). As stated earlier, patterns in the mind *can and do* influence neurons in the brain, so that mind over matter is possible, and therefore it is possible for an individual to consciously change his or her level of response to stress. Stress is a function of individual perspective and interpretation, how we perceive a situation, or the uncertainty versus control that we see in the situation (Begley, 2007).

By understanding the origin of stress and learning to manage stress we can minimize its deleterious effects. Both the excitement of learning and the fear of failure or embarrassment impact the efficiency and effectiveness of the learning process. A passion for learning opens the mind, creates possibilities, and expands the scope of interest and creativity. A fear of learning closes the mind to options and causes it to focus on safety and protection, which minimizes learning. Further, there is a strong link between an individual's emotions and his or her cognitive appraisals (LeDoux, 1996; Smith & Ellsworth, 1985). To develop understanding, see the meaning or significance of something, or recognize relationships, patterns, and probabilities requires an open mind that can explore different avenues of thought. This is difficult if fear due to excessive stress is in the background of learning (Zull, 2002).

Our rate of learning depends upon what we already know (National Research Council, 2000). A generic fear of learning may create a potential long-term degenerative spiral, resulting in continuous non-learning, the exact opposite of what would be desired. As discussed above, emotions are involved in all aspects of our living, and thus have the potential for influencing everything we do. Understanding their role in experiential learning allows the learner to take control of stress levels and turn them into learning possibilities. The recognition and belief that mind can influence the brain/body (material world) is a key concept for enhancing experiential learning (Lipton, 2005).

The items of the stress area that could potentially influence the subelements of the adult experiential learning model are as follows: (A) emotional fear inhibits learning; (B) voluntary learning promotes Theta waves (see below) that correlate with little or no stress and positive feedback; (C) stress depends on how we perceive a situation; (D) belief systems can reduce stress by reducing uncertainty; (E) stress focuses attention and takes precedence; (F) there is an optimum level of stress for learning (the inverted "U"); and (G) stress is an active monitoring system that constantly compares current events to past experiences.

Item 4–A: Emotional fear inhibits learning. Stress plays a strong role in arousal and attention, both of which significantly impact the motivational and cognitive aspects of learning. Because emotional fear spreads throughout the body, it impacts many aspects of the adult learning model. For example, sensing, feeling, awareness, attention, understanding, and meaning would all be changed in some way by high levels of emotional fear. On the converse side, a positive attitude filled with excitement and energy would enhance all of these same characteristics.

Item 4-B: Voluntary learning promotes Theta waves that correlate with little or no stress and positive feedback. Theta waves are low frequency (4-8 hertz) electrical waves generated within the brain and detected by an electroencephalograph (EEG) that measures electrical activity near the surface of the brain via electrodes on the scalp. There are a number of suggested correlates to theta waves; for example, intentional or voluntary movements, high-level processing of incoming signals, selective attention, arousal, and decision-making. As Buzsaki (2006) posits, "an inescapable conclusion is that 'will' plays a crucial role in theta rhythms" (p. 21). *Voluntary learning, as distinct from forced learning, has little or no stress attached to it and therefore fosters a much higher level of learning.* Specifically, positive learning would impact sensing, feeling, awareness, attention, understanding, and meaning as they relate to the adult learning model. As previously noted, such improved learning would most likely impact all of the aspects of the adult learning model. We are only identifying a sample of significant areas of impact.

Item 4-C: Stress depends on how we perceive a situation. As Thompson (2000) explains, "the extent to which situations are stressful is determined by how the individual understands, interprets, sees, and feels about the situation" (p. 210). Thus, stress is controllable. From a learning perspective, this item would impact awareness, attention, understanding, and meaning as well as most of the other sub-elements of the four modes of the adult experiential learning model.

Item 4-D: Belief systems can reduce stress through reducing uncertainty. Belief systems create a perspective on the world that is held to be correct and by doing so introduces a level of perceived certainty that reduces stress and increases repeatability in an individual's life. Belief systems may also narrow perspectives and thereby reduce learning. This item could impact sensing, feeling, understanding, and meaning in the adult learning model.

Item 4-E: Stress focuses attention. Stress takes precedence. This item would clearly impact the magnitude and area of one's attention relative to adult learning. If stress is too high, it may result in intense fear and the inability to act. This may reduce learning via many of the subelements.

Item 4-F: There is an optimum level of stress for learning (the inverted "U"). This level is somewhere between a positive attitude and a strong motivation to learn (arousal), and some level of fear of learning or the learning situation. Among sub-elements, it could impact problem solving, creativity, and anticipation in the abstract conceptualization learning mode.

Item 4-G: Stress is an active monitoring system that constantly compares current events to past experiences. Three subelements of the adult learning model that could be affected by this item would be anticipation, act on environment, and object-based logic. For example, in anticipating the outcomes of some planned action developed from abstract conceptualization, an individual would think about past examples of similar situations and estimate the problems and potential issues, that is, what stress may occur as a result of the action.

Area 5: Creativity

Creativity is an inherent capability of every brain (Hobson, 1999; Cristos, 2003). As described earlier, learning consists of building new patterns within the mind that represent ideas, concepts, and capabilities, and processes that are internally imagined, or represent some interpretation of external reality. According to Stonier, (1997) thinking involves the association of different patterns within the mind/brain. Since memory is distributed throughout the brain, these associative processes may contain random associations that can result in new ideas, concepts, or approaches. This is considered as ordinary creativity and can be very valuable when it occurs during any of the four modes of the adult experiential learning model. This process represents a form of self-learning initiated during the reflective observation or abstract conceptualism modes (Andreasen, 2005).

These new patterns may represent insights or increased understanding of a situation, or perhaps a clarification of the meaning of a situation. They may come from the unconscious mind "playing with" ideas that are experienced during the night. This is most likely the source of the adage, "we need to sleep on it." Since much processing is done by the unconscious during sleep (as presented earlier), learning can be enhanced by making use of the mind's capability for creativity. Such practices as meditation, lucid dreaming, and hemispheric synchronization (see Chapter 21) can serve to improve creativity and problem solving (Andreasen, 2005). Other practices such as changing one's frame of reference may also create new ways of viewing problems. Andreasen suggests there are five circumstances that create cradles of creativity (Andreasen, 2005). These are (1) an atmosphere of intellectual freedom and excitement; (2) a critical mass of creative minds; (3) free and fair competition; (4) mentors and patrons; and (5) at least some economic prosperity.

Extraordinary creativity relates to certain individuals who have the capacity to repeatedly create novel ideas or processes that push the limit on understanding or application. These are the highly creative people who keep an open mind, maintain a high curiosity, and investigate many paths toward new possibilities. These people have a particular mental capability and capacity for challenging the status quo and seeing things from unique perspectives (Andreasen, 2005).

There are many techniques, both individual and group processes that serve to open the mind to new possibilities and stimulate creative thinking. Such processes are all forms of learning with some being from concrete experience, dialogue, or social interaction; others from internal reflection and comprehension. In either case, if learners understand the dangers of assuming they already "know" the answer, they may deliberately keep an open mind and improve both the efficiency and the effectiveness of their learning and their creativity. Becoming aware that every mind is capable of creativity (Hobson, 1999; Christos, 2003), and that the rules and practices of creative thinking are available to anyone, opens the door for learners to enhance their creativity and learning capacity.

The items of creativity that could influence experiential learning are as follows: (A) an enriched environment can produce a personal internal reflective world of imagination and creativity; (B) conscious and unconscious patterns are involved with creativity; (C) the unconscious produces flashes of insight; (D) volleying between conscious and unconscious thinking increases creativity; (E) meditation quiets the mind; (F) extraordinary creativity can be developed; (G) free flow and randomness of mixing patterns can create new patterns; and (H) accidental associations.

Item 5-A: An enriched environment can produce a personal internal reflective world of imagination and creativity. This item is part of the environment, and as such may affect a number of the aspects of concrete experience and active experimentation. A rich environment entering the mind/brain/body through experiences stimulates the mind to associate patterns and create new possibilities.

Item 5-B: Conscious and unconscious patterns are involved with creativity. Creativity can impact a number of aspects in the adult learning model. We specifically indicate awareness and unleashed intuition as being part of creativity.

Item 5-C: The unconscious produces flashes of insight. Christos (2003) notes that spurious memories can generate new ideas that combine in different ways to make new associations. In addition to others, this item would affect intuition and meaning.

Item 5-D: Volleying between the conscious and the unconscious increases creativity. "New ideas are generated through the process of shifting from conscious to unconscious as the mind contemplates and searches for solutions" (Christos, 2003, p. 90). The process of shifting between conscious and unconscious thinking would make use of the memories and knowledge in the unconscious and the goals and thinking of the conscious mind. This would increase the chances of associating conscious ideas to create new ones. While this occurs in the transition from the waking state to the sleeping state (and vice versa), to do this while awake requires some level of control and discipline in implementation.

Item 5-E: Meditation quiets the mind. Meditation requires some level of control and discipline, and it can significantly enhance the ability to focus attention. In this context, quieting the mind means to reduce the noise that "bedevils the untrained mind, in which an individual's focus darts from one sight or sound or thought to another like a hyperactive dragonfly, and replace it with attentional stability and clarity" (Begley, 2007, p. 214). This item allows the mind to focus attention on potential relationships that may create new ideas.

Item 5-F: Extraordinary creativity can be developed. A basic operation of the brain is that of associating patterns within the mind to create new patterns (thoughts, ideas, and concepts), what is referred to as ordinary creativity. Andreasen (2005) believes that everyone possesses ordinary creativity: the creation of new ways of doing things in their daily lives through discussing new ideas and developing insights and deeper understanding. In this sense *all learning is creating*. Extraordinary creativity refers to highly creative people who often receive ideas through flashes of insights and moments of inspiration. Andreasen (2005) forwards that "Extraordinarily creative people go into a state at the edge of chaos, where ideas float, soar, collide and collect" (p.159). This item would relate to concepts, ideas, and logic; building models and theories; control and discipline; and focusing attention.

Item 5-G: Free-flow and randomly mixing patterns create new patterns. This relates directly to creativity and is one way of the interaction among neuronal networks and patterns to create new ideas.

Item 5-H: Accidental associations can create new patterns. This also clearly relates to creativity as part of abstract conceptualization. This makes the point that creativity can happen by accident within an active mind that plays with ideas, connections, and their relationships.

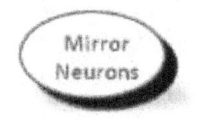

Area 6: Mirror Neurons

Mirror neurons are a more recently discovered phenomenon in the brain. They relate to the ease and speed with which we understand simple actions. Research on experiments with Macaque monkeys that began in the early 1990s indicated that the activation of subsets of neurons in brain-motor areas appeared to represent actions. The initial experiments had one monkey grasp an object (an orange) while the experimenters monitored what went on inside an observer monkey's brain. Over the past 10 years many variations of this have verified that an observer's neurons fire (or mirror) the actor's neurons. Testing has moved from monkeys to great apes to humans. Non-invasive measurement techniques such as fMRI have enabled the experiments on humans to be greatly expanded.

These measurements have included mirror neurons in humans located in the frontal lobe and in the parietal lobe, which include Broca's area, a key area for human language (Iacoboni, 2008). Emotional mirrors have been discovered using fMRI by,

> Feeling disgust activated similar parts of the brain when human volunteers experienced the emotion while smelling a disgusting odor or when the same subjects watched a film clip of someone else disgusted. (Rizzolatti, 2006, p. 60)

As Rizzolatti (2006) described, "subsets of neurons in human and monkey brains respond when an individual performs certain actions and also when the subject observes others performing the same movements" (p. 56). In other words, *the same neurons fire in the brain of an observer as fire in the individual performing an action.* These neurons provide an internal experience that replicates that of another's experience, thereby experiencing another individual's act, intentions, and/or emotions. These researchers also found that the mirror neuron system responded to the intentional component of an action as well as the action itself (Rizzolatti, 2006).

Carrying this idea further, Iacoboni proposes that mirror neurons facilitate the direct and immediate comprehension of another's behavior without going through complex cognitive processes. This makes the learning process more efficient because it can instantly transfer not only visuals but emotions and intentions as well. Mirror neurons also serve as a means of learning through imitation, which is "a very important means by which we learn and transmit skills, language and culture" (Rizzolatti, 2006, p. 61). Often a significant part of learning requires good social communication, which includes parity and direct comprehension. Parity indicates that the meaning within the message is similar for both the sender and the receiver. Direct comprehension means that no previous agreement between individuals is needed for them to understand each other. From the neuroscience perspective, both of these aspects of communication seem to be inherent in the neural organization of individuals (Rizzolatti, 2006).

The question becomes how this phenomenon aids experiential learning. One answer is that it serves to explain how actionable tacit knowledge can be transferred between individuals and the potential of mimicry to facilitate learning. A second aspect is to be aware that when we are mentally simulating another's behavior, we must not modulate that simulation through our own internal evaluation and perspectives. The capacity to re-create feelings, perspectives, and empathy with people by reliving their experiences can greatly aid learning, providing we understand what is happening and its potential for misinterpretation. In terms of enhancing experiential learning, understanding the mirror neuron effect provides the opportunity to increase the efficiency and effectiveness of that learning.

The items in the mirror neuron area that could potentially influence experiential learning are as follows: (A) cognitive mimicry that transfers active behavior and other cultural norms; (B) rapid transfer of information that bypasses cognition; (C) through reliving we recreate feelings, perspectives, and other phenomenon that we observe;

(D) we understand other people's behavior by mentally simulating it; (E) neurons create the same patterns when we see something as when we do it; (F) what we see we become ready to do; and (G) mirror neurons facilitate neural resonance between observed actions and executing actions.

Item 6-A: Cognitive mimicry that transfers active behavior and other cultural norms. Zull (2002) notes that mirror neurons are a form of cognitive mimicry that transfers active behavior and, most likely, other cultural norms. When we see something happening our mind creates the same patterns of neurons that we would use to enact the same thing ourselves. This would be related to the sensing, feeling, and attention in concrete experience subelements of the adult experiential learning model.

Item 6-B: Rapid transfer of tacit knowledge (bypasses cognition). By creating the same neuronal pattern in your mind that is in the mind of another person, the need for cognitive thinking is bypassed and tacit knowledge may be immediately transferred. This would affect understanding and meaning in reflective observation, and speed up the learning process.

Item 6-C: Through reliving we recreate the feelings, perspectives and other phenomena that we observe. Nelson et al., (2006) offer that we understand other people's behavior by mentally simulating it. Among other subelements, this would impact sensing and concepts, ideas, and logic in the adult learning model.

Item 6-D: We may understand other people's behavior by mentally simulating it. This would relate to understanding, meaning, and truth/how things work in reflective observation, and to heightened boundary conditions in active experimentation.

Item 6-E: Neurons create the same pattern when we see some action being taken as when we do it. This affects sensing, focusing, attention, and sensory feedback to the brain. Understanding this phenomenon allows the learner to make better use of learning opportunities. It also explains why our intuition can be right.

Item 6-F: What we see we become ready to do. Because we may have instant recognition and understanding of an external phenomenon via mirror neurons, reaction time can be significantly enhanced as well as our learning. This relates to heightened boundary conditions in the sense of providing instant awareness and understanding of objects and boundaries, permitting faster responses when needed.

Item 6-G: Mirror neurons facilitate neural resonance between observed actions and executing actions. By neural resonance we mean a positive, mutually reinforcing relationship between two people interacting with each other. An individual may interact with another individual more efficiently and effectively because of the understanding and affection developed from the mutually reinforcing relationship between the two. For example, we may be able to understand another's feelings and/or intended actions because (through mirror neurons) we generate similar feelings and/or intended actions (or reactions). Mirror neurons may facilitate a quick, positive relationship between the observer and the observed.

Area 7: Anticipating the Future

One aspect of the operation of the mind that enhances the abstract conceptualization learning process is that the neocortex is designed to continuously predict the near-term future (Hawkins, 2004). The mind stores memories of situations, and when similar situations arise these memories are pulled up and used to create solutions. For example, if you walk over to a table and pick up a glass of water, your mind is telling your body that it is going to pick up a glass of water and the body automatically solves the problem of *how* to move the arm and pick up the glass. The mind does not make all the calculations necessary to do this, which in terms of complexity would be beyond the capability of current computers. What it does do is go to the memory of past experiences and select the appropriate ones, recombining them to fit the situation at hand. This is based on Hawkin's (2004) theory that "the brain doesn't compute the answers to problems; it retrieves the answers from memory." In essence, he says that "the answers were stored in memory a long time ago" (p. 68).

As an example, the mind/brain could not possibly do all of the calculations to compute the movements needed for a baseball outfielder to run and catch a baseball. Instead, the sighting of the ball automatically recalls the appropriate memory. The memory is then adjusted as it is recalled to meet the specific situation (Hawkins, 2004). In this case the outfielder's movements are guided by a simple heuristic: Keep the angle between the ball and the outfielder constant.

When applied to complicated or complex situations, this storing of solutions in memory may be very effective or disastrous, depending on the level of experience of the decision-maker. This is where experts can excel by using the patterns from previous experience obtained by "living with similar situations." This is also where the mind learns and embeds multiple examples of patterns of behavior or configurations and structures. This knowledge, often created and stored in the unconscious and referred to as intuition, may provide a capability of anticipating the future outcomes of specific actions. By learning patterns and storing them in hierarchical relationships (Ratey, 2001), experts become capable of solving problems and taking effective action far beyond what others are capable of (P.E. Ross, 2006). By hierarchical relationship is meant that some elements are in an abstract sense "above or below" others. This is not a physical relationship but depends on how the two are connected to one another (Kuntz, 1968). For example, referring to the six layers of neurons in the cortex Hawkins (2004) states that,

> In the cortex, lower areas feed information up to higher areas by way of a certain neural pattern of connectivity, while higher areas send feedback down to lower areas using a different connection path. (p. 45)

As an example of a memory hierarchy, consider a child learning to read: first memorizing individual letters, then individual simple words, then learning complex multi-syllable words. Each step starts slowly and awkwardly, then progresses with effort to efficient reading and understanding. At that point we do not actually see each letter but recognize entire words and then phrases and sentences and higher levels of meaning. A similar hierarchy exists in the cortex where, during early learning, the recognition of letters occurs at high levels (V or VI) of the cortex; after reading competence is achieved letter recognition would stay at the lower levels (I or II), and "the higher regions of the cortex have learned complex objects like words and phrases" (Hawkins, 2004, pp. 166-167). These higher levels of the cortex then contain the invariant forms (Hawkins, 2004).

The development of such expertise, often through "effortful learning" falls under the field of competency theory and essentially creates the neuronal patterns in the mind such that they are connected and structured in a manner, which allows their selection and application for different situations. This is the neural equivalent of deep knowledge or expertise. While the four modes of the adult experiential model for learning apply, it is their detailed processes of implementation that creates knowledge. Through deliberate and carefully practiced learning processes, experts develop a robust and deep understanding of a subject area and are able to use past learning and memories to complete incoming information in a manner that leads to both the anticipation of the outcome of a given action and to the implementation of the actions needed to achieve the desired outcome.

Experts do not store a huge amount of details and once outside of their domain of expertise, they are no smarter than anyone else (P.E. Ross, 2006). This capacity to re-create knowledge for each situational need, instead of trying to store a large amount of detailed information, is important for effective learning. As Kolb (1984) and others have noted, the mind is oriented toward understanding and meaning, not just the memorization of facts. It remembers, and can replicate sequences such as songs or stories much easier and longer than data, or random information. The mind/brain unconsciously tailors internal information and knowledge to incoming information by storing high-level patterns and mixing them with the incoming information to adapt to the situation at hand, and thereby creates understanding, meaning, insight, new ideas, judgments, and the anticipated outcome of intended actions.

The items of anticipating the future area that could potentially influence the four modes of the adult learning model are as follows: (a) the neocortex constantly tries to predict the next experience; (b) memory stores invariant forms (used to predict the future); (c) mind/brain unconsciously tailors internal knowledge to the situation at hand; (d) mind uses past learning and memories to complete incoming information; and (e) the mind/brain creates an internal representation of the world.

Item 7-A: The neocortex constantly tries to predict the next experience. This aspect of anticipating the future is part of understanding and meaning in reflective observation and of anticipating in the abstract conceptualization mode. Buzsaki (2006) says, "brains are foretelling devices and their predictive powers emerge from the very rhythms they perpetually generate" (p. vii). This concept of prediction can become a valuable learning tool.

Using what has been learned to anticipate the outcome of one's actions and comparing the anticipated outcome to the actual outcome provides a measure of the quality of the learning process or its outcome, that is, knowledge. This creates a feedback loop that when implemented can enhance learning (Marquardt, 1999). In some applications this is referred to as Action Learning.

Some relationships of these items (neuroscience findings) to experiential learning are explored below.

Item 7-B: Memory stores invariant forms (used to predict the future). These invariant forms represent the generic meaning stored in memory and are useful in anticipating future actions. They also serve to interpret sensory feedback such as the recognition of friends from a distance.

Item 7-C: The mind/brain unconsciously tailors internal knowledge to the situation at hand. As Hawkins (2004) forwards, the hierarchical and nested structure of the cortex mirrors the structure of the external world and by doing so creates a set of memories that can be pulled together to interpret a situation. This capability makes understanding and the creation of meaning more efficient and accurate. It also helps the brain focus attention and uses immediate sensory feedback to the brain to assess its own effectiveness.

Item 7-D: The mind uses past learning and memories to complete incoming information. The capacity to complete incoming information from past experience enhances both efficiency and the effectiveness of learning. It impacts the ability to create meaning during reflective observation as well as problem solving and anticipating the outcomes of actions during abstract conceptualization.

Item 7-E: The mind/brain creates an internal representation of the world. This internal representation of the world impacts most of the subelements of the four modes of the adult experiential learning model. The validity and the scope of this internal model would affect the learner's capacity to deal with specific learning situations. A high accuracy of this internal model would make learning more efficient and effective.

Area 9: Social Support

Language and significant social relationships shape the brain (Cozolino, 2002). Cozolino also posits that the two powerful processes of social interaction and affective attunement contribute to "both the evolution and the sculpting of the brain ... [since they] stimulate the brain to grow, organize and integrate" (pp. 213, 293). See Marion Diamond's research regarding the relationship of a good social environment and the physiological increases in cortex thickness addressed in area 13, neuroscience findings on aging.

Cozolino and Sprokay (2006) believe that, "the attention of a caring, aware mentor may support plasticity that leads to better, more meaningful learning" (p. 13). They further offer that, "We appear to experience optimal development and integration in a context of a balance of nurturance and optimal stress" (p. 62).

A safe and empathic relationship can establish an emotional and neurobiological context that is conducive to neural reorganization. Such a context acts as a buffer and scaffolding, within which the learner can more easily tolerate the stress needed for neural reorganization (Cozolino, 2002). As Taylor (2006) explains,

> Adults who would create (or re-create) neural networks associated with the development of a more complex epistemology need emotional support for the discomfort that will also certainly be part of that process. (p. 82)

The effects of social forces are often not in conscious awareness. LeDoux (1996) says that the present social situation and physical environment are part of what is connected. He finds that,

> People normally do all sorts of things for reasons that they are not consciously aware of (because the behavior is produced by brain systems that operate unconsciously). And that one of the main jobs of consciousness is to keep our life tied together into a coherent story, a self-concept. It does this by generating explanations of behavior on the basis of our Self image, memories of the past, expectations of the future, the present social situation and the physical environment in which the behavior is produced. (p. 33)

The above indicates that a positive social relationship and a corresponding environment support individual learning through the creation of internal perspectives and feelings that facilitate pattern generation and the development of meaning by the learner. The biological impact resulting from interactions with an attuned other can significantly enhance learning. Experiential learning is not just a function of the incoming information. The overall environment, a trusted other, and the conscious and unconscious state of the learner all have a role in the final efficiency and effectiveness of learning that occurs. By being aware of these factors, learners may be able to change the local physical environment, improve communications with others, or perhaps position and adjust their own internal feelings and perspectives to maximize their learning. While the role of a mentor or trusted other is significant, as is the environment, Caine and Caine (2006) emphasize that the role of the individual in this relationship is also critical:

> In order to adequately understand any concept, or acquiring any mastery of a skill or domain, a person has to make sense of things for himself or herself, irrespective of how much others know and how much a coach, mentor or teacher tries to help. We have also argued that although there is an indispensable social aspect to the construction of meaning, there's also an irreducible individual element. (p. 54)

The items of the social support area that could potentially influence experiential learning are as follows: (A) language and social relationships build and shape the brain; (B) adults developing complex neural patterns need emotional support to offset the discomfort of this process; (C) affective attunement contributes to the evolution and sculpting of the brain; and (D) the brain actually needs to seek out an affectively attuned other for maximum learning.

Item 9-A: Language and social relationships build and shape the brain. This item could significantly impact the sensing aspect of concrete experience and the concepts, ideas, and logic of abstract conceptualization in the adult learning model. Good social relationships enhance learning through a reduction of stress, a shared language, and the use and understanding of concepts, metaphors, anecdotes, and stories.

Item 9-B: Adults developing complex neural patterns need emotional support to offset discomfort of this process. Taylor (2006) suggests that this support is

needed by individuals developing complex knowledge. Such emotional support will enhance the feelings of an individual during concrete experience, and also aid in the creation and understanding of concepts and ideas during abstract conceptualization.

Item 9-C: Affective attunement contributes to the evolution and sculpting of the brain. Affective attunement involves a mentor, coach, or another significant individual who is trusted and capable of resonance with the learner. When this happens, a dialogue with such an individual can greatly help the learner in understanding, developing meaning, anticipating the future with respect to actions, and receiving sensory feedback.

As these new patterns are created in the mind, they in turn impact and change the structure of the brain. All of these influence subelements of the four modes of the adult experiential learning model.

Item 9-D: The brain actually needs to seek out an affectively attuned other for learning. As Johnson explains, affective attunement reduces fear, and creates a positive environment and motivation to learn (Johnson, 2006). Being open to learning helps one integrate and look for unity as one reflects and opens up to sensory feedback during active experimentation.

Chapter 14
(Group 3)
Lifelong Learning
Social Interaction, Epigenetics, Plasticity
Exercise and Health, Aging

By way of review, recall that we conveniently divide the 13 areas of neuroscience findings into three groups:

Group 1 is made up of the unconscious (1), memory (2), and emotion (3), and represents a foundational group that is always involved in learning.

Group 2 represents findings that influence learning in specific situations. It includes stress (4), creativity (5), mirror neurons (6), anticipating the future (7), and social support (9).

Group 3 supports the capacity for, and enhancement of, lifelong learning. This group is made up of social interaction (8), epigenetics (10), plasticity (11), exercise and health (12), and aging (13).

Each area below begins with a brief description of the findings based on the discussion in Chapters 6-10, then ends with a breakdown of specific concepts (or items) that relate to the subelements of the four modes of the adult experiential learning model.

Area 8: Social Interaction

Johnson (2006) offers that "physical mechanisms have evolved to enable us to get the knowledge we need in order to keep emotionally and physically safe". Whether in dialogue, discussion, debate, or casual conversations we can learn a great deal by talking and listening to others. This helps keep learners mentally and physically safe in the sense that interaction with others may provide an atmosphere for relaxed yet challenging conversations, thereby supporting learning. For example, if a mentor creates a safe, trusting relationship and a good holding environment, the learner will be better able to recognize the mentor's thinking as they move through the development journey (Johnson, 2006). These two processes, a trusting relationship and a good holding environment, "stimulate the brain to grow, organize and integrate" (Cozolino, 2002, p. 213). During this process the learner's neurotransmitters in the frontal cortex are stimulated, leading to greater brain plasticity and increased neuronal networking—leading to meaningful learning (Cozolino, 2002). Tallis (2002) suggests that unconscious learning most likely influences people's social preferences. In his words,

> Human beings are constantly forming positive or negative opinions of others, and often have minimal social contact. If challenged, opinions can be justified, but such justifications frequently take the form of post hoc rationalization. Some of course are laughably transparent. (Tallis, 2002, p. 129)

According to Bownds, social interaction influences the expression of genes through the reaction and behavior of the learner. Gene expression in infants is influenced by sensing and behavior appropriate for its environment. Clusters of nerve cells in the brainstem distribute neurotransmitters (serotonin, acetylcholine) to areas of the cortex and influence both the growth of the brain during development and its behavior and plasticity in adults (Bownds, 1999). Which supporting neuronal pathways become permanent depends on the usefulness of the behavior in enhancing survival and reproduction.

It becomes clear that the nature of the social interaction plays an important role in determining learning. The specific social interaction that influences the neural structure, and the stress level of the individual will affect the nature and amount of learning that results. From the learner's perspective this phenomenon suggests that the learner create and manage positive and beneficial social interactions wherever possible. Being aware of this phenomenon is a first step toward effective management of the social learning process. When there is trust between two individuals, information and knowledge can be transferred with minimum distortion and high efficiency.

The items of the social interaction area that could potentially influence experiential learning are as follows: (A) physical mechanisms have developed in our brain to enable us to learn through social interaction; (B) physical and mental exercise and social bonding are significant sources of stimulation of the brain; and (C) social interaction mechanisms foster engagement in affective attunement; considering the intentions of others; understanding what another person is thinking and thinking about how we want to interact.

Item 8-A: Physical mechanisms have developed in our brain to enable us to learn through social interactions. Johnson (2006) says that these physical mechanisms have evolved to enable us to get the knowledge we need to keep emotionally and physically safe. These mechanisms would enable us to, "(1) engage in affective attunement or empathic interaction and language, (2) consider the intentions of the other, (3) try to understand what another mind is thinking, and (4) think about how we want to interact" (Johnson, 2006, p. 65). The physical mechanisms for this capability come from mirror neurons (see area 6 above) and also from adaptive oscillators. As mentioned above, mirror neurons aid in stimulating other people's states of mind. As Stern (2004) proposes, "This 'participation' in another's mental life creates a sense of feeling/sharing with/understanding the person's intentions and feelings" (p. 79). This sense of close and trusting relationship is very supportive of learning.

Another mechanism that aids in the synchronism of two individuals is the adaptive oscillators that are part of our physiology. These oscillators are created by stable feedback loops of neurons. They may bring an individual's rate of neural firing into sync with another individual. This is when two people relate well to each other and learn to anticipate each other's actions (Stern, 2004). Buzsaki calls this phenomenon mutual entrainment, meaning a measure of stability that oscillators have when they lock in with each other (Buzsaki, 2006). Such situations, when they occur, may enhance the sensing, feeling, and awareness in the concrete experience phase of the adult experiential learning model.

Item 8-B: Physical and mental exercise and social bonding are significant sources of stimulation of the brain. This statement by Amen (2005) highlights the importance of physical exercise for the health of the brain, mental exercise for the health of the mind, and social bonding. Physical exercise provides oxygen and increased blood to the brain. Studies have shown that a higher concentration of oxygen in the blood significantly improves cognitive performance in learners, for example tests demonstrated that individuals were able to recall more words from a list and perform visual and spatial tasks faster. Their cognitive abilities changed directly with the amount of oxygen in their brains (Chung et al., 2004; Scholey et al., 1999). In Sousa (2006) social bonding carries with it a positive, trusting relationship that allows the learner to take risks and not be concerned with mistakes made during learning. It also encourages an open mind and willingness to listen and learn from a trusted other. During this process, the learner's neurotransmitters in the prefrontal cortex (dopamine, serotonin, and norepinephrine) are stimulated and lead to increased neuronal networking and meaningful learning (Cozolino, 2002). While these would apply to many subelements of the adult experiential learning model, we highlight the following: awareness, attention and concepts, ideas, and logic.

Item 8-C: Social interaction mechanisms foster the engagement in affective attunement, consider the intentions of others, understand what another person is thinking and think about how we want to interact. As Johnson (2006) explains, "according to social cognitive neuroscience, the brain actually needs to seek out an affectively attuned other if it is to learn" (p. 65). Affective attunement reduces fear, a significant impediment to learning. These mechanisms support learning situations by enhancing understanding, meaning, truth and how things work, and anticipating the outcomes of actions.

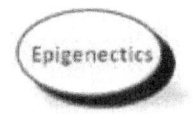

Area 10: Epigenetics

Lipton (2005) forwards that science is in the process of shattering myths and rewriting the belief that we are controlled by our genes. Epigenetics, the study of mechanisms by which the environment influences gene activity provides strong indication that we as individuals may significantly influence our destiny through our own decisions and our ability to influence gene expression (Lipton, 2005). Epigenetics refers to processes that alter gene activity, but *do not* change the DNA sequence. They may lead to modifications that can be transmitted to daughter cells. Lipton (2005) posits that,

> Genes are simply molecular blueprints used in the construction of cells, tissues and organs. The environment serves as a "contractor" who reads and engages those genetic blueprints and is ultimately responsible for the character of a cell's life. It is a single cell's "awareness" of the environment, not its genes, that sets into motion the mechanisms of life. (p. 15)

Thus, the genome is more fluid and responsive to its environment than was previously thought (Zull, 2002). In addition, the neural organization of our brain is not set in stone at birth (Byrnes, 2001).

There is no doubt that in some areas genes play a significant role in our development. However, findings from neuroscience research provides evidence that learners have the opportunity and challenge to make independent decisions and take actions to significantly influence and direct their learning and personal development. The myth that genes control destiny is no longer valid, and therefore this myth should no longer inhibit individuals from developing themselves to the maximum extent possible. Epigenetics suggests is that if the learner chooses positive and relevant beliefs toward learning that individual will indeed be able to learn (Begley, 2007; Bownds, 1999; Lipton, 2005; Rose, 2005). Thus, the power of the will and the choice of beliefs are in the hands of the individual. It is no longer reasonable to sidestep personal responsibility under the guise that genes control destiny.

No one can order another mind to be creative, to think, to explore or even to learn; only the individual themself can make those decisions. What epigenetics findings indicate is that there is more freedom and influence in taking those actions than was previously thought. All brains are made of the same chemicals, the same types of neurons, the same myelin sheaths, and the same proteins. Thus, we might wonder why there is such variation in individual learning capacities. As neuroscience removes one myth after another it becomes clear that, aside from disease or physical damage, the role of nurturing and the environment have significantly more impact on the learning capacity of the individual than previously thought.

The items of the epigenetics area that could potentially influence experiential learning are as follows: (A) genes are not destiny (the environment can change the actions of genes via nonexpression), (B) what we believe leads to what and how we think, which leads to our knowledge, which leads to our actions, which determine success, and (C) genes are operating options, modulated by inputs from the internal environment within the body that results from thoughts and behavior.

Item 10-A: Genes are not destiny. The environment can change the actions of genes via non-expression. This area on epigenetics does not necessarily directly impact many aspects of the adult experiential learning model. However, it plays a significant role in alerting learners to the influence they have on their own learning, which can significantly enhance learning efficiency. What has been discovered is that gene expression is significantly influenced by the local environment of the cells, which to some extent is under the control of individuals. As Lipton (2005) describes, "the belief that we are frail, chemical machines controlled by genes is giving way to an understanding that we are powerful creators of our lives and the world in which we live" (p. 17). And, as, C.A. Ross (2006) proposes, "genes for brain growth and development are turned on and off by the environment in a complex, rich set of feedback loops" (p. 32).

Item 10-B: What we believe leads to what we think leads to our knowledge base, which leads to our actions, which determines success. If we believe that we cannot do something, our thoughts, feelings, and actions will be such that, at best, it will be much more difficult to accomplish the objective. If we believe we can accomplish something, we are much more likely to be successful, and this results from choice, not genes.

This statement is derived from several areas of thinking among the researchers reviewed. It presents a chain of logic that ties our beliefs to our actions and our successes—or failures. Our beliefs heavily influence our mindset or frame of reference—the direction from which we perceive, reflect, and comprehend an external experience or situation. Thus, beliefs influence how we interpret and feel about the information that comes into our senses, what insights we develop, what ideas we create and what parts of the incoming information we are most aware of. From these reflective observation and abstract conceptualization processes, we create our understanding and meaning of the external world. How we see the external world and how we emotionally feel about external events drives our actions and reactions. How we act and react to our external environment influences whether we are successful or not, that is, whether we achieve our goals or not. All these latter ideas may affect many of the subelements of the adult experiential learning model.

Item 10-C: Genes are operating options modulated by inputs from the environment, resulting in behavior. The environment, referred to here is predominantly the local environment of the cells within the body. However, the environment of the cells is in turn determined by the environment of local subsystems of the body. These subsystems (such as the amygdala relating to the emotions) may play a significant role in conditioning learners to understand and take action on the influence and capability they have in determining their own success.

Environmental influences such as nutrition, stress, and emotions, released into the bloodstream, can modify genes through chemicals without changing their basic blueprint. This finding also emphasizes the importance of good nutrition, stress control, and emotional management in maximizing learning efficacy.

Area 11: Plasticity

The brain maintains a high degree of plasticity, changing itself in response to experience and learning. It has been shaped by evolution to adapt to the changes in its external environment. The sources of this ability are changes in the brain's chemistry and in its architecture (Buonomano & Merzenich, 1998, pp. 11-12). This process of neural plasticity comes from the ability of neurons to change their structure and relationships according to environmental demands or personal decisions and actions. Plasticity is increased through the production of neurotransmitters and the role of growth hormones, which facilitate neural connections and cortical organization (Cozolino & Sprokay, 2006; Cowan & Kandel, 2001; Zhu & Waite, 1998). In 2000, Eric Kandel won the Nobel Prize for showing that when individuals learn, the wiring (neuronal patterns, connections, and synapse strengths) in their brain changes. He showed that when even simple information came into the brain it created a physical alteration of the *structure of neurons* that participate in the process. Thus we are all continuously altering the patterns and structure of the connections in our brains. The conclusion is significant; thoughts change the physiological structure of our brains. This plasticity results from the connection between the mind (patterns in the brain) and the physical world (atoms and molecules of the brain). What and how we think and believe impacts our physical bodies (Medina, 2008; Kandel, 2006).

From a learning viewpoint, brain plasticity opens the door to the possibility of continuously learning and adapting to external environments and internal needs. This phenomenon, applying to all physiologically healthy individuals, means that *everyone has the potential to improve themselves by learning and modifying the structure of their brains*. It also reminds us of the importance of what and how we think, which not only drives our actions, but also influences our brains and minds that we will live and learn with in the future. Plasticity opens the door for anyone at any age to improve his or her mind/brain through learning and thinking. While many individuals may have a natural affinity for music, mathematics, or storytelling, plasticity tells us that *any individual who desires can develop and improve his or her capacity* in other areas of the brain's functioning. It also implies that the vast literature on different ways of thinking, creativity, competency development, analysis and so on. may be open to any individual with sufficient motivation, interest, and dedication.

The items of the plasticity area that could potentially influence experiential learning are as follows: (A) plasticity is the result of the relationship between neural patterns in the mind and the physical world—what we think and believe impacts our physical bodies; (B) learning depends on modification of the brain's chemistry and architecture; (C) thoughts change the structure of the brain and the brain structure influences the creation of thoughts; (D) maximum learning occurs when there are optimum levels of arousal, initiating neural plasticity; and (E) an enriched environment increases the formation and survival of new neurons.

Item 11-A: Plasticity is a result of the connection between neural patterns in the mind and the physical world—what we think and believe impacts our physical bodies. Evolution has created a brain that can adapt and readapt to a changing world (Buonomano & Merzenich, 1998). This is neural plasticity, the ability of neurons to change their structure and relationships, depending on environmental demands and personal decisions and actions. Relative to concrete experience, such plasticity can broaden the scope of sensing as well as feelings.

Item 11-B: Learning depends on modification of the brain's chemistry and architecture. While not closely related to the subelements of the adult experiential learning model, this knowledge can help learners recognize their potential for building knowledge, influencing their own brain, and developing in whatever direction they choose. Thus, in one sense it has the potential to enhance any or all of the subelements.

Item 11-C: Thoughts change the structure of the brain, and brain structure influences the creation of new thoughts. This feedback loop highlights the recognition of the interdependence and self-organization of the mind and brain in the sense that each influences the other. This also reminds one of the importance of both physical and mental health. This duality can help awareness, understanding, meaning, creativity, and anticipation, all subelements of the adult experiential learning model.

Item 11-D: Maximum learning occurs when there are moderate levels of arousal –thereby initiating neural plasticity. Moderate levels of arousal (a state of high attention without debilitating anxiety) initiate neural plasticity by producing neurotransmitters and growth hormones, which literally build connections. As Cozolino and Sprokay (2006) confirm, "learning is enhanced through dopamine, serotonin, norepinephrine and endogenous endorphin production" (p. 14). Maximizing learning could improve the areas of problem solving, creativity, and anticipating the future.

Item 11-E: An enriched environment increases the formation and survival of new neurons. Such an enriched environment can influence both the nature of the experience of the learner and his or her learning efficacy. Begley (2007) describes this phenomenon as a striking finding in neuroplasticity that "exposure to an enriched environment leads to a striking increase in new neurons, along with a substantial improvement in behavioral performance" (p. 58).

Exercise and Health

Area 12: Exercise and Health

Physical exercise plays a significant role in the mental and physical operation of the mind/brain. Exercise increases blood flow, bringing glucose as an energy source for neuron operation and also provides oxygen to take up the toxic electrons (Medina, 2008). Exercise stimulates neurogenesis, the creation of new neurons in certain locations in the brain, and exerts a protective effect on hippocampal neurons, thus heightening brain activity. The hippocampus is part of the limbic system and plays a strong role in consolidating learning and moving information from working memory to long-term memory (Amen, 2005). During this process the hippocampus, "constantly checks information relayed to working memory and compares it to stored experiences" (Sousa, 2006, p. 19). This process integrates the various incoming information and creates higher-level images, concepts, understanding, and meaning. Stonier (1997) addresses this process of creating meaning as follows: An incoming piece of information (pattern) is combined (associated) with information (patterns) from memory. When these patterns are linked successfully, the incoming information becomes meaningful. That is the incoming information is put into a context that represents broader understanding and meaningful information (p. 187).

Exercise boosts brainpower and stimulates the proteins that keep neurons connecting with each other (Medina, 2008). From the "use it or lose it" concept discussed earlier, we can now see that to build learning capacity, the learner needs to exercise both body and mind on a regular basis.

Another finding from neuroscience is that volition is very important for neuron activity, and hence for learning. Begley (2007) offers that the effects of running on neurogenesis and learning are highly dependent on volition . She says that forced exercise does not promote neurogenesis, while voluntary exercise is marked by the absence of stress and does promote neurogenesis. Recall the above discussion of stress and its relevance to learning. Here again we run into the significance of beliefs. Lipton (2005) forwards that, "your beliefs act like filters on a camera, changing how you see the world. And your biology adapts to those beliefs" (p. 143).

To understand the connection between beliefs (patterns in the mind) and the physiology of the brain, consider the following story: You have just received a phone call from the local police telling you that your daughter has been killed in an automobile accident. Now envision your feelings, emotions, and behavior, the changes in your body, your actions, and so on. These are all real and can be observed and measured. Ten minutes later you receive a second call from the same policeman who tells you that there was a mistake and it was not your daughter who was killed. Now imagine the change in your behavior and feelings. All of this was created by your own thoughts and feelings. Your daughter was perfectly fine and healthy the entire time. All of your changes were created by beliefs and thoughts within you own mind. Beliefs and biology are not independent; they are intimately connected through the relationship of patterns of the mind (in the brain) and the physiology of the brain. Patterns of neuron firings and changing synaptic strengths can create and release hormones that can change the body. Since creating and associating thoughts in the mind are the domain of learning and these thought patterns exist in the physiological structure of the brain, learning and neuroscience are irrevocably interrelated. Exercising the mind by mental activity and the physiology of the brain by physical activity provides optimum growth and health in both areas, leading to improved learning efficacy.

Physical exercise plays a significant role in maintaining a healthy brain, which in turn can support a healthy mind. We can thus understand the duality of the challenge of maximizing learning. On the one hand, the material part of the brain, the neurons and chemistry, must be kept healthy and capable of doing their part. On the other hand, how the learner interfaces with the external world and the way he or she goes about learning, creating, and mixing patterns of his or her brain neurons will influence the state of the mind/brain during the life of the learner.

Thus, the material brain can influence the creation, association, and exercise of the brain patterns at the same time these patterns can influence the architecture of the brain. What patterns are created, how many, and how often they are utilized is influenced by the physical and mental environment within which the learner lives, and the learner's decisions and actions. We can thus perceive the self-organization of the environment—learner feedback loop as being perturbed by both environmental changes and the learner's actions and reactions. The items of the exercise area that could potentially influence experiential learning are as follows: (A) volition is necessary for maximum benefit from physical exercise (forced exercise does not promote neurogenesis); (B) meditation and other mental exercises can change feelings, attitudes, and mindsets; (C) exercise increases brainpower (direct connection between exercise and blood flow and oxygen to the brain); (D) Physical activity increases the number (and health) of neurons; and (E) positive and negative beliefs can significantly affect learning.

Item 12-A: Volition is necessary for benefit. Forced exercise does not promote neurogenesis. Volition is taken to mean, "the act of making a conscious choice or decision" (*American Heritage Dictionary*, 2006, p. 1928). This item addresses the importance of physical exercise on the health of the brain and therefore learning effectiveness. According to Medina, our brains were built for walking about 12 miles a day or the equivalent exercise. Exercise keeps neurons connecting and brings glucose for energy to the brain. As Medina (2008) states, "A lifetime of exercise can result in a sometimes astonishing elevation of cognitive performance, compared to those more sedentary" (p. 14).

Item 12-B: Meditation and other mental exercises can change feelings, attitudes and mindsets. Goldberg (2005) suggests that mental exercise can stimulate neuronal growth, and this might be a pattern for growth in other parts of the brain. Mental exercises would likely influence many aspects of the adult experiential learning model.

Item 12-C: Exercise increases brainpower. There is a direct connection between exercise and blood flow and oxygen to the brain. As Medina (2008) explains, consistent exercise reduces the lifetime risk for a number of elderly mental problems such as dementia and Alzheimer's.

Item 12-D: Physical activity increases the number (and health) of neurons. This is the finding from neuroscience that has a generic effect throughout the brain and hence the improved health of the brain would have different effects on different subelements of an adult experiential learning model. Begley (2007) has offered that, "It has become a truism that the better connected a brain is, the better it is, period, enabling the mind it runs to connect new facts with old, to retrieve memories, and even to see links among seemingly disparate facts, the foundation for creativity" (p. 69).

Item 12-E: Positive and negative beliefs affect every aspect of life. This is a finding that has widespread application throughout experiential learning. Positive and negative beliefs not only impact our health, but also most aspects of our lives. When we recognize how powerful our beliefs are, we hold the key to freedom and we can change our minds (Lipton, 2005).

Area 13: Aging

During the past few decades, research has been conducted to understand the changes in the mind/brain that occur during aging. Today there is a relatively comprehensive picture of the changes occurring in the aging brain. Historically there has been a widespread belief that as individuals grow older, their mental powers decrease due to the continuous loss of neurons. Recent research contradicts this myth. It is now clear that, barring diseases, accidents, or genetic issues, so long as individuals use their mind/brain and continue to actively exercise and think, their brain capacity will maintain a good capability in healthy bodies. Although neurons do continue to die as one ages, they also can be created in some parts of the brain as long as it stays active. It is reasonable to assume elderly people should be able to use their brains and minds as long as they keep them active throughout their lives (Amen, 2005; Goldberg, 2005; Sapolsky, 1999).

Marion Diamond has spent 30 years researching brain health, using middle-aged rats, the equivalent of 60-year-old humans, as her test subjects. Why rats? Diamond (2001) posits that "The laboratory rat is an excellent model for brain research. The rat brain has the same basic pattern of brain structure as humans" (p. 9). Her research approach was to use young, middle aged, and elderly rats and compare their cortex thickness—an indicator of neuron number and size, dendrite growth, and synaptic growth using before-and-after experiments. For example, she repeatedly compared rats in an enriched environment with those in an impoverished environment and found that the rats living in the enriched environment showed an increase in cortical thickness in the frontal area compared to the impoverished rats. In the visual cortex there was a 7 percent difference in thickness between those living in enriched and those living in impoverished environments.

Other tests showed that if the rats lived together cortical thickness also increased compared to rats living alone, but not as much as rats housed together in an enriched environment, demonstrating the importance of the sociability factor. When the researchers held and stroked the rats every day their average lifespan increased from 600 days to 900 days, demonstrating the importance of care and nurturing (Diamond, 2001).

Recall the use it or lose it idea previously discussed. No matter what the age, any set of neuron circuits that do not get used will tend to grow weaker. While older people may not be able to memorize new facts as easily as younger individuals, their frontal lobes are considerably more developed and as a result they know what to focus on and how it may be useful to them. Amen (2005) also explains that the best mental exercise is new learning, acquiring new understanding and knowledge, and doing things that they have never done before. In one research program known as the Nuns study, researchers studied 801 nuns, priests, and other clergy engaged in mentally stimulating endeavors over a period of five years. The result was that those subjects who increased their mental activity during the five years "reduced their chances of developing Alzheimer's disease by one-third" (Amen, 2005, p. 114). These subjects also reduced their age-related decline in mental abilities by 50 percent and in concentration and attention span by 60 percent.

The implications of these findings are significant because it opens the door for older people to take advantage of their true mental capacity throughout life. The other value of this finding is that anyone at any age, if they so choose, can begin actively using their minds and improving their capacity to learn, no matter what their past learning history had been. Now that we understand and realize that aging need not degrade mental capacities, *anyone who desires to continue learning throughout life can do so.* When this happens, the payoffs would seem to be potentially very large.

A sample of the items of the aging area that could potentially influence experiential learning are as follows: (A) at any age mental exercise has a global positive effect on the brain; (B) the best mental exercise to slow the effects of aging is new learning and doing things you've never done before; (C) despite certain cognitive losses, the engaged, mature brain can make effective decisions at more intuitive levels; and (D) physical exercise reduces cognitive decline and dementia in older people.

Item 13-A: At any age, mental exercise has a global positive effect on the brain. It has been shown that as long as individuals use their brain and continue to actively think, barring age-related diseases, their brain capacity can maintain a good capability. While neurons continue to die as one ages, in several areas of the brain they can also continue to be created so long as the brain is active. For example, the hippocampus produces new neurons after birth and continues to do so well into old age (Sapolsky, 1999).

Item 13-B: The best mental exercise to slow aging is new learning and doing things you've never done before. Exercising the mind in multiple areas of thinking will strengthen the overall brain. New learning creates new connections, new patterns, and strengthens existing connections in the brain. No learning allows these connections to weaken. Thus, mental exercise at every age has a global, positive effect on the brain (Amen, 2005). This item has the potential for broad influence on experiential learning.

Item 13-C: Despite certain cognitive losses, the engaged, mature brain can make effective decisions at more intuitive levels. Goldberg (2005) points out that the aging brain can accomplish mental feats that are different than younger brains. He makes the point that although older people forget names, facts, and words, they have the capability of remembering high-level patterns and meaningful insights that we often consider as wisdom. This capability would impact many of the subelements of the adult experiential learning model.

Item 13-D: Physical exercise reduces cognitive decline and dementia in older people. As stated earlier, exercise promotes blood flow, providing energy to the brain cells. In some respects, 50-year-olds will do better than 18-year-olds in academic studies because their frontal lobes, which include the prefrontal cortex, are better developed. It is the frontal lobes that help individuals pay attention and ask better questions (Amen, 2005).

Chapter 15
Assessing the Findings

Careful consideration of the potential influences that each of the 13 neuroscience findings area items have on the subelements of the four modes of the historic experiential learning model, individually developed in Chapters 11-14, suggests the need to expand our baseline experiential learning model. *A key learning point is that the external environment plays an important role in supporting learning efficacy.*

As previously introduced, Kolb's (1984) experiential learning model offers a four-mode process of learning that moves from concrete experience to reflection to comprehension to action. These processes continue in the overlay of neuroscience areas in the Kolb/Zull (Zull, 2002) model as described in Chapter 4. This is not to imply that the learning process is sequential, nor was this forwarded by Kolb or Zull. Clearly, the mind often jumps around as it experiences numerous incoming signals and tries to accommodate and understand external inputs.

Assessing the Items

For your reference, the subelements for the four modes of the adult experiential learning model and the characteristics of the four enhancement values are provided in Table 15-1 below.

Tables 15-2 through 15-4 below show the overall results from Appendices 1 through 13 of the neuroscience area items as they relate to the four modes of the adult experiential learning model sub-elements. The charts are organized in the groupings in which they appeared in Chapter 12 (Group 1), Chapter 13 (Group 2) and Chapter 14 (Group 4). As presented in these chapters, these groupings are as follows:

Group 1 in **Table 15-2** is made up of the unconscious (1), memory (2), and emotion (3), and represents a foundational group that is always involved in learning.

Group 2 in **Table 15-3** represents findings that influence learning in specific situations. It includes stress (4), creativity (5), mirror neurons (6), anticipating the future (7), and social support (9).

Group 3 in **Table 15-4** supports the capacity for, and enhancement of, lifelong learning. This group is made up of social interaction (8), epigenetics (10), plasticity (11), health and exercise (12), and aging (13).

Table 15-1. *The four modes and their subelements and the characteristics of the four enhancement values.*

EXPERIENTIAL LEARNING SUBELEMENTS	ENHANCEMENT VALUES
1. Experience (grasping through apprehension) a) Sensing b) Feeling c) Awareness d) Attention e) Intuition 2. Reflective observation a) Understanding b) Meaning c) Truth and how things happen d) Intuition e) Integrate and look for unity 3. Abstract conceptualization a) Concepts, ideas, logic b) Problem solving c) Creativity d) Build models and theories e) Anticipation f) Control, rigor, discipline 4. Action a) Act on the environment b) Focus attention c) Object based logic d) Heightened boundary perception e) Sensory feedback to brain	a. Efficiency (speed and effort) 1) Speed of learning 2) Flexibility of learning (different ways of learning) 3) Minimum use of time, energy, memory b. Effectiveness (scope and quality) 1) Understanding (incoming information) 2) Meaning (significance of incoming information) 3) Insight (recognizing relationships, patterns, possibilities and probabilities) 4) Creativity (creating ideas, processes, actions) 5) Anticipation 6) Take effective action c. Meta-Learning (understanding the process) 1) Understand learning process 2) Understand phases of learning 3) Able to adapt learning process 4) Understand context of learning 5) Understand personal learning characteristics d. Sustainable learning (long-tem learning capacity) 1) Adaptability (capability to adapt learning process) 2) Robust (capability to handle broad range of learning technologies) 3) Healthy mind (what has been learned, beliefs) 4) Resilience (self-efficacy, inner strength) 5) Continuous learning

The left-hand column of each table lists the four adult experiential learning model modes and their subelements. Recall from Figure 11-1, the representative concept map for plasticity used as an example in Chapter 11, that the arrows indicating relations between neuroscience finding area items and specific adult experiential learning model subelements are meant to demonstrate *possible ways* that the items can influence and/or enhance the Kolb model subelements. Any given instance would be dependent on the specific situation (and learner) and cannot be predetermined. (See the discussion of knowledge in Chapter 3.) Therefore, the data provided in Tables 15-2 through 15-4 provide a broad overview of the potential influence of the 13 neuroscience area items on the subelements of the four modes of the experiential learning model.

The horizontal axis of the tables shows the groupings provided above for the 13 neuroscience findings areas. The letters within the chart represent the specific item in each neuroscience area. For example, in the upper left quadrant of the table the top sub-element is "sensing" and the first entry is "A" representing Item 1-A, which is identified in the Chapter 12 discussion section as, "The unconscious brain is always processing."

Further, remember that thinking is not a sequential process but is rather a mixing and bouncing around among the subelements of the four modes. Tables 15-2 through 15-4 provide additional *nominal examples* of possible neuroscience findings and their impact on learning. As forwarded above, each learning experience will be context sensitive and situation dependent and highly contingent upon the learner's awareness and utilization of what each of the neuroscience items could offer, such that, in practice, each individual learner and learning situation would *produce their own table of influence.*

Table 15-2. *Potential influence of neuroscience items (Group 1). This table provides an example of the potential influences of the neuroscience items on the sub-elements of the adult experiential learning model. The table summarizes the connections discussed in Chapter 12.*

AREAS OF NS FINDINGS:	UNCONSCIOUS	MEMORY	EMOTION
CONCRETE EXPERIENCE (Total: 65)	(1)	(2)	(3)
Sensing	A	A,B	E
Feeling	A	A,B	C,E
Awareness	A	C	C,F
Attention	-	C,D,E	A,F
Intuition	A	A	C
REFLECTIVE OBSERVATION (Total: 68)			
Understanding	C	D,E	A,B,D,G
Meaning	C,D	A,E	A,B,D,G
Truth/How things work	B,C	D	A,G
Intuition	A,E	-	C
Integrated/Look for unity	-	D,F	-
ABSTRACT CONCEPTUALIZATION (Total: 60)			
Concepts, ideas, logic	E	G,H	-
Problem solving	B	G,H	C
Creativity	F	F,G	-
Build models/theories	E	G,H	-
Anticipation	C	I,J	B
Control, rigor, discipline	G	I,J	E
ACTIVE EXPERIMENTATION (Total: 36)			
Act on environment	D,G	I	E
Focus attention	H	J	F
Object based logic	G	-	-
Heightened boundary perception	H	-	-
Sensory feedback	F	-	G
TOTALS	23	28	25

Table 15-3. *Potential influence of neuroscience items (Group 2). This table provides an example of the potential influences of the neuroscience items on the sub-elements of the adult experiential learning model. The table summarizes the connections discussed in Chapter 13.*

AREAS OF NS FINDINGS:	STRESS	CREATIVITY	MIRROR NEURONS	ANTICIPATING	SOCIAL SUPPORT
CONCRETE EXPERIENCE (Total: 65)					
Sensing	A,B,D	A	A,C,E	-	A
Feeling	A,B,D	A	A	-	B
Awareness	A,B,C	B	-	-	-
Attention	A,C,E	-	A	A	-
Intuition	-	A,B,C	-	A	-
REFLECTIVE OBSERVATION (Total: 68)					
Understanding	A,B,D	A	B,D	A,C	A,C
Meaning	A,B,C,D	C	B,D	A,B,C,D	C
Truth/How things work	-	-	D	-	-
Intuition	-	B,C,G	-	-	-
Integrated/Look for unity	-	-	-	E	D
ABSTRACT CONCEPTUALIZATION (Total: 60)					
Concepts, ideas, logic	-	A,G	C	-	A,B
Problem solving	F	-	-	D	-
Creativity	F	D,E,G	-	-	B
Build models/theories	-	G	-	-	-
Anticipation	F,G	-	-	A,B,D,E	C
Control, rigor, discipline	-	D,F,G	-	-	-
ACTIVE EXPERIMENTATION (Total: 36)					
Act on environment	G	-	F,G	C	-
Focus attention	E	H	E,G	C	-
Object based logic	G	-	-	-	-
Heightened boundary perception	-	-	D,F	E	-
Sensory feedback	-	G	E	B	C,D
TOTALS	22	18	18	13	14

152 | Expanding the Self

Table 15-4. *Potential influence of neuroscience items (Group 3). This table provides an example of the potential influences of the neuroscience items on the sub-elements of the adult experiential learning model. The table summarizes the connections discussed in Chapter 14.*

AREAS OF NS FINDINGS:	SOCIAL INTERACTION	EPIGENETICS	PLASTICITY	EXERCISE	AGING
CONCRETE EXPERIENCE (Total: 65)					
Sensing	A	-	A	A	B
Feeling	A	-	A	B	-
Awareness	A,B	A	C	B	A
Attention	B	A	-	A	A
Intuition	-	-	-	-	-
REFLECTIVE OBSERVATION (Total: 68)					
Understanding	C	A,B	-	A	-
Meaning	C	B	A,C	B	B
Truth/How things work	C	-	A,C	-	-
Intuition	-	-	-	C	C
Integrated/Look for unity	-	B	-	-	-
ABSTRACT CONCEPTUALIZATION (Total: 60)					
Concepts, ideas, logic	B	B	-	C	B
Problem solving	C	-	C,E	C	C
Creativity	B	-	D	C	B,C
Build models/theories	-	B	C,D	-	-
Anticipation	-	-	-	-	-
Control, rigor, discipline	C	-	D	-	-
ACTIVE EXPERIMENTATION (Total: 36)					
Act on environment	-	B	-	B	D
Focus attention	-	C	E	-	D
Object based logic	-	-	-	-	-
Heightened boundary perception	-	-	-	-	-
Sensory feedback	C	-	-	-	-
TOTALS	13	10	14	11	11

We now briefly consider a broad interpretation of the overall results presented in Tables 15-2 through 15-4. Looking at each column and totaling the number of letters provides an indication of which items, and how many items in each neuroscience finding area, impact the adult experiential learning model. This allows the ranking of the 13 neuroscience areas in terms of the number of items that impact the model.

The highest impact neuroscience area is *memory* (as shown on the bottom line entitled "totals"). (See Chapter 12.) The second highest area is *stress*, with the impact of these areas continuing in this order: *emotion, unconscious, creativity, anticipating the future, mirror neurons, social interaction, plasticity, social support, exercise, aging* and *epigenetics*. Note that this ranking is by number of items and *not by the depth or scope of the impact of each item*. These totals are meant to provide a rough idea of the relative influence in this example. They are not strong measures and cannot be transferred to other learning situations.

Reflecting further on Tables 15-2 through 15-4, it appears that the right-hand region of Group 2 (Table 15-3) and all of Group 3 (Table 15-4) have less influence on sub-elements of the adult experiential learning model. This is most likely because these areas have a general influence, which would not show up because of the way the table was constructed. Looking at Group 1 (Table 15-2) and the left region of Group 2 (Table 15-3) in the areas of concrete experience and reflective observation, we can see that there are a lot of influences from the four largest neuroscience finding areas: *the unconscious, memory, emotion*, and *stress*. This region shows a total of 65 items. If we take the same approach for the region encompassing abstract conceptualization and active experimentation (looking at the areas of *the unconscious, memory, emotion,* and *stress*), we find 37 items.

Assessing the chart from a different perspective, we find that the total number of items in the region of **concrete experience** is 65, the total number of items in the region of **reflective observation** is 68, the total number of items in the region of **abstract conceptualization** is 55, and the total number of items in the region of **active experimentation** is 31. From the viewpoint of the numbers of items that support each mode, this model (with the limitations as stated above) would suggest that these findings from neuroscience have the *least support* for the action phase. This does not consider the process of continuous feedback during the implementation of action. Under these conditions, neuroscience, if understood by the learner, would likely be able to influence and enhance learning throughout the modes of the learning process.

The ICALS Model

The Kolb/Zull model considers the external environment only from the perspective of incoming information through concrete experience and outgoing actions. As a consequence, there is minimal recognition of the give and take that frequently occurs between the learner and the environment during the learning process, that is, social engagement in terms of social interaction and social support.

Figure 15-1 below represents our new baseline model that takes into account the environment and social engagement, the *Kolb/Zull/Bennet Expanded Experiential Learning Model*. Also shown in Figure 15-1 are the 13 areas of neuroscience findings discussed in Chapter 11 that were identified in Chapters 6-10 and detailed in Chapter 12-14. By taking into account the 13 areas of neuroscience findings shown in the expanded model, we can then identify specific items in each area that could enhance experiential learning.

Figure 15-1. *The expanded Kolb/Zull/Bennet experiential learning model. Built on the combination of Kolb's experiential learning model, Zull's physiological overlay, the environment, including social engagement, and the 13 areas of neuroscience that could enhance experiential learning. Note: This model serves as a stepping stone to the ICALS Model presented in Chapter 4, which brings in the concept of Self.*

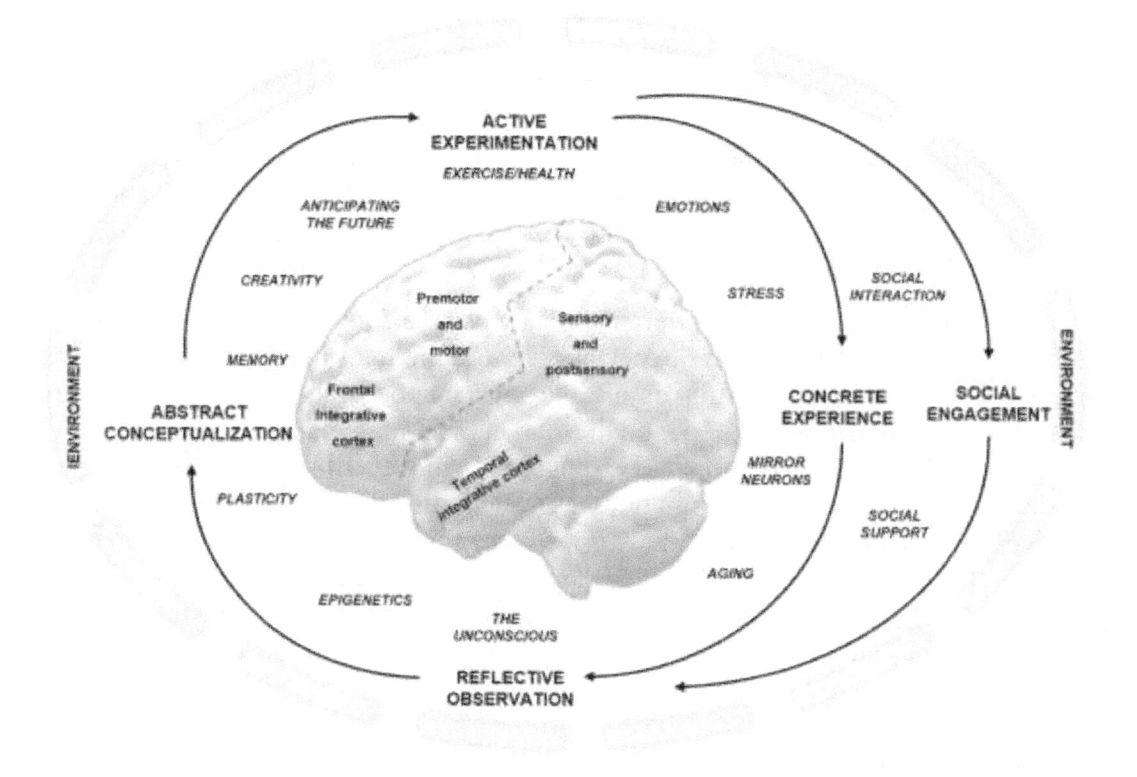

The expanded experiential learning model also responds to some of the criticism introduced in Chapter 4 associated with the original Kolb model. Specifically, including the environment and social engagement as a fifth mode offers the opportunity to take into account: (a) the process nature of experience, responding to the criticism forwarded by Hopkins (1993); (b) the impact of various cultural experiences and conditions (responding to the criticism forwarded by Anderson (1988); and (c) the concern that there is too little emphasis on the social and institutional aspects (responding to Holman et al., 1997 and Reynolds, 1999).

This expanded Kolb/Zull/Bennet experiential learning model, serves as the framework for assessing the 13 neuroscience finding areas with respect to their potential contribution to the experiential learning process.

The Environment

Two areas of neuroscience findings closely related to the environment were social interaction and social support. In addition to these two items, eight other related items emerged from the areas of stress, creativity, mirror neurons, anticipating the future, and plasticity. These items are listed in Table 15-5, below.

Table 15-5. *Items related to the environment.*

4-F	There is an optimum level of stress or learning (the inverted "U").
5-A	An enriched environment produces a personal internal reflective world of imagination and creativity.
6-A	Cognitive mimicry that transfers active behavior and other cultural norms.
6-B	Rapid transfer of knowledge bypassing cognition.
7-E	Brain-mind creates an internal representation of the world.
8-A	Physical mechanisms have developed in our brain to enable us to learn through social interactions.
9-C	Affective attunement contributes to the evolution and sculpting of the brain.
9-D	Optimal development results from a balance of nurturance and optimal stress.
10-B	The internal environment of the leader reads and engages the genetic blueprints and is ultimately responsible for the character of the cell's life.
10-D	Genes are operating options tested by inputs from the environment, resulting in behavior.
10-F	Environmental Influences such as nutrition, stress and emotions can modify genes without changing their basic blueprint.
11-E	An enriched environment increases the formation and survival of new neurons.

Our example of the environment was focused on the social aspects, that is, engagement with other people. This certainly makes sense. People do not often learn in isolation, but are very much engaged in a continuous process of what is often referred to as social learning. This is detailed in Chapter 10. An example of environmental influence that is *not* social in nature is the use of space design and plants, art and furnishing to help create an enriched environment. Another example is augmentation; computer technology, web services and social media all offer platforms that may stimulate and support learning.

Further, the environment can be considered in terms of external and internal. While Table 15-5 refers primarily to the external environment, there are several elements connected to genes that are related to the internal environment of the learner, that is, the biology, physiology, function, and form of the mind/brain/body of the learner. Depending on the individual learner and the context and specific learning process used, each of these items may enhance the learning process. For example, affective attunement—contributing to the evolution and sculpting of the brain—may have a significant impact on learning *if* the attunement is available and *if* the environment is conducive to the attunement. Under these conditions, attunement can significantly increase the efficiency and the effectiveness of the learning process. If learners appreciate and understand the value and contribution of the attunement relationship, they may be in a position to manage their learning related to the attunement process. Thus, they also may be able to *improve their efficiency and effectiveness of learning* in a specific situation. This brings us to a discussion of the role of Self.

The Self

From the learner's perspective, the *Self* is a particularly important concept to be inserted into the learning model. Note that the concept of Self was implied by, but not explicit in, the Kolb/Zull model. A number of neuroscience findings relate specifically to the Self.

The unconscious, the memory, and the emotions play important roles relative to the quality of the learning, that is, the output of the learning process. Since a large portion of these three areas operate in the unconscious (perhaps unavailable to the conscious Self), it becomes important to recognize both the limits and the opportunities for maximizing the learning process.

Considering identified neuroscience items that relate to experiential learning, but not directly to the expanded Experiential Learning Model, we find that while they all certainly related to Self, they fall into three general groupings: Self (Table 15-6), Continuous Learning (Table 15-7) and Health and Exercise (Table 15-8).

Table 15-6. *Items related to Self.*

4-D	Belief systems can reduce stress through reducing uncertainty.
4-F	There is an optimum level between arousal and stress for learning.
4-G	Individuals can consciously change their level of response to stress.
5-H	The mind/brain is a self-organizing system that can create neural links (pattern associations) on a millisecond time scale.

As can be seen, there are a number of disparate items in Table 15-4, although they are all related to the individual Self.

Table 15-7 (Continuous Learning) has a number of items dealing with memory and the effect of learning on the brain's chemistry and architecture. Each of these items represents specific information relating to the learning process. For example, the value of using stories as a vehicle for communicating and learning (Denning, 2000; O'Halloran, 2000; Wolff, 1999; Mellon, 1992; MacIntyre, 1981; Taylor, 1996) is recognized by a wide number of people who may not recognize that its efficacy comes from the generic process the mind uses to create and remember information. That process is the association of patterns in a manner such that stories are easily recalled because of their meaning and the flow of the story (Bennet & Bennet, 2008c; Schank, 1995). Storytelling is used in Chapter 22 as an example of the Self as a social learner.

Table 15-7. *Items related to continuous learning.*

2-E	Memory recall is improved through temporal sequences of associative patterns, i.e., stories and songs.
2-H	Memory patterns cannot be erased at will.
2-I	Memory patterns decay slowly with time.
11-B	Learning depends on modification of the brain's chemistry and architecture.

Another example is Item 2-I (Chapter 12), **Memory patterns decay slowly with time**. Recognizing this as a neuroscience finding, a learner might develop the habit of continuously monitoring the most important aspects of his or her knowledge and setting up a means of recalling and remembering them periodically to prevent the decay. Examples would be underlining when reading, taking notes, applying what was learned as soon as possible, or re-reading books or articles that were very important (Bennet, 2014).

Table 15-8 (Health and Exercise) provides a list of items that relate to the health of the mind/brain. These are a number of specific ideas and suggested actions that can enhance learning. For example, the idea that volition versus forced exercise makes a big difference in neurogenesis is probably unknown to most people. Yet it offers an opportunity for enhancing learning in terms of effectiveness and aging. As can be seen, these tables offer some specific ideas or practices that would aid individual learners, depending upon the context and the specific learning process used.

Table 15-8. *Items related to health and exercise.*

12-A	Volition is necessary for benefit from exercise. Forced exercise does not promote neurogenesis.
12-B	Meditation and other mental exercises can change feelings, attitudes and mindsets.
12-C	Exercise increases brain effectiveness. There is a direct connection between exercise and blood flow and oxygen to brain.
12-D	Physical activity increases the number (and health) of neurons.
12-E	Use it or lose it (brain cells).
12-F	Positive and negative beliefs affect every aspect of life.
13-A	At any age mental exercise has a global positive effect on your brain.
13-B	The best mental exercise to slow the effects aging is new learning and doing things you've never done before.
13-C	Despite certain cognitive losses, the engaged, mature brain can make effective decisions at more intuitive levels.
13-D	Physical exercise reduces the probability of dementia in older people.
13-E	If you exercise all areas of the brain you can increase the health of all areas of the brain.

In summary, looking at Tables 15-5 through 15-8 above, we can consider them as addressing two specific areas: one area related to the environment and, as a subset of the environment but a significant learning factor, social engagement, and a second area related to the Self. The importance of Self, as an explicit element of the model, emerged as we focused on the 13 neuroscience findings in Chapters 12-14. Neuroscience findings related to the Self also include Continuous Learning and Exercise and Health.

Neuroscience findings related to the environment included not only the external environment (non-living), but also social interaction and social bonding, from which emerged the fifth mode of the expanded Experiential Learning Model, *Social Engagement*. Including both the Self, the external environment, and social engagement as a fifth mode of learning allows a broader perspective of possible enhancements to the learning process. Hence, we now move beyond the expanded Experiential Learning Model to a further enhanced model which brings in the expanded elements of Self as a principal part of the experiential learning process, what we describe as the *Intelligent Complex Adaptive Learning System* (ICALS), which is introduced in Chapter 5 and detailed in Chapter 16.

Section V
Building the ICALS Theory and Model

We begin this section with an 1890 quote from *Principles of Psychology* by William James:

> *Millions of items . . . present to my senses never properly enter my experience. Why? Because they have no interest for me. My experience is what I agree to attend to. . . Everyone knows what attention is. It is taking possession by the mind in clear and vivid form of one out of what seem several simultaneous objects or trains of thought. Focalization, concentration of consciousness are of its essence. It implies withdrawal from some things in order to deal effectively with others.*

Section V delves into the new experiential learning theory and model, taking a closer look at the concept of the Intelligent Complex Adaptive Learning System. Chapter 16 delves into the idea of self-organized learning and explores the idea of experiential learning as a complex adaptive system. We then reintroduce the ICALS Theory and Model.

In Chapter 17 we look closely at the five modes of learning in the ICALS Theory and Model, building on Kolb's (1984) rigorous development of the first four modes. Putting it all together, each mode is briefly described, and then connected to items from the neuroscience findings that relate to that specific mode.

Chapter 16
The Intelligent Complex Adaptive Learning System

In Chapter 5 we introduced the ICALS Theory and Model, and in Chapters 6 through 14 we explored findings from neuroscience that impact experiential learning, showing the importance of social engagement, the environment and Self in experiential learning. We now take a closer look at the concept of the Intelligent Complex Adaptive Learning System.

A system is *a group of elements or objects, their attributes, the relationships among them, and some boundary that allows one to distinguish whether an element is inside or outside the system*. Elements of a system may be almost anything: parts of a television set, computers connected to a network, people within an organization, neurons within a brain, patterns of the mind, ideas within a system of thought, etc. The nature and number of elements and their relationships to each other are very important in determining a given system's behavior. Almost everything can be viewed as a system. For example, the following are all systems because they have many parts and many relationships: automobiles, ER teams in a hospital, cities, organizations, pipes on a submarine, ant colonies, and individuals.

The definition of complexity was introduced in the discussion of foundational language in Chapter 2. The Santa Fe Group says complexity "refers to the condition of the universe which is integrated and yet too rich and varied for us to understand in simple, mechanistic or linear ways ... complexity deals with the nature of emergence, innovation, learning and adaptation" (Battram, 1996, p. 12). Considering the immense number of interconnections that exist among the 100 billion neurons in the brain with roughly 10,000 connections per neuron, it seems clear that the mind/brain/body is a highly complex system.

> Considering the immense number of interconnections that exist among the 100 billion neurons in the brain with roughly 10,000 connections per neuron, it seems clear that the mind/brain/body is a highly complex system.

Adaptation is the process by which an organization improves its ability to survive and grow through internal adjustments. Adaptation may be responsive, internally adjusting to external forces, or it may be proactive, internally changing so that it can influence the external environment. Humans do both.

Intelligence is *the capacity for reasoning and understanding or an aptitude for grasping truths*. Wiig (1993) broadens this to include the individual's ability to think, reason, understand and act. Recall that learning is the creation of knowledge, with knowledge defined as the capacity (potential or actual) to *take effective action*. Stonier (1997) and McMaster (1996) consider intelligence as the ability to set and achieve goals. This is consistent with the concept of taking effective action. Hawkins (2004) connects intelligence to prediction when he posits, "It is the ability to make predictions about the future that is the crux of intelligence" (p. 6). Thus we are focusing on *how the individual interacts within and with its environment* in anticipation of the outcomes of that interaction. In this context, intelligent activity represents a perfect state of interaction where intent, purpose, direction, values and expected outcomes are clearly understood and communicated among all parties, reflecting wisdom and achieving a higher truth Bennet & Bennet, 2015a). Knowledge is in service to intelligent activity. Because the effectiveness of all knowledge is context sensitive and situation dependent, knowledge is shifting and changing in concert with our environment and the demands placed upon us. The incompleteness of knowledge that is never perfect serves as an incentive for the continuous human journey of learning and the exploration of ideas. See Bennet & Bennet (2004) for an in-depth treatment of intelligent behavior.

Self-Organized Learning

Enhancing the learning process raises the question of learning from what perspective? Taking a systems perspective brings home the point that it is a *self-organizing* complex adaptive system. Bennet and Bennet (2004, p. 291) have proposed that "a self-organizing complex system is one in which the agents (individuals) have a high degree of freedom to organize themselves to better achieve their local objectives." Dropping down one level to the individual learner, the agents become various subsystems of the mind/brain/body. As Battram forwards,

> In 'self-organized learning' the self-organizing is taking place inside the learner's brain (which is a complex adaptive system in its own right) rather than in a networked group of individuals (Battram, 1996, p. 145).

We expand Battram's statement to include the body because the brain and the body are tightly connected through the flow of chemicals such as hormones and neuropeptides (Pert, 1997). In addition, the neuronal signals flow throughout the central nervous system and the flow of blood continuously provides energy to the brain and the body. Simultaneously, the mind and brain are connected via the physiology of the brain and the neuronal patterns created through incoming signals and the thinking processes.

The environment is closely connected to the mind/brain/body via incoming information and exchanges of energy with the body and from physical interactions between the body and its environment. Thus a holistic view indicates that the environment, mind, brain, and body all represent complex adaptive systems which co-evolve through various levels of sensing, information and energy transfer, and some level of mutual structural adaptation. In considering the brain as a self-organizing system, Buzsaki (2006) explains that,

The brain is perpetually active even in the absence of environmental and body-derived stimuli. In fact, a main argument put forward in this book is that most of the brain's activity is generated from within, and perturbations of this default pattern by external inputs at any given time often causes only a minor departure from its robust, internally controlled program. Yet these perturbations are absolutely essential for adapting the brain's internal operations to perform useful computations. (p. 10)

It is clear that individual learning takes place via significant interplay among the various subsystems of the body and the environment. Many systems and subsystems of the individual work together to create an effective learning system. While the Self may represent one unifying perspective of the individual through consciousness, it does not control all subsystems of the mind/brain/body. As detailed in Chapters 6-10, feelings, memories, belief systems, past knowledge, motivation, and immediate goals influence learning effectiveness.

> Individual learning takes place via significant interplay among the various subsystems of the body and the environment.

Understanding the learner as a self-organizing Intelligent Complex Adaptive Learning System gives caution to teachers and organizations that would control, direct, or mandate learning. A self-organizing complex adaptive system can rarely be controlled by force—rather, it must be guided and nurtured by supportive influence. Thus, a theory of adult learning has to take into account *the learner's capacity to self-organize and internally guide his or her learning* as well as the major factors of the mind/brain/body that impact the learning process, and the individual's autobiography, motivation, and beliefs about his or her learning efficacy.

Since learning is context sensitive and content dependent, and unpredictability is a characteristic of complex systems, there is no assurance of *how much* learning will occur. However, the results of this research indicate there are specific aspects of the learning process that can *reduce that unpredictability*. For example, learning will be enhanced when it occurs near the top of the inverted "U" of the arousal/stress curve (see Chapter 8), indicating that the learner has good motivation but not too much stress. Another example is that the beliefs and attitudes of the learner will affect learning and can be under the control of the learner if he or she so chooses.

Considering the roles of emotion, memory, the unconscious, and stress in experiential learning (see Chapter 12 and Chapter 13), one can understand why learning is not always a rational process. From a creativity viewpoint, playing with ideas and using intuition, feelings, and estimates of the future outcome of actions to create potential solutions to problems (see Chapters 13 and Chapter 14) provides a significant advantage to the learner.

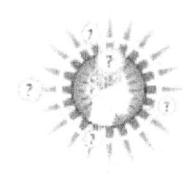

REFLECT:
Do I believe I am a learner?
Am I motivated to learn? Why am I not motivated to learn?

Exploring Experiential Learning as a Complex Adaptive Learning System

Figure 16-1, shown below, is a concept diagram providing a simplified picture of some of the interconnections among the 13 areas of neuroscience findings and an expanded experiential learning model.

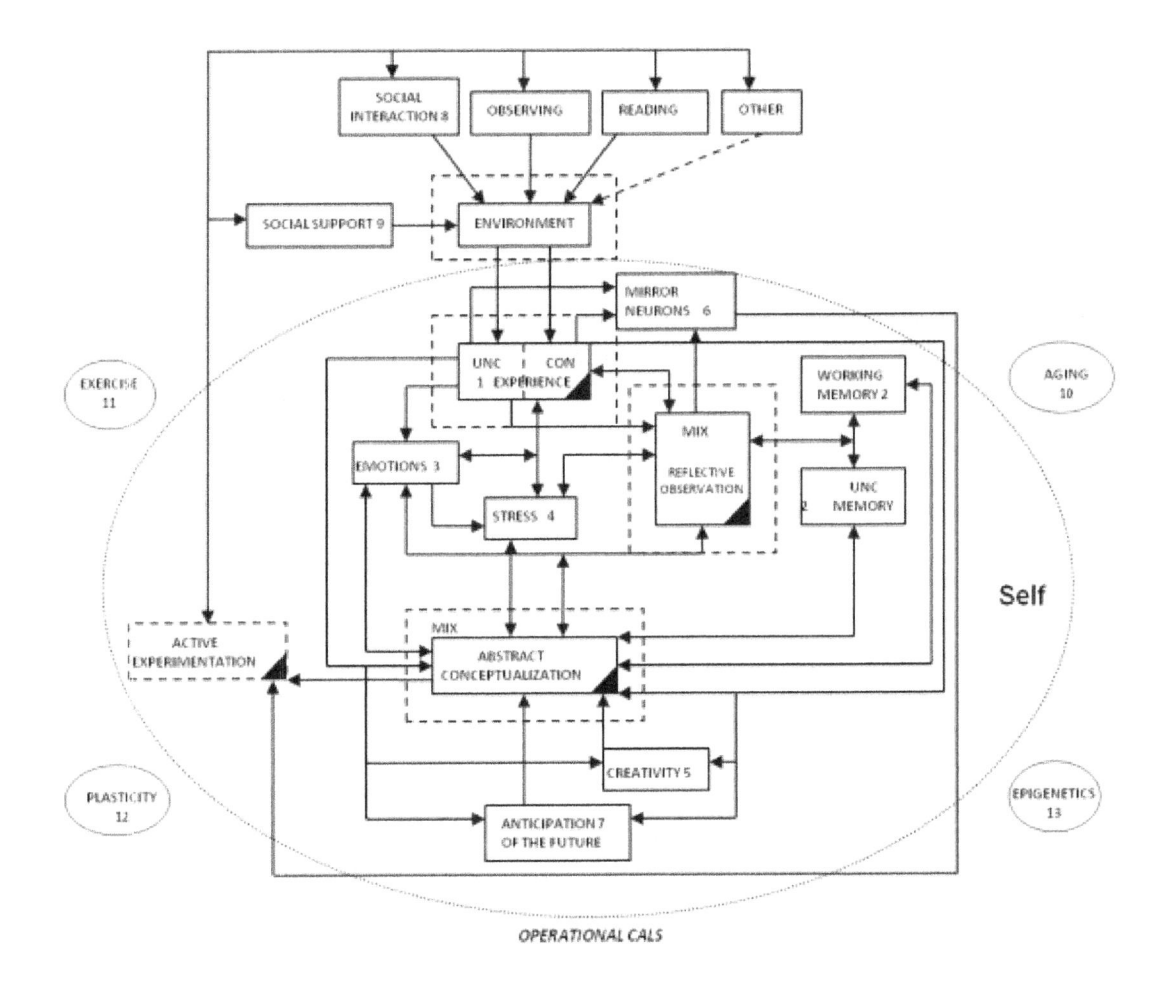

Figure 16-1. *A concept diagram highlighting some interactions among the 13 neuroscience areas and the expanded Kolb/Zull/Bennet model. This highly simplified model illustrates the self-organization and complexity of the human mind/brain/body.*

164 | Expanding the Self

The arrowheads of the various connections indicate the direction of influence. Starting at the lower left with the box labeled "active experimentation," actions influence and are influenced by the social support and social interaction areas of neuroscience by tracing the paths from environment to concrete experience to reflective observation to abstract conceptualization back to active experimentation. Neuroscientific findings 1 through 9 support the operational complex adaptive learning system (CALS) and areas 10 through 13 (epigenetics, plasticity, exercise, and aging) support sustainability of the CALS.

Two other small boxes at the top and to the right labeled "observing" and "reading" remind us that an action may not be a social interaction. Each of the boxes labeled "social support" and "social interaction" and the active experimentation box at the lower left interact with the environment and the environment interacts with them.

Even though Figure 16-1 is highly simplified, we can follow the arrows around and create many potential feedback (or feed-forward) loops. Most likely these feedback and feed-forward loops provide the associations that promote the continuous self-organization of the system. In any case, the mind/brain/body represents a self-organizing, complex adaptive system.

Going back to the environment box at the top, we see the two major areas coming down into the box labeled "experience" with the left side unconscious experience and the right side conscious experience. This reminds us that the individual learner has both a conscious and an unconscious mind/brain. From the box labeled "experience" we see a large number of arrows going out of and coming into such neuroscience areas as emotions, stress, mirror neurons, and the reflection process.

In turn, the reflective observation process interacts with working memory, unconscious memory, stress, emotions, and abstract conceptualization. This mode also has a large number of inputs and outputs. It interacts with the stress, emotions, unconscious memory, working memory, mirror neurons, creativity, anticipation, and active experimentation. Abstract conceptualization also interacts with the experience mode. Although not shown in the diagram, the three major areas of unconscious, memory, and emotions are connected to almost everything in the ellipse.

The ICALS Model

We use the term *Intelligent Complex Adaptive Learning System* (ICALS) to describe these multiple and highly simplified influences, connections, and relationships within the mind/brain/body. As introduced in Chapter 5, Figure 16-2 represents this system.

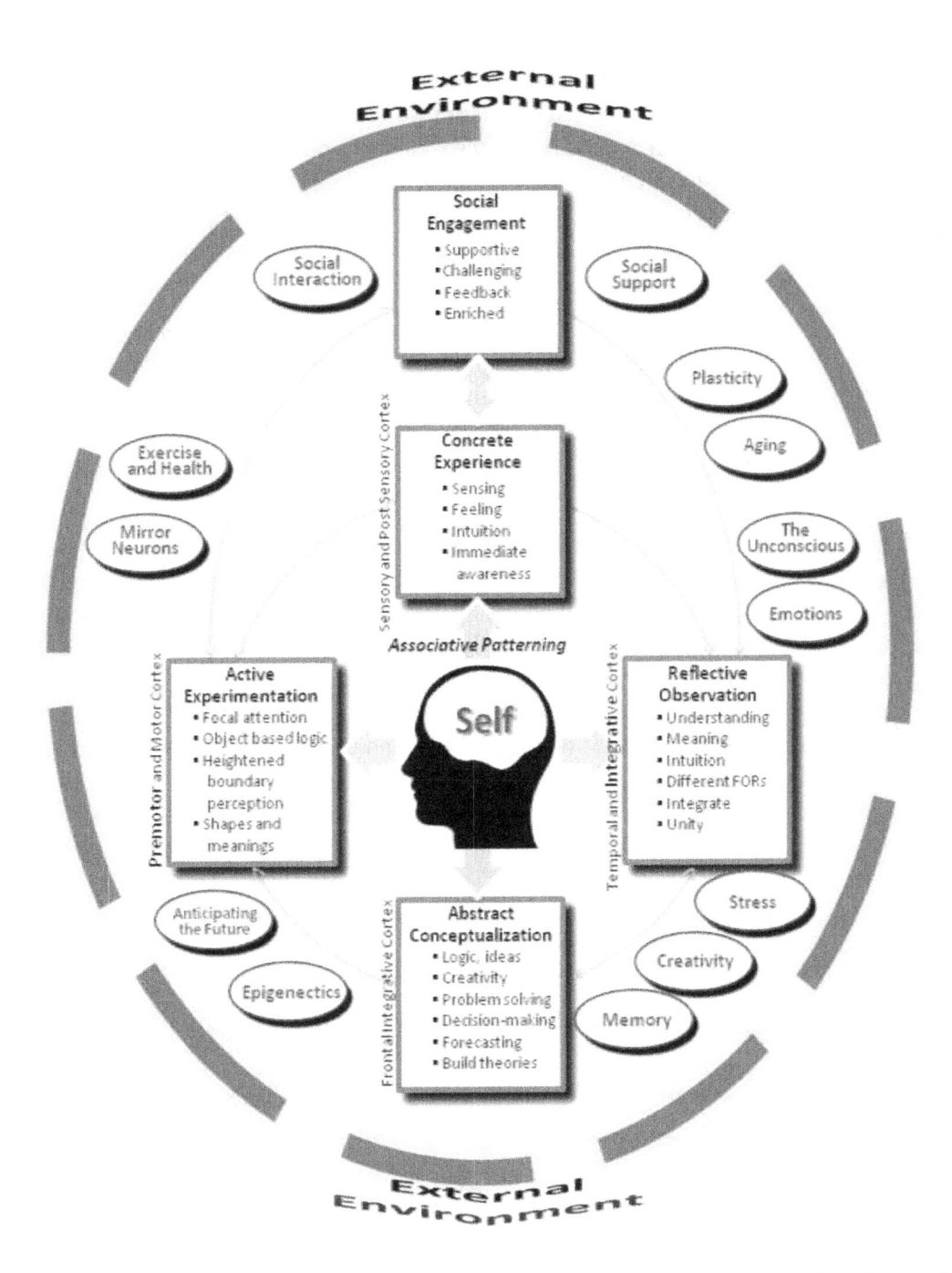

Figure 16-2. *The Intelligent Complex Adaptive Learning System (ICALS) Model considering the five modes of learning (Active Experimentation, Concrete Experience, Social Engagement, Reflective Observation and Abstract Conceptualization), the environment, and the overlay of Self.*

This model is the result of a sequence of model upgrades, beginning with the original Kolb model of experiential learning published in 1984 (built on the earlier work of Dewey, Lewin and Piaget). This model was combined with Zull's 2002 model, which brought in the brain and various parts of the brain associated with the four modes of Kolb's model. This approach was then expanded to include the 13 neuroscience findings areas and the environment. The new experiential learning model shown in Figure 16-2 includes the addition of Self and a fifth mode of learning, social engagement (social interaction and social support).

The four modes of learning in Kolb's model are concrete experience, reflective observation, abstract conceptualization and active experimentation. Although the sequence of the learning cycle appears clean, it was recognized by Kolb (1984) that as learning occurs a learner experiences many direct connections between and among all of these modes. In the ICALS Model, the fifth model of social engagement occurs with concrete experience.

Characteristics of a desirable learning environment would include supporting, challenging, feedback and richness, all of which facilitate the acquisition of knowledge during the learning process. (See Chapter 20.) Such knowledge would then improve learning capacity for the next experience. This increased knowledge becomes part of the Self, resides in the brain, and is available and accessible to support all four modes of Kolb's original learning model. In the middle of the diagram there is a line from Self coming into a box labeled knowledge creation and proficiency. There are also two lines coming from both reflective observation and abstract conceptualization. Both of these processes may create knowledge and improve learning proficiency as well as influencing the Self. (See Chapter 18 for an expanded treatment of Self.)

REFLECT:
How important is social interaction to my learning?
Why might personal complexity be a good thing?

The reflective observation box creates understanding and meaning by integrating incoming experience. Meaning is the evaluation both cognitively and emotionally of the significance or importance of the incoming experience relative to the learner, or perhaps to the context of the experience. Thus, reflective observation deals with the past and present, and uses these to understand and make sense of the incoming information. Abstract conceptualization or the comprehension box focuses on problem solving, decision-making, creativity, and forecasting the outcome of anticipated actions. Here the learner is focusing on the present and the future, and how to change the environment successfully by creating and applying knowledge. The understanding, meaning, problem solving, and decision-making developed during the reflection and comprehension modes contribute to the creation of the learner's knowledge.

At the center of the diagram the circle labeled "Self" stands for a combination of the individual Self experienced as a flowing line of conscious thought, and that part of the individual that recognizes the Self and participates in the decision-making process as part of the mind, brain, and body, or "the totality of the individual" (LeDoux, 2002, p. 26). We suggest these words with care since from the neuroscience findings the unconscious plays a significant role in participating in, and in many cases governing, the actions of the mind/brain/body, that is, the Self. There is a continuous exchange of information (neuron patterns) within the brain and body among the major functions that participate in the learning process. There are also hormones and other chemicals flowing throughout the entire body. The 13 neuroscience findings and the items within each of those areas suggest ideas, information, influence, and actions that a learner can take to enhance his or her learning capacity. These depend on the content and context of the situation, the external environment, the physiological and mental state, and the autobiography of the learner.

Because of the complexity of the mind/brain/body learning system, we have explored this system from several frames of reference, each providing its own perspective and a partial understanding of how the system works. While each frame of reference offers a perspective, and potential insights into the learning process and its complexity, we offer that a self-organizing, Intelligent Complex Adaptive Learning System engaged with its environment *cannot be understood from any one of these frames of reference*, but must be studied from multiple perspectives to allow our unconscious to create its own interpretation and meaning through all the modes of the ICALS Model.

Building on the work of Kolb (1984), Chapter 17 focuses on the five modes of the ICALS Model. In the following section, we then delve more deeply into the concepts of Self, the Self co-evolving with its environment, and the Self as a social learner.

Chapter 17
The Five Modes of Learning

The intent of this chapter is to expand on Kolb's treatment of the four learning modes in terms of their relationship to neuroscience findings and the fifth mode of the ICALS Model, social engagement. Each mode is briefly described below with examples of neuroscience findings that relate to that specific mode. See Kolb (1984) for an in-depth treatment of the original four learning modes.

Kolb's learning cycle uses the four modes of concrete experience, reflective observation, abstract conceptualization, and active experimentation to create knowledge. Thus, in his view, knowledge is the result of grasping experience, transforming it by reflection, then creating a theory or conceptual framework to better comprehend the reflected upon experience, then taking action and comparing the outcomes with expectations to get feedback. This supports Kolb's definition of learning as the process in which knowledge is created through the transformation of experience.

As previously forwarded, although the modes are connected in a circle with the arrows moving clockwise, and written in the order presented in the previous paragraph, it should *not* be inferred that the learning process always follows this order. A specific learning process, while likely starting with concrete experience, may bounce around the circle as the learner reflects, takes action, comprehends from another perspective, [interacts with others] and again reflects, and so on. Each individual's learning style, background, learning objective, and the environment influence the sequence of activities during the learning process. Kolb (1984) maintains that all four modes are equipotent contributions to the learning process.

Kolb's objective was to describe the *structural* aspects of the model, to identify the essential and long-term aspects of the learning process that determine its basic functioning rather than the details of each situational application. In his description, he addresses three aspects of his learning process: (a) its holistic structure—the interdependence of the internal components; (b) its transformation process—the way structural components transact to maintain and elaborate themselves; and (c) its process of self-regulation—how the structural system keeps its identity and integrity (Kolb, 1984).

Concrete experience and abstract conceptualization are separate, distinct, and conflicting ways of *grasping* or taking hold of a specific experience. Similarly, the two other modes, active experimentation and reflective observation, represent a second dialectic of two ways of transforming: concrete experience through reflection, and abstract conceptualization through action. According to Kolb (1984), each of these two basic dimensions "represents a dialectic opposition between two independent but mutually enhancing orientations" (p. 59). By dialectic Kolb means, "... mutually opposed and conflicting processes the results of each of which cannot be explained by the other, but whose merger through confrontation of the conflict between them results in a higher order process that transcends and encompasses them both." (Kolb, 1984, p. 29)

Figure 17-1 reflects the relationship of the original four modes—experience, reflection, comprehension and action—and the fifth mode of the ICALS Model, Social Engagement. Note that the social engagement mode refers to grasping via triggering, which refers to the associative patterning process detailed in Chapter 2. Specifically, the process would be triggered by external stimuli, incoming information from social interaction.

Further, the social engagement mode is participatory in the creation of both social knowledge and self-knowledge. Global connectivity has assured the availability of massive amounts of information and a wide diversity of thought and opinion on every subject imaginable. This shift has prompted an exponential growth in learning from each other from which the term social knowledge emerged. Self-knowledge refers to the subject/object relationship also detailed in Chapter 2.

We now briefly address each of the five modes individually and identify neuroscience findings that apply to each mode.

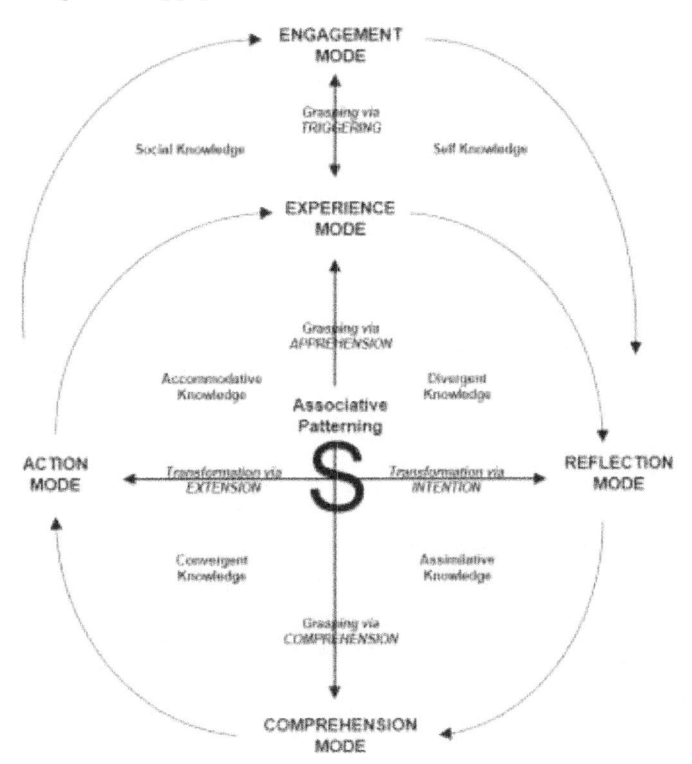

Figure 17-1. *The relationships among the five learning modes with an emphasis on the knowledges that are facilitated.*

EXPERIENCE MODE: *Concrete Experience (Apprehension)*

This mode is a form of knowing that comes from the grasping of experience by apprehension. Apprehension in this context refers to (1) an idea formed by observation or experience and (2) the ability to understand, "the power or ability to grasp the important, significance, or meaning of something" (Encarta, 1999). The philosopher Perkins (1971) says that apprehension is, "that understanding of an experience that consists in knowing what an experience is like; and we know what an experience is like by virtue of having that experience" (pp. 3-4).

Apprehension has the subelements of sensing, feeling, awareness, attention, and intuition. It is the experiencing of everything in your immediate space with an awareness that does not require thinking (Kolb, 1984). You know these things immediately and without rational or conscious thought. Such apprehensions may be tacit, that is, difficult to verbalize and communicate to others. If you change your focus, the previous apprehension vanishes and a new one comes into being. Concepts, analysis, and rational thought are rarely involved.

Feelings are a very important part of a concrete experience. Emotions are always part of the learning processes and can significantly modulate the learning process and its results. For example, during the concrete experience mode, high positive emotions can increase an individual's sensing, feeling, and awareness, as well as support focused attention. Positive emotions not only excite an individual to learn, but encourage exploration and flexibility in learning. When we are excited about something, our minds are more open and we look to building ideas and improving our understanding. On the other hand, negative emotions tend toward the opposite result. When strong negative emotions rule a situation, the learner may start to close off and become more cautious and fearful, with the result of paying less attention to learning.

As Pert (1997) details,

> Emotional states or moods are produced by the various molecules known as neuropeptide ligands, [molecules] and what we experience as an emotion or a feeling is also a mechanism for activating a particular neuronal circuit—simultaneously throughout the brain and body—which generates a behavior involving the whole creature, with all the necessary physiological changes that behavior would require. (Pert, 1997, p. 145)

Related Learning from Neuroscience Findings:

The phenomenon described in Item 3-A (**The brain can generate molecules of emotion to reinforce what is learned.**) could provide control over attention during the concrete experience. Pert (1997) offers that through self-consciousness the mind can use the brain to generate molecules of emotion and override the cognitive system. Creation of these molecules of emotion can also improve understanding and meaning, and seek truth/how things work. This could influence activities in both concrete experience and reflective observation of the Kolb/Zull model. (Item 3-A is introduced in Chapter 12.)

Other examples of neuroscience findings that impact the concrete experience include:

Item 2-A: **The brain stores only a part of the meaningful incoming sensory information. The gaps are filled in (re-created) when the memory is recalled.** This item primarily relates to the sensing aspect of concrete experience in the Kolb/Zull model. It makes the point that when we sense or feel our environment not all of the incoming information goes into memory. In fact, at best only things that are meaningful to us are usually remembered. Memory storage, recall, and recognition all occur at the level of the invariant forms, what Hawkins (2004) describes as "a form that captures the essence of relationships, not the details of the moment" (p. 82). This means that individuals cannot fully trust the details of their memory. (Item 2-A is introduced in Chapter 12.)

Item 2-C: **Less than seven hours of sleep may impair memory.** This item is shown as affecting attention and awareness in terms of concrete experience. It emphasizes the importance of adequate sleep in keeping the brain performing well enough to ensure an effective memory. (Item 2-C is introduced in Chapter 12.)

Item 6-A: **Cognitive mimicry that transfers active behavior and other cultural norms.** Zull (2002) notes that mirror neurons are a form of cognitive mimicry that transfers active behavior and, most likely, other cultural norms. When we see something happening our mind creates the same patterns of neurons that we would use to enact the same thing ourselves. This would be related to the subelements of sensing, feeling, and attention in concrete experience. (Item 6-A is introduced in Chapter 13.)

Item 11-A: **Plasticity is a result of the connection between neural patterns in the mind and the physical world—what we think and believe impacts our physical bodies.** Evolution has created a brain that can adapt and readapt to a changing world (Buonomano & Merzenich, 1998). This is neural plasticity, the ability of neurons to change their structure and relationships, depending on environmental demands and personal decisions and actions. Relative to concrete experience such plasticity can broaden the scope of sensing as well as feelings. (Item 11-A is introduced in Chapter 14.)

REFLECTION MODE: *Reflective Observation*

Reflection can be considered the act of reflecting, mental concentration, or careful consideration. Specifically, reflection refers to (1) careful thought, especially the process of reconsidering previous actions, events, or decisions and (2) an idea or thought, especially one produced by careful consideration of something (Encarta, 1999). Kolb relates the act of reflection to Jung's theory of types, specifically, his concept of introversion. According to Jung (1990), the internal world of concepts, ideas and fantasy has equal or superior status with the objective reality of the external world. However, both Jung and Diekman argue that, at least in Western society, the active mode tends to dominate the reflection mode. Kolb (1984) was convinced that the introversion/extraversion relationship could not be put in a single dimension.

According to Kolb's model, after information is taken in through concrete experience, it is reflected upon to *make sense* of the experience. Physiologically, this occurs in the back cortex where diverse information is assembled and integrated into a composite pattern that has meaning. Putting a jigsaw puzzle together might be a useful metaphor.

> In terms of the learning cycle, this integration process is what we expect to happen during "reflective observation". As implied by the term *reflective*, it may take considerable time to get everything integrated and see the full meaning of our experience. We have to think about things (reflect) and examine the images in our memory (observation). We stand back from our experience, look it over, and think about it. And what we look for is an image that fits *all* of our experience. We look for unity. (Zull, 2002, p. 154)

Reflection is often better if we can close out our external sensory experience. Reflection keeps the mind from being distracted by new information while it is thinking about old information. People often close their eyes when they are thinking. We frequently do things that don't require attention, because attention is directed inward (Zull, 2002).

The reflective observation mode has subelements consisting of understanding, meaning, truth/how things work, intuition, and integrated/look for unity.

In the brain, the temporal integrative cortex and the frontal integrative cortex make up a major part of the neocortex. Each of these two large areas of association cortices has distinct functions. The first area is in the back part of the cortex and is responsible for the association of various aspects of sensory input with each other; for example, the proper association of shape, movement, and color. As external signals come into this back area they are divided into a number of different segments and may go to a number of locations within the brain (estimated to be about 35 distinct physical locations for visual information). This is why the back cortex is said to integrate the incoming signals to allow us to make sense of them. Zull describes it as,

> Signals from different areas of the back cortex spend time just bouncing around through all the existing connections there. Some of these connections are distant, and some are weak. Some may fire right away, and others may only fire after the original input has wandered around a long time in this thicket of neurons. Pathways with the weakest of connections may still eventually be activated, but we may have to wait. Reflection is searching for connections -- literally! (Zull, 2002, p. 164)

Notice that this process may deal with the recent past where information has just come in, or perhaps the historic past if we were to reflect internally on past memories and recent questions or problems. In either case the purpose is to make sense and find meaning out of our current or recent experience, whether it is internally or externally driven, to know the who, what, where, and when of the incoming information or situation.

Although reflection is normally considered an internal thinking process, Zull suggests that a dialogue with a trusted other may also promote reflection as a natural way of learning or making sense out of experience (Zull, 2002). We agree, thus the importance of the Engagement Mode. Further, for experience to be made meaningful it needs to be related to the individual's past experiences. Reflection creates understanding and meaning by associating and integrating incoming information with information stored within memory. If the current experience is similar to a past experience (either good or bad) memory will influence the level and nature of the incoming information as it relates to the reflection and comprehension processes. This influence may significantly change the nature and interpretation of the experience. This is, of course, the associative patterning process.

Zull feels that for this to happen, time is needed for these associations to become apparent. This may happen during periods of reflection or sleep when competing sensory and motor activity is at a minimum. With time our understandings and our associations change and grow (Zull, 2002, p. 4). Recall from above that the learning process is not linear and thinking may often bounce around among the four modes.

People often reflect on images and diagrams. These images, seen during internal reflection, are created within the mind. This exercises the visual part of the brain and has led to an interesting discovery. As Zull (2002) describes it,

> We now know what parts of the brain are active when we think of an image. You could guess what these parts are by remembering that an image is a reassembled, or *unified*, set of neuronal connections .... When we reflect, we bring up images from our past experience, and these images are what we see in our mind's eye. But, in one of the most satisfying discoveries from brain imaging studies, it turns out that the part of the brain we use to see images with *our mind's eye* is the same part that we use to see them with *our real eyes*. (p.165)

Given the view of the brain afforded by brain imaging techniques, we now know that the mind can change the brain. To put it another way, the reflective process that leads to meaning has been shown to affect—and ultimately change—patterns in the brain (Liggan & Kay, 1999). Thus non-material thoughts (patterns in the brain) can and do influence the material brain. This is not a metaphysical phenomenon because patterns in the brain are patterns of physical anatomical structures of the brain. Thus another way of understanding this is to think of it as the physical brain changing itself in response to incoming signals.

Imaging studies have shown that the back cortex shows more activity in dreaming and the front cortex less activity. When we dream, our reflecting brain is at work. It sees images, hears language, and feels emotions. The amygdala is the region of the brain that monitors the emotional content of internal experience (as well as incoming sensory information), and there are often intense emotions while dreaming (Zull, 2002, p. 168).

Cozolino suggests a convenient distinction between reflective and reflexive thinking. He considers reflective language likely to require higher levels of neural network integration. As Cozolino explains, "Whereas *reflexive* language keeps our immediate attention, *reflective* language exemplifies our ability to escape from the present, gain perspective on our reflexive actions, and make decisions about what and how we would like to change" (Cozolino, 2002, pp. 293-294).

Zull suggests that we need reflection to develop complexity. We may start with a direct and sometimes relatively simple concrete experience, but that experience may grow richer as we give our brain the freedom to search for additional unknown connections. As those connections are understood, they create new neural networks within the brain. We then associate and connect the networks of our present experience to those that represent our past experience. These connections create new ideas or perspectives, thereby increasing complexity (Zull, 2002, p. 164).

Related Learning from Neuroscience Findings:

Examples of neuroscience findings that impact the concrete experience include:

Item 1-B: **The unconscious never lies**. This sub-item taken from Kandel may seem odd, but when it is realized that the unconscious is a part of the overall living individual, "lying" to Self would not make sense (Kandel, 2006). This idea relates to the truth and how things work under reflective observation. Although the intuition coming from our unconscious may not be right, it is still what our unconscious *perceives as truth*. Being aware of, and listening to, our unconscious can improve our learning scope and rate. (Item 1-B is introduced in Chapter 12.)

Item 1-C: **The unconscious can influence our thoughts and emotions without our awareness**. This affects our understanding of the making of meaning and a desire to find the truth and how things work as described under the reflective observation mode. (Item 1-C is introduced in Chapter 12.)

Item 3-B: **Emotional tags influence memory recall**. We remember things that are emotionally significant. This helps our understanding and the creation of meaning, as well as our ability to anticipate the outcomes of actions. Thus this item supports both reflective observation and abstract conceptualization. The mind solves many complex problems by recalling the core (or meaning) of past solutions. The most significant past problems have emotional tags that aid in recall. (Item 3-B is introduced in Chapter 12.)

Item 3-D: **Unconscious interpretation of a situation can influence the emotional experience**. As stated earlier, the unconscious mind is always working and, through the release of neurotransmitters it may create bodily emotional experiences. This process can impact the understanding and meaning aspects of an external experience during a learner's reflective observation. (Item 3-D is introduced in Chapter 12.)

Item 5-A: **An enriched environment can produce a personal internal reflective world of imagination and creativity**. This item is part of the environment, and as such may affect a number of the aspects of concrete experience and active experimentation in the Kolb/Zull model. A rich environment entering the mind/brain/body through experiences stimulates the mind to associate patterns and create new possibilities. (Item 5-A is introduced in Chapter 13.)

Item 6-B: **Rapid transfer of tacit knowledge (bypasses cognition)**. By creating the same neuronal pattern in your mind that is in the mind of another person, the need for cognitive thinking is bypassed and tacit knowledge may be immediately transferred. This would affect understanding and meaning in reflective observation, and speed up the learning process. (Item 6-B is introduced in Chapter 13.)

Item 6-D: **We may understand other people's behavior by mentally simulating it**. This would relate to understanding, meaning, and truth/how things work in reflective observation, and to heightened boundary conditions in active experimentation. (Item 6-D is introduced in Chapter 13.)

Item 7-D: **The mind uses past learning and memories to complete incoming information**. The capacity to complete incoming information from past experience enhances both efficiency and the effectiveness of learning. It impacts the ability to create meaning during reflective observation as well as problem solving and anticipating the outcomes of actions during abstract conceptualization. (Item 7-D is introduced in Chapter 13.)

COMPREHENSION MODE: *Abstract Conceptualization*

Comprehension is (1) the grasping of the meaning of something and (2) the intellectual ability to grasp the meaning of something (Encarta, 1999). This mode, the second way of knowing according to Kolb (1984), has subelements of concepts, ideas, logic, problem solving, creativity, building models and theories, anticipation, control, rigor, and discipline.

Abstract conceptualization or comprehension works with concepts and solves problems by recalling ideas and past experiences from memory and creating new ideas and solutions to problems (the process of associative patterning). Here both working memory and long-term memory will likely be actively involved. Working memory refers to representations of information currently in active use, such as when a person tries to remember a telephone number. If not rehearsed, the information will be forgotten within a few seconds (Haberlandt, 1998).

Comprehension allows one to create and analyze a model of the situation, and to communicate it to others. Comprehension also allows one to predict and recreate those apprehensions, and provides some level of control over situations. By observing, thinking, and careful study we come to understand our experiences. In contrasting apprehension and comprehension, Kolb quotes William James as follows: "through feelings we become acquainted with things, but only by our thoughts do we know about them. Feelings are the emotions and sensations we get from skin, muscle, viscus, eye, ear, nose, and palate. The 'thoughts' as recognized in popular parlance, are the conceptions and judgments" (James, 1890, pp. 221-2).

The philosopher Feigl suggested that there are different languages associated with the two ways of knowing. There is a phenomenal language associated with apprehension (felt qualities) and a physical language associated with comprehension (descriptive symbols). In his 1984 book, Kolb noted that since Feigl's proposed *double knowledge theory* (Feigl, 1958), much had been done in the area of neurological findings, particularly regarding the split-brain research that suggested that the left side of the brain was the logical, verbal part and the right side of the brain was the emotional, holistic part. This was thought to imply that the two ways of knowing were reflected in the physiology of the brain. Kolb offered that hemisphere-dominance research by Roger Sperry and colleagues reinforced and elaborated on the point that the two hemispheres of the brain specialized in different modes of consciousness, what he considered to be apprehension and comprehension (Kolb, 1984).

Comprehension primarily occurs in the frontal integrative cortex, also called the prefrontal cortex (or the executive brain). It is that portion of the forebrain frequently called the seat of the "self-conscious" mind processing. The self-conscious mind is self-reflective and a newly evolved "sense organ" that observes our own behaviors and emotions. The prefrontal cortex also has access to most of the information stored in our long-term memory bank. This is the part of the mind that solves problems, creates insights and new ideas or concepts. It also plans future operations, makes decisions, and anticipates the outcomes of those decisions. The prefrontal cortex is concerned with understanding the present from reflection and anticipating the future to be able to take actions as necessary.

This is where deep knowledge is created. The back cortex is primarily concerned with the past and interpreting the immediate experience. In reality individuals are likely to continuously move between reflection and comprehension (Goldberg, 2001; Lipton, 2005; Zull, 2002). While the prefrontal cortex is essential for deep understanding, problem solving, and creativity, these activities do not necessarily happen quickly. As Zull sees it, the ability to solve problems takes time for associations to become apparent (again, a reference to the associative patterning process). As noted earlier, this often happens during periods of reflection, or sleep, when competing sensory and motor activities are at a minimum, and with time, our understandings and our associations may change and grow (Zull, 2002).

Goldberg (2001) expresses the predictive aspect of the comprehending mind when he says,

> Human cognition is forward-looking, proactive rather than reactive. It is driven by goals, plans, aspirations, ambitions, and dreams, all of which pertain to the future and not the past. (p. 24)

Learning occurs when a person experiences signals from the outside world (social engagement) and the signals result in changes in the strengths of synaptic connections and/or the local biochemical and electrical properties change in complex distributed ways. Goldberg posits that the prefrontal cortex is connected to *every distinct functional unit in the brain*. This connectivity allows the prefrontal lobes to coordinate and integrate the work of the other brain functions and structures. In his perspective, the prefrontal cortex contains a map of the whole cortex. It is in the prefrontal cortex where consciousness is presumed to lie (Goldberg, 2001).

Both reflection and comprehension participate in the meaning-making process: reflection from past memories and incoming information from experience, and comprehension from the present and anticipated outcome that would result from taking actions. In both of these cases, emotions may play a significant role (LeDoux, 1996). As Zull explains,

> For the most part, things have meaning when they remind us of something in our past. When they don't, we are just puzzled. But there is another requirement. Even if we experience something that has happened to us before, it is hard to make meaning of it unless it engages our emotions. (Zull, 2002, p. 166)

Knowledge and meaning can be created by comprehension and action on the external world.

Related Learning from Neuroscience Findings:

Neuroscience findings that directly impact the comprehension mode are included below. In the area of memory there are three items:

Item 2-D: **Memories are re-created each time they are recalled and therefore never the same**. The environment influences the re-creating process. This item is shown as impacting attention, understanding, truth/how things work, and integrate/look for unity. All of these factors in the Kolb/Zull model would be very sensitive to the accuracy of memories. For example, if a specific memory was recalled as an inaccurate representation, it could significantly change the interpretation (and therefore the meaning) of the original event. (Item 2-D is introduced in Chapter 12.)

Item 2-G: **Working memory is limited.** This item could impact the Kolb/Zull model in the aspects of concepts, ideas, and logic as well as problem solving and building models and theories. Working memory is essential for having a conversation and comprehending what we are reading. However, it can get overloaded, and when it does it may cause confusion and mistakes (Christos, 2003). Because working memory is limited to roughly seven plus or minus two bits, it is very helpful to chunk patterns to improve recall (Miller, 1956). Working memory impacts concepts, ideas, and creativity as well as conceptual thinking. (Item 2-G is introduced in Chapter 12.)

Item 2-J: **Repetition increases memory recall**. This item would impact control, rigor, and discipline in abstract conceptualization and focus attention in active experimentation. This is a well-known phenomenon and goes back to Hebb's rule that *neurons that fire together wire together*. Thus, the more a given pattern is repeated the stronger the neuronal connections are and the easier a specific memory can be recalled. (Item 2-J is introduced in Chapter 12.)

Additional findings impacting comprehension include:

Item 4-F: **There is an optimum level of stress for learning (the inverted "U")**. This level is somewhere between a positive attitude and a strong motivation to learn (arousal), and some level of fear of learning or the learning situation. Among sub-elements, it could impact problem solving, creativity, and anticipation in the abstract conceptualization mode of the Kolb/Zull model. (Item 4-F is introduced in Chapter 13.)

Item 7-D: **The mind uses past learning and memories to complete incoming information**. The capacity to complete incoming information from past experience enhances both efficiency and the effectiveness of learning. It impacts the ability to create meaning during reflective observation as well as problem solving and anticipating the outcomes of actions during abstract conceptualization. (Item 7-D is introduced in Chapter 13.)

Item 9-B: **Adults developing complex neural patterns need emotional support to offset discomfort of this process**. Taylor (2006) suggests that this support is needed by individuals developing complex knowledge. Such emotional support will enhance the feelings of an individual during concrete experience, and also aid in the creation and understanding of concepts and ideas during abstract conceptualization. (Item 9-B is introduced in Chapter 14.)

ACTION MODE: *Active Experimentation*

Action refers to movement, energetic activity, something done, doing something to achieve a purpose (Encarta, 1999). The active experimentation mode, sometimes called the action mode, is intended to act upon and thereby influence the environment. Principle characteristics or sub-elements of this mode are focal attention, object-based logic; heightened boundary perception; shapes and meanings have dominance over colors and textures (Diekman, 1971).

In Chapter 3 we defined knowledge, the creation of learning, as the capacity (potential or actual) to take effective action. This ties knowledge directly to the actions we take which, through the process of associative patterning, is in the context of the instant and for the situation at hand. This means that the mind is continuously creating knowledge in response to incoming information from social engagement, that is, engagement with the environment as object as well as other individuals as objects.

Kolb says that an orientation toward active experimentation "focuses on actively influencing people and changing situations" (Kolb, 1984, p. 69), emphasizing practical application, doing, accomplishing. Note that while his model in an internal model, he speaks to actively influencing people and changing situations in the perceived external world. In other words, Kolb insinuates in his action mode the idea of social engagement in terms of external influence and change of people and situations. In the ICALS Model we will see the focus on two-way interaction with people and situations as well as the *feelings* of social support.

Related Learning from Neuroscience Findings:

Neuroscience findings that directly impact the comprehension mode are included below.

Item 1-G: **We may act for reasons we are not aware of**. This aspect of the unconscious clearly influences many subelements of active experimentation. Because of the dual roles of the conscious Self with its stream of consciousness and the large and continuously operating unconscious, our conscious mind cannot and does not control all aspects of our actions. From the perspective of this study, it is important to recognize that the unconscious significantly *affects our thinking and actions, and therefore our learning process*. (Item 1-G is introduced in Chapter 12.)

Item 1-H: **A model of the Self comes mostly from the unconscious**. Damasio believes that much of the model of the Self comes from the unconscious mind. This model creates the idea of *who* we are and the image we build up of ourselves. During active experimentation the Self interacts with objects and the external world, and hence is typically very aware of the boundaries between the individual and that external world. (Item 1-H is introduced in Chapter 12.)

Item 2-I: **Memory patterns decay slowly with time**. This depends upon the emotional and cognitive importance of the memory. When coupled with the potential errors during memory recall, it suggests that learning may be enhanced by evaluating specific material or experience for its relevance and importance to the learner. One example is to underline important passages while reading and "judge" the value (to the reader) of these passages, marking them with one to three stars in the margin. This presses the reader to *consider how important* the specific information is to his or hers own interests and goals. Repeatedly focusing attention on critical knowledge also helps solidify past knowledge. (Item 2-I is introduced in Chapter 12.)

Item 2-J: **Repetition increases memory recall**. This item would impact control, rigor, and discipline in abstract conceptualization and focus attention in active experimentation. This is a well-known phenomenon and goes back to Hebb's rule that *neurons that fire together wire together*. Thus, the more a given pattern is repeated the stronger the neuronal connections are and the easier a specific memory can be recalled. (Item 2-J is introduced in Chapter 12.)

Item 3-C: **Emotions miss details but are sensitive to meaning**. Emotions exist to alert and protect individuals from harm and to energize them to action when they have strong feelings or passions. However, emotions are concerned with the meaning of the information and not the details. Thus, this phenomenon may influence a number of aspects of the Kolb/Zull model either positively or negatively, depending on circumstances. Specifically, feeling, awareness, intuition, understanding, and meaning can all be influenced by the emotional state of the individual. Where learners can control their emotions by taking a positive attitude they can enhance their learning. (Item 3-C is introduced in Chapter 12.)

Item 4-C: **Stress depends on how we perceive a situation**. As Thompson (2000) explains, "the extent to which situations are stressful is determined by how the individual understands, interprets, sees, and feels about the situation" (p. 210). Thus, stress is controllable. From the Kolb/Zull model this item would impact awareness, attention, understanding, and meaning as well as most of the other sub-elements for Kolb's four modes. (Item 4-C is introduced in Chapter 13.)

Item 4-D: **Belief systems can reduce stress through reducing uncertainty**. Belief systems create a perspective on the world that is held to be correct and by doing so introduces a level of perceived certainty that reduces stress and increases repeatability in an individual's life. Belief systems may also narrow perspectives and thereby reduce learning. This item would impact sensing, feeling, understanding, and meaning in the Kolb/Zull model. (Item 4-D is introduced in Chapter 13.)

Item 4-G: **Stress is an active monitoring system that constantly compares current events to past experiences**. Three subelements of the Kolb/Zull model that could be affected by this item would be anticipation, act on environment, and object-based logic. For example, in anticipating the outcomes of some planned action developed from abstract conceptualization, an individual would think about past examples of similar situations and estimate the problems and potential issues, that is, what stress may occur as a result of the action. (Item 4-G is introduced in Chapter 13.)

Social Engagement (the Fifth Mode): *Triggering*

Social engagement opens up a dialogue with the environment, bringing social support and social interaction into the sphere of the Self as learner. This focus is critical as we have learned more about the workings of the mind/brain and recognized the involvement of Self in social learning.

We are social creatures. While this concept has been around for centuries, Cozolino believes that we are just waking up to this fact from a biological perspective. As he describes,

> As a species, we are just waking up to the complexity of our own brains, to say nothing of how brains are linked together. We are just beginning to understand that we have evolved as social creatures and that all of our biologies are interwoven. (Cozolino, 2006, p. 3)

There is no greater example of this than in the younger generations who are learning to co-evolve with a changing, uncertain and increasingly complex environment. Further, as noted by Tapscott (2009), global communication is eliminating the localized characteristics that are specific to young people. While there are still unique cultures and independent features, "increasingly young people around the world are becoming very much alike" in terms of generational attitudes, norms and behaviors (Tapscott, 2009, p. 27). Further, research has shown that collaborative learning is more effective in increasing academic performance than competition or individual learning (Jonassen, 2004).

Social support can be active and/or perceived. Recall that trust is very important in enhancing learning. This is because there is a cascade of biochemical processes that occurs in a secure, bonding relationship where trust has been established which promotes neural growth and learning. See Chapter 9 for a detailed discussion.

Related Learning from Neuroscience Findings:

In addition to specific neuroscience findings that relate directly to social interaction and social support, we will also explore the concept of mirror neurons and creativity in terms of their roles related to social engagement.

Neuroscience findings that directly relate to social interactions are:

Item 8-A: **Physical mechanisms have developed in our brain to enable us to learn through social interactions**. Stern (2004) says that these physical mechanisms have evolved to enable us to get the knowledge we need to keep emotionally and physically safe. These mechanisms would enable us to, "(1) engage in affective attunement or empathic interaction and language, (2) consider the intentions of the other, (3) try to understand what another mind is thinking, and (4) think about how we want to interact" (Johnson, 2006, p. 65). The physical mechanisms for this capability come from mirror neurons (see area 6 above) and also from adaptive oscillators. As mentioned above, mirror neurons aid in stimulating other peoples states of mind. As Stern (2004) proposes, "This 'participation' in another's mental life creates a sense of feeling/sharing with/understanding the person's intentions and feelings" (p. 79). This sense of close and trusting relationship is very supportive of learning.

Another mechanism that aids in the synchronism of two individuals is the adaptive oscillators that are part of our physiology. These oscillators are created by stable feedback loops of neurons. They may bring an individual's rate of neural firing into sync with another individual. This is when two people relate well to each other and learn to anticipate each other's actions (Stern, 2004). Buzsaki calls this phenomenon mutual entrainment, meaning a measure of stability that oscillators have when they lock in with each other (Buzsaki, 2006). Such situations, when they occur, may enhance the sensing, feeling, and awareness in the concrete experience phase of the Kolb/Zull model. (Item 8-A is introduced in Chapter 14.)

Item 8-B: **Physical and mental exercise and social bonding are significant sources of stimulation of the brain**. This statement by Amen (2005) highlights the importance of physical exercise for the health of the brain, mental exercise for the health of the mind, and social bonding. Physical exercise provides oxygen and increased blood to the brain. Studies have shown that a higher concentration of oxygen in the blood significantly improves cognitive performance in learners, for example tests demonstrated that individuals were able to recall more words from a list and perform visual and spatial tasks faster. Their cognitive abilities changed directly with the amount of oxygen in their brains (Chung et al., 2004; Scholey et al., 1999). In

Sousa (2006) social bonding carries with it a positive, trusting relationship that allows the learner to take risks and not be concerned with mistakes made during learning. It also encourages an open mind and willingness to listen and learn from a trusted other. During this process the learner's neurotransmitters in the prefrontal cortex (dopamine, serotonin, and norepinephrine) are stimulated and lead to increased neuronal networking and meaningful learning (Cozolino, 2002). While these would apply to many subelements of the Kolb/Zull model we highlight the following: awareness, attention and concepts, ideas, and logic. (Item 8-B is introduced in Chapter 14.)

Item 8-C: **Social interaction mechanisms foster the engagement in affective attunement, consider the intentions of others, understand what another person is thinking and think about how we want to interact**. As Johnson (2006) explains, "according to social cognitive neuroscience, the brain actually needs to seek out an affectively attuned other if it is to learn" (p. 65). Affective attunement reduces fear, a significant impediment to learning. These mechanisms support learning situations by enhancing understanding, meaning, truth and how things work, and anticipating the outcomes of actions. (Item 8-C is introduced in Chapter 14.)

Neuroscience findings that directly related to social support include:

Item 9-A: **Language and social relationships build and shape the brain**. This item could significantly impact the sensing aspect of concrete experience and the concepts, ideas, and logic of abstract conceptualization in the Kolb/Zull model. Good social relationships enhance learning through a reduction of stress, a shared language, and the use and understanding of concepts, metaphors, anecdotes, and stories. (Item 9-A is introduced in Chapter 13.)

Item 9-C: **Effective attunement contributes to the evolution and sculpting of the brain**. Effective attunement involves a mentor, coach, or another significant individual who is trusted and capable of resonance with the learner. When this happens, a dialogue with such an individual can greatly help the learner in understanding, developing meaning, anticipating the future with respect to actions, and receiving sensory feedback. As these new patterns are created in the mind, they in turn impact and change the structure of the brain. All of these influence subelements of the four modes of the Kolb/Zull model of experiential learning. (Item 9-A is introduced in Chapter 13.)

Item 9-D: **The brain actually needs to seek out an affectively attuned other for learning**. As Johnson explains, effective attunement reduces fear, and creates a positive environment and motivation to learn (Johnson, 2006). Being open to learning helps one integrate and look for unity as one reflects and opens up to sensory feedback during active experimentation. (Item 9-D is introduced in Chapter 13.)

Mirror Neurons

We now explore the phenomenon of mirror neurons and ask: How does this phenomenon aid experiential learning? One answer is that it serves to explain how actionable tacit knowledge can be transferred between individuals and the potential of mimicry to facilitate learning. A second aspect is to be aware that when we are mentally simulating another's behavior, we must not modulate that simulation through our own internal evaluation and perspectives. The capacity to re-create feelings, perspectives, and empathy with people by reliving their experiences can greatly aid learning, providing we understand what is happening and its potential for misinterpretation.

Recall that Iacoboni proposes that mirror neurons facilitate the direct and immediate comprehension of another's behavior *without going through complex cognitive processes*. This makes the learning process more efficient because it can instantly transfer not only visuals but emotions and intentions as well. Thus mirror neurons also serve as a means of learning through imitation, which is "a very important means by which we learn and transmit skills, language and culture" (Rizzolatti, 2006, p. 61). Often a significant part of learning requires good social communication, which includes parity and direct comprehension. Parity indicates that meaning within the message is similar for both the sender and the receiver. Direct comprehension means that no previous agreement between individuals is needed for them to understand each other. From the neuroscience perspective, both of these aspects of communication seem to be inherent in the neural organization of individuals (Rizzolatti, 2006). Here is what we have learned from our Neuroscience findings:

Item 6-D: **We may understand other people's behavior by mentally simulating it**. This would relate to understanding, meaning, and truth/how things work in reflective observation, and to heightened boundary conditions in active experimentation. (Item 6-D is introduced in Chapter 13.)

Item 6-G: **Mirror neurons facilitate neural resonance between observed actions and executing actions**. By neural resonance we mean a positive, mutually reinforcing relationship between two people interacting with each other. An individual may interact with another individual more efficiently and effectively because of the understanding and affection developed from the mutually reinforcing relationship between the two. For example, we may be able to understand another's feelings and/or intended actions because (through mirror neurons) we generate similar feelings and/or intended actions (or reactions). Mirror neurons may facilitate a quick, positive relationship between the observer and the observed. (Item 6-G is introduced in Chapter 13.)

Creativity

Creativity is an inherent capability of every brain (Hobson, 1999; Cristos, 2003). As described earlier, learning consists of building new patterns within the mind that represent ideas, concepts, objects, and processes that are internally imagined, or represent some interpretation of external reality. According to Stonier, (1997) thinking involves the association of different patterns within the mind/brain. Since memory is distributed throughout the brain, these associative processes may contain random associations that can result in new ideas, concepts, or approaches. This is considered as ordinary creativity and can be very valuable when it occurs during any of the four modes of Kolb's learning model. This process represents a form of self-learning initiated during the reflective observation or abstract conceptualism modes (Andreasen, 2005).

From the viewpoint of social engagement, there are group processes such as dialogue and brainstorming that serve to open the mind to new possibilities and stimulate creative thinking. The diversity of thought (ideas) that arises from social interaction can trigger the associative patterning of mind. Thus social engagement would work with internal processes in the playing out of creativity. Specifically related to social engagement, here is what we have learned from our neuroscience findings:

Item 5-A: **An enriched environment can produce a personal internal reflective world of imagination and creativity**. This item is part of the environment, and as such may affect a number of the aspects of concrete experience and active experimentation. A rich environment entering the mind/brain/body through experiences stimulates the mind to associate patterns and create new possibilities. (Item 5-A is introduced in Chapter 13.)

Overarching Findings

While all the neuroscience findings affect the learning process in some way, there are three high-level findings impacting all five modes that warrant repetition. These are:

Item 4-B: **Voluntary learning promotes Theta waves that correlate with little or no stress and positive feedback**. Theta waves are low frequency (4-8 hertz) electrical waves generated within the brain and detected by an electroencephalograph (EEG) that measures electrical activity near the surface of the brain via electrodes on the scalp. There are a number of suggested correlates to theta waves; for example, intentional or voluntary movements, high-level processing of incoming signals, selective attention, arousal, and decision-making. As Buzsaki (2006) posits, "an inescapable conclusion is that 'will' plays a crucial role in theta rhythms" (p. 21). Voluntary learning, as distinct from forced learning, has little or no stress attached to it and therefore fosters a much higher level of learning. Specifically, positive learning would impact sensing, feeling, awareness, attention, understanding, and meaning as they relate to all of the modes of the ICALS Model. (Item 4-B is introduced in Chapter 13.)

Item 11-B: **Learning depends on modification of the brain's chemistry and architecture**. This knowledge can help learners recognize their potential for building knowledge, influencing their own brain, and developing in whatever direction they choose. Thus, from this perspective it has the potential to enhance any or all of the subelements. (Item 11-B is introduced in Chapter 14.)

Item 11-C: **Thoughts change the structure of the brain, and brain structure influences the creation of new thoughts**. This feedback loop highlights the recognition of the interdependence and self-organization of the mind and the brain in the sense that each influences the other. This also reminds one of the importance of both physical and mental health. This duality can help awareness, understanding, meaning, creativity, and anticipation, and is highly impacted by social engagement. (Item 11-C is introduced in Chapter 14.)

In Summary ...

As can be seen, neuroscience findings have significantly changed the way we think about the four previously identified modes of learning, and enable us to understand the importance of the fifth mode of learning, social engagement. This is not surprising since we live in a connected world and are increasingly recognizing the power of social learning.

Section VI
Discovering the Self

Focusing on the concept of Self considerably changes the historic experiential learning model. To more deeply explore these differences, in Chapter 18 we first look at the impact of the unconscious on Self, then explore the use of the conscious self—introducing the Seashore Use of Self Model—and then think about the story of Self, the autobiographical story built up through life that helps us understand who we are and where we fit socially. Finally, using the foundational work of Schank (1995), we look at the dimensions of intelligence through the eyes of story.

Chapter 19 investigates the mind/brain/body connection, with a focus on related neuroscience findings. This is not intended as an authoritative guide; rather, to reinforce the connection between activities of the mind and activities of the body, for example, the impact of exercise on mental health. Chapter 20 looks at the Self as a complex adaptive system co-evolving with its environment. As such, our Self participates fully in co-creating the environment within which we live and learn. Demonstrating an example of the impact of our environment on learning, Chapter 21 is an in-depth study on the use of sound and music in learning.

Chapter 22 dives into the realm of Self as a social learner, beginning with a close look at social interaction and the mind/brain, then moving into a discussion of conversation, social bonding, empathy, unconscious imitation and emotional intelligence. Chapter 23, Self as the Locus of Change, asks: How can Self influence other Self's?

As we take this exciting journey into a deeper understanding of the role of Self in learning, we have shared some of our emerging insights and favorite examples. We encourage you to connect in your own personal examples as we navigate these fascinating waters.

Chapter 18
The Self

The term Self is reflective of the Hindu word *Atman* (translated in English as Self), which is in the Hindu teaching "Brahman is Atman and Atman is Brahman." Brahma is the Creator of the Universe (unknowable, infinite and transcendent) and Atman is the divine spark at the core of our being that is part of the greater whole (Brahma) (Crowley, 1999). Self may also be compared to the beliefs about the soul or spirit as is described in the Abrahamic religions—Judaism, Christianity and Islam. Jung's process of individuation involves "letting go of all the false images of ourselves that we have allowed to be built up by our environment and by the projected visions of parents, teachers, friends, and lovers." (Crowley, 1999, p. 136) *There is a Self that is deeper, wiser and more powerful than that individual who is subject to environmental perturbations.*

The concept of Self was introduced in Chapter 2. For purposes of this discussion, the **Self** (which as a principal element of the ICALS Theory and Model is capitalized in this book) is considered to be the conscious and the unconscious mind, the brain and the body. Every Self has a mind, which can be defined as:

> ... a field of possibilities in which at least one-half of the field has chosen the same direction for its choices, with these choices having the potential to further limit a smaller field that the larger could be a creator of and is therefore potentially connected to. (MacFlouer, 1999, p. 162)

From this perspective, Self can be thought of as a self-organizing complex adaptive system—including self-referential memory, self-description, self-awareness and the personality—coevolving with, and the creator of, its environment. (See Chapter 16 and Chapter 18.) As American psychologist James argues, "Although the Self might feel like a unitary thing, it has many facets—from awareness of one's own body to memories of oneself to the sense of where one fits into society." (Zimmer, 2005) Thus there is no single point within the mind/brain/body complex where we could situate Self. It is the interactions among *all* of those neuronal patterns, firings and connections that define Self. This idea of **permeation is why the Self is central in the ICALS Model** presented in Chapter 16.

In the perceived external dimensions of the body that is part of Self there are X, Y, Z (the height, width and breadth of three-dimensional space) and T (time). See Figure 18-1. This is true in both the external reality, and in the physical makeup of the brain structure, such as the neurons, axons, synapses and gleon cells that all exist in a four-dimensional space/time continuum. However, when we consider every chain or sequence of thoughts as a dimension and consider the variety and number of patterns continuously emerging in the mind, the thoughts that generate the persona of Self are beyond our ability to count. They are also multidimensional in that these internal dimensions might be represented in vector space by geometrical relationships that are orthogonal, at right angles to each other so as to operate independently (not a subset of the other), yet with the potential to be combined. Recognizing that any model is an artificial construct, these dimensions might be grouped in many ways; for example, by autonomic systems, major sub-systems, or in relationship to the conscious and unconscious.

Building on the introduction of consciousness in Chapter 2, we consider consciousness is comprised of a single, linear stream of thought patterns (Edelman & Tononi, 2000) and their relationships to each other and to the Self (MacFlouer, 1999). As such, this mechanism of awareness and understanding can be filled with mundane facts or highly charged emotions. For a pattern to be observed and recognized (brought into consciousness), it must exist for some finite period *in time*. Thus consciousness is usually aware of time, but not always. As Csikszentmihalyi has proposed, there are times when the mind is unaware of time. These are called autotelic experiences where the mind is so focused and busy, and usually highly productive, that an individual simply looses track of time (Csikszentmihalyi, 1990). In contrast, the multidimensional unconscious is not subject to a linear stream of thought (denoting time), and dreams often lack any relativity to time.

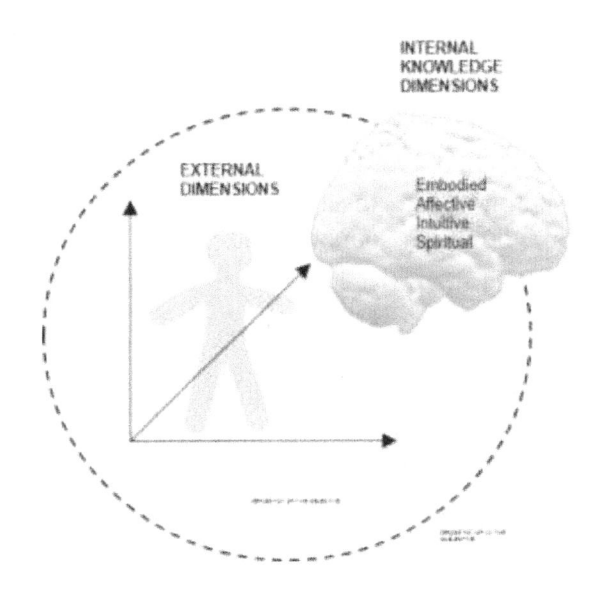

Figure 18-1. *External dimensions and internal knowledge dimensions of Self. Note that the model is counter-intuitive, bounding the external dimensions and putting no limits on internal knowledge dimensions.*

The sense of Self (consciousness) expands first through comparing itself to what it is not, seeing and recognizing differences, what can be referred to as discriminative thought. This sense of Self is eventually expanded further by detecting similarities in others and identifying with those similarities (MacFlouer, 1999). This connection can come about through pondering the purpose of life, both as a Self and from the viewpoint of the other, learning and expanding from giving and receiving energy and knowledge. This exchange and expansion will be discussed further in Chapter 22 where we explore the Self as a social learner.

The Impact of the Unconscious on Self

The term unconscious refers to *not* conscious, or occurring in the absence of conscious awareness or thought, without conscious control; involuntary or unintended (*American Heritage Dictionary*, 2006, p. 1873). People normally do all sorts of things for reasons of which they are not consciously aware (Item 1-G). As affirmed by Uleman (2005), the unconscious includes "internal qualities of mind that affect conscious thought and behavior, without being conscious themselves" (p. 3).

In our treatment, we consider the unconscious as an integrated unit comprised of unconscious functions that include the *subconscious* and the *superconscious*, with knowing the sense gained from experience that resides in the subconscious part of the mind *and* the energetic connection our mind enjoys with the superconscious. Thus, the subconscious and superconscious are both part of our unconscious resources, with the subconscious in service to and directly supporting the embodied mind/brain and the superconscious focused on tacit resources involving larger moral aspects, the emotional part of human nature and the higher development of our mental faculties. (See Chapter 25 for an expanded treatment of knowing.)

Two areas of Self pertaining to the unconscious will be discussed below: tacit knowledge and a quick review of associative patterning.

Tacit Knowledge

Knowledge—the capacity (potential or actual) to take effective action—was introduced in Chapter 3. Our focus in this section is on that knowledge residing in the unconscious, that is, tacit knowledge (Item 1-E). Tacit knowledge is the descriptive term for those connections among thoughts that cannot be pulled up in words, a knowing of what decision to make or how to do something that cannot be clearly voiced in a manner such that another person could extract and re-create that knowledge (understanding, meaning, etc.). An individual may or may not know they have tacit knowledge in relationship to something or someone; but even when it is known, the individual is unable to put it into words or visuals that can convey that knowledge. We all know things, or know what to do, yet may be unable to articulate why we know them, why they are true, or even exactly what they are. To "convey" is to cause something to be known or understood or, in this usage, to transfer information from which the receiver is able to create knowledge.

As a point of contrast, explicit knowledge is information (patterns) and processes (patterns in time) that can be called up from memory and described accurately in words and/or visuals (representations) such that another person can comprehend the knowledge that is expressed through this exchange of information. This has historically been called declarative knowledge (Anderson, 1983). Implicit knowledge is a more complicated concept, and a term not unanimously agreed-upon in the literature. This is understandable since even simple dictionary definitions—which are generally unbiased and powerful indicators of collective preference and understanding—show a considerable overlap between the terms "implicit" and "tacit," making it difficult to differentiate the two. We propose that a useful interpretation of implicit knowledge is knowledge stored in memory of which the individual is not immediately aware which, while not readily accessible, may be pulled up when triggered (associated). Triggering can occur through questions, dialogue or reflective thought, or happen as a result of an external event. In other words, implicit knowledge is knowledge that the individual does not know they have, but is self-discoverable! However, once this knowledge is surfaced, the individual may or may not have the ability to adequately describe it such that another individual could create the same knowledge; and the "why and how" may remain tacit.

A number of published psychologists have used the term implicit interchangeably with our usage of tacit, that is, with implicit representing knowledge that once acquired can be shown to effect behavior but is not available for conscious retrieval (Reber, 1993; Kirsner et al, 1998). As described in our above discussion of implicit knowledge, what is forwarded here is that the concept of implicit knowledge serves a middle ground between that which can be made explicit and that which cannot easily, if at all, be made explicit. By moving beyond the dualistic approach of explicit and tacit—that which can be declared versus that which can't be declared, and that which can be remembered versus that which can't be remembered—we posit implicit as representing the knowledge spectrum between explicit and tacit. While explicit refers to easily available, some knowledge requires a higher stimulus for association to occur but is not buried so deeply as to prevent access. This understanding opens the domain of implicit knowledge.

Tacit and explicit knowledge can be thought of as residing in "places," specifically, the unconscious and the conscious, respectively, although both are differentiated patterns spread throughout the neuronal system, that is, the volume of the brain and other parts of the central nervous system. On the other hand, implicit knowledge may reside in either the unconscious (prior to triggering, or tacit) or the conscious (when triggered, or explicit). Note there is no clean break between these three types of knowledge; rather, this is a continuum.

Calling them interactive components of cooperative processes, Reber agrees that there is no clear boundary between that which is explicit and that which is implicit (our tacit): "There is ... no reason for presuming that there exists a clean boundary between conscious and unconscious processes or a sharp division between implicit and explicit epistemic systems ..." (Reber, 1993, p. 23). Reber describes the urge to treat explicit and implicit (our tacit) as altogether different processes the "polarity fallacy" (Reber, 1993). Similarly, Matthews says that the unconscious and conscious processes are engaged in what he likes to call a "synergistic" relationship (Matthews, 1991). What this means is that the boundary between the conscious and the unconscious is somewhat porous and flexible.

Knowledge starts as tacit knowledge, that is, the initial movement of knowledge is from its origins within the Self (in the unconscious) to an outward expression (howbeit driving effective action). What does that mean? Michael Polanyi, a professor of chemistry and the social sciences, wrote in *The Tacit Dimension* that, "We start from the fact that we can know more than we can tell" (Polanyi, 1967, p 108). He called this pre-logical phase of knowing tacit knowledge, that is, knowledge that cannot be articulated (Polanyi, 1958).

Tacit knowledge can be thought of in terms of four aspects: embodied, intuitive, affective and spiritual (Bennet & Bennet, 2008c). While all of these aspects are part of Self, each represents different sources of tacit knowledge whose applicability, reliability and efficacy may vary greatly depending on the individual, the situation and the knowledge needed to take effective action. They are represented in Figure 18-2 along with explicit and implicit knowledge on the continuum of awareness.

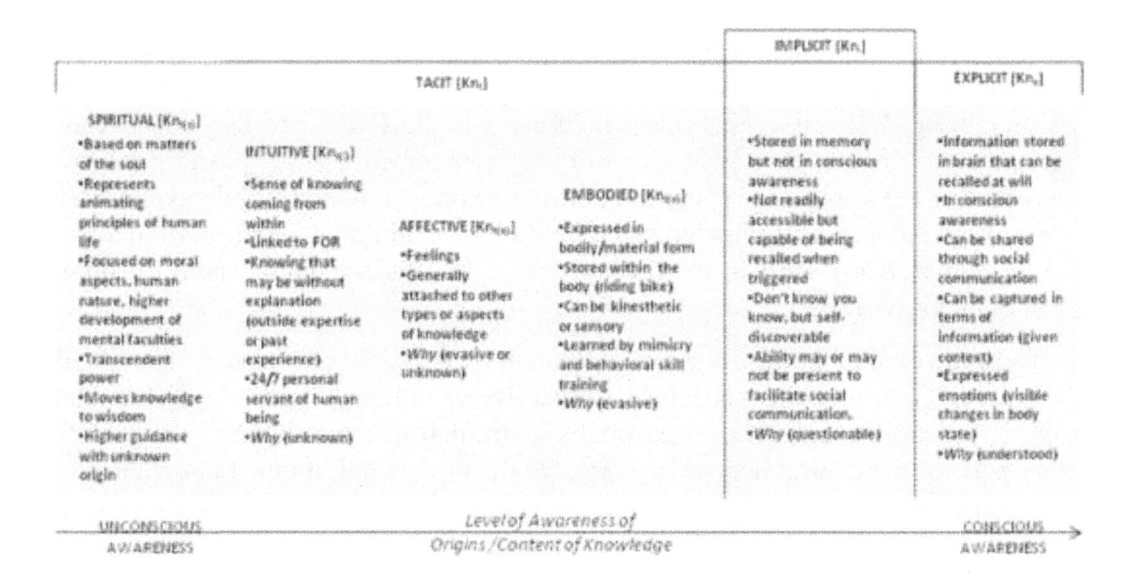

Figure 18-2. *Continuum of awareness of knowledge source/content.*

Embodied tacit knowledge is also referred to as somatic knowledge. Both kinesthetic and sensory, it can be represented in neuronal patterns stored within the body. *Kinesthetic* is related to the movement of the body and, while important to every individual every day of our lives, it is a primary focus for athletes, artists, dancers, kids and assembly-line workers. A commonly used example of tacit knowledge is knowledge of riding a bicycle. *Sensory*, by definition, is related to the five human senses through which information enters the body (sight, smell, hearing, touch and taste). An example is the smell of burning rubber from your car brakes while driving or the smell of hay in a barn. These odors can convey knowledge of whether the car brakes may need replacing (get them checked immediately), or whether the hay is mildewing (dangerous to feed horses, but fine for cows). These responses would be overt, bringing to conscious awareness the need to take effective action and driving that action to occur.

Intuitive tacit knowledge is the sense of knowing coming from inside an individual that may influence decisions and actions; yet the decision-maker or actor cannot explain *how* or *why* the action taken is the right one. The unconscious works around the clock with a processing capability many times greater than that at the conscious level. This is why as the world grows more complex, decision-makers will depend more and more on their intuitive tacit knowledge. But in order to use it, decision-makers must first be able to tap into their unconscious.

Affective tacit knowledge is connected to emotions and feelings, with emotions representing the external expression of some feelings. Feelings expressed as emotions become explicit (Damasio, 1994). Feelings that are not expressed—perhaps not even recognized—are those that fall into the area of affective tacit knowledge. Feelings as a form of knowledge have different characteristics than language or ideas, but they may lead to effective action because they can influence actions by their existence and connections with consciousness. When feelings come into conscious awareness they can play an informing role in decision-making, providing insights in a non-linguistic manner and thereby influencing decisions and actions. For example, a feeling (such as fear or an upset stomach) may occur every time a particular action is started which could prevent the decision-maker from taking that action.

Spiritual tacit knowledge can be described in terms of knowledge based on matters of the soul. The soul represents the animating principles of human life in terms of thought and action, specifically focused on its moral aspects, the emotional part of human nature, and higher development of the mental faculties (Bennet & Bennet, 2007c). While there is a "knowing" related to spiritual knowledge similar to intuition, this knowing does not include the experiential base of intuition, and it may or may not have emotional tags. The current state of the evolution of our understanding of spiritual knowledge is such that there are insufficient words to relate its transcendent power, or to define the role it plays in relationship to other tacit knowledge. Nonetheless, this area represents a form of higher guidance with unknown origin. Spiritual knowledge may be the guiding purpose, vision and values behind the creation and application of tacit knowledge. It may also be the road to moving information to knowledge and knowledge to wisdom (Bennet & Bennet, 2008d). In the context of this book, spiritual tacit knowledge represents the source of higher learning, helping decision-makers create and implement knowledge that has greater meaning and value for the common good.

Whether embodied, affective, intuitive or spiritual, tacit knowledge represents the bank account of the Self. The larger our deposits, the greater the interest, and the more we are prepared for co-evolving in a changing, uncertain and complex environment.

Associative Patterning

In Chapter 2 we introduced the concept of the mind as an associative patterner. While this material will not be repeated here, we wish to emphasize that the process of associative patterning is a process of Self, the continuous complexing and creation of knowledge that enables action in the context of the instant and for the situation at hand (Item 2-D and Item 7-C). In the ICALS Model, Self is the integrative feature of all five modes of learning, *with associative patterning the learning tool of the mind.*

Use of the Conscious Self

In Chapter 1 and as introduced at the beginning of this chapter, we have laid the groundwork for a working model of Self, which is woven throughout experiential learning. Building on this groundwork, we now look at the Self in terms of actions, that is, as reflected through unconscious effects as well as conscious awareness and choice based on an understanding of relationships among things and with our Self, which occurs in the prefrontal cortex as we observe our behaviors and emotions. We will build on the Seashore Use of Self Model (see Figure 18-3) to explore the area of conscious awareness, understanding and choice.

The Seashore Use of Self Model is highly consistent with Knowles four ways that an adult's experiences affect learning (Chapter 4), that is: (a) creating a wider range of individual differences; (b) providing a rich resource for learning; (c) creating biases that can inhibit or shape learning; and (d) providing grounding for the self-identity of adults (Knowles et al., 1998).

The Seashore Model proposes a framework that relates key factors that are important in maintaining and increasing our individual capacity as change agents, leaders, task facilitators, etc. The model considers the world as we perceive it and act on it, and the simultaneous or consequent, intentional or unintentional, change that occurs within ourselves. (Self as a agent of change is a focus of Chapter 23 and an element of the Knowing Framework described in Chapter 25.) As expressed in caricatures around the Self bubble at the left of the model, the Self is an integration of (at the unconscious level) the defensive Self, the shadow Self, the lost Self, and the robotic Self; and (at the conscious level) the performing Self, the creative Self, the beautiful Self and the evolving Self. Intentions, styles, patterns, habits, defenses and needs all contribute to the differentiation or individuation of Self.

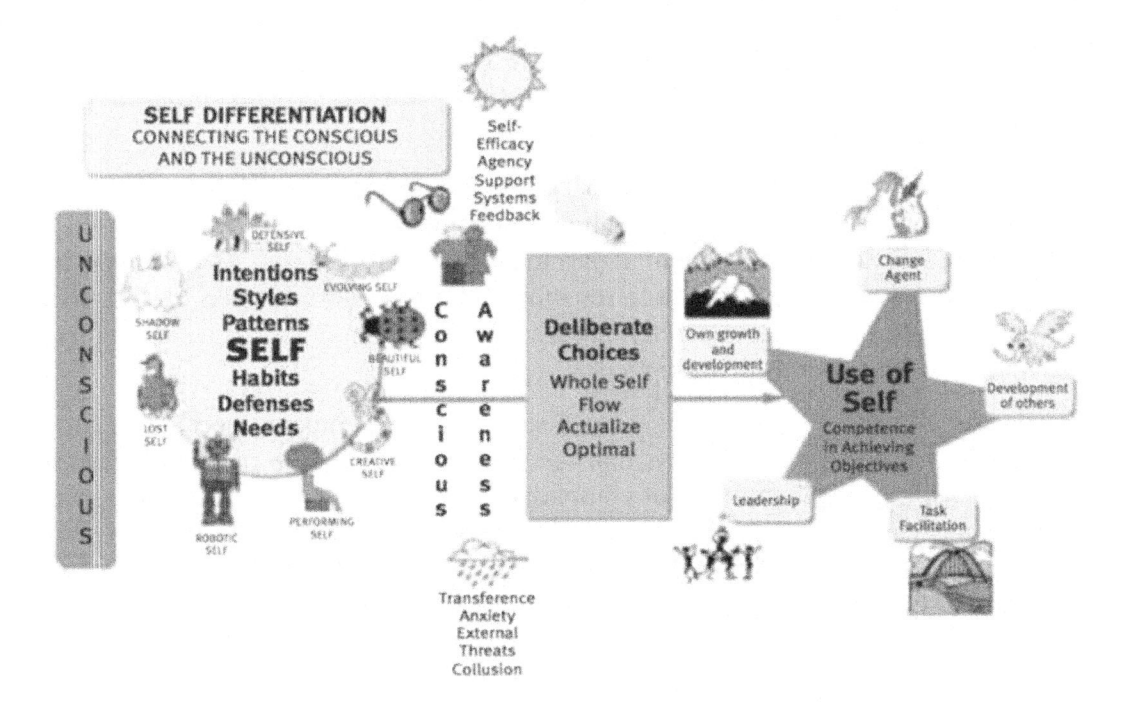

Figure 18-3. *The Seashore Use of Self Model* [1]

In this model, the individual's competence and effectiveness are functions of many elements, including self-efficacy agency, skills and the use of support systems to optimize those. Self-efficacy refers to an individual's belief that they can achieve desired ends (Item 10-B). Agency refers to the ability and capacity to act on those beliefs (knowledge). Support systems are the pool of resources (individuals, groups, organizations) that an individual can draw on selectively "to help one be at their best in moving in directions of their choice and to grow strong in the process" (Seashore et al., 2004, p. 58.).

Examples of potential barriers to conscious awareness are transference, anxiety, and external threats. Transference refers to the ability to perceive situations through the projection of oneself onto others, a process that can both potentially aid or interfere with understanding. Note that conscious awareness lays the groundwork for choice. Deliberate choices and the use of Self as a change agent—for leadership and development of others, and for task facilitation and personal development—requires an understanding of the connections and relationships among others and the Self.

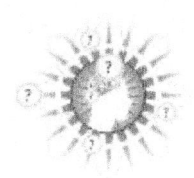

REFLECT:
When have I outwardly expressed my tacit knowledge?
Do I understand my biases?

The Story of Self

Human memories are story based. Memory recall is improved through temporal sequences of associative patterns such as stories and songs (Item 2-E). Written, oral and visual storytelling are sequential narratives in a serial fashion. As Hawkins (2004) explains that just as it is difficult to remember an entire story at once, the memory of a song is an excellent example of temporal sequences in memory. "You cannot imagine an entire song at once, only in sequence." (pp. 71-72)

While all experiences are not stories, stories are remembered because they come with many indices, multiple ways that the story is connected to memory. "The more indices, the greater the number of comparisons with prior experiences and hence the greater the learning." (Schank, 1995, p. 11) In order for memory to be effective, it must have not only the memories themselves (events, feelings, etc.), but also memory traces (or labels) that attach to previously stored memories. These indices can be decisions, conclusions, places, attitudes, beliefs, questions, etc.

One of the main jobs of consciousness is to tie our life together into a coherent story, a concept of Self (LeDoux, 1996). Moving through various life experiences, the individual singles out and accentuates what is significant and connects these events to historic events to create a narrative unity, what Long describes as a *fictionalized history*.

> [The] narrative unity which results from this process is not discovered; it is the result of selective attention, emphasis, dim remembrance, and possibly even forgetting. The person makes choices about the importance of persons and events, decides of their meanings, though there may only be a minimal awareness of the resulting order as a partially created one. These choices and decisions – like those of a novelist – are not arbitrary; they are guided by the desire for the "good story." The finished product is the "fictionalized" history of a life, neither a lie nor "the truth," but instead a work of imagination, evaluation and memory. (Long, 1986, pp. 75-92)

As introduced in Chapter 2 and mentioned in Chapter 9, the autobiographical Self—the idea of who we are, the image we build up of ourselves and where we fit socially—is built up over years of experience and constantly being remodeled, a product of continuous learning (Item 7-E). Recall that Damasio (1999) believes that much of this model is created by the unconscious. While this is undoubtedly true, it is the conscious mind that *perceives the idea of Self* and through active experimentation with objects and the external world is typically very aware of the perceived boundaries between the individual and the external world.

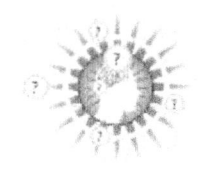

REFLECT:
Can I consciously change my level of stress?
What is my story?

It seems that evolution created the mind/brain to insure survival through its meaning-making capacity, not just its memory. For example, Hawkin's (2004) invariant forms, Sousa's (2006) point that we tend to remember things that have meaning, and the close ties between emotion, meaning, and remembering bring out aspects of the mind/brain/body that emphasize meaning (Item 3-B and Item 3-C). The narrative language and connective tissue of stories communicates the nature and shape and behavior of complex adaptive phenomena. This is because stories capture the "essence of living things, which are quintessentially complex phenomena, with multiple variables, unpredictable phase changes, and all of the characteristics that the mathematics of complexity has only recently begun to describe" (Denning, 200, p. 113). See Bennet & Bennet (2013) for an in-depth treatment of systems and complexity.

Schank (1995) goes so far as to measure intelligence in terms of the number of stories an individual has to tell, and in terms of the size of an individual's indexing and retrieval schema that provide a mechanism for determining what is relevant to current experiences, and the ability to search and find what is relevant. This is consistent with the power of the mind as an associative patterner.

Intelligent activity represents a perfect state of interaction where intent, purpose, direction, values and expected outcomes are clearly understood and communicated among all parties, reflecting wisdom and achieving a higher truth (Bennet et al., 2015a). Knowledge in service to intelligent activity. Because the effectiveness of all knowledge is context sensitive and situation dependent, knowledge is shifting and changing in concert with our environment and the demands placed upon us (Item 7-C). The incompleteness of knowledge that is never perfect serves as an incentive for the continuous human journey of learning and the exploration of ideas.

To understand how to measure intelligence, Schank (1995) outlines seven dimensions of intelligence: data finding, data manipulation, comprehension, explanation, planning, communication and integration. These seven dimensions of intelligence affect all five areas of the use of Self in the Seashore Model, that is, as a change agent, in development of others, for task facilitation, for personal growth and development, and for leadership. While we will use Schank's seven dimensions to help define the space of intelligence, and quite briefly describe these dimensions from the perspective of this book, we encourage the reader to explore Schank's work for an explanation of these dimensions from his perspective.

The first dimension of intelligence is data finding. Data finding is built on a system of unconscious labeling in response to thinking about an experience. Mulling over an experience (Item 2-J and Item 6-D) and having a strong emotional feeling about the experience (Item 3-B) builds additional indices for future recall. Further, in the associative patterning process, the richer an individual's past experiences and the more interests a person has, the more associations are possible. Schank equates this level of intelligence with the ability to search and bring up stories that are not superficially, or obviously connected to a current situation. As he says, "Higher intelligence depends upon complex perception and labeling" (Schank, 1995, p. 224).

The second dimension of intelligence is data manipulation. The mind/brain stores pictures in invariant form (Item 2-A and Item 7-B). This means that when looking at a friend or colleague that maybe the 15-20% of the features that define that individual are remembered, not the whole. Then, when the individual comes into awareness the remaining part of the picture is created in the moment at hand. Schank considers partial matching as part of everyday intelligence. An example is seeing someone who has just had a haircut, recognizing something different but still recognizing the person. Stories can also achieve partial matches with other stories. The high end of intelligence occurs when an old story is adapted to create a new story that becomes a resource to creatively cope with new situations.

The third dimension of intelligence is comprehension. There are levels of comprehension. The high level of intelligence is when meaning can be perceived in a new story even though there is no old story to which it is related, that is, finding coherence where there is no obvious coherence.

The fourth dimension of intelligence is explanation. Schank relates this to the ability to explain our failures, with the high level of intelligence considered the ability to recover from these failures and use them to prevent future failures. This entails finding the predictive rules within a failure and having the ability to apply these to future scenarios (Item 7-A). Schank contents that, "The more intelligent you are the more you will fail. Ultimately the value of failure and the explanation of failure is to come up with new rules that predict how events will turn out" (Schank, 1995, p. 232). Considering our neuroscience findings, we expand this idea of intelligence as explanation to include a deeper understanding of how things work, coupled to the discovery process inextricably connected to creativity and innovation. We now recognize the plasticity of the mind/brain and that what we focus on very much affects the co-creation of our reality (Item 11-C). Thus, in business, while certainly failures need to be acknowledged and addressed, the old methods of focusing on failures give way to the appreciative inquiry model that pushes us to discover what is right and focus and expand from that point of understanding (Item 10-B). See Bennet et al. (2015b).

The fifth dimension of intelligence is planning. At the first level of intelligence, we execute plans that are copies from others; at the second level, we adapt these plans to current situations; at the third level, we create and execute plans of our own. This higher level relates to personal creativity. Bodin (1991) breaks creative thought (or creative people) into two types: *P-creative* (psychological or personal) and *H-creative* (historical). P-creative ideas are fundamentally novel with respect to the individual mind, the person who has them, and H0-creative ideas are historically grounded, fundamentally novel with respect to the whole of recorded human history. Her point is that the H-creative ideas, which by definition are also P-creative, are the ones that are socially recognized as creative, but P-creative ideas are possible in every human being (Item 5-F). Thus, following this model, each level of intelligence in this dimension would include some amount of P-creativity.

The sixth dimension of intelligence is communication. For humans, communication is very situation dependent, intended to make a point the teller wishes to communicate. (There is a deeper discussion of context under the heading of "Conversation" in Chapter 22.) The extension of this ability is in the creation of new stories and the elaboration of old ones (Item 9-A). Schank sees the ability to go beyond simple, direct descriptions of what has happened as a higher level of intelligence. "[Intelligent people] have learned how to *generalize*, *crystallize*, and *elaborate* so that they tell stories that express insights not obvious in the original story." (Schank, 1995, p. 234) While Schank sees this crystallization-generalization aspect of intelligence as a learned skill, it is very dependent upon having stories to tell in the first place! Thus lived experience would appear to support a higher level of intelligence in this dimension.

The seventh dimension of intelligence is integration. At the first level, we all understand stories that we have been told. This element deals with not only what is remembered but also what is in the unconscious since integration is involved in the selection of what will be remembered and what is of insignificance and therefore not remembered (that is, minimal memory traces, most likely with little emotion attached). The higher level of this intelligence includes curiosity, where an individual goes beyond integrating the current with the remembered (Item 7-D) to *seeking new understanding*; this would also include an element of creativity (Item 5-D, Item 5-G and Item 5-H). The significance of integration to perceived intelligence, however, is very environmentally driven. For instance, a child who embraces everything new about computers and consistently works to integrate the current and remembered will be considered more intelligent in today's world than a child with similar capabilities who is focusing on motorcycles.

As Schank concludes,

> So, the issue with respect to stories is this: We know them, find them, reconsider them, manipulate them, use them to understand the world and to operate in the world, adapt them to new purposes, tell them in new ways, and we invent them. We live in a world of stories. Our ability to utilize these stories in novel ways is a hallmark of what we consider to be intelligence. (Schank, 1995, p. 241)

As we become aware of our autobiography, that is, from the viewpoint of the seven dimensions of intelligence, as we integrate the experiences, reflections, comprehensions, social engagements and actions of our story, we move to the position of observing the observer, floating above the drama of life and soaking in the richness of a lifetime of experiential learning. Is age the determinate of this aggregate and, accordingly, of the seventh dimension of intelligence? We think not. Short periods of time can be experientially rich, and the diversity of mind reflects the diversity of humanity. We can be sure, however, that every living creature is at some level experiencing and, hopefully, learning.

In Chapter 19 we look at the mind/brain/body connection. Chapter 20 explores the concept of Self co-evolving with the environment, Chapter 21 provides an in-depth example of the impact of the environment on learning, and Chapter 22 and Chapter 23 explore Self as a social learner and the focus of change.

Chapter 19
The Mind/Brain/Body Connection

One of the greatest gifts of being human is the innate ability to change the structure of our brain with our thoughts, which in turn influences the creation of new thoughts (Item 11-C). What does this mean? It is quite literal; we are co-creators of our Self's! Through the miracle of what we now call neuroplasticity, the human brain changes throughout our lives. Recall that the brain is the physical structure of atoms and molecules and the mind is the totality of neuronal patterns within this physical structure, that is, patterns of neurons, their connections (synapses) and the strength of those connections. It is exciting to note that this complex, interwoven and interdependent system that is the mind/brain/body is continuously changing, never repeating a pattern!

In a similar circular feedback loop of thinking and feeling, and as introduced in Chapter 6, our health impacts the workings of our mind/brain/body, and our mind/brain/body affects our health. More specifically, the health of each component of the mind/brain/body affects the health of the other two as well. See Figure 19-1.

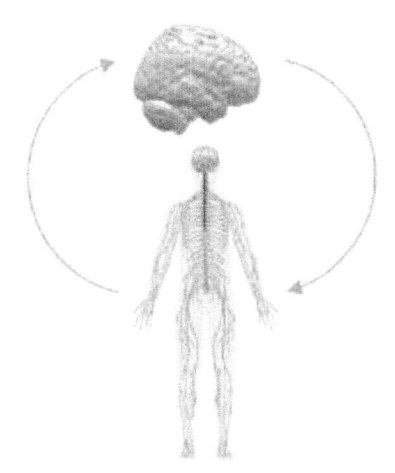

Figure 19-1. *The life-giving loop of learning and change.*

Fundamentally, developed through evolution, the brain influences the behavior of the body's cells. Thus, the brain is the central information processor for a distributed nerve network, coordinating the flow of behavior regulating signal molecules (Lipton, 2005). Lipton says to consider this when we blame our cells for health issues we experience. Recall that *what we think and believe impacts our physical bodies*. This is the wonderful discovery of neural plasticity—the ability of neurons to change their structure and relationships based on environmental demands and personal decisions and actions (Item 11-A).

Emotions

Everything is connected within the mind/brain/body in terms of energy through the arterial and veno systems. What becomes significant is the strength of neuronal connections in the central nervous system or what could be called the guidance system. Emotions play a large role in this process (Item 3-G). In this context, emotions are considered signals or labels that are, for the most part, generated unconsciously. An emotional tag is linked to all information coming into the brain. As Lipton explains,

> The evolution of the limbic system provided a unique mechanism that converted the chemical communication signals into sensations that could be experienced by all of the cells in the community. Our conscious mind experiences these *signals* as emotions. (Lipton, 2005, p. 131)

As part of the evolving learning system of Self, memories, and the emotional tags that gage the importance of those memories, become part of an individual's everyday life. The stronger the emotional tag, the greater the strength of the neuronal connections (LeDoux, 1996) and the easier to recall (Item 3-B). As Kluwe states, "Often we experience that emotionally arousing events result in better recollection of memories. It appears to us that we will not forget certain events in our life whenever they are accompanied by very pleasant or fearful emotions." (Kluwe et al., 2003, p. 19) This is true because *emotions have priority in our stream of consciousness*. Through evolution (based on survival needs) our brain has been wired such that the connections from the emotional systems to the cognitive systems are much stronger than the connections from the cognitive systems to the emotional systems. The entire body is involved in emotions (Item 3-E). As LeDoux describes, "Emotions easily bump mundane events out of awareness, but non emotional events (like thoughts) do not so easily displace emotions from the mental spotlight." (Kluwe et al., 2003, p. 51) Thus we cannot "manage" Self without an understanding of emotions, which can be considered the energetic life's blood of the learning system.

> As part of the evolving learning system of Self, memories, and the emotional tags that gage the importance of those memories, become part of an individual's everyday life.

REFLECT:
What new learning would I like to acquire?
When I remember events do I feel the emotions I felt during those events?

Brain Health

Brain health, as commonly labeled, addresses how to sustain a clear, active mind. As a key part of your overall health, it suggests the ability to concentrate, remember, plan, learn and make decisions. "It's being able to draw on the strengths of your brain—information management, logic, judgment, perspective and wisdom." (Harden, 2015, p. 1).

So, what can you do about it? The Brain Health Educator Guide put out by ACL (the Administration for Community Living), NIH (the National Institutes of Health) and CDC (the Centers for Disease Control and Prevention) cites possible risks or threats to brain health as: some medicines, or improve use of them; smoking; excessive use of alcohol; heart disease, diabetes, and other health problems; poor diet; insufficient sleep; lack of physical activity; and little social activity and being alone most of the time (ACL et al., 2015). While this makes sense also from a general health perspective, there are specific effects directly related to the brain. For example, the use of alcohol can slow or impair communication among brain cells and cause long-term changes to balance, memory and emotions, coordination and body temperature. Sleep apnea can lead to injury, high blood pressure, stroke or memory loss; all affecting brain health.

Note the criticality of social activity, that is, staying connected (Item 8-A and Item 9-D). The guide says that people who have meaningful activities feel happier and healthier (Item 8-B), and that social activities are directly linked to reduced risk of health problems such as dementia. This is not surprising since good relationships reduce stress (Item 9-A).

As we see from the Brain Health Educator Guide description above, there are increasingly wide-ranging and deep considerations when addressing brain health. In the past, there has been a tendency to view the brain and brain issues from a considerably separate viewpoint with general causal relationships to the rest of the body. Going back far enough, prevailing perspectives about the brain are rather humorous. Rita Carter, a prolific science and medical writer and brain lecturer describes the phenomenon this way:

> The human brain is like nothing else. As organs go, it is not especially prepossessing–3lb (1.4kg) or so of rounded corrugated flesh with a consistency somewhere between jelly and cold butter. It doesn't expand and shrink like the lungs, pump like the heart, or secrete visible material like the bladder. If you sliced

> off the top of someone's head and peered inside, you wouldn't see much happening at all. (Carter et.al., 2009, p. 6)

It certainly doesn't sound all that appealing! Just to make sure we get the point, Carter continues with several historical examples that demonstrated the relative unimportance of brains.

> When they mummified their dead, the ancient Egyptians scooped out the brains and threw them away, yet carefully preserved the heart. The ancient Greek philosopher, Aristotle, thought the brain was a radiator for cooling the blood. Rene Descartes, the French scientist, gave it a little more respect, concluding that is was a sort of antenna by which the spirit might commune with the body. It is only now that the full wonder of the brain is being realized. (Carter et al., 2009, p. 6)

With the nearly exponential unfolding of kaleidoscopic information and knowledge about the brain as we entered this century, a keen interest in brain health emerged. We use the term kaleidoscopic here because the count of annual research articles is in the tens of thousands from over 20 branches of neuroscience alone. Add to that a consideration for the consilience approach as introduced in Chapter 3 and what possibilities are there? What will emerge from research in such areas as quantum brain dynamics (QBD) where the brain is addressed in terms of quantum field theory? Or, more directly to the point of brain health; what can be gained by researching the brain's use of phytochemicals?

For example, nutrition and hydration have been directly tied to learning, specifically, "making connections, finding meaning and solving problems are learning tasks that require lightning-fast electrical impulses between areas of the brain" (Norman, 2015). When you are learning a biochemical process is occurring, and this process is dependent on the internal environment of the brain. For example, the formation of memory actually requires reshaping of the cell networks, a physical growth process. Neurons require good fats, protein, complex carbohydrates, water and micronutrients such as vitamins, minerals and phytonutrients, all of which are used to drive learning functions (Norman, 2015).

As you may know, phytochemicals are not nutrients, rather they are bioactive chemical components found in plants that are studied for their benefits to human health. But, wait a minute, it is too hard to keep up! We Googled "phytochemicals and the brain" and found 542,000 results in 90 seconds! Let us take, as an example, the first article found in the search on phytochemicals and the brain. The research article is entitled "Neuroprotective potential of phytochemicals" and reports research conducted by G. Phani Kumar and Farhath Khanum at the Biochemistry and Nutrition Division of the Defence Food Research Lab in Mysore, India Their research abstract begins with the following description:

> Cognitive dysfunction is a major health problem in the 21st century, and many neuropsychiatric disorders and neurodegenerative disorders, such as schizophrenia, depression, Alzheimer's Disease dementia, cerebrovascular impairment, seizure disorders, head injury and Parkinsonism, can be severely

functionally debilitating in nature. In course of time, a number of neurotransmitters and signaling molecules have been identified which have been considered as therapeutic targets. Conventional as well as newer molecules have been tried against these targets. Phytochemicals from medicinal plants play a vital role in maintaining the brain's chemical balance by influencing the function of receptors for the major inhibitory neurotransmitters. In traditional practice of medicine, several plants have been reported to treat cognitive disorders. In this review paper, we attempt to throw some light on the use of medicinal herbs to treat cognitive disorders. (Kumar & Khanum, 2012, p. 81)

Given the above brief quote on the specific subject of phytochemicals, one can imagine the magnitude and the depth of the research that is continuously forthcoming. Furthermore, this is occurring in an environment that increasingly appreciates the interconnectedness of the mind/brain/body and their function as subsystems of a fully integrated human system. A good measure of what drives this level of information and knowledge productivity is a lengthy taxonomy or listing of research issues that is driven by general categories of inquiry such as what impacts and strengthens the health of the brain, the mind, and the body as a host of the brain? What lifestyle practices will make a difference? What healthcare, medical, and personal coaching resources can one use? What diet, supplements, and pharmaceuticals should be considered?

As all of this new brain health information and knowledge comes to us at the speed of the Knowledge Age, how will we avail ourselves of what will be of greatest value? A resource that can help with this challenge is knowledge enablers. *Brain knowledge enablers facilitate acquiring, organizing, evaluating, and deciding about information and knowledge in order to create the capacity to take effective action.* Table 19-1 is a "toolkit" of brain knowledge enablers that you may find useful.

To help with your use of **My ICALS BrainKnow Toolkit**, additional information about several of the knowledge enablers is briefly discussed here. First, relating to research participation. We are at the beginning of what is a major breakthrough in medical research participation. Historically, health researchers would send out tens of thousands of invites to participate in research only to receive back a few hundred acceptances. With Apple's new ResearchKit, announced March 15, 2015, ten times the participation may be achievable in just days. Apple describes ResearchKit as an open source framework allowing researchers and developers of medical research to create powerful applications. It enables the easy creation of "visual consent flows, real-time dynamic active tasks, and surveys using a variety of customizable modules that you can build upon and share with the community" (Apple, 2015). Further, since it works seamlessly with Health Kit, researchers have access to even more relevant data such as daily step counts, calorie use and heart rate. ResearchKit and HealthKit are trademarks of Apple Inc. And, of course, they are compatible with the iPhone!

Hundreds of millions of people around the world have an iPhone in their pocket. Each one is equipped with powerful processors and advanced sensors that can track movement, take measurements, and record information — functions that are perfect for medical studies. The sheer number of them being used across the globe opens up new possibilities for researchers. With ResearchKit, researchers can easily create apps that take advantage of iPhone features to gather new types of data on a scale never available before. (Apple, 2015)

Table 19-1. *My ICALS BrainKnow Toolkit©*

Knowledge Enablers	How To Guidelines
Expanding the Self The Intelligent Complex Adaptive Learning System (ICALS) A New Adult Learning Theory	As I use the ICALS Theory and Model, I will adapt it to my level of interest. I may use it for professional or personal purposes. Whichever the case, it will empower my ability to explore, to discover, to learn, and to enjoy the journey.
My Tool List	This is my list of brain health tools that I want to learn about and/or use. I can start with the neuroscience areas and items in the ICALS Model. This list will grow over time.
My Glossary	These are the key terms that I want to have at hand. The ICALS Glossary will get me started.
My Online Resources	This is my list of resources that I will use to keep me informed about brain health research. I will watch the websites of brain health research centers that are doing solid research. I also want to keep an eye on the ACL/NIH/CDC online brain health education services and The Brain Initiative website hosted at NIH.
My Researchers and Authors	This is my list of researchers, scientists, thought leaders and authors who have solid credentials.
My Research Participation	These are research areas that I would like to watch for and participate in.
My Health Care Providers	Medical care professionals who support my BrainKnow interests and needs.
My Medical Information	My personal medical information that establishes baselines and trends. Most of my personal information will be maintained in separate online medical record systems. This will tell where to find my information and what tests I may want to have.
My BrainKnow Toolbox	The repository of My ICALS BrainKnow Toolkit. My cloud service will be available on "Any Device 24/7 Anywhere". Here is where I can store any of my BrainKnow information for lifelong learning and use. Toolkit folders are shareable for collaboration. Dropbox and Evernote are examples of suitable Cloud service options.

Again, Apple is providing this technology as open source, available to Microsoft, Samsung, Google and other companies wishing to support this new research capability. David Pogue, Yahoo Tech founder, and Emmy Award-winning technology correspondent for CBS Sunday Morning and monthly writer for *Scientific American*, provides an example of this new research capability which uses tests for Parkinson's patients normally conducted in a medical office and makes it available on a daily basis. (Pogue, 2015)

> ...Apple worked with five medical institutions, associated with places like Harvard, Stanford, and Mount Sinai in New York City, to come up with the first five ResearchKit-based apps. They represent studies of asthma, diabetes, heart disease, Parkinson's, and breast cancer. (You can enroll in the heart, breast cancer, and Parkinson's studies even if you don't have those diseases. The researchers will use your data as a control.) ...The mPower app for Parkinson's is a great example. Each day, it asks you to participate in certain activities. One asks you to say "ahhh" into the microphone for as long as you can on a single breath. One asks you to tap the screen alternately with two fingers as fast as you can. One tracks your short-term memory by testing to see if you can remember a pattern of flowers lighting up. (Pogue, 2015) [See Figure 19-2.]

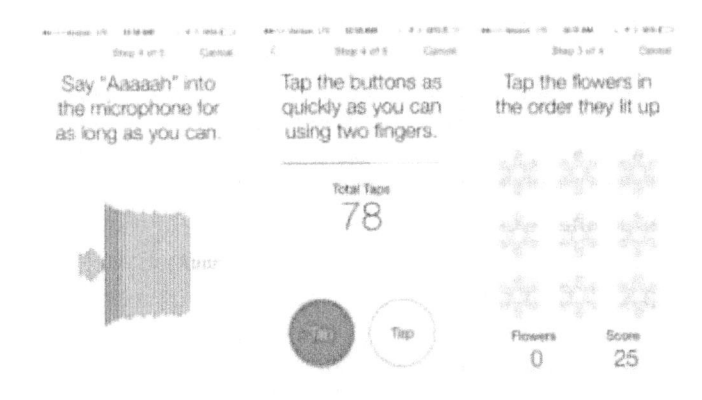

Figure 19-2. *Sample screens in ResearchKit-based apps. Open-source. (Pogue, 2015)*

As an example of staying abreast of the latest findings in nutrition and health, there is a not-for-profit magazine called *Life Extension*, published monthly, that provides articles on current research and specific findings related to health and longevity. Life Extension makes and sells vitamins at reduced rates, and uses their profits to fund research projects. Vitamins are important because after the age of 35 (or around there) our bodies may not make all of the vitamins we need. Their articles are detailed, highly professional, well referenced, and at the end many of them say: *If you have any questions on the scientific content of this article, please call a Life Extension Healthcare Advisor at* .... Similarly, a number of medical schools publish reports in the form of small books in their areas of expertise. These books are state-of-the-art; for example, there is an excellent free booklet from Johns Hopkins on how to reduce memory loss.

An interesting twist on personal life data gathering looks to the Quantified Self movement, which is also called lifelogging, body hacking and personal informatics. Using technologies such as wearable computing, individuals are able to track different aspects of their lives such as inputs (calories and carbs, or the quality of air being breathed), states (arousal and blood oxygen levels) and performance (response to mental and physical exercise, etc.) We are able to quantify biometrics that we never even knew existed! As Wikipedia (2015) describes, we can track our insulin and cortisol levels, sequence DNA, and see what microbial cells inhabit our bodies!

The Quantified Self movement uses technologies and processes for health-related functions with many related directly to brain health such as sleep patterns and sleep coaching, mood logs, qualitative information on over 500 medical conditions, etc. Certain of these resources may serve you well if you plug them into "My Research Participation" of the *BrainKnow Toolkit*. Obviously, brain health monitoring is becoming more doable. As Chapman, founder and chief director of the Center for BrainHealth at the University of Texas at Dallas, observes:

> I predict that preventive medicine will put brain health benchmark evaluations at the top of the list of best practices very soon. A brain health benchmark establishes a cognitive index of brain performance to determine current level of function and identity strengths and weaknesses. It allows you to monitor changes in your cognitive fitness as you age. There is also a proactive element to having a benchmark, since it allows you to strengthen areas of weakness and continue to build resilience to guard against cognitive decline. In short, a cognitive assessment will help you better understand how your brain works, what it needs to be more fit, and ideas about how to achieve higher brain performance. (Chapman, 2013, p. 38)

What we are witnessing is a substantial increase in the ability and in the interest in managing our own health care, including brain health. Let's go back to the ACL/NIH/CDC website and take a close look at their online document Brain Health Key Facts and Resources, (ACL NIH, CDC, 2014).

See
http://www.acl.gov/Get_Help/BrainHealth/docs/BrainHealthKeyFactsResources.pdf

This document provides a useful introduction to brain health topics. Each topic is linked to a related page that has additional content with links to the more detailed information. For example, take a look at the page related to Sleep Apnea and the detailed information that is provided. This type of guide offers a viable overview of pertinent information about various brain health topics. Hopefully, this type of information resources will be continuously updated, since we anticipate that new information will emerge at an unbelievable rate. We would also expect that the guides will need to expand in terms of scope. To that end, we foresee guides in this category that will increasingly address brain health topics that accelerate learning. To that end, let's briefly explore the impact health has on learning. This is the direct relationship that Cozolino (2006) sees between optimal health and the functioning and increasingly advanced levels of growth and integration.

Physical and Mental Exercise

As detailed in Chapter 14, physical exercise plays a significant role in the mental and physical operation of the mind/brain (Item 12-C and Item 12-D). Exercise increases blood flow, bringing glucose as an energy source for neuron operation, provides oxygen to take up the toxic electrons, and stimulates the proteins that keep neurons connecting with each other (Medina, 2008), improving the connections among brain cells and heart health as well as reducing the risk of dementia.

> The relationship between physical exercise and the brain is direct.

The relationship between physical exercise and the brain is direct. Neurons communicate using the process of neurotransmission. Electrical impulses trigger the release of messenger chemicals (neurotransmitters), which then travel across the synapse sending information to the next cell. These neurotransmitters connect verbal, emotional, visual and kinesthetic memories, and regulate levels of alertness, all correlated with the learner's current mood and behavior (Norman, 2015).

Exercise stimulates neurogenesis, that is, the growth of new neurons, exerts a protective effect on hippocampal neurons, and increases the blood flow, providing additional oxygen to the brain (see Chapter 6 for details). There is a caveat, of course, and that is it appears the effects of exercise on neurogenesis and learning is highly dependent on volition (Item 12-A). Voluntary exercise is characterized by the absence of stress and brain rhythms called theta waves (Begley, 2007). This is an important finding.

At any age, mental exercise has a global positive effect on the brain (Item 13-A). If you exercise all areas of the brain you can increase the health of all areas of the brain. Quite literally, in terms of brain activity, the phrase *use it or lose it* applies. The best mental exercise to slow the effects of aging is new learning and doing things you've never done before (Item 13-B).

For example, not only using your mind for your everyday work, but playing games, reading books, doing cross-word puzzles, and driving a taxicab in your spare time! In a lengthy study, Macguire, Woollett and Spiers found that "years of navigation experience correlated with hippocampal gray matter volume ... with right posterior gray matter volume increasing and anterior volume decreasing with more navigation experience." (Macguire et al., 2006, p. 1091.) The study took place in London, where cab drivers must complete the Knowledge of London Examination System, which requires memorizing a map of the capital (some 25,000 streets and thousands of landmarks, including the order of theaters on Shaftesbury Avenue). It is interesting to note that the example often takes 12 attempts to pass. This intense learning causes structural changes in the brain, which affects memory and increases the volume of nerve cells in the hippocampus. As can be seen, there is a direct correlation between physical and mental exercise and the operation of the mind/brain, which impacts both the conscious and unconscious processes.

Anxiety and Stress

As detailed in Chapter 13, anxiety/stress can both aid and interfere with learning, which is highly dependent on the level of arousal of the learner. Too little arousal and there is no motivation; too much arousal and stress takes over and reduces learning. Maximum learning occurs when there is a moderate level of arousal (Item 3-A). This initiates neural plasticity (Item 11-D) by increasing the production of neurotransmitters and neural growth hormones, which in turn facilitate neural connections and cortical organization.

For each individual there is at any given time an optimum level of stress that facilitates learning (Cozolino & Sprokay, 2006) (Item 4-F). Excitement—as a form of arousal—can serve as a strong motivation to drive people to learn, but not so strong that it becomes high stress moving to anxiety. For example, Merry sees adaptation not as a basic transformative change, but as having a new range of possibilities. When people are in increasingly uncertain and stressful situations they may somehow, through resilience, find new and novel forms of adaptation to responds to those situations (Merry, 1995). In other words, with a stressful external environment that represents external threats, people will naturally tend to find ways of reacting and adapting to that environment.

> For each individual there is at any given time an optimum level of stress that facilitates learning.

Plotting the learning rate on the vertical axis and stress level along the horizontal axis, we get an inverted "U" (see Figure 19-3.) The arousal/stress level, located at the center of the inverted "U", challenges the learner but does not make the learner fearful of failure or embarrassment (Akil et al., 1999). This optimal level is context sensitive and content dependent upon the situation, and is also influenced by the individual learner's history. To optimize learning in a given situation, a learner needs to understand the level of arousal/stress that challenges the individual to learn but does not reduce that learning because of fear.

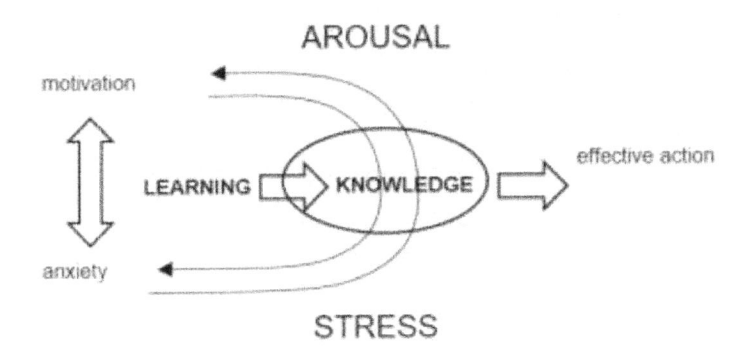

Figure 19-3. *The optimal level of anxiety/stress facilitates learning.*

Individuals can consciously change their level of response to stress (Item 4-C). Stress serves as an active monitoring system that constantly compares current events to past experiences (as part of the associative patterning process). Thus, in anticipating the outcomes of some planned action, an individual can think about past examples of similar situations and estimate the problems and potential issues (Item 7-A), that is, what stress may occur as a result of the action. As we will further explore below, *awareness and understanding of connections enable choice.*

Beliefs play a large role in this process. Beliefs change how we perceive the world, and our biology adapts to those beliefs (Lipton, 2005). As detailed in Chapter 13, belief systems can reduce stress through reducing uncertainty (Item 4-D). Note that beliefs are a cognitive process. They are built up over time as similar situations or patterns repeat themselves and are stored in invariant form at the highest levels of the neocortex.

REFLECT:
What mental exercises do I enjoy?
Can I consciously change my level of stress?

Aging

[A personal addendum from the principal author, Dr. David Bennet, who at this writing is 81 years young.]

How old do you want to be when you die?

Thinking about one's own death is hard, and most of the time we avoid the issue by not discussing the subject at all. Being a fairly intelligent human, we automatically believe we will live to a ripe old age. So, when asked how long we expect to live, we answer with a smile something like this, "I'm going to live to be 100." or "I will live long enough to see my grandchildren grow up."

While avoiding the topic is understandable, this may not be the smartest thing to do. Why? Simply because there are things you can do along life's path to increase the probability of a long life—if, and only if, you *choose* to do so. While there are no guarantees that come with birth, every thought you think, feeling you feel and action you take has the potential to affect the quality and longevity of your life!

And it's more than eating vegetables and fruits, exercising, avoiding drugs and smoking and moderating your alcohol consumption, all the things I was warned against in *my* younger years. Not to say those things aren't good ideas. For example, available data indicates that smokers die ten years younger than non-smokers. Smoke is harmful to our lungs (as well as affecting our brains), and lungs are essential for life. While everyone has the right to make their own choices, it's pretty clear that by understanding the broader, longer and deeper consequences of our behaviors—and making wise choices based on that understanding—you can make a huge difference. Moreover, you will find that any of the things that increase your brain health are very satisfying and bring new avenues of enjoyable activities to your daily life.

Many topics that we have addressed in this book fall under this same umbrella. This is why learning throughout life is so important, and with the potential offered by our mind/brain/body connection, perhaps we as a humanity have just begun to recognize the power of our Self's.

Final Thoughts

A common thread running throughout this section—throughout this book—is that **we as humans have a great deal of choice regarding our lives, and technologies and sciences are developing to support that choice**. In the area of personalized medicine, we are developing new tools to improve screening, diagnosis and treatment selection. Technologies to improve performance are used by professional sports leagues and elite military forces. The Neuroscience Imaging Center at UC San Francisco is developing therapeutic gaming that improves the cognitive functions. In other words, the boundaries between what it is to be human and the technologies that we develop are blurring.

In the next chapter we look at the Self co-evolving with the environment, and Chapter 21 provides an in-depth example by exploring the close relationship of the mind/brain and music.

Chapter 20
Co-Evolving with the Environment

The Self is a complex adaptive system. Complex adaptive systems are partially ordered systems that unfold and evolve through time. They are mostly self-organizing, while continuously learning and adapting. To survive, they are always scanning the environment, trying new approaches, creating new ideas, observing the outcomes, and changing the way they operate. In order to continuously adapt, they must operate in perpetual disequilibrium, which results in some unpredictable behavior. Having nonlinear relationships, complex adaptive systems create global properties that are called emergent because they seem to emerge from the multitude of elements and their relationships (Bennet & Bennet, 2013).

While the term co-evolve is used to describe the interdependent relationship of a host and parasite, it is quite appropriate to describe the symbiotic relationship between Self and its environment. Co-evolve refers to adaptation, and adaptation cannot occur without learning. Adaptation is the process by which a system has and applies knowledge to improve its ability to survive and grow through internal adjustments. System adaptation may be responsive, internally adjusting to external forces, or it may be proactive, internally changing so that it can influence the external environment. The Self does both. The environment is the region outside the boundary of a system; since the environment may also be considered as a system, it is sometimes referred to as the supra-system. All open systems have inputs and outputs consisting of material, energy, or information. In essence, they transform their inputs into outputs that satisfy internal purpose and environmental needs. Learning—the process of creating knowledge—uses incoming information from the environment to produce knowledge, the capacity (potential or actual) to take effective action.

> The Self co-evolves with its environment. Co-evolve refers to adaptation, and adaptation cannot occur without learning.

To help build a deeper understanding of the relationship of Self and the perceived external environment, we will first explore, from different frames of reference, the role of Self in creating reality, assuming the role of co-creator as we engage in a continuous loop of acting and learning. Second, we will look at the impact of enriched environments on learning, providing an in-depth treatment of music as an example.

Co-Creating Our Reality

As a child, that means getting a stomachache when you eat too many jelly doughnuts on your Saturday morning shopping jaunt with your dad. As a teenager, that means getting a report card that reflects the effort you've put into your homework. As an expectant mother or father, that means the looming responsibility of parenthood. But, as the years pass and the Self experiences life, reality becomes far richer and far more meaningful.

As you read these words, the information you are receiving is not an attribute of the letters or words themselves. The **print** on this page is not information, it *transmits* information. The letters and words on this page are symbols, which have learned and agreed-upon meanings connected with them. Similarly, when we speak to each other the actual words convey information. Though thoughts and feelings may also be communicated, they are quite different things than the words themselves.

Feelings, thoughts and mental images serve as the medium of exchange for creating our reality (Item 11-A). These feelings, thoughts and mental images are derived through a sense of knowing, a deep personal, subjective sense that an idea or thought is important and, when connected with other ideas or thoughts through associative patterning, insights and understanding of both ourselves and our surrounding world emerge. Knowing, or having knowledge of, has the same relationship to what is often called objective reality as that of subject and object (Bolles, 1991). Knowing is to *perceive or understand* as fact or truth while objective reality is *composed* of facts or truths, the state or quality of being real, or that which exists independently of ideas concerning it. Of course, as will be discerned shortly, that can never be entirely the case. The frame from which we understand objective reality is limited by our personal experiences, beliefs and knowledge. A deeper treatment of knowing is in Chapter 25.

> The frame from which we understand what we perceive as objective reality is limited by our personal experiences, beliefs and knowledge.

The word "limits" is often perceived in a negative connotation, but this is not necessarily the case. When referring to ideas, the limits imposed by defining our ideas within a framework helps develop a deeper understanding within that bounded domain, assists in the sharing of that understanding, and spurs on the emergence of new ideas, some even beyond the framework. In other words, limits can offer the opportunity for learning and the emergence of new ideas. A dramatic example of the value of limits can be found in the use of information technology. By placing limits (such as standards and protocols) on information technology, we are able to achieve broader interoperability among different technologies, giving more people access to more data and information.

In like manner, the symbiotic relationship between knowledge and what we perceive as objective reality can be highly productive by allowing our imaginative subjective knowledge to expand and play with ideas that may then extend our knowledge of objective reality (Emig, 1983). For instance, Einstein imagined he was riding on a light wave as he developed the general theory of relativity—which changed the way all of science understood the universe (Item 11-C). It is the imagination of artists that creates a painting with the potential of expanding hundreds of viewer's understanding and appreciation of the world. For example, consider Leonardo da Vinci's portrayal of The Last Supper painted on the wall of the refectory of the Convent of Santa Maria delle Grazie, Milan. The variety of reactions in the faces and body movements of the disciples captured by Leonardo have intrigued and inspired viewers and writers since the beginning of the 16th century. From a new objective reality, viewers often discern more about themselves and their own subjective reality, with the newly discovered subjective reality often being very different from the artist's original intent or experience.

Simultaneously, what we perceive as objective knowledge can serve as a framework upon which subjective reality can play. For example, when Darwin's theory of evolution became widely known to the public, it caused many people to change their self-image and shook the basic foundation of their very existence. The concept of Darwinian Evolution created such strong subjective feelings that repercussions can still be felt today. The mind that can use this interplay between multiple realities has the capability of extending both their subjective knowledge *and* understanding of objective reality, if indeed such a thing exists.

REFLECT:
How am I co-evolving with my environment?
What role does experiential learning play in co-evolving?

Today we live in a world where thoughts and ideas are spurred onward by an almost exponentially increasing amount of data and information accessible to everyone. In both our personal and professional lives we have become adept at responding to and anticipating change. The very act of change may create a new reality requiring new values and perspectives of life. While we clearly recognize the importance of the individual—of Self—in creating and sharing feelings, thoughts and mental images to bring about and apply new knowledge, thinking about ways we create our reality can move us from a reactive role to a proactive role, fully embracing the power of Self. An important first step in harnessing this power is to understand the different perspectives and theories about how we as humans create our reality.

Multiple Perspectives on Self Creating Reality

To explore the framework of creating reality, we will briefly look at the following perspectives: Literary, Living System, Consciousness, Scientific and Spiritual. A word of caution as we begin this exploration. As in all human constructs provided to facilitate understanding, while the discussions are representative of these perspectives, they are not the perspectives themselves. As ever, the map is not the territory.

From a Literary Perspective. The relationships among thought, language and behavior have been explored throughout man's history. The power of knowledge in the form of writing is evident in early records describing the role of the *Overseer of All the King's Works* in ancient Egypt. This Overseer, who directed the massive labor force required to build a pyramid, was a scribe. His palette and papyrus scroll were the symbols of his knowledge and of his authority, and bureaucratic lists and registers were the tools of political and economic power (Silverman, 1997, p. 90). Literature was prized because of its influence over others, and brought fame to the scribe. In short, knowledge, demonstrated by writing, was considered an authority, whether it took the form of literature, a medical recipe or a list. Whatever was written (as symbols) was considered truth, or reality.

> Knowledge, demonstrated by writing, was considered an authority, whether it took the form of literature, a medical recipe or a list.

In 1784 Hugh Blair identified a clear, close alliance between thought and language, with the spoken/written word sometimes responsible for the clarification of thought, and the clarification of thought sometimes responsible for the improvement of the word. In his words, *thought and language act and re-act upon each other mutually* and *by putting our sentiments into words, we always conceive them more distinctly*. How do I know what I mean until I hear what I am going to say? So the story goes. While tying this close connection, it is clear that Blair (2015) believes the conception of thought remains *prior in time and importance* to language.

Later theorists (Brown, Black, Bloomfield, Skinner and Quine) regarded language as a major form of behavior, a significant entity in its own right. Language as behavior is very much in contrast with language as a subordinate feature in the process of communication. In 1982, a writing text contended that *the freedom to act upon the world and to construct reality is both the aim and the process of education* (Writing, 1982). This implies that language is a powerful, if not unique, way of constructing reality and acting on the world. A number of well-known and well-published authors would agree. They describe the writing process—that is, interacting with pen and paper or, in more recent years, keyboarding—in the following words:

Francoise Sagan: "For *Bonjour Tristesse* all I started with was the idea of the character, the girl, but nothing really came of it until my pen was in hand. I have to start to write to have ideas …."

James Thurber: "I don't believe the writer should know too much where he's going. If he does, he runs into old man blueprint – old man propaganda."

Truman Capote: "But in the working-out, the writing-out, infinite surprises happen. Thank God, because the surprise, the twist, the phrase that comes at the right moment out of nowhere, is the unexpected dividend, that joyful little push that keeps a writer going."

William Faulkner: "Sometimes technique charges in and takes command of the dream before the writer himself can get his hands on it ... It [*As I Lay Dying*] was simple in that all the material was already at hand."

Gertrude Stein: "It will come if it is there and you will let it come, and if you have anything you will get a sudden creative recognition. You won't know how it was, even what it is, but it will be creation if it came out of the pen and out of you and not out of an architectural drawing of the thing you are doing ..."

(Excerpts from Cowley, 1958)

In more prosaic terms, every act of writing is an act of creating, interacting with the medium in the environment to create symbols external to Self, a release of the unconscious reality into public view. As Lakoff and Nunez note in their book, *Where Mathematics Comes From*:

> Perhaps the most fundamental, and initially the most startling, result in cognitive science is that most of our thought is unconscious – that is, fundamentally inaccessible to our direct, conscious introspection. Most everyday thinking occurs too fast and at too low a level in the mind to be thus accessible. ... We all speak in a language that has a grammar, but we do not consciously put sentences together word by word, checking consciously that we are following the grammatical rules of our language. To us, it seems easy: We just talk, and listen, and draw inferences without effort. But what goes on in our minds behind the scenes is enormously complex and largely unavailable to us. (Lakoff and Nunez, 2000, p. 27)

From a Living System Perspective. Autopoiesis is a term with Greek derivation that means self-production. The main argument of the theory is that living systems are created and reproduced in an autonomous, simultaneously open and closed self-referential manner. This means a porous boundary, where some things can come in and others are warded off. An example would be the intake and processing of food versus the rejection of foreign matter. Autopoiesis assumes everything the living system needs for self-production is already in the system (Maturana & Varela, 1987).

In epistemological terms, autopoietic systems are considered to contain their own knowledge since the system is the observer of external events. (See the discussion of subject and object in Chapter 2.) External events, such as clouds, people, buildings, etc., are all part of the individual's experience and the interpretation and description of these events are the results of the *relationships* established between our previous experience and our perceptions. From an autopoietic viewpoint, it is impossible to step out of the individual and see ourselves as a unit in an environment because what the individual sees as the external environment is still part of his experience and by no means lies outside the interface that, in theory, separates the knower from the known.

If our reality cannot be separated between ourselves and the external world, then within our own minds what we perceive and create and believe is reality. Therefore, when we actively create new realities within ourselves, they become "the" reality upon which we act, anticipate and analyze. From this internal reality, and the forthcoming actions, comes behavior in the external world that then creates a perceived reality in the minds of others. Thus, the possibility of diffusion of our own individual reality to others becomes realized and a significant external reality can be created through widespread commonality of interpretation.

From a Consciousness Perspective. The permanency of form, or reality, is an illusion, since all consciousness is a process of change. Consciousness is a process in which thoughts, images and feelings are constantly evolving. Its major characteristics are unity, optimum complexity and selectivity. Unity is necessary to make the time flow of thoughts, images and feelings coherent. Optimum complexity allows the processing of divergent signals from within the individual and from the external environment. Selectivity limits the incoming signals to those that are essential to survival or interest. What this means is that when you get incoming information from the senses, you take that information and mix it with your memories of thoughts, feelings and images related to that incoming information (the associative patterning process). The brain's ability to integrate these forms is what is called the remembered present (Edelman, 1989). The process we call consciousness is a continuous sequence of these remembered presents and the understanding of their connections and relationships to each other and our Self.

> The process we call consciousness is a continuous sequence of remembered presents and the understanding of their connections and relationships to each other and our Self.

Studies from consciousness would agree with autopoiesis in that when we receive external information, since we immediately compare it with what is already in our memory, it is the combination of these two, coupled with our own belief and value systems, that yields what we perceive as reality, an integrated mental scene. That means the individual mind participates in the creation of its own reality.

From a Scientific Perspective. Scientific inquiry assumes the existence of an objective, external reality that can be studied, understood and tested through empirical methods. Although science recognizes the potential subjectivity of individual perceptions and observations, where possible, particularly in the domains of physics and chemistry, it has built into its methodology protection mechanisms that minimize or eliminate subjectivity in areas of concern to science. Through the process of creative construction of models and theories of objective reality, filtered by empirical testing and public dialogues and debate, the best estimate of objective reality is created. While this objective reality is not "the" objective reality, it is self-consistent and for each area of its applicability it has been highly effective, leading to great advances in technology and a deeper understanding of our world and our universe.

Under these working assumptions, to some extent an individual's perception of reality can influence that reality predominantly through the psychological impact that belief has on the individual's actions. Through these actions, then, the external reality can be influenced, and therefore a self-fulfilling prophecy may be possible (Davis, 1997).

While science recognizes that individuals have different subjective realities as explained by autopoiesis and numerous psychological studies, these differences in reality do not preclude understanding the objective reality in the hard sciences. However, there are significant open questions in several areas related to the observer's impact on that objective reality.

From a Spiritual Perspective. Like the words in this book, the objects around us that make up our environment are symbols that transmit a reality with a learned, and agreed-upon, meaning. The true information is not in the object any more than thought is in words and letters. Both words and objects are methods of expression. When you speak words, and though they may express more or less your feelings, they are not your feelings. There is a gap between our thought and our expression of thought. This gap is particularly visible when we consider how often each of us begins a sentence, and don't know exactly how it's going to end. We create the thought and the language as we go along. This same gap occurs between our thoughts, feelings and mental images and the creation of objects (in space) and events (in time).

> From the Spiritual viewpoint, we form the fabric of our experience through our beliefs and expectations, which are not about reality, but are reality itself.

Spirituality sees the continuous creation of our physical environment as a method of communication and expression, with the Self in the role of co-creator. Feelings, thoughts and mental images are translated into physical reality. Feelings play a significant role in this process. The intensity of a feeling, thought or mental image is an important element in determining subsequent physical materialization; feelings—often linked to thoughts and mental images—largely build that intensity. If your mind works with high intensity, and you think in vivid mental emotional images, these are swiftly formed into physical events. We form the fabric of our experience through our beliefs and expectations, which are not about reality, but are reality itself (Roberts, 1994). This is the power of intent introduced in Chapter 2.

Ultimately, the answers to the nature of reality are to be found through an inner journey into ourselves, through ourselves and through the world we know. It is human imagination and creativity that is constantly creating the reality in which we live

(Edelman & Tononi, 2000). Each and every one of us has observed or been a part of this great creativity, which always seems greater than our physical dimension with its objective reality. This joy of creativity flows though us as effortless as our breath; and each of us uses this flow of creativity to create a unique reality, different from any other individual.

> **REFLECT:**
> *Am I fully engaging my imagination and creativity?*
> *How do I best create the reality within which I live?*

In summary, the literary perspective is that language is a powerful way of constructing reality and acting on the world. The living system and consciousness perspectives agree that the individual mind does participate in the creation of reality, and in autopoiesis a diffusion of individual reality to others can be realized. The science perspective is that parts of external reality can be understood and influenced, and therefore a self-fulfilling prophecy may be possible. The spiritual perspective is that all reality is a result of feelings, thoughts and mental images, and reality emerges dependent on the intensity of those feelings, thoughts and mental images.

Regardless of the perspective that is taken, it is clear that at some level humans are involved in the creation of the reality in which they live. Perhaps the idea of co-creation would be more descriptive as **the Self is continuously learning from that which is perceived as its environment, and using this learning to act on the reality, which they simultaneously co-create.**

Enriched Environments

As you may recall, the literature suggests that there are specific changes within the brain that occur through **enriched environments**, that is, when the surrounding environment contains many interesting and thought-provoking ideas, pictures, books, statues, etc. Byrnes sees the results of research on the effects of enriched environments on brain structure as both credible and well-established (Byrnes, 2001). Specifically, within the brain thicker cortices are created, cell bodies are larger, and dendritic branching in the brain is more extensive. These are physiological changes in response to the environment, the feelings, and the learning of the participants. These changes have been directly connected to higher levels of intelligence and performance (Begley, 2007; Byrnes, 2001; Jensen, 1998). As we learned in Item 5-A, an enriched environment can produce a personal internal reflective world of imagination and creativity.

What is an enriched environment? Asked this question 20 years ago, we would say that effective learning requires concentration; no physical, mental or emotional distractions. Our minds cannot function if they are bombarded with disturbances. From the viewpoint of the formal classroom setting, this means surroundings that are quietly attractive, passive yet comfortable. If the surroundings provide safety, positive feelings and an aura of warmth and confidence, the desired learning will likely be easier and quicker, and the results remembered longer. We would also agree that the idea of an enriched environment might be highly sensitive to the specific learner. For example, as we will see in Chapter 21, some types of music have long served as a learning aid.

Which brings us to the learners of today. Indeed, the generation of learners emerging in the workforce today are quite different from the generation of yesterday. We live in unprecedented technologically-advanced times. Unparalleled economic shifts over the last century have taken us from predominantly agrarian societies to post-industrial societies with knowledge-based economies. In terms of the scale of societal change and the need for learning and adaptation, this is the most radical environmental transformation in human history. Every aspect of our existence is impacted. Amidst the transformational challenges, including the diminished convergence with nature in the environment and the accelerated speed of change, we make some choices that potentially portend dire consequences. Nevertheless, progress and opportunity carry the day.

> In terms of the scale of societal change and the need for learning and adaptation, this is the most radical environmental transformation in human history.

At the heart of everything we create now in every field of human endeavor—in health and medicine, safety, transportation, energy, exploration, manufacturing and technological innovation, finance, education—and in whatever work we pursue, in our sociality and in our governance, *our brain/mind is augmented in increasingly unimaginable ways*. That augmentation is computers and advanced communication technologies. These two technologies are increasingly inseparable, and their relationship with us is increasingly synergistic. Already we may say that the interdependence between humans, computers, and communication systems is so rich and dynamic that technologies are shifting from a focus on specialized design and specific functionality to the dynamics and sharing of information, which in turn may result in interactive learning and, in many cases, the creation and application of knowledge.

Interactive man-machine learning not only applies to how we learn from the technologies, but also *how the technologies learn from us*. Not long ago, we hoped that the technologies would remember our previous settings, requests, and choices. When you use these technologies today, there is increasing likelihood that they will learn from what you're doing and adjust their functionalities to accommodate your mode of use. Further, various software and computer systems not only anticipate what we want, but, when we select a certain type of function or process, the system will suggest next steps or new levels of procedures. The technology gives us choices, supports us in the background, and guides us as we proceed. For example, in the 1980's when spreadsheet software was being developed, there was a strong hesitancy among many to accept the value in such tools. Now, that category of software is so sophisticated and multifaceted that it's difficult to find users who even know about, much less use, the full range of capabilities.

Imagine what computer and communication tools will be capable of in another five to ten years! It is likely current concepts of computer and communication tool performance will be displaced by far more advanced personal tools that *simultaneously enable performance while enhancing our learning*. A key factor in this kind of future is the ability of technologies to accommodate our individual needs on multiple levels.

> Not only are technologies enabling performance while enhancing our learning, they increasingly are augmenting our brain capacity and serving as teachers.

Our technologies are increasingly able to reach out to whatever we need and whomever we seek. We will spend less and less time determining what the options are and less and less time making choices, and will find it easier and easier to figure out how to engage and perform new functions and processes. In this environment, the technologies will *increasingly be augmenting our brain capacity* and serving as teachers. As Horstman describes:

> Forget book learning, physical classrooms, and didactic teaching, even physical books themselves. Brains today learn through Internet interaction, wirelessly at lightning speed and all the time, networked globally across social, political, and geographical boundaries. Scientists aren't sure exactly what that's really doing to our brains, but they're sure it's doing something, and that microprocessors that will WiFi our brains directly to the Internet are next up. (Horstman, 2010)

This isn't so far off. For example, a University of Washington (UW) research study involved brains communicating directly with each other over the Internet to play a simple video game. The participants in the research were located 800 meters apart. On the sender end, three individuals had to fire their canons at incoming rockets to defend their cities. To do this, they would think about it and their brain signals would alert the brains of their counterpart receivers, on the other end, to activate the firing button in order to fire the canons at the right moment. The receivers could not see the game and were only prompted to hit the firing button when their brains received a sender's thought. The messages from the senders would be received in less than a second. Accuracy varied between the pairs and ranged from 25 percent to 83 percent. Accurate results depended upon a sender's ability to make the right judgment about when to fire the canon. This is the Abstract description from the researchers' report:

> We describe the first direct brain-to-brain interface in humans and present results from experiments involving six different subjects. Our non-invasive interface, demonstrated originally in August 2013, combines electroencephalography (EEG) for recording brain signals with transcranial magnetic stimulation (TMS) for delivering information to the brain. We illustrate our method using a visuomotor task in which two humans must cooperate through direct brain-to-brain communication to achieve a desired goal in a computer game. The brain-to-

brain interface detects motor imagery in EEG signals recorded from one subject (the "sender") and transmits this information over the Internet to the motor cortex region of a second subject (the "receiver"). This allows the sender to cause a desired motor response in the receiver (a press on a touchpad) via TMS. We quantify the performance of the brain-to-brain interface in terms of the amount of information transmitted as well as the accuracies attained in (1) decoding the sender's signals, (2) generating a motor response from the receiver upon stimulation, and (3) achieving the overall goal in the cooperative visuomotor task. Our results provide evidence for a rudimentary form of direct information transmission from one human brain to another using non-invasive means. (Rao et al., 2014)

The UW researchers are now at the point where they can successfully replicate the experiment with walk-in participants. The full details and results of the research, with photographs, are published at PLOS ONE, an online research journal. Figure 20-1 illustrates the process:

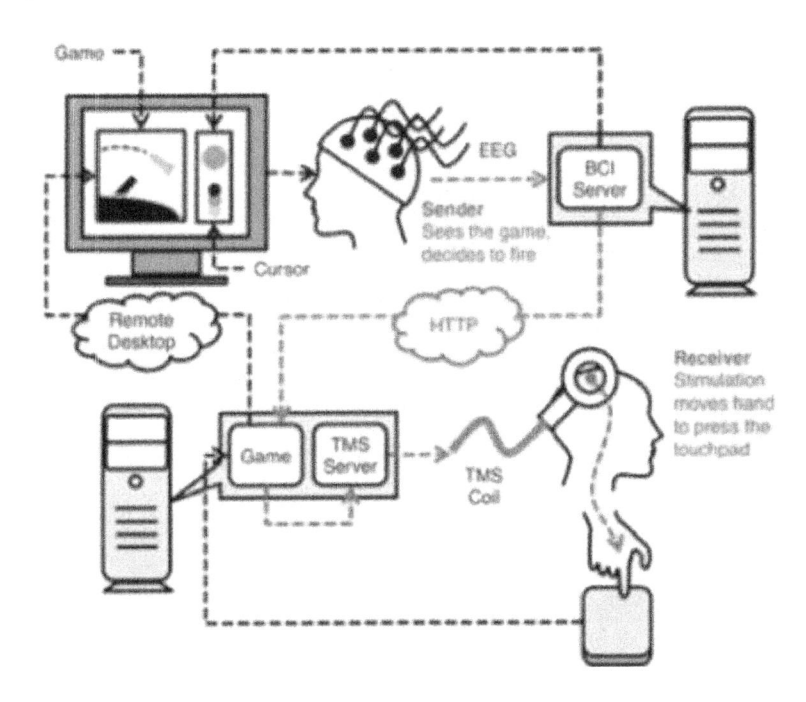

Figure 20-1. *Schematic Diagram for Direct Brain-to-Brain Interface (Rao et al, 2014, used with permission).*

While French and Spanish scientists have also conducted research with direct links; nevertheless, the UW project was the first instance where multiple pairs were successfully transmitting simultaneously. The UW research team received a $1 million grant to expand the communication process to transmit information and images. They hope the research can open up possibilities to help people teach with thought transmission. Chantel Prat, a psychologist and co-author of the research writes, "Imagine someone who's a brilliant scientist but not a brilliant teacher. Complex knowledge is hard to explain—we're limited by language" (Rao et al., 2014).

While there are other core technological enablers in our new environment, computer and communication technologies are leverage points. As we continue to interact and learn in this new environment, there will be increases in interaction speed, frequency and types; and in this environment we can—and will—resolve dire human issues, prevail against our human inadequacies, prosper in new ways, and exponentially accelerate our mind/brain capacity to learn.

Final Thoughts

We have just begun to introduce the conversation about the impact of the environment on the Self—and the impact of Self on the environment—and the learning that occurs throughout this process. To drive the importance of the environment in learning, we provide an in-depth example of the connections between music and the learner that is Self in Chapter 21.

Chapter 21
Self: Music in the Brain

[An in-depth example of the impact of the environment on learning]

When Charles Darwin wrote his *Autobiography* in 1887, he was moved to say,

> If I had to live my life again I would have made a rule to read some poetry and listen to some music at least once a week; for perhaps the parts of my brain now atrophied could thus have been kept active through use. (Amen, 2005, p. 158)

Today there's no doubt that the brain atrophies through disuse, that is, neurons die and synapses wither when they are not used (Zull, 2002), but would listening to music once a week have kept more of those neurons and synapses active and alive? And if so, what if we *participated more fully* in music-making? How could we maximize our learning?

Music and the human mind have a unique relationship that is not yet fully understood. As Hodges forwards,

> By studying the effects of music, neuroscientists are able to discover things about the brain that they cannot know through other cognitive processes. Likewise, through music we are able to discover, share, express, and know about aspects of the human experience that we cannot know through other means. Musical insights into the human condition are uniquely powerful experiences that cannot be replaced by any other form of experience. (Hodges, 2000, p. 21)

While the effect of music on the critical aspects of learning, attention and memory may be a relatively new area of focused research, the human brain may very well be hardwired for music. As Weinberger, a neuroscientist at the University of California at Irvine, says: "An increasing number of findings support the theory that the brain is specialized for the building blocks of music" (Weinberger, 1995, p. 6). Wilson, a biologist, goes even farther as he states, "...all of us have a biologic guarantee of musicianship, *the capacity to respond to and participate in the music of our environment* [emphasis added]" (Wilson, as cited in Hodges, 2000, p. 18).

> The brain may very well be hard-wired for music.

Sousa (2006) forwards that there are four proofs that support the biological basis for music: (1) it is universal (past-present, all cultures (Swain, 1997); (2) it reveals itself early in life (infants three months old can learn and remember to move an overhead crib mobile when a song is played (Fagan, et al., 1997), and within a few months can recognize melodies and tones (Weinberger, 2004; Hannon & Johnson, 2005); (3) it should exist in other animals besides humans (monkeys can form musical abstractions (Sousa, 2006)); and (4) we might expect the brain to have specialized areas for music.

Exactly where this hardwiring might be located would be difficult to say. For example, even though there is an area in adults identified as the auditory cortex, visual information goes into the auditory cortex, just as auditory information goes into the visual cortex. That is why certain types of music can stimulate memory recall and visual imagery (Nakamura *et al.*, 1999). Further, the auditory cortex is not inherently different from the visual cortex. Thus, "Brain specialization is not a function of anatomy or dictated by genes. It is a result of experience." (Begley, 2007, p. 108) This process of specialization through experience begins shortly after the time of conception, selecting and connecting. Many of the interconnections remain into adulthood, or perhaps throughout life. While these connections are not exercised in most adults—they are more like back road connections—when the brain is deprived of one sense (for example, hearing or seeing), a radical reorganization occurs in the cortex, and connections that heretofore lay dormant are used to expand the remaining senses (Begley, 2007).

In the early phases of neuronal growth, during the first few months of life, there is an explosion of synapses in preparation for learning (Edelman, 1992). Yet beginning around the age of eight months through sixteen months, tens of billions of synapses in the audio and visual cortices are lost (Zull, 2002). Chugani says that this loss is concurrent with synaptic death, with experiences determining which synapses live or die (Chugani, 1998). As Zull explains, before eight months of age synapses are being formed faster than they are being lost. Then things shift, and we begin to lose more synapses than we create (Zull, 2002). The brain is sculpting itself through interaction with its environment, with the reactions of the brain determining its own architecture.

This process of selection continues as the rest of life is played out. This is the process of learning, selecting, connecting and changing our neuronal patterns (Edelman, 1992; Zull, 2002). Music plays a core role in this process. Jensen contends that, "music can actually prime the brain's neural pathways" (Jensen, 2000b, p. 246).

As introduced in our earlier discussions of plasticity, the brain has the capacity to structurally change throughout life. As Begley describes, "The actions we take can literally expand or contract different regions of the brain, pour more juice into quiet circuits and damp down activity in buzzing ones" (Begley, 2007, p. 8). During this process, the brain is expanding areas for functions used more frequently and shrinking areas devoted to activities that are rarely performed.

> The process of learning, selecting, connecting and change our neuronal patterns continues as life is played out.

Further, in the late 1990's neuroscientific research discovered that the structure of the brain can change as a result of the thoughts we have. As Dobbs' explains, the neurons that are scattered throughout key parts of the brain "fire not only as we perform a certain action, but also when we watch someone else perform that action" (Dobbs, 2007, p. 22). These are mirror neurons, a form of mimicry that bypasses cognition by transferring actions, behaviors and most likely other cultural norms quickly and efficiently. Thus when we *see* something being enacted, our mind creates the same patterns that we would use to enact that "something" ourselves. Because people have stored representations of songs and sounds in their long-term memory, music can be imagined. When a tune is moving through your mind it is activating the same cells as if you were hearing it from the outside world. Further, as we have noted, when you are internally imagining a tune, the visual cortex is also stimulated such that visual patterns are occurring as well (Sousa, 2006).

Not all of these findings were known when music and acoustic pioneer Alfred Tomatis (1983) forwarded the analogy that sound provides an electrical charge to energize the brain. He described cells in the cortex of the brain as cells acting like small batteries, generating the electricity viewed in an EEG printout. What he discovered that was amazing is that these batteries were not charged by the metabolism, but rather through sound from an external source. With the discovery of mirror neurons (see Chapter 13), this would mean that imagining tunes is also providing a charge. These early Tomatis studies found that sound impacted posture, energy flow, attitude and muscle tone, and that the greatest impact was in the 8000 hertz frequency range (Tomatis, 1983; Jensen, 2000b). Other research took this further, suggesting that low-frequency tones caused a discharge of mental and physical energy, and certain higher tones powered up the brain (Clynes, 1982; Zatorre, 1997).

Researcher Frances Rauscher (1997), contends that music appreciation and abstract reasoning have the same neural firing patterns. However, this was observed in research that occurred several years after her earlier studies introducing the controversial Mozart Effect, and setting in motion a growing interest in the relationship of music and learning.

The Mozart Effect

The Mozart Effect emerged in 1993 with a brief paper published in *Nature* by Frances Rauscher, Gordon Shaw and Katherine Ky. To discover whether a brief exposure to certain music increased cognitive ability, the researchers divided 36 college students into three groups and used standard intelligence subtests to measure spatial/temporal reasoning. Spatial/temporal reasoning is considered "the ability to form mental images from physical objects, or to see patterns in time and space" (Sousa, 2006, p. 224). During the subtests one group worked in silence, one group listened to a tape of relaxation instructions, and the third group listened to a Mozart piano sonata (specifically, Mozart's *Sonata for Two Pianos in D*). There were significantly higher results in the Mozart group, although the effect was brief, lasting only 10-15 minutes (Rauscher *et al*., 1993).

The Mozart Effect quickly became a meme, taking on a life of its own completely out of context of the findings. Perhaps this was because it was the first study relating music and mental spatial reasoning, suggesting that listening to music actually increased brain performance. There ensued high media coverage with the emphasis placed on the most sensational findings. However, the details of the study—specifically, that these findings were limited to spatial reasoning not general intelligence, and that the effect was short-lived (10-15 minutes)—were not part of the meme.

In 1995, Rauscher, Shaw and Ky performed a follow-on study that was more extensive than the first. This five-day study involved 79 college students who were pretested for their level of spatial/temporal reasoning prior to three listening experiences and then post-tested. While it was found that all students benefited (again, for a short period of time), the greatest benefits accrued to those students who had tested the lowest on spatial/temporal reasoning at the beginning of the experiment (Rauscher et al., 1993).

By now, other groups were exploring the Mozart Effect. The results were similar to the earlier results, again for a short period of time (Rideout & Laubach, 1996; Rideout & Taylor, 1997; Rideout *et al*., 1998; Wilson & Brown, 1997). However, a series of similar studies with slightly different approaches demonstrated no relevant differences between the group listening to Mozart and the control group (Steele et al., 1999a, 1999b; Chabris, 1999). Still another study began with the premise that the complex melodic variations in Mozart's sonata provided greater stimulation to the frontal cortex than simpler music. When this theory was tested it was discovered that the Mozart sonata activated the auditory as well as the frontal cortex in all of the subjects, thus suggesting a neurological basis for the Mozart Effect (Muftuler et al., 1999). Other specific case results were emerging. For example, Johnson et al., (1998) reported improvement in spatial-temporal reasoning in an Alzheimer's patient; and Hughes et al. (1999) reported that a Mozart sonata reduced brain seizures.

REFLECT:
Do I play music behind me when I'm reading?
What do I see when I imagine a favorite tune?

As the exaggerated sensation of the initial finding began to sink into disillusionment, other researchers were building more understanding of the effect. For example, it was determined that while listening to Mozart *before* testing might improve spatial/temporal reasoning, listening to Mozart *during* testing could cause neural competition through interference with the brain's neural firing patterns (Felix, 1993). Studies expanded to include other musical pieces. The University of Texas Imaging Center in San Antonio discovered that "other subsets of music actually helped the experimental subjects do far better than did listening to Mozart" (Jensen, 2000b, p. 247). Thus, it was determined that the effect was not caused by the specific music of Mozart as much as the rhythms, tones or patterns of Mozart's music that enhanced learning (Jensen, 2000b). This is consistent with earlier work by researcher King (1991) who suggested that there is no statistically significant different between New Age music or Baroque music in the effectiveness of inducing alpha states for learning (approximately 8-13 Hz), that is, they both enhance learning. However, Georgi Lozanov, a pioneer of accelerated learning, had said that classical and romantic music (circa 1750-1825 and 1820-1900, respectively) provided a *better background* for introducing new information (Lozanov, 1991), and Clynes (1982) had recognized *a greater consistency in body pulse response to classical music* than rock music, which means that the response to classical music was more predictable.

> It was determined that it was the rhythms, tones or patterns of Mozart's music that enhanced learning.

Considering the exaggerated early claims publicized without context and based on highly situation-dependent and context-sensitive studies, and the differences in findings among various research groups, it is easy to understand why the Mozart Effect has proved so controversial. Note that the Mozart Effect emerged from studies involving adults (not children) and that it involved short periods of listening to specific music and doing specific subtasks to measure spatial/temporal reasoning. In these studies, effects from long-term listening were not studied or assessed, nor were the richer long-term involvement of learning and playing music. This brings us to a discussion of transfer effects.

Transfer Effects

The question of if and how music improves the mind is often couched as a question of transfer effects. This refers to the transfer of learning that occurs when improvement of one cognitive ability or motor skill is facilitated by prior learning or practice in another area (Weinberger, 1999). For example, riding a bike, often used to represent embodied tacit knowledge (Bennet & Bennet, 2008c; 2015a), is a motor skill (in descriptive terms, learning to maintain balance while moving forward while peddling) that can facilitate learning to skate or ski.

In cognitive and brain sciences the transfer of learning is a fundamental issue. While it has been argued that simply using a brain region for one activity does not necessarily increase competence in other skills or activities based in the same region (Coch et al., 2007), with our recent understanding of the power of thought patterns, one discipline is not completely independent of another (Hetland, 2000). For example, a melody can act as a vehicle for a powerful communication transfer at both the conscious and non-conscious level (Jensen, 2000b). Thus, "Music acts as a premium signal carrier, whose rhythms, patterns, contrasts, and varying tonalities encode any new information" (Webb & Webb, 1990). By "encode" is meant to facilitate remembering. An example is the *Alphabet Song* sung to the tune of *Twinkle, Twinkle Little Star*.

There are different spectral types of real sounds coming from a myriad of sources. Periodic sounds that give a strong sense of pitch are harmonic (sung vowels, trumpets, flutes); those which have a weak or ambiguous sense of pitch are inharmonic (bells, gongs, some drums); and sound that has a sense of high or low but no clear sense of pitch is noise (consonants, some percussion instruments, and initial attacks of both harmonic and inharmonic sounds) (Soundlab, 2008). Specific sounds we hear may include different spectral types; music often includes all three. For example, when hearing a church vocal soloist, the noise of a strong consonant is followed by a sung vowel (harmonic). It is also noteworthy that the same part of the brain that *hears pitch* (the temporal lobe) is also involved in *understanding speech* (Amen, 2005). Thus specific combinations of sound may carry specific meaning by triggering memories or feelings whether or not they have words connected to them.

Research findings indicate that music actually increases certain brain functions that improve other cognitive tasks. Perhaps one of the most stunning results in the literature was achieved by a professional musician in North Carolina who was music director of the Winston-Salem Triad Symphony Orchestra. The music director arranged for a woodwind quintet to play two or three half-hour programs per week at a local elementary school for three years: the first year playing for all first graders; the second year playing for all first and second graders; and the third year playing for all first, second and third graders. Note that 70 percent of the students at the elementary school received free or reduced-price lunches. Prior to the study, first through fifth graders had an average composite IQ score of 92 and more than 60 percent of third graders tested below their grade level. Three years into the program, testing of the third graders exposed to the quintet music for three years showed remarkable differences, with 85 percent of this group testing *above grade level for reading* and 89 percent testing *above grade level for math* (Campbell, 2000).

> Research findings indicate that music actually increases certain brain functions that improve other cognitive tasks.

The limbic system and subcortical region of the brain—the part of the brain involved in long-term memory—are engaged in musical and emotional responses. Therefore, when information is tied to music, it has a better chance of being encoded in long-term memory (Jensen, 2000b). Context-dependent-memory connected to music is not a new idea. In a study at Texas A&M University examining the role of background instrumental music, music turned out to be an important contextual element. Subjects had the best recall when music was played during learning and that same music was played during recall (Godden & Baddeley, 1975). This was confirmed in a 1993 study monitoring cortical and verbal responses to harmonic and melodic intervals in adults knowledgeable in music. The results showed consistent brain responses to intervals, whether isolated harmonic intervals, pairs of melodic intervals, or pairs of harmonic intervals. These results indicated that intervals may be viewed as meaningful words (Cohen et al., 1993).

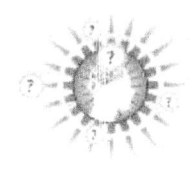

> **REFLECT:**
> *Do I have a strong reaction to any specific sounds?*
> *What would it be like to sing familiar tunes using ideas I am trying to learn?*

It has also been found that background music enhances the efficiency of individuals who work with their hands. For example, in a study of surgeons it was found that background music increased their alertness and concentration (Restack, 2003). The music that surgeons said worked best was not "easy-listening"; rather, that music was (in order of preference): Vivaldi's *Four Seasons*, Beethoven's *Violin Concerto Op. 61*, Bach's *Brandenburg Concertos*, and Wagner's *Ride of the Valkyries*. The use of background music during surgery did not cause interference and competition since music and skilled manual activities activate different parts of the brain (Restak, 2003). This, of course, is similar to the use of background music in the classroom or in places of work.

Dowling, a music researcher, believes that music learning affects other learning for different reasons. Building on the concepts of declarative memory and procedural memory, he says that music combines mind and body processes into one experience. For example, by integrating mental activities and sensory-motor experiences (like moving, singing or participating rhythmically in the acquisition of new information, and for our doctors in the example above their hand movements) learning occurs "on a much more sophisticated and profound level" (Campbell, 2000, p. 173). Conversely, it has also been found that stimulating music can serve as a distraction and interfere with cognitive performance (Hallam, 2002). Thus, much as determined in the early Mozart studies, *different types of music produce different effects in different people* in regard to learning.

Impact of Musical Instruction

Substantiating the long-held "knowing" that music is beneficial to human beings, Hodges outlines five basic premises that establish a link between the human brain and the ability to learn. The first two confirm our earlier discussion of the brain as being hardwired for—or at least having a proclivity for—music. The latter three are pertinent to our forthcoming discussion of the impact of musical instruction on the learning mind/brain. As Hodges forwards (with some paraphrasing): (1) the human brain has the ability to respond to and participate in music; (2) the musical brain operates at birth and persists throughout life; (3) early and ongoing musical training affects the organization of the musical brain; (4) the musical brain consists of extensive neural systems involving widely distributed, but locally specialized regions of the brain; and (5) the musical brain is highly resilient (Hodges, 2000, p. 18).

There are hundreds of studies that confirm that creating music and playing music, especially when started at an early age, provide many more cerebral advantages than listening to music. In a study involving 90 boys between the ages of 6 and 15, it was discovered that musically-trained students had better verbal memory but showed no differences in visual memory. Thus, musical training appeared to improve the ability of the Broca's and Wernicke's areas to handle verbal learning. Further, the memory benefits appeared long-lasting. When students who dropped out of music training were tested a year later, it was found that they had retained the verbal memory advantage gained while in music training (Ho et al., 2003).

Music and mathematics are closely related in brain activity (Abeles & Sanders, 2005; Catterall et al., 1999; Graziano et al., 1999; Kay, 2000; Schmithhorst & Holland, 2004; Vaughn, 2000). Mathematical concepts basic to music include patterns, counting, geometry, rations and proportions, equivalent fractions, and sequences (Sousa, 2006). For example, musicians learn to recognize patterns of chords, notes and key changes to create and vary melodies, and by inverting those patterns they create counterpoint, forming different kinds of harmonies. As further examples, musical beats and rests are counted, instrument finger positions form geometrical shapes, reading music requires an understanding of ratios and proportions (duration and relativity of notes), and a musical interval (sequence) is the difference between two frequencies (known as the beat frequency) (Sousa, 2006).

> Mathematical concepts basic to music include patterns, counting, geometry, rations and proportions, equivalent fractions, and sequences.

In the brain music is stored in a pitch-invariant form, that is, the important relationships (patterns) in the song are stored, not the actual notes. This can be demonstrated by an individual's ability to recognize a melody regardless of the key in which it is played (with different notes being played than those stored in memory). As Hawkins and Blakeslee detail,

> This means that each rendition of the 'same' melody in a new key is actually an entirely different sequence of notes! Each rendition stimulates an entirely different set of locations on your cochlea, causing an entirely different set of spatial-temporal patterns to stream up into your auditory cortex ... and yet you perceive the same melody in each case. (Hawkins & Blakeslee, 2004, pp. 80-81)

Unless you have perfect pitch, it is difficult to differentiate the two different keys. This means that—similar to other thought patterns—the natural approach to music storage, recall and recognition occurs at the level of invariant forms. Invariant form refers to the brain's internal representation of an external form. This representation does not change even though the stimuli informing you it's there is in a constant state of flux (Hawkins & Blakeslee, 2004).

A 1993 study at the University of Vienna revealed the extent that different regions of the human brain cooperate when composing music (this also occurred in some listeners). Professor Hellmuth Petsche and his associates determined that brain wave coherence occurred at many sites throughout the cerebral cortex (Petsche, 1993). For some forms of music, the correlation between the left and right frontal lobes increases, that is, brain waves become more similar between the frontal lobes of the two hemispheres (Tatsuya et al., 1997). For example, in a study involving exposure of four-year-old children to one hour of music per day over a six month period, brain bioelectric activity data indicated an enhancement of the coherence function (Flohr et al., 2000).

REFLECT:
Do I easily recognize patterns, proportions and sequences?
Could this have been influenced by early musical experiences?

In a study of the relationship of coherence and degree of musical training, subjects with music training exhibited significantly more EEG coherence within and between hemispheres than those without such training in a control group (Johnson et al., 1996). In other words, it appeared musical training increased the number of functional interconnections in the brain. Specifically, the researchers suggested that greater coherence in musicians, "... may reflect a specialized organization of brain activity in subjects with music training for enabling the experiences of ordered acoustic patterns" (Johnson et al., 1996, p. 582).

Further, in a study between 30 professional classical musicians and 30 non-musician controls matched for age, sex and handedness, MRI scans revealed that there was a positive relationship between corpus callosum size and the number of fibers crossing through it, indicating a difference in inter-hemispheric communication between musicians and controls (Schlaug et al., 1995; Springer & Deutsch, 1997). In other words, the two hemispheres of the brain of the musicians had a larger number of connections than those of the control group. Thus, as Jenson confirms, "Music ... may be a valuable tool for the integration of thinking across both brain hemispheres" (Jensen, 2000b, p. 246). And as summed up by Thompson, brain function is enhanced through increased cross-callosal communication between the two hemispheres of the brain (Thompson, 2008).

Musicians have structural changes that are "profound and seemingly permanent" (Sousa, 2006, p. 224). As Sousa describes, "the auditory cortex, the motor cortex, the cerebellum, and the corpus callosum are larger in musicians than in non-musicians" (Sousa, 2006, p. 224). This, of course, moves beyond being able to discern different tonal and visual patterns to acquiring new motor skills. Since the brains of musicians and non-musicians are structurally different yet studies of 5 to 7-year-olds beginning music lessons show no pre-existing differences (Restak, 2003; Sousa, 2006; Norton et al., 2005), *it appears that most musicians are made, not born.* An example is perfect pitch, the ability to name individual tones. Perfect pitch is not an inherited phenomenon. Restak (2003) discovered that perfect pitch can be acquired by average children between three and five years of age when given appropriate training. Structural brain changes occur along with the development of perfect pitch, and continue as musical talent matures (Restak, 2003).

We have now answered two of our introductory questions: listening to music regularly, along with replaying tunes in our brains, helps keep our neurons and synapses active and alive. Listening to the *right* music does appear to facilitate learning. Further, participating more fully in music-making appears to provide additional cerebral advantages. *But, as we will discover, some music offers an even greater opportunity to heighten our conscious awareness in terms of sensory inputs, expand our awareness of, and access to, that which we have gathered and stored in our unconscious, and grow and expand our mental capacity and capabilities.*

Since music has its own frequencies, it can either resonate or be in conflict with the body's rhythms. The pulse (heart beat) of the listener tends to synchronize with the beat of the music being heard (the faster the music, the faster the heartbeat). When this resonance occurs the individual learns better. As Jensen confirms, "When both are resonating on the same frequency, we fall 'in sync,' we learn better, and we're more aware and alert" (Jensen, 2000b). This is a starting point for further exploring brain coherence.

Hemispheric Synchronization

Hemispheric synchronization is the use of sound coupled with a binaural beat to bring both hemispheres of the brain into unison (Bennet & Bennet, 2008f). Binaural beats were identified in 1839 by H.W. Dove, a German experimenter. In the human mind, binaural beats are detected with carrier tones (audio tones of slightly different frequencies, one to each ear) below approximately 1500 Hz (Oster, 1973). The mind perceives the frequency differences of the sound coming into each ear, mixing the two sounds to produce a fluctuating rhythm and thereby creating a beat or difference frequency. Because each side of the body sends signals to the opposite hemisphere of the brain, both hemispheres must work together to "hear" the difference frequency.

This perceived rhythm originates in the brainstem (Oster, 1973) and is neurologically routed to the reticular formation (Swann et al., 1982), then moving to the cortex where it can be measured as a frequency-following response (Hink et al., 1980; Marsh et al., 1975; Smith et al., 1978). This inter-hemispheric communication is the setting for brain-wave coherence, which facilitates whole-brain cognition (Ritchey, 2003), that is, an integration of left- and right-brain functioning (Carroll, 1986).

What can occur during hemispheric synchronization is a physiologically reduced state of arousal while maintaining conscious awareness (Atwater, 2004; Fischer, 1971; Delmonte, 1984; Goleman, 1988; Jevning et al., 1992; Mavromatis, 1991; West, 1980), and the capacity to reach the unconscious creative state described above through the window of consciousness. For example, listening to a special song in your life can draw out deep feelings and memories buried in your unconscious. Further, inter-hemispheric communication was introduced as a setting for achieving brainwave coherence (a doorway into the unconscious), providing greater access to knowledge (informing) and knowledge (proceeding), thereby facilitating learning (Bennet & Bennet, 2008f). By reference the ideas forwarded in this work are included here.

In 1971 Robert Monroe—an engineer, founder of The Monroe Institute, and arguably the leading pioneer of achieving learning through expanded forms of consciousness—developed audiotapes with specific beat frequencies which create synchronized rhythmic patterns of concentration called Hemi-Sync®. Repeated experiments occurred with individual brain activity observed. The following correlations between brain waves and consciousness were used: Beta waves (approximately 13-26 Hz) and focused alertness and increased analytical capabilities; Alpha waves (approximately 8-13 Hz) and unfocused alertness; Theta waves (approximately 4-8 Hz) and a deep relaxation; and Delta waves (approximately 0.5-4 Hz) and deep sleep. While it was discovered that theta waves provided the best learning state and beta waves the best problem solving state, this posed a problem. Theta is the state of short duration right before and right after sleep (Monroe Institute, 1985). This problem was solved by superimposing a beta signal on the theta, which produced a relaxed alertness (Bullard, 2003).

This is consistent with the findings from neurobiological research that *efficient learning is related to a decrease in brain activation* often accompanied by a shift of activation from the prefrontal regions to those regions relevant to the processing of particular tasks (the phenomenon known as the anterior-posterior shift).

REFLECT:
Do I resonate with certain types of music?
In what part of my body do I "listen" to and "feel" music?

The first meta-music developed combining theta and beta waves (*Remembrance* by J.S. Epperson) was released in 1994 (Bullard, 2003). A second meta-music piece combining theta and beta waves, released that same year (*Einstein's Dream*, also by Epperson), was based on a modification of Mozart's *Sonata for Two Pianos in D Major*, **the same piece used in the initial study which produced the controversial Mozart Effect.** This version, however, had embedded combinations of sounds to encourage whole brain coherence. (See Bullard & Bennet, 2013, for an in-depth treatment of the use of designer music for learning.)

Thus, the Monroe Institute was developing and releasing audiotapes (and then CDs and MP3s) specifically designed to help the left and right hemispheres of the brain work together, both providing meditation support (Item 5-E), and resulting in increased concentration, learning and memory (Jensen, 2000b). While the range and number of similar music products has expanded over the past years, the many years of both scientific and anecdotal evidence available about the use of this product provides a plethora of material from which to explore the benefits of brain coherence as it relates to learning. Thus we will briefly explore the context around this technology.

The Hemi-Sync®[1] Experience

There are dozens of recorded studies dated during the 1980's that looked at the relationship of Hemi-Sync® and learning, some specifically focused on educational applications. For example, at a government training school the use of Hemi-Sync® to focus and hold attention was found to increase mental-motor skills by 75 percent (Waldkoetter, 1982). In a general psychology class, Edrington (1983) discovered that students who listened to verbal information (definitions and terms peculiar to the field of psychology) with a Hemi-Sync® background signal (4 ± .2 Hz) scored significantly higher than the control group on five of six tests.

In 1986, Dr. Gregory Carroll presented the results of a study on the effectiveness of hemispheric synchronization of the brain as a learning tool in the identification of musical intervals. While the results of the experimental group were 5.54 percent higher than the control group, this was not considered significant. However, a surprise finding was that individuals in the experimental group had a tendency to achieve higher scores on their post-tests than on their pre-tests. The effect was in both the number of individuals and the amount of individual change. Only 28 percent of the individual responses in the control group post-tests were higher than their pre-tests, while 54 percent of the experimental group did much better (Carroll, 1986). This suggests that Hemi-Sync® signals **sustained their levels of concentration during the course of the 40-minute tape sessions**, considerably longer than what occurred (when it occurred) in the Mozart Effect studies.

Hemi-Sync® has consistently proven effective in improving enriched learning environments through sensory integration (Morris, 1990), enhanced memory (Kennerly, 1994), and improved creativity (Hiew, 1995) as well as increasing concentration and focus (Atwater, 2004; Bullard, 2003). There is also a large body of observational research. For example, after 14 years of using music as part of his practice, medical doctor Brian Dailey found that the use of sound (specifically, Hemi-Sync®) not only had a therapeutic effect for his patients with a variety of illnesses, but could be extremely effective in assisting healthy

> Hemi-Sync® has consistently proven effective in improving enriched learning environments through sensory integration.

individuals with concentration, insight, intuition, creativity and meditation (Mason, 2004). This short review has not included the many studies specifically addressing the impact of music, and in particular Hemi-Sync®, on patients with brain damage or learning disorders, which is outside the focus of this book.

In a recent study on the benefits of long-term participation in The Monroe Institute programs[2] involving more than 700 self-selected participants,[3] it was shown that greater experience with Hemi-Sync® increased self-efficacy and life satisfaction (Danielson, 2008) at a state of development similar to that of self-transforming (Kegan, 1982). As described in the research results,

> Individuals at this stage of development recognize the limitations in any perspective and more willingly engage others for the challenge it poses to their worldview as the means for growing more expansive in their experiences—to consciously grow beyond where they are rather than merely having it happen to them as a function of circumstances. (Danielson, 2008, p. 25)

The 700 study participants (all adults) were evenly divided between single program participation (SPP) and multiple program participation (MPP) (indicating increased usage over a longer period of time). SPP means one week of continuous emersion using Hemi-Sync® technology; MPP means multiple weeks of continuous emersion, separated by time periods ranging from weeks to years. Following their Hemi-Sync® experiences, participants reported remarkable results. For example, the following percentages of participants *strongly agreed* (on a five-point Likert scale) to the following statements:

*I have a more expansive vision of how the parts of my life relate to a whole (25.29% SPP, 61.3% MPP)

*I am actively involved in my own personal development (30.65% SPP, 62.45% MPP)

*I take actions that are more true to my sense of Self (18.77% SPP, 45.21% MPP)

*I have been able to resolve an important issue or challenge in my life (11.88% SPP, 32.57% MPP)

*I am more productive at work (4.6% SPP, 14.18% MPP)

*I have a clear sense of further development I need to accomplish (29.5% SPP, 40.23% MPP)

*I am more successful in my career (6.56% SPP, 17.97% MPP)

Clearly, Hemi-Sync® supports a long-term development program for "those interested in playing on the boundaries of human growth and development ... who want to see positive change in their lives" (Danielson, 2008, p. 25).

Final Thoughts

As can be seen, for the past 30 years, and perhaps longer, there have been studies in the mainstream touting the connections between music and mind/brain activity from the viewpoints of psychology, music, education, etc., and another expanding set of studies not as mainstream from the viewpoint of consciousness. As our thought and understanding as a species is expanding, these areas of focus are openly acknowledging each other and learning together. It is no longer necessary or desirable to limit our thoughts to one frame of reference, nor to place boundaries on our mental capacity and ability to expand or contract that capacity.

Further, we have seen evidence that changes in brain organization and function occur with the acquisition of musical skills. From the external viewpoint, whether as a listener or participant, music clearly offers the potential to strengthen and increase the inter-connections across the hemispheres of our brain. As an example, the sound technology of Hemi-Sync® offers the potential to achieve brain coherence, thus facilitating whole-brain cognition.

> Music clearly offers the potential to strengthen and increase the inter-connections across the hemispheres of our brain.

This is not to say that sound, music, Mozart or Hemi-Sync® offer a panacea for learning. Let's not produce the disappointment of creating a meme without context. When asked what to expect from the Hemi-Sync® experience, engineer and developer Robert Monroe responded,

> As much or as little as you put into it. Some discover themselves and thus live more completely, more constructively. Others reach levels of awareness so profound that one such experience is enough for a lifetime. Still others become seekers-after-truth and add an on-going adventure to their daily activity. (Monroe, 2007)

We've come full circle. As we can see through this extensive example of the Self in an environment of music and sound, there is a continuous thread of learning connecting the mind/brain and the environment. This learning value to the Self is discoverable through beauty, aesthetics, literature, fine cuisines, and through connecting with nature and any surroundings positively engaging the human senses. But the amount, quality and direction of that learning—and the environments in which we live that impact that learning—are choices. Yes, Charles Darwin, regularly listening to music—and, even better, participating in music-making—would have undoubtedly kept more neurons alive and active, and synapses intact.

Now our opportunity is to fully exploit this understanding in our organizations, in our communities, and in our everyday lives.

Chapter 22
The Self as a Social Learner

As life has unfolded around us, we now understand that "all of our biologies are interwoven" (Cozolino, 2006, p. 3). Cozolino pushes this thought even further as he suggests that scientists need to understand that neither a single neuron nor an individual human brain exists in nature. "Without mutually stimulating interactions, people and neurons wither and die." The human brain is designed to think socially. Think about *your* everyday life; we form and reform social groups and relationships every day of our life.

When Darwin first published his book in 1859, *On the Origin of Species,* he voiced conclusions regarding the superior strength of individuals. His conclusion, "survival of the fittest", became an accepted business mantra leading to and supporting hard competition. What is lesser known is that later in life in his book, *The Descent of Man*, Darwin had realized his mistake. As he summarized, "Those communities which included the greatest number of the most sympathetic members would flourish best and rear the greatest number of offspring." (Darwin, 1998, p. 110) In the early 20th century, Russian naturalist Peter Kropotkin had discovered from his own observations that "cooperation and unity, rather than survival of the fittest, are the keys to the success of a species." (Kropotkin, 1902) John Swomley, a professor emeritus of Social Ethics at the St. Paul School of Theology, bluntly stated in direct contradiction to Darwin's earlier work that cooperation is the "key factor in evolution and survival." (Swomley, 2000, p. 20). (Excerpted from Bennet et al., 2015b.)

When we explore the workings of the mind/brain, this is not surprising. Mahoney and Restak look at the neuron as a model for corporate success, a design based on networking. "Our identity as social creatures is hardwired into the very structure of our brain ... this pattern of interconnectedness and sociability exists at every level of brain function." (Mahoney & Restak, 1998, p. 42)

> "Our identity as social creatures is hardwired into the very structure of our brain ... at every level of brain function."

Gazzaniga (2008) feels that, metaphorically, humans are much more of a sociological entity than a single Self. The basis of this sociability is the continuous communication occurring among neurons. In 1998 the Nobel Prize in Physiology or Medicine was awarded to three scientists for their work on cell signaling, now described as Redox signaling. Our bodies use this Redox process—the process of exchanging electrons between atoms—to signal and communicate on an atomic level in order to coordinate the defense, repair and replacement of tissue (Naidu, 2013).

While there are many ways to learn—self-reflection, observing others, our own instincts, etc.—in our networked world the art of communication and social networking has become an essential part of our organizations and communities. Global connectivity has assured the availability of massive amounts of information and a wide diversity of thought and opinion on every subject imaginable, and the ability to share this information with others. This shift has prompted an exponential growth in learning from each other, with a plethora of new ideas emerging from the creative imaginings of people and the bisociation of ideas.

Social learning theory emerged in the 1960's—long before the advent of the Internet—with the work of Bandura (1963; 1977). It was Bandura who recognized that current learning approaches discounted the influence of social variables. He posited that learning could occur purely through observation *or* direct instruction *in addition to* the observation of rewards and punishments, or vicarious reinforcement.

The key tenets of social learning theory are:

1. Learning is not purely behavioral; it is a cognitive process taking place in a social context.

2. Learning occurs by observing a behavior and the consequences of the behavior (vicarious reinforcement).

3. Learning involves observation, extraction of information from those observations, and making decisions about the performance of the behavior (modeling). Thus learning can occur without an observable change in behavior.

4. Reinforcement plays a role in learning, but is not entirely responsible for learning.

5. The learner is not a passive recipient of information. Cognition, environment, and behavior all mutually influence each other (reciprocal determinism). (Grusec & Lytton, 1992, p. 5)

As can be seen, Bandura's work moved us closer to understanding the full impact of social learning. Nevertheless, as reflected in earlier chapters of this book, it wasn't until the late 1990's that neuroscience brought us to a deeper understanding of social learning.

To consider learning as the creation of knowledge more fully in a social setting, we first review our understanding of knowledge. Building on our earlier discussion, knowledge can be thought of as theories, beliefs, practices and experiences coupled with a whole neighborhood of associated concepts, facts, and processes that together create the understanding, meaning and insight (to take effective action) that we consider knowledge. If an individual receiving information from a knowledgeable person cannot recreate the invariant forms and neighborhood, or modulate their own invariant forms and neighborhood, then little or no learning will occur (Item 7-B). Consequently, knowledge will not be shared, that is, the receiver has not recreated the sender's knowledge, nor are they likely to create their own comparable knowledge.

Knowledge is dependent on context. In fact, it represents an understanding of situations *in context*. This includes insights into the relationships within a system, and the ability to identify leverage points and weaknesses to recognize meaning in a specific situation, and to anticipate future implications of actions taken to resolve problems. Shared understanding is taken to mean the movement of knowledge from one person to the other, recognizing that what passes in the air when two people are having a conversation is information in the form of changes in air pressure. These patterns of change may be understood by the perceiver if the language and its nuances are known, but the changes in air pressure do not represent understanding, meaning or the capacity to anticipate the consequences of actions. The perceiver must be able to take the information patterns and—interpreting them through context—re-create the knowledge that the source intended. In other words, under perfect circumstances, *the content and context (information) originating at the source resonate with the perceiver such that the intended knowledge can be re-created by the perceiver* (Item 9-A).

> Knowledge represents an understanding of situations *in context.*

REFLECT:
Are there times when I hear words without understanding them?
Are the professionals in my field easy to understand?

As introduced in Chapter 3, it is convenient to think about knowledge as having three levels—surface, shallow and deep—although, of course, this would be a continuum of sorts, and highly context sensitive and situation dependent. *Surface knowledge* is predominantly, but not exclusively, information. It can be stored in books and computers, and the mind/brain. *Shallow knowledge* is when you have information plus some understanding, meaning and sense-making. To make meaning requires context, which the individual creates from mixing incoming information with their own internally-stored information. *Shallow knowledge is the realm of social knowledge,* and as such this focus overlaps with social learning theory (Bennet & Bennet, 2013). For *deep knowledge,* the individual has developed and integrated, many if not all, of the following seven components: understanding, meaning, intuition, insight, creativity, judgment, and the ability to anticipate the outcome of actions taken. This is lived experience, the realm of the expert who has learned to detect patterns and evaluate their importance in anticipating the behavior of situations that are too complex for the conscious mind to understand. Our focus in this chapter is primarily on shallow knowledge.

242 | Expanding the Self

Further, it is important to recognize that all knowledge is imperfect and/or incomplete intelligence. Intelligent activity represents *a perfect state of interaction* where intent, purpose, direction, values and expected outcomes are clearly understood and communicated among all parties, reflecting wisdom and achieving a higher truth. This is the activity toward which social engagement strives. Because the effectiveness of all knowledge is context sensitive and situation dependent, knowledge is shifting and changing in concert with our environment and the demands placed upon us. In a specific situation, the incompleteness of knowledge that is never perfect serves as an incentive for the continuous human journey of learning and the exploration of new ideas.

Social Interaction and the Mind/Brain

When two people meet, there may be a large amount of information (and only information) exchanged between them. Visibly, when they first see each other, light waves (or photons) travel between them, communicating patterns of movement, colors, pictures such as facial expressions, and sound waves as they talk or walk. Each person automatically creates in their own mind images, thoughts, feelings and an overall "sense" regarding the entire situation, including the surrounding environment. Much of this information is automatically processed by our unconscious, sometimes influencing our behavior and feelings before we become conscious of them.

All of this is primarily information (ordered patterns) or, at best, surface knowledge. It is not shallow or deep knowledge; these latter knowledges can only be created by each person within their own minds, shallow through interaction and the building of context, and deep by reflection over time in related situations within a specific domain of knowledge such that patterns emerge.

We each have a unique autobiography that includes different beliefs and personal goals. To create knowledge (understanding, meaning, insights, etc.), incoming information is mixed with our own internal thought patterns. This is the process of associative patterns introduced in Chapter 2. This mixing process becomes more effective when there is a conversation, a dialogue or affirmative inquiry process, between two or more people, enabling the movement from surface to shallow knowledge through the sharing of context.

A significant part of learning requires good ***social communication***, which includes parity and direct comprehension. Parity indicates that meaning within the message is similar for both the sender and the receiver. Direct comprehension means that no previous agreement between individuals is needed for them to understand each other. From the neuroscience perspective, both of these aspects of communication seem to be inherent in the neural organization of individuals (Rizzolatti, 2006).

Recall that we now know that people are in continuous, two-way interaction with those around them, with the brain continuously changing in response. While this communication can happen through physical changes such as facial expressions and eye contact or hand and body movements, there are also energy exchanges. For example, even with your eyes closed and no input from the other physical senses, the human can sense/feel strong emotions such as joy at a wedding or sadness at a funeral.

While context always plays a large role in social learning, or the creation of shallow knowledge, as the shared knowledge moves from surface to shallow more context and deeper relationships are involved to facilitate the exchange. See Figure 22-1. Below we further explore social interactions, in terms of conversation and storytelling, and social bonding, in terms of affective attunement and empathy. From a larger perspective, we will then touch on emotional intelligence, collaborative entanglement, idea resonance and unconscious imitation before ending with an exploration of Self in a social setting a locus of change.

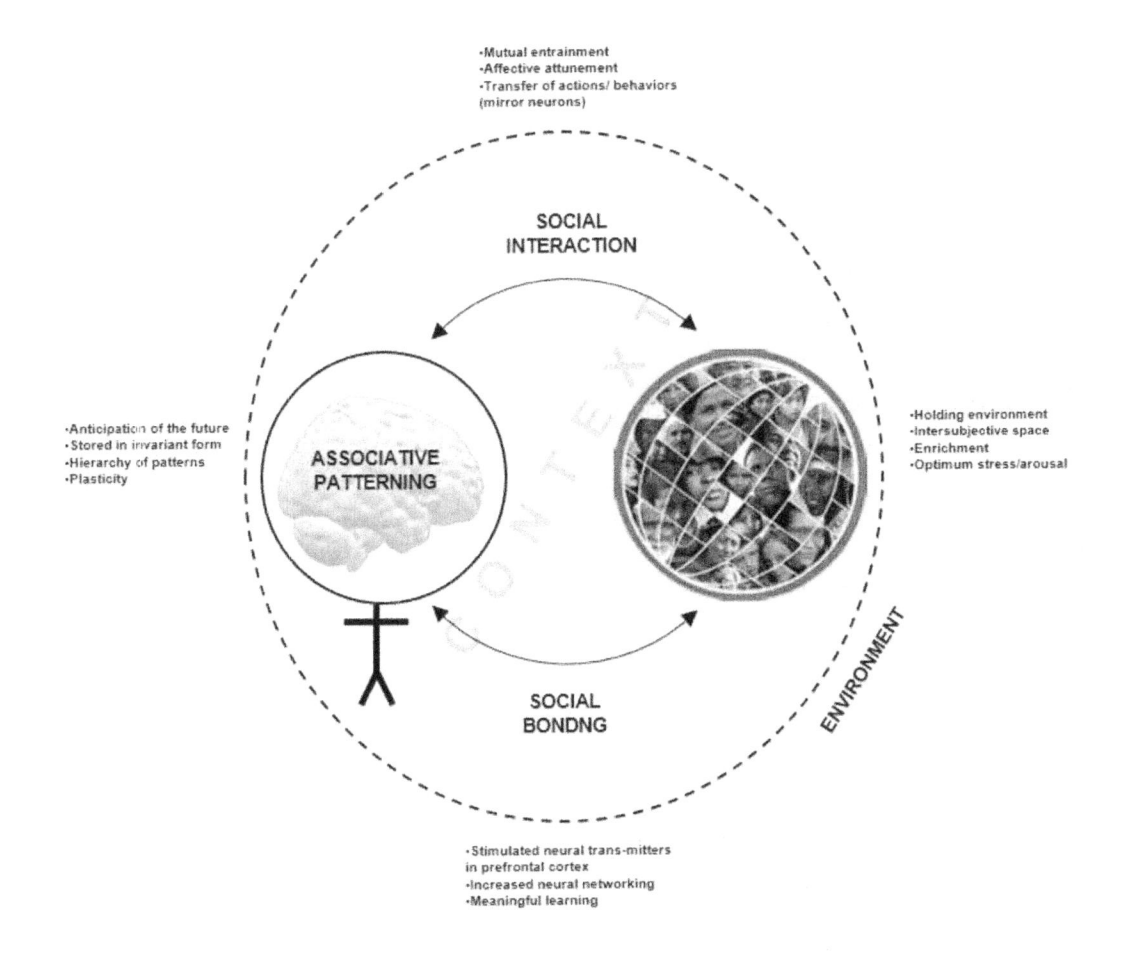

Figure 22-1. *Social Learning, or the Social Creation of Knowledge.*

Conversation

The innate ability to evoke meaning through understanding—to evaluate, judge and decide—is what distinguishes the human mind from other life forms. This ability enables people to discriminate and discern—to see similarities and differences, form patterns from particulars, and create and store knowledge purposefully. In this human process for creating meaning and understanding from external stimuli, *context shapes content*. Bennet et al. (2015a) suggest eight primary avenues of context patterns that may directly impact the message: (1) the content, (2) setting or situation, (3) silent attention/presence, (4) non-voiced communications patterns, (5) the system, (6) personal context, (7) unconscious processes and (8) the overarching pattern context. These contexts are present and influential to various degrees depending on the specific social situation. While their influence on learning may be through the participant's unconscious, they are there.

> The innate ability to evoke meaning through understanding—to evaluate, judge and decide—is what distinguishes the human mind from other life forms.

Context 1 focuses on the content itself: the specific nouns and verbs selected, the adjectives and adverbs used in the primary expression, and the structure of the sentence that support this expression.

Context 2 focuses on the setting or situation surrounding the content. Contexts 1 and 2 are informational in nature and directly tied to the use and rules of language.

Context 3 is that which is not expressed, what we call silent attention/presence. Attention represents awareness and focus; presence represents immediate proximity in terms of time or space. In the presence of another, even in silence the perceiver is embedded in an unseen dialogue based on past and perceived future interactions. Silence has language in terms of meaning, i.e., when somebody does *not* answer a question, they are communicating more than their non-words.

Context 4 includes the non-verbal, non-voiced communication patterns that inevitably exist in conjunction with the content, whether in face-to-face interactions, hand written exchanges, or virtual networking. These are associated information signals that involve interdependent encoding (expression) from the source, and decoding (interpretation) of the receiver. This might include visual or vocal cues, or social media expressions such as " :) ".

Context 5 is focused on the system within which the interaction takes place, the mutually-shared common information and patterns with meaning *within the system*. The context of the system would include an understanding, either consciously or unconsciously, of the boundaries, elements, relationships and forces within the system.

Context 6 is the personal context, which includes beliefs, values, experiences, and feelings that emerge into conscious awareness. This includes positions that we take that are locked into our conscious mind, unconscious patterns that are made conscious by the emerging content of the message, and the core values and beliefs that rise to our awareness by virtue of "feelings."

Context 7 is the impact of unconscious processes. These unconscious impacts can be thought of in terms of the unconscious response to external stimuli (environment); experiences and feelings (memories) not in conscious awareness; and empathetic processes that can mirror behavior. Context 6 and 7 work together.

Context 8 is the overarching pattern context, higher levels of patterns of significance that emerge in the mind. These include the unconscious—and sometimes conscious—connecting of Contexts 1 through 7 to develop a pattern of understanding or behavior; and the development and recognition of patterns of patterns among different interactions over time.

Whether promulgated by the conscious or unconscious mind, the higher the number of related patterns, the higher the possibility of resonance between the source and perceiver and the greater the level of shared understanding. See Bennet et al (2015a) for a deeper treatment of shared context.

Conversation as an art dates back to the ancient Greeks with Socrates and continues into the electronic age. Conversations are "defining moments that literally shape our lives, shape our relationships, and shape our world" (Patterson et al, 2012, Foreward). Because our unconscious is multidimensional and considerably more powerful as a processor than our conscious stream, conversations that we engage in today are planting the seeds for decisions we will make in the future. The unconscious has a powerful memory system just waiting to be triggered as needed to address the instant at hand. Yet most people do not fully value their daily conversations.

One type of conversation is dialogue, the capacity of a group to suspend assumptions and enter into a genuine thinking and learning experience together. Dialogue is frequently viewed as the collaborative sharing and development of understanding. It can include both inquiry and discussion, but all participants must suspend judgment and not seek their own outcomes and answers. The process stresses the examination of underlying assumptions and listening deeply to the Self and others to develop a collective meaning. According to Senge (1990), dialogue involves gathering and unfolding meaning that comes from many parts, as well as inquiring into assumptions, learning through inquiry and disclosure, and creating a shared meaning among group members. More formally, David Bohm (1992) developed dialogue as a specific group process to create a situation in which members participate as coequals in inquiring and learning, creating a common understanding and shared perception of a given situation or topic.

When two Self's engage in conversation as complex adaptive systems, the wonderful property of emergence is at play, resulting in the whole being greater than the sum of the parts. Feelings, thoughts and new ideas come into being, resulting in a strong bonding, which supports learning.

REFLECT:
How important is context in my conversations?
Do I notice and response to non-verbal cues?

Social Bonding

Social forces clearly affect every aspect of our lives. Our personal story—the very way we observe and experiment with the world—forms the basis of our personal theoretical framework with which we make sense of the world (Item 7-E). As Rose (2005, p. 9) says, this framework has been "shaped by the history of our subject, by the power and limits of available technology, and by the social forces that have formed and continue to form that history."

Studies in social neuroscience have affirmed that over the course of evolution, physical mechanisms have developed in our brains to enable us to **learn through social interactions** (Item 8-A). Johnson (2006) suggests that these mechanisms, which have evolved to keep us emotionally and physically safe, enable us to:

(1) Engage in affective attunement or empathic interaction and language,

(2) Consider the intentions of the other,

(3) Try to understand what another mind is thinking, and

(4) Think about how we want to interact. (Johnson, 2006, p. 65)

Affective attunement involves learning from a trusted other. Recall that affective attunement reduces fear, which is a significant impediment to learning, and that the Self actually seeks out an affectively attuned other to learn (Johnson, 2006). Thus, affective attunement can have a significant impact on learning (Item 9-C). With this recognition comes the opportunity to self-manage the learning process in terms of improving efficiency and effectiveness of learning in a specific situation.

For example, engaging in mentoring activities. As the field of knowledge management has helped bring the focus of organizations back to a focus on people and their knowledge as a strategic resource, new words such as verication have accented the importance of affective attunement to learning. To "vericate" is to consult a trusted other, that is, honoring the intelligence emerging with deep knowledge in a specific domain (Bennet & Bennet, 2004). In the learning domain, this is Dewey's concept of educators having a "sympathetic understanding of individuals as individuals" (Dewey, 1997, p. 39). Andreasen cites mentoring as one of the elements that helps create a cultural environment to nurture creativity. From a broader perspective, the five circumstances that create what she calls a "cradle of creativity" include an atmosphere of intellectual freedom and excitement; a critical mass of creative minds; free and fair

> To *vericate* is to consult a trusted other, that is, honoring the intelligence emerging with deep knowledge in a specific domain.

competition, mentors, and patrons, and at least some economic prosperity. As she concludes, "If we seek to find social and cultural environmental factors that help to create the creative brain, these must be considered to be important ones" (Andreasen, 2005, p. 131).

Cozolino (2002) says that the efficacy of the mentoring relationship—a balance of support and challenge—is supported by the literature on brain function. "We appear to experience optimal development and integration in a context of a balance of nurturance and optimal stress" (p. 62).

Social bonding aids in learning, that is, reducing individual fears and creating trust such that the Self is much more open to incoming information, creating a desire to understand, and thereby re-create, the knowledge of the sender. This trusting relationship also encourages an open mind and willingness to learn, and allows the learner to take risks and not be concerned with mistakes made during learning (Sousa, 2006).

Cozolino (2002) says that along with language, *significant social relationships* stimulate learning and knowledge creation and shape the brain (Item 9A). He offers that the two powerful processes of social interaction and affective attunement, when involving a trusted other, contribute to "both the evolution and sculpting of the brain ... [since they] stimulate the brain to grow, organize and integrate" (Cozolino, 2002, p. 213).

REFLECT:
Do I learn from those whom I trust?
Who do I consult to vericate my ideas?

Following a study of unconscious communications which supported the fact that people are in constant interaction with those around them, although often unconsciously, Cozolino and Sprokay say that one possible implication of this finding of specific interest is the fact that "the attention of a caring mentor may support the plasticity that leads to better, more meaningful learning" (Cozolino & Sprokay, 2006, p. 13). Recall that plasticity refers to the fact that new ideas change the patterns in the mind, which changes the physiology of the brain (Item 11-A). Also, changes in the physical brain can change the patterns of neurons and thereby thoughts of the mind. As we live, learn and change through experience, our mind/brain also changes both physically and pattern-wise. Thus the mind/brain is said to have a great deal of "plasticity." Similarly, referring to recent discoveries in cognitive neuroscience and social cognitive neuroscience, Johnson (2006) says that educators and mentors of adults recognize "the neurological effects and importance of creating a trusting relationship, a holding environment, and an intersubjective space" (p. 68) where such things as reflection and abstract thinking can occur.

Fear has been identified as an impediment to learning and knowledge sharing throughout the field of adult learning (Brookfield, 1987; Daloz, 1986, 1999; Mezirow, 1991; Perry, 1970/1988) (Item 4-A). The limbic system, the primitive part of the human brain, and in particular its amygdala, is the origin of survival and fear responses.

The literature is extensive on the need for a safe and empathic relationship to facilitate learning and knowledge sharing. Cozolino says that for complex levels of self-awareness, that is, those that involve higher brain functions and potential changes in neural networks, learning cannot be accomplished when an individual feels anxious and defensive (Cozolino, 2002). Specifically, he says that a safe and empathic relationship can establish an emotional and neurobiological context that is conducive to neural reorganization. "It serves as a buffer and scaffolding within which [an adult] can better tolerate the stress required for neural reorganization" (Cozolino, 2002, p. 291). Taylor explains that,

> A safe and empathic relationship establishes an emotional and neurobiological context that is conducive to neural reorganization.

> Adults who would create (or recreate) neural networks associated with development of a more complex epistemology need emotional support for the discomfort that will also certainly be part of that process. (Taylor, 2006, p. 82)

From a neuroscience perspective, ***trust in a relationship*** enhances the sharing of knowledge, especially regarding shallow and deep knowledge. When a secure, bonding relationship in which trust has been established occurs, the learner's neurotransmitters in the prefrontal cortex (dopamine, serotonin, and norepinephrine) are stimulated and lead to increased neuronal networking and meaningful learning (Cozolino, 2002). Schore describes this as "a cascade of biochemical processes, stimulating and enhancing the growth and connectivity of neural networks throughout the brain" (Schore, 1994, as cited in Cozolino, 2002, p. 191). **Thus, a caring, affirming relationship promotes neural growth and knowledge creation.** Such physiological changes can quickly influence the attitude and expectations of people involved in social knowledge sharing and learning.

Without such trust and bonding, a listener tends to defend his or her own pre-established beliefs, theories, frames of reference, and self-image. Under normal situations, we tend to defend our beliefs and how we see the world. This defense may accept some incoming information, reject other, and change some. When these distortions occur, the incoming information can no longer represent the knowledge of the sender and therefore it is not shared. New knowledge that challenges or contradicts what we already know also tends to threaten our concept of Self, and thereby creates defensive reactions that minimize or negate learning. Our mind concentrates on "defending itself" and does not have time for listening or taking the other person's view and understanding.

On the other hand, if a trusting, nurturing relationship exists between two or more people, a safe environment can be created that eliminates or minimizes potential threats to the learner. Daloz (1986) refers to such a situation as a holding environment (in Johnson, 2006, p. 64). When such a relationship is created, the receiver can build a new sense of Self while building the sender's knowledge out of the information that moves from the sender to the receiver. Such knowledge may not be identical to the sender's knowledge because the mind/ brain of each participant is different. However, when the knowledge sharing is successful, the knowledge in each person may be equally capable of taking effective action even though their understanding, meaning and insight may differ in some ways.

The effects of social forces, of course, are often not in conscious awareness. The role of the conscious is to connect it all together. Recall that we considered "consciousness" from the viewpoint of both Edelman & Tononi (2000) and MacFlouer (1999), that is, as a linear stream of thought patterns, and understanding their relationships to each other and to the Self. LeDoux (1996, p. 33) says that the present social situation and physical environment are part of what is connected, and that a primary job of consciousness is "to keep our life tied together into a coherent story, a self-concept", that is, our autobiography.

Empathy

Cozolino (2006, p. 203) calls empathy a hypothesis that we make based on a combination of visceral, emotional and cognitive information, a "muddle of resonance, attunement, and sympathy." Kohut (1984) says empathy is objectively trying to experience the inner life of another (Item 8-C). Riggio (2015) describes three different types of empathy: (1) a cognitive-based form called *perspective-taking*, that is, see the world through someone else's eyes; (2) literally feeling another's emotions form called *personal distress,* caused by "emotional contagion"; and (3) recognition of another's emotional state and feeling in tune with it called *empathic concern.*

Interestingly enough, from a neuroscience viewpoint, the physiological basis for empathy is so inherent in brain function that is has been extensively documented in scientific experiments with other tested primates. For example, Masserman (1964) reported that in a study of rhesus monkeys when one money pulled a chain for food, a shock was given to that monkey's companion. The monkey who pulled the chain refused to pull it again for 12 days, that is, the primates would literally choose to starve themselves rather than inflict pain on their companions. de Waal (2009) feels that empathy is nature's lessons for a kinder society.

> From a neuroscience viewpoint, the physiological basis for empathy is inherent in brain function.

A key proponent of empathy is feeling, and Riggio (2015) thinks that in reality we all have some level of each type. However, it is when the boundaries between Self and the other blur, and the inner states of the other are assumed to be identical with the Self, that empathy is replaced by what Cozolino (2006) calls identification or fusion, lacking perspective and an awareness of boundaries.

Although the neurobiology of empathy is still in its early development, the insula—described as the limbic integration cortex (Augustine, 1996) lying beneath the temporal and frontal lobes—appears to "play an important role in both the experience of Self and our ability to distinguish between ourselves and others" (Cozolino, 2006, p. 206). Beyond basic sensations, the left insula is involved in the evaluation of eye gaze direction, the response to fearful faces and the observation of facial expression of the other (Carr et al., 2003; Kawashima et al., 1999). Further research has found that the insula mediates the extreme limits of emotions, ranging from severe pain to passionate love (Andersson et al., 1997; Calder et al., 2003).

Cozolino (2006) says that the insula cortex and anterior cingulate link hearts and minds and that this is best demonstrated when watching others experience pain.

> These two regions become activated either when we experience pain, or when a loved one experiences pain. The degree of activation of these two structures has been shown to correlate with measures of empathy (Singer et al., 2004; Jackson et al., 2005). Thus, whereas the insula cortex has played a small role in the history of neurology and neuroscience until this point, it appears to have a bright future as a central component of the developing social brain. (Cozolino, 2006, p. 208)

These findings suggest that through feelings there is an active link between our own bodies and minds and the bodies and minds of those around us. Thus the feelings that we each perceive in the course of our daily living may be affected by, or even belong to, those around us.

Unconscious Imitation

Closely related to the concept of empathy is unconscious imitation. As the Self perceives the actions of others in its environment, there is a stream of learning occurring, primarily in the unconscious (Item 6-F). As Rizzolatti (2006) described, "subsets of neurons in human and monkey brains respond when an individual performs certain actions and also when the subject observes others performing the same movements" (p. 56). In other words, the same neurons fire in the brain of an observer as fire in the individual performing an action (Item 6-E). As introduced and detailed in Chapter 13 on mirror neurons, these neurons provide an internal experience that replicates that of another's experience, thereby experiencing another individual's act, intentions, and/or emotions (Item 6-C). The researchers also found that the mirror neuron system responded to the intentional component of an action as well as the action itself (Rizzolatti, 2006).

Carrying this idea further, Iacoboni (2008) proposes that mirror neurons facilitate the direct and immediate comprehension of another's behavior without going through complex cognitive processes (Item 6-B). This makes the learning process more efficient because it can instantly transfer not only visuals, but emotions and intentions as well. Mirror neurons also serve as a means of learning through imitation, which is "a very important means by which we learn and transmit skills, language and culture" (Rizzolatti, 2006, p. 61).

Mirror neurons aid in stimulating other people's states of mind. As Stern (2004) proposes, "This 'participation' in another's mental life creates a sense of feeling/sharing with/understanding the person's intentions and feelings" (p. 79). Blakemore and Frith describe the phenomenon called mirror neurons as,

> Simply observing someone moving activates similar brain areas to those activated by producing movements oneself. The brain's motor regions become active by the mere observation of movements even if the observer remains completely still. (Blakemore & Frith, 2005, pp. 160-161)

As Dobbs (2007, p. 22) further explains, "These neurons are scattered throughout key parts of the brain—the premotor cortex and centers for language, empathy and pain—and fire not only as we perform a certain action, but also when we watch someone else perform that action.

Zull (2002) suggests that mirror neurons are a form of cognitive mimicry that transfers actions, behaviors and most likely other cultural norms (Item 6-A). Thus when we *see* something being enacted, our mind creates the same patterns that we would use to enact that "something" ourselves. It would appear that mirror neurons represent a neuroscientific mechanism for the transfer of tacit knowledge between individuals or throughout a culture. Siegel suggests that mirror neurons are the way in which our social brain processes and precedes the intentional or goal-directed action of others. Thus mirror neurons link our perception to the priming of the motor systems that engage the same action. In other words, "what we see, we become ready to do, to mirror other's actions and our own behaviors" (Siegel, 2007, p. 347).

REFLECT:
Are there others whose behavior I learn from?
Can I see the world from another person's perspective?

Emotional Intelligence

Coming to the attention of the workplace at the turn of the century, emotional intelligence is very much connected with social learning. Goleman (2000) defines emotional intelligence as the ability to *effectively manage ourselves and our relationships*. Focused on learning more about ourselves and others, Goleman identifies four components of emotional intelligence at work: self-awareness; self-management; social awareness; and social skill. Since the publication of Goleman's first book, there has been considerable research in this area, and today EQ is recognized as a basic requirement for effective use of the Self. As can be seen, emotional intelligence is a primary aspect of Self-development, especially in terms of social engagement, and managing ourselves and our relationships.

A power of emotions is their sensitivity to meaning (Item 3-C). Emotions exist to alert and protect individuals from harm and to energize them to action when they have strong feelings or passions. However, emotions are concerned with the meaning of the information and not the details. This is because emotions bypass slower cognitive functions such as conscious thought. All incoming signals and information are immediately passed to the amygdala, where they are assessed for potential harm to the individual. The amygdala places a tag on the signal that gives it a level of emotional importance (Adolphs, 2004; Zull, 2002). If the incoming information is considered dangerous to the individual, the amygdala immediately starts the body's response, such as pulling a hand away from a hot stove or an instant response to a difficult situation. In parallel, but slower than the amygdala's quick response, the incoming information is processed and cognitively interpreted as usual. Thus the automatic reaction has occurred prior to conscious awareness or thought. From this short description, it is easy to see how important self-awareness and self-management are in social learning.

A business tool that has emerged as an example of the importance of social networking is *Relationship Network Management* (RNM). The relationship network is a matrix of people that consists of the sum of an individual's relationships, those people with whom the individual interacts, or has interacted with in the past, and with whom there is a connection or significant association. In short, all those with whom you have repeated interactions and comfortable conversations. The global mind described by Peter Russell (1995) compares how the evolution of the telephone system and the Internet system have increased the connectedness of people and, as a result, their thought patterns. A thought leader participating in a research study cited by Bennet et al. (2015a) expanded this to include *contactivity*, which includes context and other senses.

Successful relationship networks are built on interdependency, trust, openness, flow and equitability (Bennet & Bennet, 2004). The bottom line is that when we recognize the value of relationships and our interactions across our relationship network, we can learn to consciously manage it by (1) identifying the people with whom you interact regularly; (2) consciously choosing to develop, expand and actively sustain those positive relationships in terms of thought, feelings and actions; and (3) staying open to sharing and learning through our relationship network.

In Chapter 23 we provide several examples of the use of Self as an agent of change in social settings.

Chapter 23
Self as the Locus of Change

How can Self influence other Self's? How can we share our knowledge—understanding, insights, meaning, intuition, creativity, judgment and the ability to anticipate the outcome of our actions—with others such that they, in turn, can share with others?

In Chapter 18 we introduced the concept of Self as an Agent of Change, a core element of the Seashore Use of Self Model. We've presented findings from neuroscience regarding plasticity, the ability of our thoughts and beliefs to change the structure of our brains, which in turn affects our thoughts. Then in Chapter 22 we began to explore the social learner, honoring the fifth mode of the ICALS Model, social engagement. We now touch on the impact of our Self on others as they learn. We begin with the telling of stories, which offers the potential for deep learning. We then briefly touch on the idea of collaborative entanglement, that is, interactive communities learning together, and on the concept of idea resonance emerging from global connectivity, forever changing the way we build value in relationships. Finally, we look at the cycle of experience and the elements of individual change as a tool for Self as the locus of change in a social setting.

The Telling of Stories

Stories are an invitation to human relationship and, thereby, to meaning. "Let me tell you a story ..." is the oldest invitation in the human experience (Taylor, 1996, p. 1). Stories in printed form have a very different reality than those told orally. Printed stories are set in a firm context that may be explored again and again and again as the reader thinks about the work in different modes and explores the meaning of the writer. Steve Denning looks at this availability as a kind of logarithmic table, "scarcely more alive than the abstract reasoning for which we have set them aside." (Denning, 2000, p. 137) Denning feels that the force of the story is not in the story itself, but in the telling of the story, with the teller expressing understanding and eliciting understanding from the listener (Item 2-E).

A focus on the story alone, to the exclusion of the interaction between the storyteller and the listener, misses the point of storytelling. It is **the interaction**

of the storyteller with the listeners and the communal meaning that emerges from the interaction. (Denning, 2000, p. 137)

Long agrees with Denning. He thinks that stories work better and are more fun when they are shared verbally. He points out that storytelling was originally an oral art, with stories passed by word of mouth for generations. Long (1986, p. 5) states that "there is qualitative difference that can easily be detected when a story is read to instead of told to someone."

Similarly, Macguire reminds us that storytelling is a *vocal* art. He points out that a written story needs to be organized around a single epiphany or turning point and that, when you tell a story, there is a narrative string of events that gets spun in the tale. It is also a "folk" art that emerges naturally from us. This is quite different than an actor interpreting a role from a script, bringing a character to life within a theatrical context. Rather, storytelling involves speaking from the heart, bringing a story to life from a human context, opposed to a theatrical one. "Storytelling is at its best when the story can't be separated from the teller." (Macguire,1998, p. 135) Cassady agrees. *Storytelling is considered an oral art form that provides a means of preserving and transmitting ideas, images, motives, and emotions that are universal* (Cassady, 1990).

Why 'story/teller'? Because they cannot be separated. The story is the teller is the story/teller. Unlike the printed word, a story that is told cannot be recorded accurately on paper. So much depends on other things—on the background of the teller, on the interpretation of emotions, on the way a listener responds, on the state of the teller's thoughts, perceptions, feelings. On the teller's abilities. (Cassady, 1990, p. 5)

Much like theatre, dance and music, the "art" occurs during the presentation, and like any art form, the purpose is sharing, to entertain, present knowledge, or teach behavior and morals. This would include such things as vocal inflection, movement, or the use of cue cards and props. A told story paints a picture, using rhythmic patterns, is pleasing to listen to, is enjoyable and educational. "At its best it goes beyond truth in that it illustrates life and so is bigger than life" (Cassady, 1990, p. 8).

Since oral stories are not copyrighted, they can be adjusted in any way the storyteller feels is appropriate. The storyteller can change the point of view, change the time period, rearrange the plot, add or delete characters or lengthen or shorten the story. When considering changes to a story, Cassady reminds us that in the telling there must be clear-cut differences between good and evil, perhaps built on archetypical characters personifying certain traits or characteristics, without too much dependency on long descriptive passage, but rather on narration, or getting the story told (Cassady, 1990, p. 6).

An oral story cannot be recorded accurately on paper. So much of the telling depends on other things—the background of the teller, the interpretation of emotions, the way the listener responds, the teller's and listener's thoughts, perceptions, feelings, and/or the teller's abilities. Storytelling, then, is defined as an oral art form that provides a means of preserving and transmitting ideas, images, motives, and emotions that are universal. (Cassady, 1990, p.5)

In *Oral Cultures Past and Present: Rappin' and Homer*, Edwards and Sienkewica, who studied the oral tradition from ancient Greeks through the contemporary era, present the argument that oral storytelling and literature are poles of a single continuum. But instead of presenting the oral and written as dichotomous, they look at them as two parts of the same whole. They go on to say that an *understanding of the social context of the story is vital*. The issue becomes "not only oral versus written but also how to preserve the vital elements of culture when a folk tale is retold—whether on paper or in performance." (Leotta, 1997, p. 41)

The Native American Tradition. Stories from Native American tribes form a large number of tales from the oral traditions of North America, serving as cultural foundations for their tribes. They are meant to be repeated over and over from generation to generation.

> Now I will tell you stories of what happened long ago. There was a world before this. The things that I am going to tell about happened in that world. Some of you will remember every word that I say, some will remember a part of the words, and some will forget them all – I think this will be the way, but each man must do the best he can ... You must keep these stories as long as the world lasts; tell them to your children and grandchildren generation after generation ..." (Feldman, 1965, Preface)

At the root of Indian stories as Indian culture, are the concepts of "reciprocity and the right relation to the earth" (Bruchac, 1997, pp. 12-15). Native American tales are not only meaningful and memorable, but have exciting details that attract both storytellers and audiences alike. For example, Iroquois stories are filled with such wonderful creatures as stone giants, monster bears, flying heads, magical dwarfs, and vampire skeletons. But with the telling of these stories comes a responsibility to ensure an understanding of the *context* of these stories. These stories are not meant to exist in isolation from the culture of the people to whom they were addressed. They have a strong relationship with the sacred, and were intended to serve as lessons and communication tools.

Bruchac believes the storyteller of Native American Stories must also have an awareness of the place and proper use of stories. There "appears to be a continent-wide tradition that all Native American myths and legends are to be told only at certain times and in certain ways." (Bruchac, 1997, p. 14) An example is the Anishinabe medicine woman and storyteller who begins every story with an offering of tobacco to the ancestors, and then begins each story in song.

Stories were to be told only during winter months in most North American tribes, and, in many cases, only at night. Also, to mention the names of certain characters in the stories outside of the story itself was considered bad luck. For example, some California Indian tribes say that if you mention the name of Coyote outside the story he will come visit you and cause mischief. Enforcement of these traditions is not through human means, but through the powers of nature. For example, the Iroquoi say that if you tell stories in summertime a bee will fly into your dwelling lodge and sting you. In like manner, the Abenaki believe that if you tell stories during the growing season, snakes will come into your house.

REFLECT:
How do stories stimulate your learning?
Do you every tell stories to get a point across?

The Setting of the Telling. Today **timing** is still important in storytelling. As Shakespeare said, "Ripeness is all."[1] While Prusak does not agree that timing is everything, he does say that it is important, that stories need a context, to be told at a particular time and place (Brown, et al., 2004, p. 24). Generally, stories have a **context** and hence the telling of them is more effective in specific settings for specific purposes. For example, some stories are told for social bonding, as signals, to understand history or direct the future, to spark change, or to help understand ourselves and make sense of life. Denning's list of the functions that stories play in organizations would include: entertaining, conveying information, nurturing communities, promoting innovation, preserving organizations and changing organizations (Brown, et al, 2004, p. 110).

Macguire says that the way to develop the skill for storytelling is to tell stories. As Robin Moore says, "Inside each of us is a natural-born storyteller, waiting to be released." (Macguire, 1998, p. 128) Macguire says the ideal way to go about creating personal stories is to speak our inner stories out loud, telling stories to ourselves so that we can hear them and feel them taking shape, then telling them over and over again. In other words, a told story is one that is meant to be more open, interactive, lively, homespun, with spontaneously emerging elements. They convey the teller's on-the-spot energy, mood, imagination, judgment, appearance, and gestures; the audience's perceived needs and cues; the circumstance surrounding the telling occasion; and the influence of the physical setting. (Macguire, 1998, p. 139) While the storyteller should have a clear sense of the milestones that need to be reached—and where to begin and where to end—the pace, rhythm and time space of each telling has to be suited to the particular occasion of the telling.

While leaning more towards storytelling in terms of a theatrical story, Cassady nonetheless believes that the storyteller must *understand* the story and make it their own. In other words, the storyteller engages in a step-by-step analysis of the story: (1) **characterization**, understanding the characters and why they do what they do, their important traits and background, their emotions, and their motives; (2) **theme**, what the story means overall and what it is saying to the audience; (3) **mood**, the overall feeling of the story itself versus the feelings of the characters in the story, and the mood conveyed to listeners; (4) **organization of plot** if there is one, although even stories without a plot have high points, recognizing the inciting incident, the rising action and the climax, and the protagonist and antagonist, the meeting of two opposing forces; (5) **universality**, figuring out how the story relates to the human condition (needs and wants), and its relevance to the listener's life; (6) **symbolism,** going beyond the actual words, what the words represent; (7) **imagery**, while short in a told story, needs to go beyond the words to help listeners visualize or taste or smell; (8) **voice**, considering quality, rate and variety pauses and length of pauses, emphasis, in other words how a particular passage should be spoken; and (9) **use of words**, not only familiar with the words in a story but understanding their meaning and pronunciation, even if you're not going to use them, because in order to choose synonyms you have to understand the original sense of the words. As Cassady reminds us, "The more you understand your story, the more chance you have of making it meaningful for an audience. So it's a good idea to go through the steps discussed in addition to considering anything else you think is important." (Cassady, 1990, p. 100)

In discussing delivery of a story, Simmons notes that when you speak words are less than 15 percent of what listeners "hear." Listeners are receiving messages from the storyteller's face, posture, hands, clothes, eye movements, timing, tone and other unpredictable factors like a storyteller's haircut or where they work or what they have to say or their accent, etc. Simmons goes on to point out that an *individual is a story* to whomever they meet (Simmons, 2001, p. 86).

For example, a modest use of hands can add value to a message by creating props, drawing scenery, increasing the intensity of an emotion or intentionally sending an incongruent message. Facial expressions can communicate, in a split second, emotion at a deeper level than the cultural norm! The same presence and movement of the body can convey a sense of confidence to one listener and arrogance to another. Sounds can be used to convey a sense of reality or to produce smells and tastes and emotions—pursing the lips to create the wind, chattering teeth to illustrate cold, etc. Timing and pauses add meaning and variety. Silence can be more powerful than verbals, and tone can ultimately override every other message, making or breaking the influence of the storyteller (Simmons, 2001). For the storyteller, this would mean on a "bad tone" day any storytelling would be for naught. Finally, Simmons provides "do's and don'ts" for storytellers, which certainly make sense for any presenter: don't act superior, don't bore your listeners, don't scare people or make them feel guilty, do connect at the level of humanity, and do leave them feeling hopeful.

Introducing Collaborative Entanglement

Biological systems are remarkably smarter in their support of the body than we are in sustaining our work places and communities. Fortunately, we can learn and *are* learning from ourselves in this sense, and whether we reflect on this learning in the form of a reality or as an analogy is insignificant as long as we keep learning and creating knowledge (Bennet & Bennet, 2008c).

In a social setting new thoughts and behaviors proposed through personal reflection emerge and then build on other's thoughts and behaviors, becoming mixed with yet another set of thoughts and behaviors from the community, and so on (Item 8-A). We call this mixing, entwining and creation of unpredictable associations the *process of entanglement*; the knowledge creation process in a group or community that works very much as does the human mind/brain.

Collaborative entanglement as a social phenomenon can be analogous to the natural activities of the brain, with the brain representing the researcher and the stakeholder community representing the knowledge beneficiary. All the living and learning of the host human is recorded in the brain, stored among some hundred billion neurons that are continuously moving between firing and idling, creating and re-creating patterns. Information is coming into the individual through the senses, which, assuming for the sake of our analogy, resonates with internal patterns that have strong synaptic connections. When resonance occurs, the incoming information is consistent with the individual's frame of reference and belief systems. As this incoming information is complexed (the associative patterning process) it may connect with, and to some degree may bring into conscious awareness, deep knowledge. The unconscious continues this process 24/7, with new knowledge stored in the unconscious and perhaps emerging at the conscious level.

Little wonder that, as we moved into the new century, new modes of interacting together such as professional communities and global social networks, integrating both voice and visual formats, blossomed in the business environment.

Idea Resonance

Consistent with the increased availability of information, primarily surface knowledge as knowledge (informing), and the resultant coupling of knowledge and creativity, an emergent quality of our new paradigm is idea resonance. With the proliferation of hierarchies and bureaucracies in the 1900's, idea resonance is built primarily on relationships, that is, the valuing of ideas based on attunement with trusted and respected others who were personally known to the decision-maker. As organizations grew more powerful, there was an expansion to include value built on respect and trust of structure, that is, work associates in "my" organization, and external "experts" who were identified as successful by "my work associates" and the world in general, and recognized as experts in "my" domain of knowledge. While this resonance still often included an attunement with specific people, there was a larger resonance beginning to occur based on purpose and ideas.

In the global social networks of recent years—and consistent with an expanding focus on innovation—we have moved fully into the venue of idea resonance, that is, value built on relationship of, respect for and resonance with ideas (Item 11-C). As we increasingly become aware, "Exposure to a greater diversity of perspectives and knowledge increases the quality of ideas, leading to better innovation results." (Carpenter, 2009) See Figure 23-1.

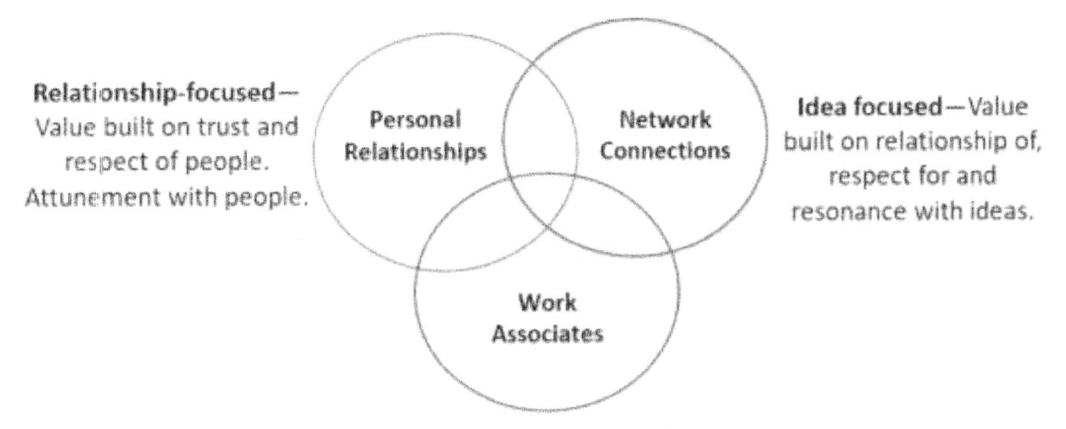

Relationship-focused—Value built on trust and respect of people. Attunement with people.

Personal Relationships

Network Connections

Idea focused—Value built on relationship of, respect for and resonance with ideas.

Work Associates

Relationship and idea-focused—Value built on respect and trust of structure and people. Resonance with purpose, structure and ideas. Possible attunement with people.

Figure 23-1. *The movement from a focus on value built on trust and respect of people to value built on the relationships of, respect for and resonance with ideas.*

This global shift toward expansion of, and dependency on, social knowledge is clearly demonstrated by the new generation of decision-makers. Through continuous connectivity and engagement in conversation and dialogue (a search for meaning), the tech savvy generations have developed—and continue to develop—a wide array of shallow knowledge. (See Bennet et al. (2015b) for a deeper treatment of idea resonance.)

Awareness and Beyond

As an individual engages in a significant interchange with Self, another person or a group of people, the *cycle of experience* (Gestalt theory) begins with awareness, then moves through the phases of energy, action, contact and withdrawal (Nevis, 1987; Polster & Polster, 1973). When partnered with learning, awareness lays the groundwork for physiological, psychological and spiritual change. As Lipton states, "It is a single cell's 'awareness' of the environment, not its genes, that sets into motion the mechanisms of life." (Lipton, 2005, p. 15) This expresses how important the environment is to Self. We now know more assuredly that we are the creators of our lives and the world within which we live. As Byrnes professes, "The neural organization of an adult brain is not set in stone at birth" (Byrnes, 2001, p. 171) (see Chapter 14) (Item 10-A).

Similarly, awareness is the first stage of the Bennet Individual Change Model (Bennet & Bennet, 2008b). Awareness means that something has come into your attention; it has been mentally engaged. Attention is a cerebral phenomenon, which the scientist Michael Posner hypothesized as caused by three separable but integrated systems in the brain (Medina, 2008). The first system is the Alerting or Arousal Network, a surveillance and monitoring system paying attention to the environment in the condition of Intrinsic Alertness (what would be the amygdala). When something unusual is detected, this Intrinsic Alertness transforms into specific attention or Phasic Alertness.

> The individual change model moves through the stages of awareness, understanding, believing, feeling, ownership and empowerment (knowledge and courage).

The second system is the Orienting Network—representing an increase in neuronal firings and connections with incoming information patterns engaged with an emotional tag—which uses the senses to gain more information about the subject of the alert. The third system is the Executive Network—engagement of the executive function in the frontal cortex—which is the stage where a response is, or is not, determined (Medina, 2008).

Note that in a social setting the interactions in which we engage have the potential to stimulate awareness, as well as affect other levels of change. One part of the brain that *may keep individuals from paying attention* is the amygdala, the part of the brain where incoming sensory input is continuously screened for potentially dangerous situations. If a threat is sensed, the amygdala immediately sends a signal that sets in motion a quick action, such as the fight or flight response, before the cortex understands what has happened. As Zull details, when a threat is sensed, "our actions will not be controlled by our sensory cortex that breaks things down into details, but by our survival shortcut through the amygdala, which is fast but misses details" (Zull, 2002, p. 141). Inversely, Begley notes that attention, one of the parameters of successful learning, also pumps up neuronal activity. She says that, "Attention is real, in the sense that it takes a physical form capable of affecting the physical activity [and therefore the structure] of the brain" (Begley, 2007, p. 158).

Following awareness in the Bennet Individual Change Model are: understanding, believing, feeling good, ownership and empowerment (internal and external; confidence and knowledge). To choose to change and direct that change we must *understand* the connections and relationships among things, the actions needed and the expected outcomes that drive the need for change. Understanding includes the description of the situation and its information content that provides the *who, what, where* and *when*. It involves the frame of reference of the individual—the individuated Self—including assumptions and presuppositions. As the system that is the Self becomes more complicated or complex, which happens naturally through the process of living, the behaviors and characteristics of the Self change, requiring different approaches to understanding (Wilson, 1998; Bennet & Bennet, 2004). As Chickering et al. (2005) forward, where deep learning is necessary, we create and re-create our own personal understanding.

Building on awareness and understanding, an individual must *believe* that the actions are real and will work as understood. Believing something means that the individual accepts what they are aware of as a truth. It really exists. Beliefs are cognitive, fundamental neural patterns, which over time are associated with many other patterns, and may dominate those patterns. These are central and strong patterns in the mind created by autobiographical experiences and closely related to emotions. Our beliefs significantly impact our attitudes, what we think about various subjects, and how we act. Thus, believing that actions are real and will work is closely linked to our personal history of experiences.

Beliefs are frequently hidden from conscious thought and thereby can drive actions without cognitive awareness. Consciously seeking and building awareness and understanding of our underlying belief set, what Senge (1990) refers to as our mental models, we have a greater opportunity for intentional, conscious and deliberate choices that will result in desired outcomes. Transformational learning is a common expression used for a strong disoriented experience that results in an individual realizing that their beliefs and underlying assumptions are no longer valid or appropriate for a given aspect of reality. When this occurs, we typically have double-loop learning—a rapid shift in the frame of reference, the mindset or perspective of the individual relative to some experience.

> Beliefs are frequently hidden from conscious thought and thereby can drive actions without cognitive awareness.

Given awareness, understanding and believing, the individual must then *feel good* about taking action. These feelings are what make the action important to the individual and worthy of their efforts. Referencing our earlier findings, Zull (2002) considers emotions the foundation of learning, with the chemicals of emotion modifying the strength and contribution of each part of the learning cycle, directly impacting the signaling systems in each affected neuron. Similarly, Blackmore (2004) reminds us that reason cannot operate without emotions. Plotkin (1994) says that emotional content is almost always present in verbal and non-verbal communication. We push that even further. All information coming into the body moves through the amygdala, that part of the brain that is,

... important both for the acquisition and for the on-line processing of emotional stimuli ... [with] Its processing encompassing both the elicitation of emotional responses in the body and changes in other cognitive processes, such as attention and memory. (Adolphs, 2004, p. 1026)

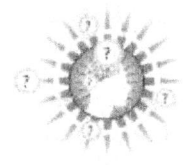

REFLECT:
Do I feel good about new actions that I take?
Has an event where you interact with others ever caused you to change your beliefs?

Recall that as incoming information moves through the amygdala, what we call an emotional "tag" is attached. If the incoming information is perceived as life-threatening, then the amygdala takes immediate control, making a decision and acting on that decision before the individual is consciously aware of the threat! Haberlandt (1998) says that there is no such thing as a behavior or thought not impacted by emotions in some way. Even simple responses to information signals can be linked to multiple emotional neurotransmitters. As Mulvihill points out, because emotions are integrally linked with incoming information from all the senses, "it becomes clear that there is no thought, memory, or knowledge which is 'objective,' or 'detached' from the personal experience of knowing (Mulvihill, 2003, p. 322).

Unfortunately, even this emotional tagging and sense of knowing may not be enough to initiate action. An individual must also feel *ownership* of the action—a personal responsibility to act—and *empowered* to take action, that is, has the knowledge and confidence (internal empowerment), and the right and freedom (perceived external empowerment) to take the action (Self efficacy).

Knowledge empowers people. For purposes of this book, empowerment is considered the investing of power, or to supply an ability, to enable (*American Heritage Dictionary*, 2006). Thus, being empowered includes having *knowledge* of how, when and where to take the desired action. From learning theory, we know that individuals who *believe* they can learn, can learn (Lipton, 2005). Extrapolating this concept to empowerment, a person who believes they are empowered and can accomplish some task or worthwhile goal will have a much higher probability of success than an individual who does not believe they are empowered to do so (Bennet & Bennet, 2007a). *The value of empowerment lies simultaneously in the freedom and the responsibility given to individuals to accomplish something—both by Self and perceived external authorities—and in the internal recognition of the personal capacity and capability to do so.*

> Self empowerment includes the knowledge of how to act ... and the courage to act.

In Chapter 12, we introduced the concept that the brain can generate molecules of emotion to reinforce what is learned. This is a choice, where through self-consciousness the mind uses the brain to generate molecules of emotion and override the cognitive system (Pert, 1997). This phenomenon can not only provide control over attention during concrete experience, but also improve understanding and meaning and seek truth or how things work. For example, through an awareness of biases and the presence of values against having these, an individual can exercise control over these biases (LeDoux, 1996). This process relates directly to the high degree of plasticity of the brain, which is able to change itself in response to experience and learning.

In the sense of Self as an agent of change in a social setting, the individual change model suggests questions that need to be asked, and actions that need to be taken. For example, in an organizational setting if a change strategy has been promulgated widely throughout all levels of the organization by senior leadership, then it could be assumed that employees are generally aware of the desired change and have a level of understanding about it. The question would be: Do they believe it is a good idea? Do they believe it will work? If success examples in other organizations with similar products and/or processes have been brought up and discussed, or other evidence of the power and potential of the change effort has been provided, then the question would be: How do the employees feel about this change? Of course, these feelings are very much based on employee questions such as: How will it impact my work? Is this something added to an already overwhelming work load? If successful, will this phase out my job? These, then, become the questions, which need to be addressed through words and actions. Once assured that employees feel good about the change, that is, they are not threatened by it and perhaps it will make their job easier or enable them to do a better job, then the question becomes: Do they have ownership of it? Once this issue is addressed the question becomes: Are they empowered to act? This is not empowerment by job description. This is self-empowerment in terms of: Do I have the knowledge and skills necessary to act, and am I confident to act? As can be seen there is tremendous power in working through this model to support change in a social setting.

Final Thoughts

In the last six chapters we have spent considerable time further exploring the concepts of Self, the environment and social engagement, repeating a few of the neuroscience findings in this context, and adding both simple and complicated examples to stimulate recognition of the importance of these concepts to the ICALS Theory and Model of experiential learning. We now take a deep breath, and in the next two chapters bring in two concepts critical to learning in terms of both individuation and the social life of Self: wisdom and knowing.

Section VII
A Crescendo of Capacity

Recall that knowledge is defined as a capacity. What does that mean? It becomes clearer as we have explored the concept of associative patterning, acknowledging that knowledge, which is context sensitive and situation dependent, is created by the Self in the instant at hand. Thus a crescendo of capacity expands the Self' potential for learning.

In this final section we first explore the wisdom of learning in Chapter 24. In a way, this is the affirmation of the value of evolution as humans have co-evolved with their environment. In another sense, coupled with a strong value set, learning has the potential to move the learner toward wisdom as more and more patterns are observed and experienced, and as an understanding grows of the relationships among those patterns and Self. This is consciousness expanding.

The second part of Chapter 24 are the guidelines for learning that have emerged from this work. We encourage those who are not interested in the discourse on wisdom to jump to the second half of the chapter. These guidelines are worth the jump.

Chapter 25 addresses more fully the concept of knowledge and knowing, tying this to experiential learning, and looking towards the future. Chapter 26 is a small glimpse of this future. We do not even begin to suggest that this book—or any book—provides the answers for the future—for that future is emerging even as we complete the writing of this sentence. As we go through life, we run into a wide range of experiences and situations that challenge us with respect to understanding and taking action.

What we *do* propose is that **fully developing an appreciation of the power of learning and knowledge** will help us recognize and engage in the amazing shifts that are occurring as humanity moves into a new time of "Lightenment".

Chapter 24
The Wisdom of Learning

Wisdom is universally a lofty consideration and too often we sense that it eludes us. The more that we seek it, the more we understand that it comes through learning. Moreover, the true irony is that wisdom brings with it the desire to learn more. Here, this Wisdom of Learning chapter holds three perspectives—it's wise to seek learning, there are wise ways to cultivate our learning, and learning will bring wisdom into our thinking. To that end, the following provides definitions and background related to wisdom. Then, to support learning and wisdom development, **nine guidelines for learners are offered that are based on the neuroscience findings surfaced in this research**.

As Tom Stonier, a theoretical biologist, was developing a workable theory of information in the 90's, along the way he discovered new relationships between information and the physical universe of matter and energy (Stonier, 1990; 1992; 1997). Simultaneously, an intense interest in neuroscience research was spurred onward by the creation and sophistication of brain measurement instrumentation. For the first time we could see what is happening in the mind/brain as we process information and act on that information. In the mind/brain there is no cause-and-effect relationship between information and knowledge; knowledge is an emergent phenomenon. Recall that it is through the interaction and selection (complexing) among many ideas, concepts and patterns of thought, all consisting of information, that knowledge is birthed.

Also during the late 90's, the body of research focused on wisdom was rapidly expanding. In the early years of knowledge management, a number of authors argued that wisdom was the end of a continuum made up of data → information → knowledge → wisdom. But as Peter Russell explains,

> Various people have pointed to the progression of data to information to knowledge ... continuing the progression suggests that something derived from knowledge leads to the emergence of a new level, what we call wisdom. But what is it that knowledge gives us that takes us beyond knowledge? Through knowledge we learn how to act in our own better interests. Will this decision lead to greater well-being, or greater suffering? What is the kindest way to respond in this situation? Wisdom reflects the values and criteria that we apply to our knowledge. Its essence is discernment. Discernment of right from wrong. Helpful from harmful. Truth from delusion. (Russell, 2007)

Remembering that knowledge is the outcome of learning, let us further explore this connection between knowledge and wisdom.

Definitions and Descriptions

A rich diversity of definitions and descriptions abound for wisdom. Focusing on work occurring around the turn of this century, Csikszentmihalyi and Nakamura (2005) described wisdom as referring to two distinct phenomena. The first was the *content* of wisdom (information and/or knowledge) and the second an individual's *capacity to think or act* wisely. Since the second part defines itself by itself, this invites a deeper exploration. Focusing on the content of wisdom, Clayton and Birren (1980) said that individuals perceived wisdom differently when socio-demographic variables were changed, that is, as we now recognize about knowledge, they considered wisdom as developed over time from a series of events context sensitive and situation dependent in terms of culture and locality. Similarly, the works of Holliday and Changler (1986), Erikson (1998), Sternberg (1998), Jarvis (1992), Kramer and Bacelar (1994), Bennett-Woods (1997), and Merriam and Caffarella (1999) all take the position that wisdom is grounded in life's rich experiences,

> ... [wisdom] therefore is developed through the process of aging ... wisdom seems to consist of the ability to move away from absolute truths, to be reflective to make sound judgments related to our daily existence, whatever our circumstances. (Merriam & Caffarella, 1999, p. 165)

Some core words associated with wisdom that appear throughout the literature include: *understanding* (Clayton & Birren, 1980; Chandler & Holliday, 1990; Orwoll & Perlmutter, 1990); *empathy* (Clayton & Birren, 1980; Csikszentmihalyi & Rathunde, 1990; Chandler & Holliday, 1990; Levitt, 1999; Shedlock & Cornelius, 2000); *knowledge* (Baltes & Smith, 1990; Clayton & Birren, 1980; Sternberg, 1998; Shedlock & Cornelius, 2000); *knows Self* (Chandler & Holiday, 1990; Levitt, 1999; Damon, 2000; Stevens, 2000; Shedlock & Cornelius, 2000); *living in balance* (Birren & Fisher, 1990; Meacham, 1990); *understanding* (Clayton & Barren, 1980; Chandler & Holliday, 1990; Levitt, 1999; Stevens, 2000); and *systemic thinking* (Chandler & Holliday, 1990; Stevens, 2000; Shedlock & Cornelius, 2000). Macdonald describes this systemic thinking as "acting with the well-being of the whole in mind" (Macdonald, 1996, p. 1).

Trumpa (1991) sees wisdom as a state of consciousness with the qualities of spaciousness, friendliness, warmth, softness and joy. Woodman and Dickinson (1996) see wisdom as the state of consciousness that allows the spiritual Self to be active. Similarly, in a comparative study of two groups, one characterized as elderly and one characterized as creative, Orwoll and Perlmutter (1990) discovered that wisdom was associated with advanced self-development and self-transcendence.

Wisdom also appears to have an affective component (Brown, 2000). The neurobiological roots of this were confirmed by Sherman (2000) who discovered that some brain-damaged patients who lacked wisdom also lacked the evaluative affects used to choose a course of action (make a decision).

268 | Expanding the Self

A number of writers have considered wisdom as a part of intelligence (Smith et al., 1987; Dittmann-Kohli & Baltes, 1990). Baltes and Smith (1990) go on to say that wisdom is "a highly developed body of factual and procedural knowledge and judgment dealing with what we call the 'fundamental pragmatics of life'." In contrast, from qualitative research with Buddhist monks, Levitt (1999) said that the monks tended toward a spiritual definition and believed that all people were capable of wisdom, regardless of their intellect.

Around the turn of the century, the U.S. Department of the Navy placed knowledge at the beginning and wisdom near the end of their change model based on the seven levels of consciousness (Porter, et al, 2003; Bennet & Bennet, 2004). See Figure 24-1. The change model consists of the following progression to facilitate increased connectedness and heightened consciousness: (1) closed structured concepts, (2) focused by limited sharing, (3) awareness and connectedness through sharing, (4) creating concepts and sharing these concepts with others, (5) advancement of new knowledge shared with humanity at large, (6) creating wisdom, teaching, and leading, and (7) creating (and sharing) new thoughts in a fully aware and conscious process.[1]

In the earlier levels of this model, value is absent since the positive or negative value of knowledge is context sensitive and situation dependent. However, prior to reaching level 6 Creating Wisdom, Teaching and Leading, there is the insertion of value framed in the context of the greater good.

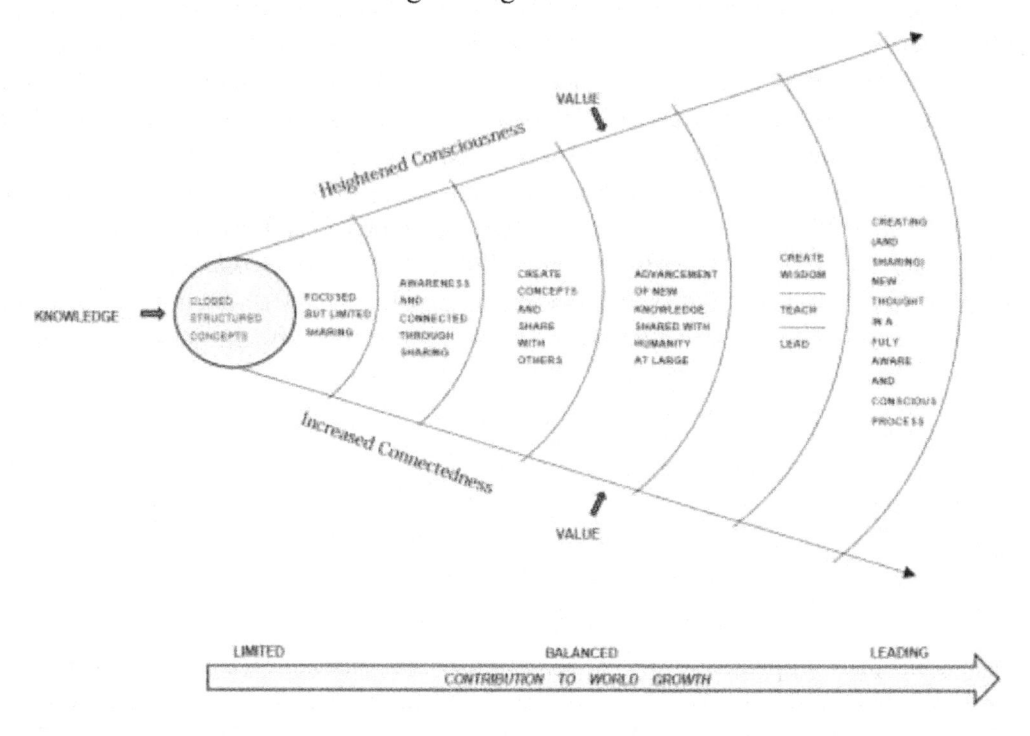

Figure 24-1. *The growth of knowledge and sharing (a change model used in the US Department of Navy based on the seven levels of consciousness).*

Please note that values are knowledge (Bennet & Bennet, 2015a) and are context sensitive and situation dependent—developed over time and highly responsive to culture. The model specifically focused on the new decision-maker emerging from a global culture. As connections increase and consciousness expands there is recognition of a higher value of knowledge, that is, moving beyond the individual to groups, to communities, to a global value. *This is the direction and connection to wisdom.* Note that this relationship to others is also a factor in our description of intelligent activity, which activity reflects wisdom.[2]

Nussbaum (2000) forwards that all knowledge, and by extension learning, is in the service of wisdom. Nelson (2004) says that wisdom is the knowledge of the essential nature of reality. Further, similar to what was expressed in the Navy model, Sternberg defines wisdom as "the application of tacit knowledge as mediated by values toward the goal of achieving a common good" (Sternberg, 1998, p. 353), thus suggesting that tacit knowledge is a prerequisite for developing wisdom and, as suggested in the previous paragraph, *wisdom is defined in a social rather than individual context*. This is an important distinction of wisdom, although in everyday language the term "wise" is often used in service to the individual. Note that over time, what is considered "wise" only from an individual perspective leads to separation, self-service, and learning limitations as the individual identifies with the knowledge they create. Looking from the functional viewpoint of the mind/brain as an associative patterner, it would appear that information (as patterns of energy) is intended to flow from person to person, triggering experiential learning and expansion. This would indeed place learning in service to wisdom and insinuate its connection to a greater social good.

REFLECT:
How can I bring more wisdom into my life?
What is the relationship between wisdom and learning?

Wisdom as Patterns

Goldberg, a clinical professor of neurology, raises the question: If memory and mental focus decline with age, why is it that our wisdom and competence grow? After validating these two propositions, he answers the question by asserting that *tacit knowledge* does not suffer appreciable decline with age because it represents high-level patterns of procedural knowledge—knowledge of solving problems (Goldberg, 2005). These are *patterns that represent chunks or groups of other patterns.* If a mind has been active throughout life, these high-level patterns represent competence, insight and deep (tacit) knowledge that may be considered wisdom. Thus while memory, specific facts and attention may decline with age, the knowledge of how to solve problems or what needs to be done in a specific situation does not appear to decline. Tacit knowledge and wisdom may remain strong and even continue to grow with age. What this also implies is that tacit knowledge—particularly as we age—is primarily process knowledge, or knowledge (proceeding).

Murphy (2000) points out that wisdom is at home in several levels of the hierarchy of complexity. As she observes, "understanding of a phenomenon at each level of the hierarchy can be enhanced by relating it to its neighboring levels" (Murphy, 2000, p. 7). Schloss explains that the levels of a hierarchy are interrelated via feedback loops; increased understanding results from following these feedback loops from one level to another and back again (Schloss, 2000). Similarly, Erikson says that a sense of the complexity of living is an attribute of wisdom. A wise person embraces the,

> ... sense of the complexity of living, of relationships, of all negotiations. There is certainly no immediate, discernible, and absolute right and wrong, just as light and dark are separated by innumerable shadings ... [the] interweaving of time and space, light and dark, and the complexity of human nature suggests that ... this wholeness of perception to be given partially and realized, must of necessity be made up of a merging of the sensual, the logical, and the aesthetic perceptions of the individual. (Erikson, 1988, p. 184)

As Can Be Noted in this Brief Treatment ...

The concept of wisdom is clearly related to knowledge—and in particular to tacit knowledge—and has also been related to the phenomenon of consciousness. Wisdom is clearly connected with systemic, hierarchical thinking, and the complexity of human nature has been brought into the discussion. Most importantly, wisdom is not in isolation; it appears to deal with the cognitive and emotional, personal and social, as well as the moral and religious aspects of life, very much based on the interconnectedness of people.

As Costa sums up in *Working Wisdom*:

> Wisdom is the combination of knowledge and experience, but it is more than just the sum of these parts. Wisdom involves the mind and the heart, logic and intuition, left brain and right brain, but it is more than either reason, or creativity, or both. **Wisdom involves a sense of balance, an equilibrium derived from a strong, pervasive *moral* conviction ... the conviction and guidance provided by the obligations that flow from a profound sense of interdependence.** In essence, wisdom grows through the learning of more knowledge, and the practiced experience of day-to-day life—both filtered through a code of moral conviction. (Costa, 1995, p. 3)

From Ordinary to Extraordinary Consciousness

To quickly lay the groundwork for understanding our usage of consciousness, we provide representative viewpoints from several fields. The psychologist William James said that consciousness was the name of a non-entity in that it stands for the function of knowing (a process) (McDermott, 1977). The psychologist J. Allan Hobson considers consciousness as awareness of the world, the body and the Self (Hobson, 1999). In neuroscience terms, this would be the sensitivity to outside stimuli as translated through the brain and neuron connections into patterns that to the mind represent thoughts. The Nobel Laureate physiologist Gerald Edelman considered consciousness as a process of the flow of thoughts, images, feelings and emotions (Edelman & Tononi, 2000). The spiritualist Ramon describes consciousness as the "energized pool of intent from which all human experience springs" (Ramon, 1997, p. 48).

As introduced in Chapter 2 and reiterated several times in this book, we agree that consciousness is a process, and not a state. It is private, continuous, always-changing, and felt to be a sequential set of ideas, thoughts, images, feelings and perceptions (Bennet, 2001) with an understanding of the relationships among these ideas, thoughts, images, feelings and perceptions and the Self (MacFlouer, 1999). It is the sum total of who we are, what we believe, how we act and the things we do, so it's all of our actions, thoughts and words (Dunning, 2014). A high-level property of consciousness is its unity. The mind is continually integrating the incoming signals from the environment as well as connecting many different processing areas within the brain and combining them into a coherent flow of conscious thinking or feeling. When we see a snapshot of the visible world, it appears as a coherent, unified whole.

REFLECT:
How is wisdom cultivated in my unconscious?
Am I conscious of my consciousness?

Ordinary consciousness represents the customary or typical state of consciousness, that which is common to everyday usage, if consciousness could possibly be considered common! Polanyi sees tacit knowledge as *not* part of one's ordinary consciousness (Polanyi, 1958); thus, tacit knowledge resides in the unconscious. To access tacit knowledge, the individual needs to move beyond ordinary consciousness to what we call *extraordinary consciousness*, acquiring a greater sensitivity to information stored in the unconscious in order to facilitate the awareness and application of that information and knowledge. Extraordinary consciousness may be created through such techniques as meditation, lucid dreaming, guided visualization, hemispheric synchronization (see Chapter 21), and other ways of quieting the conscious mind, and by doing so allowing and encouraging *accessibility* to information in the unconscious. Such techniques create a heightened sensitivity to, awareness of, and connection with our unconscious mind with its memory and thought processes.

On the other hand, consciousness appears to be a flow, with extraordinary consciousness representing increased sensitivity to awareness of tacit knowledge. As a process, consciousness represents a characteristic of the human mind to be *aware* of the nature and structure of information and understanding its relationship to Self. Moving beyond ordinary consciousness to extraordinary consciousness would increase this awareness and understanding.

In the discussion of wisdom above, recall that Csikszentmihalyi and Nakamura (1990) described wisdom as referring to two distinct phenomena: the *content* of wisdom and the *capacity* to think or act wisely. This parallels our understanding of knowledge as both knowledge (informing) and knowledge (proceeding), an information component and a process component. Knowledge and wisdom would then both deal with the *nature and structure of information*, with nature being, or representing, the quality or constitution of information and structure being (or representing) the process of building new information, learning. Wisdom represents **higher discernment** and the use of tacit knowledge to provide new, situation-dependent, context-sensitive knowledge—perhaps taking the form of intuition. The tacit knowledge driving what is surfaced would be both knowledge (informing) and knowledge (proceeding), although as noted by Goldberg (2005), primarily knowledge (proceeding).

> Extraordinary consciousness represents increased sensitivity to awareness of tacit knowledge.

Further, wisdom has been repeatedly related to systemic thinking and **the recognition of a higher order of interdependence in the hierarchy of life**, perhaps even the universe. Similarly, extraordinary consciousness delimits ordinary consciousness, increasing sensitivity to, and awareness of, that which is tacit—that which is in the unconscious—whether embodied, affective, intuitive or spiritual (see Chapter 18). It is important to recall that these tacit knowledges are inter-linked; humans are holistic decision-makers. With this larger sensitivity and awareness of that which is tacit comes increased understanding of the interdependence associated with patterns of information, some of which would be patterns of patterns, possibly hierarchical in nature, although they might be represented by any three-dimensional patterns in space.

Figure 24-2 provides a visual representation of the relationships among knowledge, consciousness and extraordinary consciousness. The dotted lines represent a movement from ordinary consciousness into extraordinary consciousness, at whatever level that may occur. The wavy lines represent the fluctuating boundary between explicit and tacit knowledge, with implicit knowledge describing that which was thought tacit but triggered into consciousness by external events (incoming information).

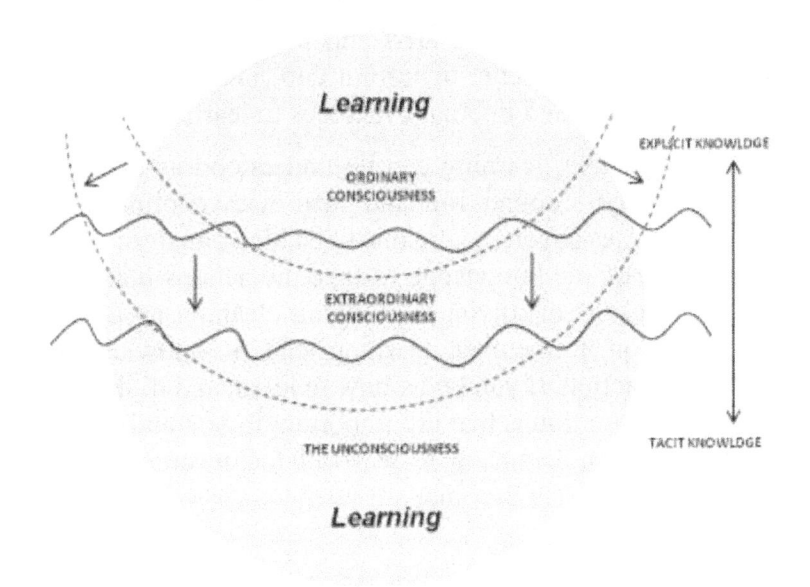

Figure 24-2. *Conceptual model relating knowledge and consciousness.*

While there is much thinking and experimentation needed to truly understand wisdom, it is increasingly clear that extraordinary consciousness—expanding our sensitivity and awareness of that which is tacit—appears to open the door to expanded wisdom.

Seeking and Cultivating Learning and Wisdom

Our world is changing, sometimes rapidly, sometimes randomly and sometimes dangerously. At the same time, it is easy for an individual, a family, a city, a country or even our world to turn away, ignore, and let things go as they will. The attitude is likely to be "Let others do something." or "Nothing will really happen." Throughout life, the rationale is sometimes "It's too early to do anything." or "Let someone else take care of it." Or perhaps, "We have enough of our own problems." Thus, the world, on its own, continues with its changes, problems, and directions. Since citizens and leaders often do not know what is going on, or what may happen in the near term, ignoring the possibilities and/or the probabilities often seem the easiest way!! Unfortunately, this is how families break up, accidents happen, cities deteriorate and nations start wars.

The future is rarely predictable and as "CUCA"—change, uncertainty, complexity, anxiety—is an indicator of the present *and* most likely the future, it is extremely difficult, if not impossible, to anticipate what will happen in the future. But all hope is not lost, because although prediction is never 100 percent correct, continuous and well directed areas of learning can give the alert and provide the proactive individual, family, and organization a much better opportunity to "take effective action." To do this we can develop the ability and internal capacities to learn.

From a broader perspective, learning can be understood as the capacity to take effective action. As we go through life and deal with continuous change, new opportunities, and sometimes adversity, we must be able to analyze the situations and through our learning, create the knowledge to take the actions that will achieve our objectives. That action results in solving a problem, cleaning up a bad situation, or creating a desired situation. Remember, learning leads to knowledge, which is the capacity to take effective action. If you know how to learn, and if, in fact, you take the time and effort to learn those things that are important to you and your life, you will then have a high probability of being able to deal with the uncertainties and challenges that the future may bring. *That* is wisdom.

Guidelines for Learning

A significant conclusion from this research is that adults, should they desire, have much more control over their learning than they may realize. Many of the popular and presumably scientific myths have been falsified with scientific evidence. Examples of myth busters that this study has addressed are **neuroplasticity**, destroying the myth that brains are rigid and fixed at birth, the possibility of **continuous learning throughout life,** destroying the myth that the brain must decay with age and that older people cannot learn, and **the phenomenon of epigenetics,** destroying the myth that "genes are destiny". **The role of the unconscious and the importance of exercise** also expands the potential impact individuals have over their own learning.

This new evidence opens the door for adult learners to develop themselves in whatever way they desire, that is, we have choices. At the same time, parents have the impetus to support their children's learning through their understanding of the importance and relevance of the family environment and social engagement in aiding brain development. In short, all have the innate potential to expand, improve and develop their minds/brains and significantly improve their learning capacity and hence their knowledge. Adults who heretofore thought they were not capable of learning could perceive their future and themselves in an entirely different light as they become aware of—and believe in—the power of their minds and the new learning possibilities this research has identified.

All this centers on the power of Self, which undergirds all the modes of learning. Further, by designating social engagement as the fifth learning mode, we acknowledge and honor the global nature of social learning that continues to expand as we move squarely into this new millennium. Social engagement offers resources and new ideas through a continuous dialogue with the environment in which we live.

> The power of self undergirds all the modes of learning.

As a beginning step toward a new theory of learning, nine guidelines for learners are offered below. These guidelines, based on the neuroscience findings surfaced in this research, are a high-level perspective for adult learners as they acquire and apply knowledge and consider implementing their own self-development. These guidelines are concerned with (1) the infinite potential of the human mind, (2) the powerful role of beliefs, (3) the influence of the environment, (4) the responsibility of knowledge, (5) the power of the unconscious, (6) the wisdom of age, (7) the drive for certainty, (8) the sacredness of values, and (9) "The Paradox."

1. The Infinite Potential of the Human Mind

This research identifies a number of neuroscientific findings that signify the almost unbounded limits of the human mind. While, to our understanding, no one knows the number of neurons and synapses that may be involved in any specific thought or idea, given some reasonable assumptions it is easy to show that the number of possible thoughts in the human mind becomes extremely large, larger than 10^{79}—the estimated number of particles in the universe. The plasticity of the mind/brain, the ability of thoughts to change the physiological architecture of the brain and to impact the entire body, its potential efficacy throughout our lives, and its penchant for growth and development are clear evidence of the potential and magnificence of this mind/brain we carry with us throughout life.

The effects of a positive environment, good nutrition and health, and regular exercise also provide evidence of the high potential of all individuals. What this indicates is that parents have more influence, and therefore more responsibility, for the support and guidance of their children and their children's environment. It also indicates that adults, no matter where they start, have the tremendous possibility and opportunity to learn, grow, and develop as individual human beings. From a survival—and perhaps sustainability—perspective, taking advantage of our potential as individuals, families, organizations, and nations may be our most important contribution to the existence and advancement of the human race, and perhaps the survival of all of Earth's life forms.

The Republic of Singapore, named the most admired knowledge city in the world in both 2007 and 2008, recognized the need to restructure their complete educational system. As Wong et al. (2006) describe, "The educational system was restructured in the last few years in order to foster greater creativity and instill higher-order (i.e., analytical, creative, and systems) thinking skills amongst its school children. There is now a substantial reduction in curriculum content and student assessment in favor of team learning, problem solving and process skills acquisition" (p. 91). These authors also note that the objective is to create a future workforce capable of advanced, continuous learning, un-learning, and relearning. As neuroscience and its related sciences continue to contribute to our knowledge of human learning, we will be able to take better and better advantage of that with which we have been gifted.

2. The Powerful Role of Beliefs

As described earlier in this study, the mind/brain learns through mixing incoming information patterns with internally existing patterns of information and knowledge, thereby creating new patterns that represent understanding and meaning (the process of associative patterning). These internal patterns are significantly influenced by the beliefs and theories created and held by ;the Self. Lipton (2005) makes the point that both positive and negative beliefs impact every aspect of our life, including our health. Because of their power to influence our decisions and actions, beliefs have influence over our learning. A good representation of this idea is that *if an individual believes that they cannot learn, then in fact, they will not be able to learn*. For example, when social relationships and attitudes cause an individual to feel incapable of learning, they experience a self-fulfilling prophecy. On the other hand, if an individual believes they can learn, then in fact, they can and will be able to learn, moving through environmental influence to personal decisions, to beliefs, to frames of reference, to understanding, to knowledge, to action.

Thus an individual's attitudes toward their own capability and efficacy of learning is critical to their capacity to learn. It is for this reason that we should seriously consider and question our own beliefs to see if they are aligned with our personal objectives and values. If not, then we may want to reinvestigate the basis and assumptions that drive these beliefs and expand our awareness to the possibility of beliefs more in alignment with our learning goals.

Another role of beliefs is influencing health. The biologist Lipton (2005, p. 144) forwards that, "If you choose to see a world full of love, your body will respond by growing in health. If you choose to live in a dark world full of fear, your body's health will be compromised as you physiologically close yourself down in a protection response." Referring to his own book, *The Biology of Belief*, Lipton (2005) says that the secret of life is all about learning to harness our own minds to promote and accelerate growth.

3. The Influence of the Environment

Influence can be thought of as a power to sway or affect. Recall the discussion of the autopoietic co-evolution of the learner and the environment in Chapter 10. This relationship may significantly influence the learner's stress level, self-confidence, and tentativeness or interest in any specific learning. Here is where the learner must recognize what is happening and seek to modify or change the environment to better enable successful learning. At the same time, an individual having a dialogue with another learner needs to recognize the importance of the environment relative to the efficacy of either party's learning process. Often the environmental influence is through embodied experiences without conscious awareness. Other paths to the unconscious include affective, intuitive and spiritual—all contributing to learning (Bennet & Bennet, 2008a; 2015a). Placing the potential effects of the learning environment, both good and bad, next to the potential power of the human mind places the responsibility for learning and personal development directly in the hands of the adult learner, not the environment.

Another aspect that came up in this study is the local environment within which cells exist throughout the body. From epigenetics it becomes clear that the local environment of the cell could have significant influence on whether or not the DNA of the cell was expressed. This means that genes do not have to be destiny and that an individual should in some cases be able to influence the potential effect of their genetic heritage, and some of the influences may be passed on to their offspring. As Church (2006) says, "There is mounting evidence that invisible factors of consciousness and intention—such as our beliefs, feelings, prayers, and attitudes—play an important role in the epigenetic control of genes." (p. 57)

4. The Responsibility of Knowledge

This guideline comes from the recognition that most societies hold individuals responsible for their actions. Knowledge has been defined as the capacity to take effective action and learning is the creation and application of knowledge. In other words, those individuals who learn and create knowledge have a duty to implement that knowledge responsibly. As Meacham (1995) posits, "The essence of wisdom...lies not in what is known but rather in the manner in which that knowledge is held and in how that knowledge is put to use" (p. 185). Whether that knowledge relates to a small situation or to a world crisis, whoever holds that knowledge has a responsibility to act appropriately and wisely. This is where wisdom, fairness and responsibility come into play. Knowledge alone has no constraints; but knowledge is not alone when it is applied in the real world. Here humans, as a part of all life, have strong responsibilities towards other life forms and the planet we live on. Thus, since learning creates knowledge, both learning and knowledge include responsibility for application, both pragmatically and ethically.

If we consider deep knowledge, that is, individuals with high expertise in a specific area, one would expect them to have an even higher responsibility in implementing such knowledge. However, with deep knowledge—or perceived deep knowledge—also comes a caution. We are not our knowledge; indeed, the ICALS is a continuous learning function of the human. Since knowledge is context sensitive and situation dependent, it is incomplete, that is, what worked in one situation may not work in another and, as the environment shifts and changes, new knowledge is continuously emerging. Thus as a learner and part of a global network of learners we carry the additional responsibility of social engagement, to enable learning through sharing and taking action for the broader and higher good of our families, friends and civilization and all other life on the planet.

5. The Power of the Unconscious

Power means the ability or capacity to perform or act effectively, as well as the ability or official capacity to exercise control (*American Heritage Dictionary*, 2006). As we have seen in this study, the unconscious mind plays a significant role in experiential learning. The brain is always processing information, mostly through the unconscious. When we sleep, we often reflect on the previous day's information. Rock (2004) suggests that at night the unconscious evaluates the information that has come in that day for its relative importance and discards the unimportant information while storing what is important . Kandel (2007) notes that the unconscious never lies, but it can make mistakes. This is not surprising since our unconscious is a part of who we are and exists to aid in our survival. The unconscious influences our thoughts and emotions without our being fully aware of it. This may be a good thing if we watch what we take in, but as Marshall (2005, p. 11) so eloquently warns,

> *Beware of the stories you read or tell; subtly, at night. Beneath the waters of consciousness, they are altering your world.*

The unconscious processing of incoming information is significantly greater than conscious processing and includes the memory and autonomous systems with the exception of part of working memory. All tacit knowledge is created and stored in the unconscious. It is the source of dreams, intuition, judgment, knowing, and much creativity. By recognizing, respecting, and working with our unconscious we can improve our capacity to learn, think, make decisions, and take effective actions. However, much more research needs to be done in understanding and explaining the operation and influence of the unconscious in learning.

There is considerable interest and dialogue with respect to the existence of the reality of free will. The relations between the conscious Self, the unconscious, and memory and emotion are likely to play a large role in our learning capacity and intuitively it makes sense that these four phenomena will play a central role in any strong theory of adult learning. The connecting link would likely be through the internal relations within a complex adaptive, self-organizing learning system.

In our book, *The Course of Knowledge: A 21st Century Theory* (MQIPress, 2015), we present a deep treatment of tacit knowledge with a chapter dedicated to engaging tacit knowledge. For those interested in exploring the inner realms of tacit, this is a good starting point.

6. The Wisdom of Age

Expanding on our earlier treatment of wisdom, Meacham says that wisdom is not beliefs, attitudes, or sets of facts, rather wisdom is *the attitude taken by individuals toward their beliefs, values and knowledge*. Similarly, Sternberg (1998) posits that **"The essence of wisdom is not in what is known but in how that knowledge is held and put to use"** (p. 188). According to Goldberg, age can bring along with it wisdom, if the individual so chooses. For the mind/brain to maintain its functional capacity, it must continuously be used throughout life. Ideally, all parts of the brain should be exercised both mentally and physically. While the total neuronal population of the brain may decrease with age, some parts of the brain will continue to create new neurons. Goldberg claims that the patterns that represent significant meaning and value, those patterns referred to as wisdom, tend to remain independent of age (Goldberg, 2001, 2005). This, of course, depends on the nature of the mental and physical life lived by the individual. Thus we may conclude that wise individuals are not just lucky individuals, they are the people who *continue to learn and work to develop and apply knowledge for higher-level purposes*.

7. The Drive for Certainty

Drive means to push, propel, or press forward; to supply a motive force or power to cause to function. From an evolutionary perspective, survival can be seen as lifelong learning and a search for certainty in a changing, uncertain, and increasingly complex world. One solution to this challenge is the capacity to understand the environment and develop the capability to anticipate its immediate future. As discussed above, this is one function of learning, namely, to be able to take effective actions for survival. Theories, beliefs, and assumptions are used to build mental models or frames of reference to understand the environment. These then form a framework for new learning as well as for guiding actions. If the beliefs are consistent with the external environment, the believers are rewarded through effective actions and empowerment.

Beliefs may also serve to narrow the field of perceived possibilities that could occur in the external world and, if they are strong, absolute beliefs, they can create the potential illusion of certainty. Unfortunately, such adverse drives for certainty serve to limit learning capacity and seek to maintain the status quo—an almost impossible task in today's world. There is no risk aversion, there is only risk management. *Risk requires learning, learning creates knowledge, knowledge leads to action, and action needs wisdom. They are all connected in circular spirals that determine the quality of our lives and the existence of our planet.*

8. The Sacredness of Values

One interpretation of sacred means dedicated or devoted exclusively to a single use, purpose, or person (*American Heritage Dictionary*, 2006). Although this research does not deal directly with values, they are inherent in all learning and knowledge (Bennet & Bennet, 2015a). Two of the above guidelines relate responsibility and wisdom to learning. Recall the set of relationships: beliefs influence thinking, which influences understanding, which creates knowledge, which directs actions, which impacts the environment. Actions are related to the environment and two other guidelines immediately call up responsibility and wisdom, which in turn are closely related to values. Wisdom suggests what the objective should be, knowledge says what needs to be done to achieve the objective, and values provide guidance on how it should be achieved and what should not be done, which in a sense leads back to wisdom.

One surprise during this research was the central role that learning and the learning process play in a great many aspects of our lives. We cannot escape the role of—and benefits of—learning in our lives, yet we often ignore it. The questions are: What shall we learn? How should we learn? What can we do with our learning? And what are our responsibilities if we have knowledge? Learning is too important to the future of the world to be left to teachers, schools, industry or governments. It must become the responsibility and the activity of every individual!

9. "The Paradox"

Einstein reminds us that everything should be as simple as possible and no simpler. Mountain Quest Institute, the research location for the authors, posits that before you can simplify something, you had better understand its complexity (Bennet & Bennet, 2013). Yet the world continues to change and increase in complexity at a faster and faster rate. So how do we understand the world and its complexity well enough to be able to improve our knowledge and effectiveness of learning? And how can we learn faster and better, thereby keeping up with our world and its increasing complexity? This is the paradox and the challenge of the future! The simplicity is in the patterns—learning, knowledge, responsibility, values and wisdom are our most effective solution. Seeking to embrace complexity by creating deep knowledge and maximizing our own autobiographies, meta-learning, and learning processes as part of our growth and development will help us catch up with exponentially exploding complexity while always keeping in mind the need and importance of wisdom.

REFLECT:
How can I use these guidelines to enable my learning?
What nuggets from this book can I share with others?

Chapter 25
Knowledge and Knowing

The infinite potential of the human mind is not limited by the boundaries of the human neural system, nor by that which can be sensed by the five physical senses of hearing, seeing, tasting, smelling and feeling. There is an additional internal sense that we call knowing.

Every decision, and the actions that decision drives, is a learning experience that builds on its predecessors by broadening the sources of knowledge creation and the capacity to create knowledge in different ways. For example, as an individual engages in more and more conversations across the Internet in search of meaning, thought connections occur that cause an expansion of shallow knowledge. As we are aware, *knowledge begets knowledge*. In a global interactive environment, the more that is understood, the more that can be created and understood. **This is how ICALS, our personal learning system, works.** As we tap into our internal resources, *knowledge enables knowing, and knowing supports and enhances the creation of knowledge*.

A Quick Review

We have alluded to the concept of "knowing" earlier in this book and have described it in various terms. For example, in *Assumption 3* of the Preface we say: Complex systems can rarely be understood by analytical thinking or deductive reasoning alone. Therefore, deep knowledge created from effortful practice, the development of intuition and tacit knowledge through experience and continuous learning, and *the recognition of, and sensitivity to, our inner knowing* is required. And in *Assumption 8* we say: Given the limitations of our own perceptions and understanding, we consider and explore areas and phenomena that move beyond our paradigms and beliefs regarding learning and knowledge to *the larger area of knowing beyond the activity of our cognitive functions to consider the energy patterns within which humanity is immersed.*

In Chapter 2 (Learning from the Inside Out) we write: The mind is the seat of consciousness, enabling awareness of *our self as a knower*, as an observer and learner, and as one who takes action. But knowing, observing, learning and taking action are not static, nor is the Self. And later in Chapter 2 we provide a quote: Mulvihill (2003) notes that during the initial processing and linking of information from the different senses, "it becomes clear that there is no thought, memory, or knowledge which is 'objective,' or 'detached' from the personal experience of knowing" (p. 322). And still later in Chapter 2, knowing was identified as one of the four forces of the organization:

the force of direction, the force of intent, the force of knowledge and the force of knowing. Knowing expands knowledge, bolsters intent, and signals the organization or individual whether the actions and directions are on track.

In Chapter 3, intuition is defined as *the act or faculty of knowing or sensing without the use of rational processes*; immediate cognition (*American Heritage Dictionary*, 2006, p. 919), and in Chapter 5 we state that there is a sense of knowing that emerges from the unconscious that may or may not be linked to the external environment, although it certainly emerges from the internal environment of Self.

When exploring emotions in Chapter 8 we quote Mulvihill (2003) as saying:

> Because the neurotransmitters which carry messages of emotion, are integrally linked with the [incoming] information, during both the initial processing and the linking with information from the different senses, it becomes clear that there is no thought, memory, or knowledge which is "objective," or "detached" from *the personal experience of knowing*. (p. 322)

In that same chapter, while exploring neuroscience findings related to the unconscious, we quote Gigerenzer (2007) as saying: "The intelligence of the unconscious is in knowing, without thinking, which rule is likely to work in which situation." (p. 19) And later in that chapter we state that: These examples indicate the existence of an unconscious mind that is capable of thinking and recognizing patterns; in other words, the unconscious ability to *learn and know what to do without conscious awareness* (Berry & Broadbent, 1984). This is also *one source of tacit knowledge*, when the individual intuitively understands and knows something yet is unable to articulate the reasons or evidence for knowing (Polanyi, 1958; Bennet et al., 2015a; Bennet & Bennet, 2013).

Unconscious Connection

The word and concept of "knowing" can be used in so many ways in our language. But as is insinuated in the review above, we focus on a concept here that is beyond Self, yet informing Self. We consider knowing, connected at the core of Self, as a *sense* that is supported by our tacit knowledge. Perhaps it can poetically be best described as: *seeing beyond images, hearing beyond words, sensing beyond appearances, and feeling beyond emotions*.

Figure 25-1 is a nominal graphic showing the continuous feedback loops between knowledge and knowing. Thinking about (potential) and experiencing (actual) effective action (knowledge) supports development of embodied, intuitive and affective tacit knowledge. Knowing begins with expanding our five external senses and increasing our ability to consciously integrate these sensory inputs with our tacit knowledge (embodied, intuitive and affective), that knowledge created by past learning experiences residing in the unconscious that is *entangled with* the flow of spiritual tacit knowledge continuously available to each of us. (Definitions of these tacit knowledges are presented in Chapter 18.) In other words, knowing is the *sense* gained from experience that resides in the *unconscious*, including the energetic connection our mind enjoys with the *superconscious*.

When we recognize and use our sense of knowing—regardless of its origin—we are tapping into our tacit knowledge to inform our decisions and actions. These decisions and actions, and the feedback from taking those actions, in turn expand our knowledge base, much of which over time will become future tacit resources. Since our internal sense of knowing draws collectively from all areas of our tacit knowledge, the more we open to this inner sense, respond accordingly, and observe and reflect on feedback (reflective observation), the more our inner resources move beyond limited perceptions which may be connected to embedded childhood memories.

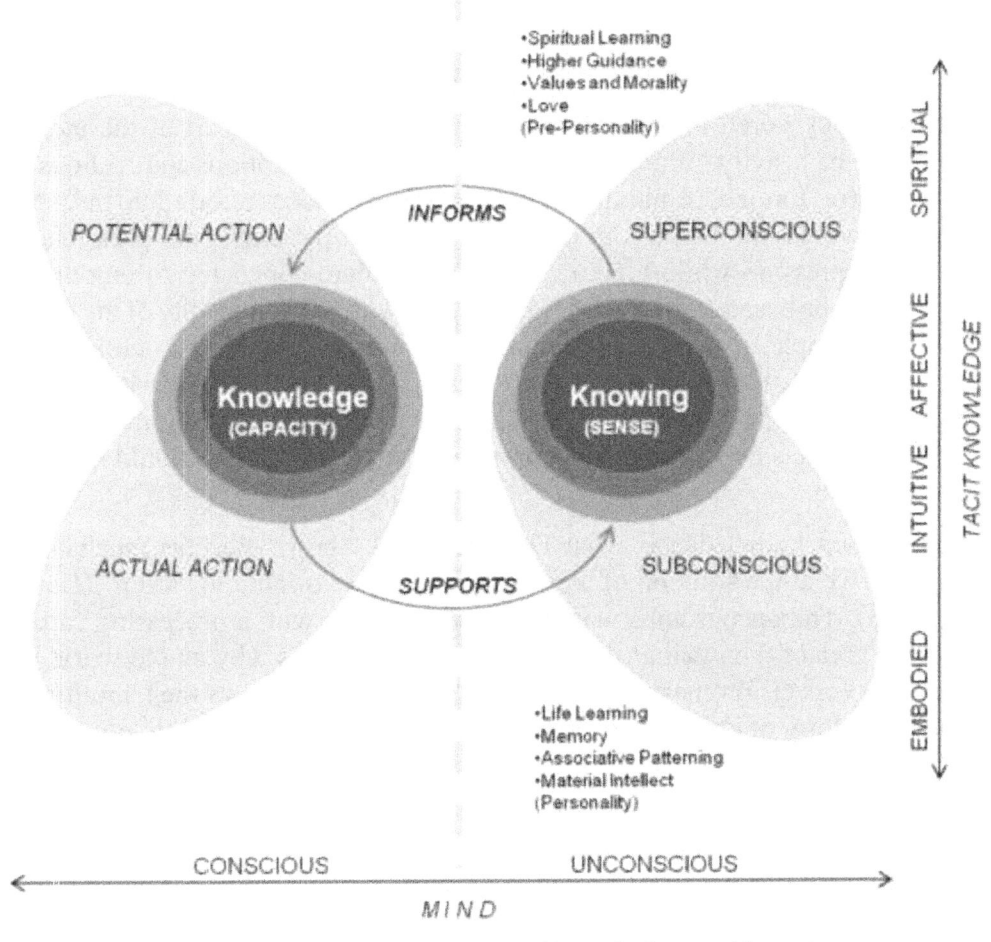

Figure 25-1. *The eternal loop of knowledge and knowing.*

The subconscious and superconscious are both part of our unconscious resources, with the subconscious directly supporting the embodied mind/brain and the superconscious focused on tacit resources involving larger moral aspects, the emotional part of human nature and the higher development of our mental faculties. When engaged by an intelligent mind, which has moved beyond logic into conscious processing based on trust and recognition of the connectedness and interdependence of humanity, these resources are immeasurable.

In Figure 25-1, the descriptive terms for the subconscious include life learning, memory, associative patterning, and material intellect. The subconscious is an autonomic system serving a life-support function. We all must realize that as part of the Self, **the human *subconscious* is in service to the conscious mind**. It is not intended to dominate an individual's decision-making; rather, to serve as an information resource and a guidance system. The subconscious expands as it integrates and connects (complexes) all that we put into it through our five external senses. *It is at the conscious mind level that we develop our intellect and make choices that serve as the framework for our subconscious processing.*

The memories stored in the subconscious are very much a part of the individual Self, and may be heavily influenced by an individual's perceptions and feelings at the time they were formed. Embodied tacit knowledge, also referred to as somatic knowledge, would be based on repeated physical patterns and preferences of personality expression while affective tacit knowledge, connected to emotions and feelings, would be based on the feelings connected with the personality of the decision-maker. For example, if there was a traumatic event that occurred in childhood that produced a feeling of "helplessness," there might be neuronal patterns later in life that are triggered that reproduce this feeling when the adult encounters a similar situation. While these feelings may have been appropriate for the child, they would rarely be of service to the adult.

Intuitive tacit knowledge is what Damasio calls "the mysterious mechanism by which we arrive at the solution of a problem without reasoning toward it" (Damasio, 1994, p. 188). The unconscious works around the clock with a processing capability many times greater than that at the conscious level. This is why as the world grows more complex, decision-makers will depend more and more on their intuitive tacit knowledge. A form of knowing, deep tacit knowledge is created within our minds (or hearts or guts) over time through experience, contemplation, and unconscious processing such that it becomes a natural part of our being—not just something consciously learned, stored, and retrieved (Bennet & Bennet, 2007e). In other words, intuitive tacit knowledge is the result of continuous learning through experience!

REFLECT:
What is the relationship between knowledge and knowing?
Do I value my intuitive tacit knowledge?

Looking again at Figure 25-1, the superconscious is described with the terms spiritual learning, higher guidance, values and morality, and love. An aspect of considering the larger perspective is the expanding idea that there is something else in existence that is powerful and pervasive. In a number of world religions, attention is given to external communications "inspiring" the human mind. For example, in Christianity some adhere to the idea of the light of Christ or the Spirit of Truth as a universal influence available to all. Additionally, the role of the Holy Ghost for individual guidance is so fundamental that this is a communication resource attributed directly to deity. From another perspective, thinking in terms of the Earth as an ecosystem and the interconnectivity of humanity, this view might look something like the energy field described by the French geologist/paleontologist, Pierre Teilhard de Chardin as "a human sphere, a sphere of reflection, of conscious invention, of conscious souls" (de Chardin, 1966, p. 63) The word "noosphere" is a neologism that employs "noos", the Greek word for "mind". Today more and more literature is employing the word "quantum", whether or whether not understanding anything whatsoever of the concept. Still, new words trigger new thoughts and, building on the concept of the particle/wave theory, that is, until energy is focused upon it, has the potential for both, the concept of quantum bodes well for empowering people.

The superconscious is also characterized as "pre-personality" to emphasize that there are no personal translators such as beliefs and mental models attached to this form of knowing. The flow of information from the superconscious is very much focused on the moment at hand and does not bring with it any awareness patterns that could cloud the individual's full field of perception.

Spiritual learning is in service to both the conscious and unconscious. It connects through the unconscious and opens the door to the Self being more receptive to the superconscious. Spiritual learning is the process of elevating the mind as related to intellect and matters of the soul to increase the capacity for effective thought and action. The four primary dimensions of the human are the physical (body), mental (mind), emotional (emotions) and spiritual (soul). In spiritual learning all four dimensions come into play to create a knowing, with insights often taking the form of transformative knowledge. For example, in times of warfare there are numerous recorded instances where military personnel under fire have known what movements to make without detailed knowledge of the terrain or enemy troop movement.

In a study exploring the concept of spiritual learning and, specifically, how human characteristics that are spiritual in nature contribute to the learning process, it was discovered there was a positive correlation between representative spiritual characteristics and human learning (Bennet et al., 2015b). There were a number of emergent themes in this study, which can be loosely described as shifting frames of reference, moving toward wisdom, priming for learning, enriching relationships, and animating for learning. See Figure 25-2.

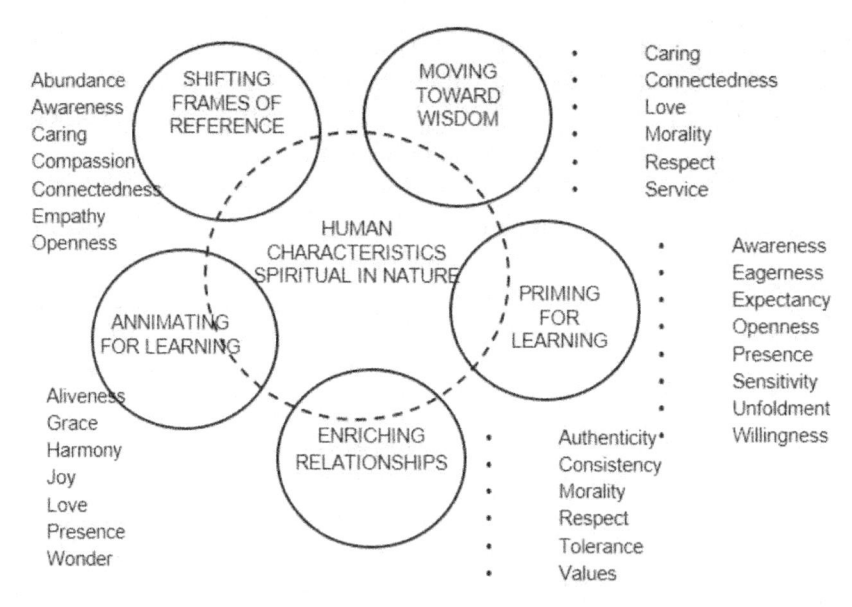

Figure 25-2. *Spiritual characteristics and spiritual learning.*

This correlation between spiritual characteristics and human learning makes sense, of course, since there are overarching connections between the concepts of spirituality and learning that are embedded by virtue of the concepts themselves. For example, Teasdale explains, "Being spiritual suggests a personal commitment to a process of inner development that engages us in our totality ... the spiritual person is committed to growth as an essential ongoing life goal." (Teasdale, 1999, pp. 17-18) In other words, learning (growth) is a life goal of spirituality. Therefore, it follows that human characteristics that are spiritual in nature would contribute to learning.

Critical Areas of Knowing

The Knowing Framework encompasses three critical areas: Knowing our Self, Knowing the "other", and Knowing the situation (the context of the environment).

Knowing our Self includes understanding, loving and trusting our Self. Alexander Pope, in his essay on man (1732-3), noted that: "Know then thyself, presume not God to scan; the proper study of mankind is man." We often think we know ourselves, but, in reality, this is an ongoing discovery. To really understand our own biases, perceptions, capabilities, etc., each of us must look inside and, as objectively as possible, ask ourselves, who we are, what our limitations are, what our strengths are, and what jewels and baggage do we carry from our years of experience. This includes deep reflection on our Self in terms of beliefs, values, dreams and purpose for being, and appreciation for the unique beings that we are. It includes understanding our goals, objectives, strengths and weaknesses in thought and action, and internal defenses and limitations

Rarely do we *take ourselves out of ourselves and look at ourselves*. But without an objective understanding of our own values, beliefs, and biases, we are continually in danger of misunderstanding the interpretation we apply to the external world. Our motives, expectations, decisions, and beliefs are frequently driven by internal forces of which we are substantially unaware. For example, our emotional state plays a strong role in determining how we make decisions and what we decide. Further, knowing our Self means recognizing that we are a social being, part of the large ecosystem some call *Gaia* and inextricably connected to other social beings around the world, which brings us to the second critical element: *Knowing others*.

We live in a connected world, spending most of our waking life with other people, and often continuing that interaction in our dreams! There is amazing diversity in the world, so much to learn and share with others. Whether in love or at war, people are always in relationships and must grapple with the sense of "other" in accordance with their beliefs, values and dreams. The power of social engagement in the experiential learning process emerged in the neuroscience findings.

The third critical area is that of *knowing the situation* in as objective and realistic a manner as possible, understanding the situation, problem, or challenge in context. In the military this is called situational awareness and includes areas such as culture, goals and objectives, thinking patterns, internal inconsistencies, capabilities, strategies and tactics, and political motivations. The current dynamics of our environment, the multiple forces involved, the complexity of relationships, the many aspects of events that are governed by human emotion, and the unprecedented amount of available data and information make situational awareness a challenging but essential phenomenon in many aspects of our daily lives. In the book *Decision-Making in The New Reality: Complexity, Knowledge and Knowing* (Bennet & Bennet, 2013), we discuss complex decision-making in terms of the complexity of situations, the complexity of decisions and the complexity of actions. *It is easy to understand why we describe the experiential learner of today as an Intelligent Complex Adaptive Learning System, that is, a learner who can co-evolve with a changing, uncertain and increasingly complex environment!*

As we move away from predictable patterns susceptible to logic, decision-makers must become increasingly reliant on their "gut" instinct, an internal sense of knowing combined with high situational awareness. Knowing then becomes key to decision-making at all levels. The mental skills honed in knowing help learners identify, interpret, make decisions, and take appropriate action in response to current situational assessments. By exploring our sense of knowing we expand our understanding of our Self, improve our awareness of the external world, learn how to tap into internal resources, and increase our learning skills to affect internal and external change.

Principles of Knowing

The knowing framework provides ideas for developing deep knowledge within the Self and sharing that knowledge with others to create new levels of understanding and learning, and new capacities.

To assist in achieving high situational awareness, the concept of knowing focuses on the cognitive capabilities of observing and perceiving a situation; the cognitive processing that must occur to understand the external world and make maximum use of our internal cognitive capabilities; and the mechanism for creating deep knowledge and acting on that knowledge via the Self as an agent of change. The knowing framework was first developed at the turn of the century for the U.S. Department of the Navy (Porter et al, 2002). See Figure 25-3.

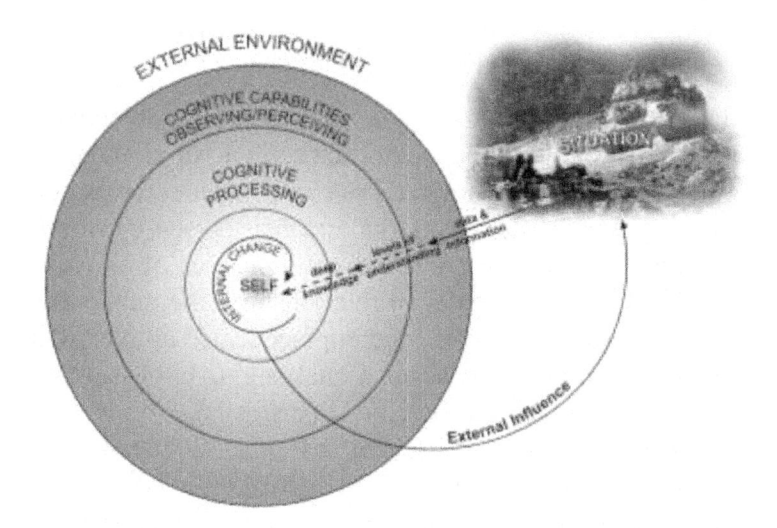

Figure 25-3. *Developing the concept of knowing.*

There are a number of recognized basic truths that drove its development. These truths became the principles upon which the knowing framework is based. These are:

(1) Making decisions in an increasingly complex environment requires new ways of thinking and expanded learning capacity.

(2) All the information in the world is useless if the decision-maker who needs it cannot process it, learn from it, and connect it to their own internal values, knowledge, and wisdom.

(3) We don't know all that we know.

(4) Each of us has knowledge far beyond that which is in our conscious mind. Put another way, we know more than we know we know, with much of our experience and knowledge residing in the unconscious mind.

(5) By exercising our internal and external sensory capabilities, we can increase our capacity to learn and know.

(6) Support capabilities of organizational knowing include organizational learning, knowledge centricity, common values and language, coherent vision, whole-brain learning, openness of communications, effective collaboration, and the free flow of ideas.

The Knowing Framework

The **Cognitive Capabilities** include observing, collecting and interpreting data and information, and building knowledge relative to the situation. The six areas addressed in the knowing framework are: listening, noticing, scanning, sensing, patterning, and integrating. These areas represent means by which we perceive the external world and make sense of it. We will explore the area of listening as an example.

Listening sets the stage for the other five cognitive capabilities. Listening involves more than hearing; it is a sensing greater than sound. It is a neurological cognitive process involving stimuli received by the auditory system. The linguist Roland Barthes distinguished the difference between hearing and listening when he says: "Hearing is a physiological phenomenon; listening is a psychological act." What this means is that there is a choice involved in listening in terms of the listener choosing to interpret sound waves to potentially create understanding and meaning (Barthes, 1985). There are three levels of listening: alerting, deciphering and understanding. Alerting is picking up on environmental sound cues. Deciphering is relating the sound cues to meaning. Understanding is focused on the impact of the sound on another person. Active listening is intentionally focusing on who is speaking in order to take full advantage of verbal and non-verbal cues.

In developing active listening, imagine how you can use all your senses to focus on what is being said. One way to do this is to role-play, imagining you are in their shoes and feeling the words. Active listening means fully participating, acknowledging the thoughts you are hearing with your body, encouraging the train of thought, actively asking questions when the timing is appropriate. The childhood game of pass the word is an example of a fun way to improve listening skills. A group sits in a circle and whispers a message one to the next until it comes back to the originator. A variation on this theme is Chinese Whispers where a group makes a line and starts a different message from each end, crossing somewhere in the middle and making it to the opposite end before sharing the messages back with the originators. Another good group exercise is a "your turn" exercise, where one individual begins speaking, and another person picks up the topic, and so forth. Not knowing whether you are next in line to speak develops some good listening skills.

What we don't hear cannot trigger our knowing. Awareness of our environment is not enough. We must listen to the flow of sound and search out meaning, understanding and implications.

The **Cognitive Processes** in our mind/brain support the cognitive capabilities. These include visualizing, intuiting, valuing, choosing, and setting intent. These five internal cognitive processes greatly improve our power to understand the external world and to make maximum use of our internal thinking capabilities, transforming our observations into understanding. We will explore *choosing* as an example.

Choosing involves making judgments, that is, conclusions and interpretations developed through the use of rules-of-thumb, facts, knowledge, experiences, emotions and intuition. While not necessarily widely recognized, judgments are used far more than logic or rational thinking in making decisions. This is because all but the simplest decisions occur in a context in which there is insufficient, noisy inputs, or perhaps too much information to make rational conclusions. Judgment makes maximum use of heuristics, meta-knowing, and verication.

Heuristics represent the rules-of-thumb developed over time and through experience in a given field. They are shortcuts to thinking that are applicable to specific situations. Their value is speed of conclusions and their usefulness rests on consistency of the environment and repeatability of situations. Thus, they are both powerful and dangerous. Dangerous because the situation or environment, when changing, may quickly invalidate former reliable heuristics and historically create the phenomenon of always solving the last problem; yet powerful because they represent efficient and rapid ways of making decisions where the situation is known and the heuristics apply.

Meta-knowing is knowing about knowing, that is, understanding how we know things and how we go about knowing things. With this knowledge, one can more effectively go about learning and knowing in new situations as they evolve over time. Such power and flexibility greatly improve the quality of our choices. Meta-knowing is closely tied to our natural internal processes of learning and behaving as well as knowing how to make the most effective use of available external data, information, and knowledge and intuit that which is not available. An interesting aspect of meta-knowing is the way that certain errors in judgment are common to many people. Just being aware of these mistakes can reduce their occurrence. For example, we tend to give much more weight to specific, concrete information than to conceptual or abstract information. (See Kahneman et al., 1982, for details.)

Verication is the process by which we can improve the probability of making good choices by working with trusted others and using *their* experience and knowing to validate and improve the level of our judgmental effectiveness. Again, this could be done via a trusted colleague or through effective team creativity and decision-making.

> **REFLECT:**
> *Recall a time when you tapped into your sense of knowing. How did this occur?*

Self as an Agent of Change is the third area of the knowing framework. It is a mechanism for creating deep knowledge, a level of understanding consistent with the external world and our internal framework. This expands on the work done by Seashore (2004; 2001) that is introduced in Chapter 18. As the unconscious continuously associates information (associative patterning), the Self as an agent of change takes the emergent deep knowledge and uses it for the dual purpose of our personal learning and growth, and for making changes in the external world. This is consistent with our treatment of Self co-evolving with the environment presented in Chapter 20 and the example in Chapter 21.

Recall that deep knowledge consists of beliefs, facts, truths, assumptions, and understanding of an area that is so thoroughly embedded in the mind that we are often not consciously aware of the knowledge. To create deep knowledge an individual has to "live" within that domain of knowledge, continuously interacting, thinking, learning, and experiencing that part of the world until the knowledge truly becomes a natural part of the inner being. An example would be immersion in a foreign country to learn to fluently speak the language and absorb the culture. A person with deep knowledge would be able to think in the language without any internal translation, and would not need their native language to understand that internal thinking.

In the knowing framework there are ten elements related to Self as an agent of change. Five of these elements are internal: know thyself, mental models, emotional intelligence, learning and forgetting, and mental defenses; and five of these elements are external: modeling behaviors, knowledge sharing, dialogue, storytelling, and the art of persuasion. We will explore *learning and letting go* as an example.

Since humans have limited processing capability and the mind is easily overloaded and tends to cling to its past experience and knowledge, "letting go" becomes as important as learning. Letting go is the art of being able to let go of what was known and true in the past. Being able to recognize the limitations and inappropriateness of past assumptions, beliefs, and knowledge is essential before creating new mental models and for understanding ourselves as we grow. It is *one of the hardest acts of the human mind* because it threatens our self-image and may shake even our core belief systems.

The biggest barrier to learning and letting go arises from our own individual ability to develop invisible defenses against changing our beliefs. These self-imposed mental defenses have been eloquently described by Chris Argyris (1990). The essence of his conclusion is that the mind creates built-in defense mechanisms to support belief systems and experience. These defense mechanisms are invisible to the individual and may be quite difficult to expose in a real-world situation. They are a widespread example of not knowing what we know, thus providing invisible barriers to change. Several authors have estimated that information and knowledge double approximately every nine months. If this estimate is even close, the problems of saturation will continue to make our ability to acquire deep knowledge even more challenging. We must learn how to filter data and information through vision, values, goals, and purposes, using intuition and judgment as our tools. This discernment and discretion within the deepest level of our minds provides a proactive aspect of filtering, thereby setting up purposeful mental defenses that reduce complexity and provide conditional safeguards to an otherwise open system. This is a fundamental way in which the Self can simplify a situation by eliminating extraneous and undesirable information and knowledge coming from the external world.

While the complete knowing framework has not been made a part of this book, it is detailed in Bennet and Bennet (2013) and Bennet et al. (2015a).

It's a New World

We all have been touched by the expanding climate of increasing change, uncertainty and complexity. As we co-evolve with our environment, new characteristics and ways of thinking and being are emerging both in seasoned learners and in our younger generations. One of these characteristics could be described by the expression *knowing*, being open to the fullness of who we are. Now, the expanding global network of connectivity and communication with our Self and the world is presenting profound ways for developing a deeper sense of knowing. We, indeed, are coming to know a new way of learning and being in a new world.

Chapter 26
Living a New Frame of Reference[1]
(A story of the future)

I was snuggled deep into the flannel sheets under several layers of soft blankets and a quilt while outside a light covering of snow reflected a bright night sky. The temperature had plummeted during the night.

In that dreamy state of well-being and warmth there was a soft tapping on my forehead. Tap. Tap. Tap. A gentle movement of my hair. Tap. Tap. Tap. I reached up to brush it off and felt the soft padding of our large tabby's left foot. Cat Walker. My hand reached to his head and rubbed down across his neck. He was not to be dissuaded. Tap. Tap. Tap.

Rolling out of the covers on automatic, I hit the cool rug with my bare feet and ambled around the corner to the cat bowl, opening a small dark blue can and responsibly dishing out a spoonful of his favorite food into his dish. Then, accordingly, a habit of age, went along the top landing for a quick bathroom trip and a drink of water. As I headed back toward the bedroom, I noted that Cat Walker had not touched the food; indeed, a second cat, Zeusi, who had been a starved stray several years ago—but was no longer—was heading toward the bowl. Woops! She was overweight and couldn't stop eating, so this was not a good idea. Where was Cat Walker? Since he was nowhere to be found, I picked up the dish, covered it, and left it in the coolness for later.

Back to bed. The sheets felt wonderful and sleep was immediate. I was on a campus; the school where I had sent my child, not a child I know in this lifetime (mine are now grown), rather a young teen, a daughter? Since I am awake in my dreams, I thought: *This must be my inner child.*

As an educator, I was concerned about the methodologies and curricula of the school. What subjects were required? What activities were available? What standard tests did they use? How did they grade these kids? What did our children know when they graduated? And traveling through my head were so many more of the everyday kind of questions we ask of our school systems. What kind of education was I paying for? Hmmm. Since emersion and experience trump all the words in the world, I decided to live with my kid at school for a while and get some answers. And since it was still night, and still cold, I was cuddled in warm flannel sheets next to my ... daughter?

Tap. Tap. Tap. There it was again. As I woke, my half-grown child had tired of sleeping and gone off to a class, some activity, I didn't know exactly what. But the covers were warm and it was cold outside, so I wrapped them around my face. Tap. Tap. Tap. On the top of my head. There was the cat again. *Oh, no, I get your game now. You aren't really hungry.* Only he stayed and insisted. *Okay, okay.* I swung out of bed and repeated my earlier routine. Again, he was not there, only the second cat, to whom this time I gave a bite of food. A quick bathroom trip, a glass of water, and back into the covers while there was still some darkness left.

Back on campus, my now mid-teen child came into the room. How did those years pass while I was sleeping? Only half awake, I asked where *she* had been. *This really interesting class on brain chemicals and emotions*, she responded. Hmmm. Didn't realize her interests lay in that direction. *Then I went over and polished a skate board I want to try out later today, during afternoon games.* Hmmm. Didn't know she liked skateboarding. They have games every afternoon? *And I stopped by a dance class before playing some numbers games with a really cute guy who likes physics.* Hmmm. Guy?! She's clearly growing up. That's a lot. Had I really been asleep that long? *Are you still tired mom? You're missing all the fun.* My eyes had closed again—so I pulled them open and looked her direction. She was leaving, again. *I'm going to go check out this class on ancient literature ... at least it sounds ancient, a really great writer named Beowolf.* Beowolf? That rang a bell. When did she become interested in literature?

I closed my eyes, but did not go back to sleep. Tap. Tap. Tap. I dragged myself from the bed. That wasn't quite as difficult as I thought it would be. I was still on the campus. Awake now, warmly dressed, I walked outside. It was a beautiful day. The dusting of snow across the campus had melted into the ground and there were laughing, playing children of all ages moving among the buildings and parks and playgrounds. I quickly followed the paths and quietly walked into the back of the common room of the administrative building. An educator facilitator was there with some older children. *Now students*, the facilitator lightly reminded, *there are some very special learning opportunities available to you this semester. Be sure and take advantage of those classes if they offer something you would like to learn. Choose well. You will be graduating in the Spring. And if there is an area that you have passion around that we have not offered, let's have a conversation and we will find additional resources for you. Meanwhile, everyone enjoy the day!*

The children were leaving now; only they all seemed older now. College Age? From my point of observation, they seemed to float out the door. How do I mean that? Well, there was a buoyancy about them, a healthiness, an eagerness, and laughter. They interacted continuously, either verbally or silently sending signals to each other, signals that I seemed to be able to pick up and read. From one, *What do I want to learn today?* From another, *I can't wait to try this creative numbers class out.* From another, *Did you see the new Asian recipe book from Thailand? I'm going to have a cooking experience today.* From another, *There's a new organizational accounting system based on feelings that I want to learn about.* And from another, *They brought in an old 1966 Pontiac GTO to work on.* Excitedly, *We're going to take it apart and put it back together.*

It was then that I saw the Head Master of the school. There was a bright aluminum object in his hand that caught my attention, about ten inches long, cylindrical. He caught my glance and smiled, walking over my direction. *Here*, handing me the object. The cool energy of it caused a quick jolt, and my eyes opened wider. Was I still asleep? No, I don't think so. I was still on campus and the Head Master was right in front of me. I rubbed my hand over the smooth wall of the cylinder and felt energy move into my hand, up my wrist, traveling up my arm. Confused, I looked up at the Head Master. He responded, *A Universal connector that helps us fill the gaps between our mind/body capabilities, the opening of our hearts, and the wonderful learning energies available to us from the Cosmos. When you were attracted to it, I knew you could feel the energies. Are you open to learning, then? It is a choice.*

When had I not been open to learning? For a moment I felt back into the flannel sheets and covered my head. Tap. Tap. Tap. *Wake up and Experience. Wake up and Be.* Then I was again standing in front of the Head Master.

Open to learning? *Yes*, I silently answered. *Yes, yes, yes.*

Sit with it a moment, said the Master nodding at the Universal connector as he moved toward the Learning Facilitator who was waiting a few feet away, and engaged her in conversation. I sat at a small desk nearby. There was a stack of various sizes of colored paper and writing and drawing utensils atop the desk. Almost reverently, I placed the cylinder against a multi-colored page and drew a line down one side with a wide-tip pen that issued a gold leaf residue. The reflection of the gold bounced against the brightness of the cylinder, highlighting an energy glow that had moved into my awareness and was expanding. Yes, I could feel the connections. I could feel myself opening up. I could feel the energy building. Silently I repeated a favorite mantra, *I am open to receive; I am open to experiencing; I am open to learning*. Only, now I wasn't *saying* it, I was *feeling* it. *It was me*. The energy that had moved up my arm glided around my shoulder and through my chest, rhythmically engaging my heartbeat, then lightly floating upwards into my head. There was a swirling, a dancing, an awakening. Had I ever felt so alive? So hungry to learn?

Through misty eyes I saw my now-grown child come through the front door into the building. She walked up to me smiling. The words from her glowing face answered so many questions. *Hello, mom. Welcome to my world.*

REFLECT:
Do I tap into the learner I am?
What will the learning environment look like for future generations?

Glossary

absorption ... A change strategy that brings a complex system into a larger complex system so that the two can intermix, thereby resolving the original issue by dissolving the problem system.

Abstract Conceptualization (AC) ... A mode in the experiential learning process where learning involves using theories, logic and ideas, rather than feelings, to understand problems or situations. (See Chapter 17.)

action learning ... A learning by doing approach with continuous feedback loops. A process involving a small group of people solving real problems while simultaneously focusing on what they are learning and how that learning benefits the whole (Marquardt, 1999).

Active Experimentation (AE) ... A mode in the experiential learning process, where learning takes an active form - experimenting with changing situations. The learner takes a practical approach and is concerned with what really works, as opposed to simply watching a situation. (See Chapter 17.)

affective attunement ... Open emotional state involving learning from a trusted other. The notion of affective attunement is connected to Dewey's observations that an educator needs to "have that sympathetic understanding of individuals as individuals which gives him an idea of what is actually going on in the minds of those who are learning" (Dewey, [1938] 1997, p. 39). As Johnson (2006) explains, "According to social cognitive neuroscience, the brain actually needs to seek out an affectively attuned other if it is to learn. Affective attunement alleviates fear" (p. 65).

amplification ... An evolutionary approach where a variety of actions are tried to determine which ones succeed, then building upon (amplifying) those that are successful.

amygdala ... The region of the brain that monitors the emotional content of internal experience (as well as incoming sensory information).

apprehension ... "...the manner in which a part of something that is perceived as an external experience can stimulate a much more complete or richer internal experience of the 'whole' of that thing to be conjured up" (Moon, 2004, p. 23); "... that understanding of an experience that consists in knowing what an experience is like; and we know what an experience is like by virtue of having that experience" (Perkins, 1971, pp. 3-4).

associative patterning ... The continuous process of learning by creating new patterns in the mind/brain; the complexing of incoming external information with internal information, creating new neuronal patterns that may represent understanding, meaning, and/or the anticipation of the consequences of actions, in other words, knowledge (Stonier, 1997; Bennet & Bennet, 2008).

attractors ... Attractors indicate where a system is going (Battram, 1996). (See Chapter 2.)

autobiographical Self ... The idea of *who* we are, the image we build up of ourselves and where we fit socially.

autopoietic ... Literally meaning self-making—the way living organisms recreate and maintain themselves (Battram, 1996).

boundary management ... Managing influences around the boundary of the system, where a system interacts with its environment.

capacity ... Volume; amount; used with learning to express a learning capability, open to learning more.

collaborative entanglement ... the continuous interaction, movement of information, and sharing and learning of knowledge resulting in a community movement toward a higher level of awareness, understanding and meaning. Such a process builds both explicit and implicit knowledge and creates a learning, trust and bonding that may energize and accelerate community progress. (See Chapter 23.)

complexing ... The mixing together of internal knowledge and memories and external information to create new knowledge.

complexity ... Describes a system that can take on many states and has so many interconnections and causal paths that they cannot be identified and overall system behavior cannot be predicted. This is primarily due to the nonlinear relationships, time delays, and immensely large number of individual causal relationships. As defined by Santa Fe Institute: The condition of the universe which is integrated and yet too rich and varied for us to understand in simple, common mechanistic or linear ways. We can understand many parts of the universe in these ways but the larger and more intricately related phenomena can only be understood by principles and patterns—not in detail. Complexity deals with emergence, innovation, learning and adaptation (Battram, 1996, p. 12).

complex adaptive system ... A system composed of a large number of self-organizing components that seek to maximize their own goals but operate according to rules and in the context of relationships with other components and the deterministic and inherently unpredictable external world.

concrete ... An actual or specific thing or instance, something that exists in reality and is perceptible by the senses (*American Heritage Dictionary*, 2006, p. 485).

Concrete Experience (CE) ... A mode in the experiential learning model; a form of knowing that comes from the grasping of experience by apprehension. Apprehension in this context refers to (1) an idea formed by observation or experience and (2) the ability to understand, "the power or ability to grasp the important, significance, or meaning of something" (Encarta, 1999). The philosopher Perkins (1971) says that apprehension is, "that understanding of an experience that consists in knowing what an experience is like; and we know what an experience is like by virtue of having that experience" (pp. 3-4). (See Chapter 17.)

consciousness ... A process, a sequential set of ideas, thoughts, images, feelings and perceptions and an understanding of the connections and relationships among them.

consilience ... The bringing together of two or more disciplines or when two or more inductions drawn from different disciplines come into agreement. A "jumping together" of knowledge through the linking of facts and fact-based theory across disciplines to create a common groundwork of explanation (Wilson, 1998).

Constructivism ... The process of making sense of our world; how people build understanding and construct meaning from their experience, whether it is individual or social (Merriam et al., 2007; Mezirow et al., 2000).

creativity ... The ability to create new ideas, concepts or capabilities that has not been created before (p. 118); the emergence of new or original patterns (ideas, concepts or actions) that "typically have three components: originality, utility and some kind of product" (Andreasen, 2005, p. 17) (p. 21). Creativity is inherent in the basic operation of the nervous system (Hobson, 1999).

CUCA ... A characterization of the global trend toward: increasing **C**hange, rising **U**ncertainty, growing **C**omplexity and ubiquitous **A**nxiety—or CUCA (Bennet & Bennet, 2004; 2013).

data ... Isolated or disconnected bits of information (Stonier, 1990; 1997).

declarative memory (also explicit memory) ... The recollection of those memories that in principle can be consciously retrieved and reported (Kluwe, 2003; Markowitsch, 1999, 2000; Schacter, 1996; Squire & Knowlton, 1995).

deep knowledge ... The capacity to understand situations, recognize their meaning and implications, identify underlying problems (versus symptoms), create solutions, make decisions and implement effective actions. Thus, deep knowledge has the following attributes: understanding, meaning, insight, creativity, judgment and the ability to anticipate the outcomes of actions.

deep learning ... The continuous creation and re-creation of our own personal understanding (Chickering et al., 2005).

dialectic ... "... mutually opposed and conflicting processes the result of each of which cannot be explained by the other, but whose merger through confrontation of the conflict between them results in a higher order process that transcends and encompasses them both" (Kolb, 1984, p. 249).

EEG ... Electroencephalograph (EEG), a noninvasive technique that measures the average electrical activity of large populations of neurons (Nicolelis & Chapin, 2007).

emergence ... A property of a system that its separate parts do not have (Axelrod & Cohen, 1999).

emotion ... "A mental state that arises spontaneously rather than through conscious effort and is often accompanied by physiological changes ..." (*American Heritage Dictionary*, 2006); "... the familiar human experiences of anger, fear, and sadness, as well as joy, contentment, and courage ... also basic sensations such as pleasure and pain, as well as the 'drive states' ... such as hunger and thirst" (Pert, 1997, p. 131).

Emotional Intelligence ... The ability to effectively manage ourselves and our relationships. Includes self-awareness, self-management, social awareness and social skill (Goleman, 2000). (See Chapter 22.)

empathy ... Objectively trying to experience the inner life of another (Kohut, 1984). "A hypothesis that we make based on a combination of visceral, emotional and cognitive information, a "muddle of resonance, attunement, and sympathy" (Cozolino (2006, p. 203). (See Chapter 22.)

enhance ... Taken to mean: (1) to make more effective; (2) to make more efficient; (3) to improve meta-learning; and (4) to make more sustainable.

environment ... Generally taken to mean the world within which we live, referring to the external, natural world and/or the social and physical conditions that surround us. The internal environment refers to the thoughts and feelings of Self.

epigenetics ... Literally meaning control above genetics. The study of the molecular mechanisms by which the environment influences gene activity (Lipton, 2005).

essence of emotions ... The collection of changes in the body state such as skin color, body posture and facial expressions that are induced by nerve cell terminals (Damasio, 1994).

experience ... An "apprehension" (ability to understand) of an object, thought, or emotion through the senses or mind; an event, or series of events, participated in or lived through (*American Heritage Dictionary*, 2006); the "total response of the learner to a situation or event: what the learner thinks, feels, does or concludes at the time or immediately thereafter" (Boud, et al., 1994, p. 18).

experiential learning ... The creation and application of information and knowledge. Learning is defined through experience. The experience may be either primary (through sense experiences) or secondary (mediated experiences) (Jarvis, 2004).

feelings ... The private, mental experience of an emotion (Damasio, 1999); internal signals experienced by the conscious mind.

fMRI ... Functional magnetic resonance imaging; used for neuroimaging to produce precise measurements of brain structures (Hyman, 2007).

gene expression ... When DNA information within a gene is released and influences its surrounding environment. See epigenetics.

Hemi-Sync® ... A short term for hemispheric synchronization; the term patented by Robert Monroe to describe the Hemispheric Synchronization auditory-guidance system, a binaural-beat sound technology that demonstrated changes in focused states of consciousness in over 30 years of study. (See Chapter 21.)

hippocampus ... Part of the limbic system that plays a significant role in consolidating learning and moving information from working memory to long-term memory.

idea resonance ... Value built through social interactions based on relationship of, respect for and resonance with ideas.

information ... A basic property of the Universe; the result of organization expressed by any non-random pattern or set of patterns (Stonier, 1990, 1997). Information has no meaning until some organism recognizes and interprets the patterns (Bennet & Bennet, 2008c; 2015a). (See Chapter 3.)

insight ... The capacity to discern the true nature of a situation; penetration. The act or outcome of grasping the inward or hidden nature of things or of perceiving in an intuitive manner (*American Heritage Dictionary*, 2006, p. 906). Insight is also the result of searching for new relationships between concepts in one domain with those in another domain (Crandall, et al., 2006).

intelligence ... The "... capacity to remember and predict patterns in the world, including language, mathematics, physical properties of objects, and social situations" (Hawkins, 2004, p. 97).

intelligent activity ... represents *a perfect state of interaction* where intent, purpose, direction, values and expected outcomes are clearly understood and communicated among all parties, reflecting wisdom and achieving a higher truth.

Intelligent Complex Adaptive Learning System (ICALS) ... The adult experiential learning process that carries within its behavior many of the characteristics of complexity such as non-linear relationships, emergence, feedback loops, time delays, tipping points, power laws, correlations, unpredictability and butterfly effects (Battram, 1996; Buchanan, 2004; Gell-Mann, 1994; Gladwell, 2000). As such it can be influenced through boundary management, absorption, optimum complexity, simplification, sense and respond, amplification and seeding. (See Chapter 5 and Chapter 16.)

intention ... The source with which we are doing something, the act or instance of mentally and emotionally setting a specific course of action or result, a determination to act in some specific way. Intention includes the purpose and attitude toward the *effect* of one's action, the outcome, with purpose implying having a goal in mind or the determination to achieve something and attitude encompassing loyalty and dedication to achieving that goal. (Introduced in Chapter 2.)

intersubjective space ... Those parts of the mind/brain where reflection and abstract thinking can occur.

intuition ... The act or faculty of knowing or sensing without the use of rational processes; immediate cognition (*American Heritage Dictionary*, 2006, p. 919).

invariant ... A form that "captures the essence of relationships, not the details of the moment" (Hawkins, 2004, p. 82). The core of a picture stored in the representations brain that represent the basic source of recognition and understanding of the broader patterns. The higher-level pattern stored in the brain that could be described as a pattern of patterns with possibly both hierarchical and associative relationships to other patterns. See "apprehension".

knowing ... An internal sense supported by our tacit knowledge. Poetically described as: seeing beyond images, hearing beyond words, sensing beyond appearances, and feeling beyond emotions. (See Chapter 25.)

knowledge ... The capacity (potential or actual) to take effective action under varied and uncertain circumstances. Knowledge can be considered as having some or all of the following six attributes: understanding, meaning, insight, creativity, prediction and action.

knowledge (informing) ... The information (or content) part of knowledge, that is, information that is used as part of the knowledge process. While it is still generically information (organized patterns), it is special because of its structure and relationships with other information. Represents insights, meaning, understanding, expectations, theories and principles that support or lead to effective action. (See Chapter 3.)

knowledge (proceeding) ... The process and action part of knowledge, that is, the process of selecting, associating and applying the relevant information--which is knowledge (informing)—from which specific actions can be identified and implemented, that is, actions that result in some acceptable outcome. (See Chapter 3.)

learning ... "The process whereby knowledge is created through the transformation of experience" (Kolb, 1984, p. 38).

Lightenment ... Transcending the limitations of the past in order to embrace new ways of living and learning in a globally and collaboratively entangled connectedness.

meaning ... The significance created in the mind/brain of the learner by relating the new incoming information of a perceived situation to the current cognitive structures of the learner (Pardoe, 2000).

mediated experience ... Where information is communicated primarily through words or pictures and although there is a direct sense experience between the contributor, it is not a direct experience with the phenomenon itself (Jarvis, 2004). Examples include conversations, listening to the media or instructor, lectures, debates, group or team discussions or reading books.

meme ... "... taken to be something, like a skill, technique or useful idea that we have copied from someone else, such as how to make a fire, how to use tools, how to grow crops, ... or just a piece of information or knowledge generally" (Christos, 2003, p. 73 from Blackmore, 1999).

memory systems ... Refers to the full set of memory patterns stored throughout the mind/brain/body.

mind/brain ... Term used to connote the combination of the physiological brain and the patterns of neuron firings and synaptic connections (the mind) that exist in and are created by the brain.

mirror neurons ... Neurons that provide an internal experience that replicates that of another's experience, enabling an individual to experience another individual's act, intentions, and/or emotions. (Introduced in Chapter 13.)

model ... A schematic description of a system, theory, or phenomena that accounts for its known or inferred properties and may be used for further study on its characteristics (*American Heritage Dictionary*, 2006, p. 1130).

Mozart Effect ... A term emerging from research involving spatial/temporal reasoning where one group listening to a Mozart piano sonata had significantly higher results on standard intelligence subtests. (See Chapter 21.)

neural Darwinism ... A competition of thoughts coming into consciousness.

neuroanatomy ... The branch of anatomy that deals with the nervous system.

neurogenesis ... The ability of the brain to generate new neurons.

neurons ... A cell made up of a cell body, axon and dendrites that transmit nerve impulses that is the basic functional unit of the nervous system.

neuropeptides ... Any peptide in the brain that acts as a messenger molecule distributing information throughout the organism (Pert, 1997).

neuropeptide receptors ... Molecules made up of proteins that attach themselves to the surface of cells and function as sensing molecules picking up information from other molecules in the fluid flowing around the cell (Pert, 1997).

neurotransmitters ... carry messages of emotion. They are integrally linked with incoming information (Mulvihill, 2003).

nonreferential ... Intentional focus on a state (versus an object).

optimum complexity ... That level of variety needed to manage the complexity of the present and deal with the anticipated future level (Bennet & Bennet, 2004).

passion ... Those desires, behaviors, and thoughts that suggest urges with considerable force (Frijda, 2000).

pattern ... Connections or relationships that convey a consistent thought; a design that can be replicated.

plasticity of the brain ... The ability of the brain to change its physical structure in response to changing thoughts.

practical experience ... The experience that occurs when there is a direct, undiluted relationships with the phenomenon and the learner. When the signals, patterns and information from the environment come directly into the learner's embodied senses, thereby initiating internal bodily sensations that may be perceived and apprehended by the learner (Jarvis, 2004).

prediction ... The anticipation or expectation of solutions to, and the outcomes of proposed actions on some situation. As used here prediction does not imply certainty but rather is the best estimate or expectation that an individual has for identifying the outcome of their actions.

prefrontal cortex ... Also called the frontal integrative cortex. That portion of the forebrain frequently called the seat of the "self-conscious" mind processing, a sense organ that observes our own behaviors and emotions. The prefrontal cortex also has access to most of the information stored in our long-term memory bank. This is the part of the mind that solves problems, creates insights and new ideas or concepts, plans future operations, makes decisions and anticipates the outcomes of those decisions.

problem ... A situation that presents complexity or difficulty.

procedural memory (also implicit memory; tacit) ... Memories that cannot be consciously retrieved and reported. Procedural memory includes skills and habits, priming, classical and operant conditioning and non-associative learning, that is, habituation and sensitization (Kluwe, 2003).

protein synthesis ... The combining of separate proteins to form a new protein.

referential ... Intentional focus on an object.

Reflective Observation (RO) ... A mode in the experiential learning process where after information is taken in through concrete experience, it is reflected upon to *make sense* of the experience. (See Chapter 17.)

seeding ... The process of nurturing emergence through a set of simultaneous actions that move the system in a desired direction.

Self ... A subjective mind exploring the world from the inside out; *Who* we are, the image of ourselves and where we fit socially. The mind is the seat of consciousness, enabling awareness of our Self as a knower, as an observer and learner, and as one who takes action. There is no single point within the mind/brain/body complex where we could situate Self. It is the interactions among *all* our neuronal patterns, firings and connections that define Self. (Introduced in Chapter 2; readdressed in Chapter 18; and theme continues through Chapter 23.)

sense and respond ... A testing approach where a situation is first observed, then perturbed in some manner, and the response to that perturbation studied, thereby providing a learning process to understand system behavior.

sense-making ... Constructivism or the Constructivist orientation; how people build understanding and construct meaning from their experience, whether it is individual or social (Merriam et al., 2007; Mezirow et al., 2000).

simplification ... Reducing the number of parts and connections in a system. Reduces the uncertainty, but may miss core issues and often creates system backlash, resulting in counter intuitive system behavior.

Social Engagement (SE) ... A mode in the experiential learning process (added in ICALS) where Social engagement opens up a dialogue with the environment, triggering thoughts and emotions and bringing social support and social interaction into the sphere of the Self as learner. This focus is critical as we have learned more about the workings of the mind/brain and recognized the involvement of Self in social learning. (See Chapter 17.)

spirit ... The vital principal or animating force within living beings.

substrate of emotion ... The biochemical network of communication between brain and body including neuropeptides, their receptors, the brain, glands and immune system (Pert, 1997) (pp. 96-97).

surface learning ... Learning that "...relies primarily on short term memorization—cramming facts, data, concepts and information to pass quizzes and exams (Chickering et al., 2005, pp. 132-133).

symptom ... An indication that there is a problem, but in itself is not the source or cause of the problem (*American Heritage Dictionary*, 2006).

synapses ... The structure that allows information in the form of an electrical charge or chemical signal to flow from one neuron to another neuron.

system ... A collection of interrelated parts that work together as a whole.

tacit knowledge ... The descriptive term for those connections among thoughts that cannot be pulled up in words, a knowing of what decision to make or how to do something that cannot be clearly voiced in a manner such that another person could extract and re-create that knowledge (understanding, meaning, etc.) Tacit knowledge can be thought of in terms of four aspects: embodied, intuitive, affective and spiritual (Bennet & Bennet, 2008c). While all of these aspects are part of Self, each represents different sources of tacit knowledge whose applicability, reliability and efficacy may vary greatly depending on the individual, the situation and the knowledge needed to take effective action. (See Chapter 18.)

tags ... Short for "emotional tags". A term indicating that the amygdala "tags" or puts some level of danger or importance on the incoming signal indicated by release of hormones throughout the body (LeDoux, 1996).

Theory ... "...a set of interrelated concepts that explain some aspect of the field in a parsimonious manner" (Merriam, et al., 2007, p. 79). Knowles gives another perspective of a theory as a "comprehensive, coherent, and internally consistent system of ideas about a set of phenomena" (Knowles, et al., 1998, p. 10). These are both consistent with our understanding of theory. (See Chapter 3.)

theta waves ... Brain rhythms that have a frequency of six to twelve cycles per second that are present when you pay close attention to something but not when you eat or drink or are otherwise on automatic pilot (Begley, 2007).

TMS ... Transcranial magnetic stimulation. Uses head mounted wire coils that send very short but strong magnetic pulses directly into specific brain regions that induce low level electric currents into the brain's neural circuits.

unconscious ... "... the many things that the brain does that are not available to consciousness" (LeDoux, 2002, p. 11); "... internal qualities of mind that affect conscious thought and behavior, without being conscious themselves" (Uleman, 2005, p. 3); includes the subconscious and superconscious (Bennet & Bennet, 2013). See Chapter 12 and Chapter 25.

unconscious imitation ... The unconscious replication of another's actions, behaviors, emotions. Related to mirror neurons. (See Chapter 21.)

understanding ... The description of the situation and its information content that provides the *who, what, where, when, how* and *why*. It involves the frame of reference of the observer, including assumptions and presuppositions.

variety ... A measure of complexity and represents the number of possible states that a complex system can have. Variety represents the number of options or possible actions that an organization has when interacting with another organization.

wisdom ... "Wisdom is the combination of knowledge and experience, but it is more than just the sum of these parts. Wisdom involves the mind and the heart, logic and intuition, left brain and right brain, but it is more than either reason, or creativity, or both. Wisdom involves a sense of balance, an equilibrium derived from a strong, pervasive *moral* conviction ... the conviction and guidance provided by the obligations that flow from a profound sense of interdependence. In essence, wisdom grows through the learning of more knowledge, and the practiced experience of day-to-day life—both filtered through a code of moral conviction." (Costa, 1995, p. 3) (See Chapter 24.)

Endnotes

Chapter 2
[1] Dr. William Tiller, Professor Emeritus of Materials Science and Engineering, Stanford University, is the author of *Science and Human Transformation* (Tiller, 2007), a book on esoteric concepts such as subtle energies that work beyond the four fundamental forces which he believes act in concert with human consciousness.

In his words, what Tiller (2007) discovered is that there are two unique levels of physical reality. The "normal level" of substance is the electric, atomic, and molecular level, what most of us think of and perceive as the physical reality. However, Tiller proposes that a second level of substance exists at what he describes as the magnetic information level. While these two levels always interpenetrate each other, under "normal" conditions they do not interact; they are in an "uncoupled" state. Intention changes this condition, causing these two levels to interact, or move into a "coupled" state. Where humans are concerned, Tiller forwards that what an individual intends for himself with a strong sustained desire is what that individual will eventually become.

He appeared in *What the Bleep Do We Know*? See www.tillerfoundation.com for a complete list of published material and downloadable white papers.

Chapter 17
[1] While used as a short term for hemispheric synchronization, Hemi-Sync is also the term patented by Robert Monroe to describe the Hemi-Sync auditory-guidance system, a binaural-beat sound technology that demonstrated changes in focused states of consciousness in over 30 years of study.

2 Released in early 2008 at the Monroe Institute.

3 More than 20,000 people worldwide have participated in formal Hemi-Sync programs at the Institute. An equivalent number of people have participated in outreach programs, which are conducted in English, Spanish, French, German and Japanese.

Chapter 18
[1] For many years Charles Seashore, Ph.D. served as chair of the faculty of the doctoral program in Human and Organizational Development of the Fielding Graduate University and a founding member of the faculty in the American University/NTL Institute Master's program in Organizational Development. Charlie's passion was the Self as an Agent of Change. As Charlie said, "We are always making choices. Even when we say, 'I don't think I had a choice', we are choosing." He asked us to take the opportunity to explore ways of increasing our awareness, our consciousness, so that we could make conscious, intentional decisions instead of operating on "automatic pilot" or finding ourselves stuck without accessible options. In a simple context, Charlie encouraged us to live fully.

Chapter 22
[1] In order of growth toward wisdom and beyond, the seven levels of consciousness focus on: (1) structured concepts: material, ideological, causative; (2) spiritual concepts: focused and limited love at the personal level; (3) spiritual concepts: soul as part of a larger structure, awareness and connectedness through giving; (4) senses other souls: giving what is needed by others so they can create virtue; balance, humility and hierarchy of thought and need in giving virtue; (5) spiritual awareness: planetary level, advancement of new knowledge communicated to humanity and re-communicated in mental framework; contribution to development of civilization to assist in creating virtue; (6) understanding soul as part of God (wisdom): creating virtue, teaching in soul capacity, leading; and (7) awareness of soul as a functional part of God: creating more of God in a fully aware and conscious method (MacFlouer, 1999).

[2] Intelligent activity represents a perfect state of interaction where intent, purpose, direction, values and expected outcomes are clearly understood and communicated among all parties, reflecting wisdom and achieving a higher truth. Intelligent activity was introduced as Assumption 4 in the Foreward.

Chapter 23
[1] William Shakespeare: *King Lear*, Act V, Scene 2.

Chapter 24
[1] Dr. Alex Bennet is Co-Founder of the Mountain Quest Institute, a research and retreat center located in the Allegheny Mountains of West Virginia. See www.mountainquestinn.com and www.mountainquestinstitute.com She is a Professor at the Bangkok University Institute for Knowledge and Innovation Management and teaches at Rotterdam School of Management, Erasmus University, in the Netherlands. Dr. Bennet is awake in her dreams, experiencing, feeling and fully engaged, with insights often emerging from these sequences. This short narrative describes such a sequence that occurred while she was heavily focused helping to bring this book into reality. Alex can be reached at alex@mountainquestinstitute.com

References

Abeles, H.F. & Sanders, E.M. (2005). Final Assessment Report: New Jersey Symphony Orchestra's Early Strings Program, Center for Arts Education Research. New York: Columbia University.

Abrahams, P. (Ed.) (2015). *How the Brain Works: Understanding Brain Function, Thought, and Personality*. New York: Metro Books.

Adams, J. K. (1957). "Laboratory Studies of Behavior without Awareness" in *Psychological Bulletin, 54*, 383-405.

Adolphs, R. (2004). "Processing of Emotional and Social Information by the Human Amygdala" in M. S. Gazzaniga (Ed.), *The Cognitive Neurosciences III*. Cambridge, MA: The Bradford Press, 1017-1030.

Akil, H., Campeau, S., Cullinan, W., Lechan, R., Toni, R., Watson, S., & Moore, R. (1999). Neuroendocrine System I: Overview—Thyroid and Adrenal Axis in M. Zigmond, F. Bloom, S. Landis, J. Roberts, & L. Squire (Eds.), *Fundamentals of Neuroscience*. New York: Academic Press, 1127-1150.

Amen, D. G. (2005). *Making a Good Brain Great*. New York: Harmony Books.

Amen, D.G. (2012). *Use Your Brain to Change Your Age: Secrets to Look, Feel, and Think Younger Every Day*. New York: Crown Archetype.

American Heritage Dictionary of the English Language (4th ed.). (2006). Boston: Houghton Mifflin.

Anderson, J. A. (1988). "Cognitive Styles and Multicultural Populations" in *Journal of Teacher Education, 39*(1), 2-9.

Anderson, J.R. (1983). *The Architecture of Cognition*. Cambridge, MA: Harvard University Press.

Anderson, J. R. (2004). *Cognitive Psychology and Its Implications*. New York: Worth.

Andersson, J.L., Lilja, A., Hartvig, P., Langstrom, B., Gordh, T., Handwerker, H., et al. (1997). "Somatotopic Organization along the Central Sulcus, for Pain Localization in Humans, as Revealed by Positron Emission Tomography" in *Experimental Brain Research, 117*, 192-199.

Andreasen, N. C. (2005). *The Creating Brain: The Neuroscience of Genius*. New York: The Dana Foundation.

Apple (2015). Open Source material downloaded 10/07/15 from http://www.apple.com/researchkit/?cid=wwa-us-kwg-iphone

Argyris, C. (1990). *Overcoming Organizational Defenses: Facilitating Organizational Learning*. Englewood Cliffs, NJ: Prentice Hall.

Ascoli, G. A. (Ed.). (2002). *Computational Neuroanatomy: Principles and Methods*. Totowa, NJ: Humana Press.

Atherton, J. S. (2005). "Learning and Teaching: Reflection and Reflective Practice." Retrieved September 2006 from http://www.learningandteaching.info/learning/reflecti.htm

Atwater, F. H. (2004). *The Hemi-Sync Process*. Faber, VA: The Monroe Institute.

Augustine, J.R. (1996). "Circuitry and Functional Aspects of the Insular Lobe in Primates, including Humans" in *Brain Research Reviews, 22*, 229-244.

Ausubel, D. (1968). *Educational Psychology: A Cognitive View*. New York: Holt, Rinehart Winston.

Axelrod, R. & Cohen, M. D. (1999). *Harnessing Complexity: Organizational Implications of a Scientific Frontier*. New York: The Free Press.

Baltes, P.B. & Smith, J. (1990). "Toward a Psychology of Wisdom and Its Ontogenesis", in Sternberg, R.J. (Ed.), *Wisdom: Its Nature, Origins, and Development*. Cambridge: Cambridge University Press.

Bandura, A. (1977). *Social Learning Theory*. Oxford, England: prentice-Hall.

Bandura, A. (1963). *Social Learning and Personality Development*. New York: Holt, Rinehart and Winston.

Bargh, J. A. (2005). "Bypassing the Will: Towards Demystifying the Nonconscious Control of Social Behavior" in R.R. Hassan, J.S. Uleman, & J.A. Bargh (Eds.), *The New Unconscious*. New York: Oxford University Press, 39.

Barthes, R. (1985). *In the Responsibility of Forms*. New York: Hill and Wang.

Battram, A. (1996). *Navigating Complexity: The Essential Guide to Complexity Theory in Business and Management*. Sterling, VA: The Industrial Society

Battro, A.M., Fischer, K.W. & Lena, P.J. (Eds.) (2013). *The Educated Brain: Essays in Neuroeducation*. New York: Cambridge University Press.

Bear, M. F., Connors, B. W. & Paradiso, M. A. (2001). *Neuroscience: Exploring the Brain* (2nd ed.). Baltimore: Lippincott, Williams & Wilkins.

Beggs, J. M., Brown, T. J., Byrne, J. H., Crow, T., LeDoux, J. E., LeBar, K. & Thompson, R. J. (1999). "Learning and Memory: Basic Mechanisms" in M. Zigmond, F. Bloom, S. Landis, J. Roberts & L. Squire (Eds.), *Fundamental Neuroscience*. New York: Academic Press, 1411-1454.

Begley, S. (2007). *Train Your Mind Change Your Brain: How a New Science Reveals Our Extraordinary Potential to Transform Ourselves*. New York: Ballantine Books.

Bennet, A. (2005). *Exploring Aspects of Knowledge Management that Contribute to the Passion Expressed by Its Thought Leaders*. Frost, WV: Self-published. Retrievable from http://www.mountainquestinstitute.com

Bennet, A. & Bennet, D. (2004). *Organizational Survival in the New World: The Intelligent Complex Adaptive System*. New York: Elsevier.

Bennet, A., & Bennet, D. (2006). "Learning as Associative Patterning" in *VINE: The Journal of Information and Knowledge Management Systems*, Vol. 36, No. 4, 371-376.

Bennet, A., & Bennet, D. (2007a). *Knowledge Mobilization in the Social Sciences and Humanities: Moving from Research to Action*. Frost, WV: MQIPress.

Bennet, A. & Bennet, D. (2007b). "From Stories to Strategy: Putting Organizational Learning to Work" in *VINE: The Journal of Information and Knowledge Management Systems*, 37 (4).

Bennet, A. & Bennet, D. (2007c). "The Knowledge and Knowing of Spiritual Learning" in *VINE: The Journal of Information and Knowledge Management Systems*, 37 (2), pp. 150-168.

Bennet, A. & Bennet, D. (2008a). "The Decision-Making Process for Complex Situations in a Complex Environment" in C.W. Holsapple & F. Burstein (Eds.), *Handbook on Decision Support Systems*. New York: Springer-Verlag, 3-20.

Bennet, A. & Bennet, D. (2008b). "A New Change Model: Factors for Initiating and Implementing Personal Action Learning" in *VINE: The Journal of Information and Knowledge Management Systems*, 38 (4), 378-387.

Bennet, A. & Bennet, D. (2008d). "Moving from Knowledge to Wisdom, from Ordinary Consciousness to Extraordinary Consciousness" in *VINE: The Journal of Information and Knowledge Management Systems*, 38 (1), 7-15.

Bennet, A. & Bennet, D. (2008f). "The Human Knowledge System: Music and Brain Coherence" in *VINE: The Journal of Information and Knowledge Management Systems*, 38 (3), 277-295.

Bennet, A. & Bennet, D. (2013). *Decision-Making in the New Reality: Complexity, Knowledge and Knowing*. Frost, WV: MQIPress.

Bennet, A., Bennet, D. with Avedisian, J. (2015a). *The Course of Knowledge: A 21st Century Theory*. Frost, WV: MQIPress.

Bennet, A., Bennet, D. with Lewis, J. (2015b). *Leading with the Future in Mind: Knowledge and Emergent Leadership*. Frost, WV: MQIPress.

Bennet, D. (2014). "Learning How to Learn". Downloaded July 1, 2014, from http://www.mountainquestinstitute.com/#learning.html

Bennet, D. (2009). *Exploring Recent Findings in Neuroscience that Can Enhance Adult Learning*. A dissertation submitted to Fielding Graduate University.

Bennet, D. (2006). "Expanding the Knowledge Paradigm" in *VINE: The Journal of Information and Knowledge Management Systems*, 36 (2), 175-181.

Bennet, D. (2001). "Loosening the World Knot", unpublished paper available at www.mountainquestinstitute.com

Bennet, D. & Bennet, A. (2010). "Social Learning from the Inside Out: The Creation and Sharing of Knowledge from the Mind/Brain Perspective" in Girard, John & Girard, JoAnn (2010). *Social Knowledge: Using Social Media to Know What You Know*. Hershey, PA: IGI Global, 1-23.

Bennet, D., & Bennet, A. (2008c). "Engaging Tacit Knowledge in Support of Organizational Learning" in *VINE: The Journal of Information and Knowledge Systems*, 38 (1), 72-94.

Bennet, D. & Bennet, A. (2008e). Associative Patterning: The Unconscious Life of an Organization" in J.P. Girard (Ed.) *Organizational Memory*. Hershey, PA: ICI Global, 201-224.

Bennett-Woods, D. (1997). "Reflections on wisdom", unpublished paper, University of Northern Colorado.

Berry, D. C., & Broadbent, D. E. (1984). "On the Relationship between Task Performance and Associated Verbalizable Knowledge" in *Quarterly Journal of Experimental Psychology*, 36A, 209-231.

Birkerts, S. (1994). *The Gutenberg Elegies: The Fate of Reading in an Electronic Age*. Boston: Faber and Faber.

Birren, J.E. and Fisher, L.M. (1990). "The elements of wisdom: Overview and integration", in Sternberg, R.J. (Ed.), *Wisdom: Its Nature, Origins, and Development*, Cambridge University Press, Cambridge, England.

Blackmore, S. (2004). *Consciousness: An introduction*. New York, NY: Oxford University Press.

Blackmore, S. (1999). *The Meme Machine*. Oxford, UK: Oxford University Press.

Blair, Hugh (2015). Readings on Sentence Structure from Hugh Blair From Lectures on Rhetoric and Belles Lettres Downloaded 09 13 2015 from http://academic.macewan.ca/einarssonr/files/2009/10/On-Sentence-Structure-by-Blair1.pdf

Blakemore, S., & Frith, Y. (2005). *The Learning Brain: Lessons for Education*. Malden, MA: Blackwell.

Bloom, F. E. (2007). "Best of the brain from Scientific American: Mind, Matter, and Tomorrow's Brain. New York: Dana Press.

Bloom, F. E., Fischer, B. A., Landis, S. C., Roberts, J. L., Squire, L. R., & Zigmond, M. J. (1999). Fundamentals of Neuroscience in M. J. Zigmond, F. E. Bloom, B. A. Landis, S. C. Roberts, & L. R. Squire (Eds.), *Fundamental Neuroscience*. San Diego, CA: Academic Press, 3-8.

Bobe, R., et al. (2002). "Faunal Change, Environmental Variability and Late Pliocene Hominin Evolution." *Journal of Human Evolution 42*, No. 4 (2002).

Boden, M. (1991). *The Creative Mind, Myths & Mechanisms*. London: Basic Books.

Bohm, D. (1992). Thought as a system. London: Routledge.

Bohm, D. (1980). *Wholeness and the Implicate Order*, Routledge & Kegal Paul, London.

Bolles, E. (1991). *A Second Way of Knowing: The Riddle of Human Perceptions*. New York: Prentice Hall Press.

Boud, D., Keogh, R., & Walker, D. (Eds.) (1994). *Reflection: Turning Experience into Learning*. New York: Routledge Falmer.

Bownds, M. D. (1999). *The Biology of Mind: Origins and Structures of Mind, Brain, and Consciousness*. Bethesda, MD: Fitzgerald Science Press.

Brean, J. (2014). "A billion-dollar European Effort to Model the Brain in a Supercomputer is in Danger of Collapsing." Downloaded 09/19/2015 from http://news.nationalpost.com/news/a-billion-dollar-european-effort-to-model-the-human-brain-in-a-supercomputer-is-in-danger-of-collapsing

Brookfield, S. D. (1987). *Developing Critical Thinkers*. San Francisco: Jossey-Bass.

Brown, J.S., Denning, S., Groh, K. & L. Prusak (2004). *Storytelling in Organizations*. Oxford: Elsevier.

Brown, J.S. & Duguid, P. (2000). *The Social Life of Information*. Boston: Harvard Business School Press.

Brown, W.S. (2000). "Wisdom and Human Neurocognitive Systems: Perceiving and Practicing the Laws of Life" in Brown, W.S. (Ed.), *Understanding Wisdom: Sources, Science and Society*. Philadelphia, PA: Templeton Foundation Press.
Bruchac, J. (1997). "Storytelling and the Sacred: On the Uses of Native American Stories" in *Storytelling Magazine*. Special Edition, September.
Buchanan, M. (2004, Spring). "Power Laws and the New Science of Complexity Management" in *Strategy + Business, 34*, 70-79.
Buks, E., Schuster, R. Heiblum, M., Mahalu, D & Umansky, V. (1998). "Dephasing in Electron Interference by a 'Which-Path' Detector" in *Nature* (Vol. 391) February 26, 871-874.
Bullard, B. (2003). "Metamusic: Music for inner space", Hemi-Sync® Journal, Vol. XXI, Nos. 3 & 4, pp. i-v.
Bullard, B. & Bennet, A. (2013). *REMEMBRANCE: Pathways to Expanded Learning with Music and Metamusic®*. Frost, WV: MQIPress.
Buonomano, D. V. & Merzenich, M. M. (1998). "Cortical Plasticity: From Synapses to Maps" in *Annual Review of Neuroscience, 21*, 149-186.
Buzsaki, G. (2006). *Rhythms of the Brain*. New York: Oxford University Press.
Byrnes, J.P. (2007). "Some Ways in which Neuroscientific Research Can Be Relevant to Education" in Coch, D., Fischer, K.W. and Dawson, G., *Human Behavior, Learning and the Developing Brain: Typical Development*. New York: The Guilford Press.
Byrnes, J. P. (2001). *Minds, Brains, and Learning: Understanding the Psychological and Educational Relevance of Neuroscientific Research*. New York: The Guilford Press.
Caine, G., & Caine, R. N. (2006). "Meaningful Learning and the Executive Functions of the Brain" in S. Johnson & K. Taylor (Eds.), *The Neuroscience of Adult Learning: New Directions for Adult and Continuing Education*. San Francisco: Jossey-Bass.
Calaprice, A. (2000). *The Expanded Quotable Einstein*. Princeton NJ: Princeton, University Press.
Campbell, D. (2000). *Heal Yourself with Sound and Music*, Sounds True, Boulder, CO.
Cannon, W. B. (1929). *Bodily Changes in Pain, Hunger, Fear and Rage*. (Vol. 2). New York: Appleton.
Carlsson, B., Keane, P., & Martin, J. B. (1976). *R&D Organizations as Learning Systems*. Sloan Management Review, 21-31.
Carpenter (2009). "Designing for innovation through competitive collaboration". Downloaded on 11/02/14 from http://www.cloudave.com/1036/designing-for-innovation-through-competitive-collaboration/
Carr, L., Iacoboni, M., Dubeau, M.C., Mazziotta, J.C. & Lenzi, G.L. (2003). "Neural Mechanisms of Empathy in Humans: A Relay from Neural Systems for Imitation to Limbic Areas" in *Proceedings of the National Academy of Sciences*, USA, 100, 5497-5502.
Carroll, G. D. (1986). *Brain Hemisphere Synchronization and Musical Learning*, reprint of paper published by University of North Carolina at Greensboro, NC.
Carter, R. (2002). *Exploring Consciousness*. Berkeley: University of California Press.
Carter, R., Aldredge, S., Martyn, P. & Parker, S. (2009). *The Human Brain Book: An Illustrated Guide to Its Structure, Function, and Disorders*. New York: DK Publishing.
Cassady, M. (1990). *Storytelling Step by Step*. San Jose, CA: Resource Publications, Inc.
Catterall, J., Chapleau, R. & Iwanga, J. (1999). "Involvement in the Arts and Human Development: Extending an Analysis of General Associations and Introducing the Special Cases of Intense Involvement in Music and in Theater Arts" in Monograph Series No. 11, Americans for the Arts, Washington, D.C.
Chabris, C. (1999). "A Quantitative Meta-Analysis of Mozart studies" in *Nature, 400*, 826-827.
Chandler, M.J. & Holliday, S. (1990). "Wisdom in a Postapocalyptic Age" in Sternberg, R.J. (Ed.), *Wisdom: Its Nature, Origins, and Development*. Cambridge, England: Cambridge University Press.
Chapman, S.B. & Kirkland, S. (2013). *Making Your Brain Smarter*. New York, NY: Simon & Schuster.

Chickering, A. W. (1977). *Experience and Learning: An Introduction to Experiential Learning.* New Rochelle, NY: Change Magazine Press.

Chickering, A. W., Dalton, J. C., & Stamm, L. (2005). *Encouraging Authenticity & Spirituality in Higher Education.* San Francisco: Jossey-Bass.

Christos, G. (2003). *Memory and Dreams: The Creative Human Mind.* New Brunswick, NJ: Rutgers University Press.

Chugani, H.T. (1998). "Biological Basis of Emotion: Brain Systems and Brain Development" in *Pediatrics* (Vol. 102, No. 5), 1225-1229.

Chung, S., Tack, G., Lee, B., Eom, G., Lee, S., & Sohn, J. (2004). "The Effect of 30 Oxygen on Visuospatial Performance and Brain Activation: An fMRI Study" in *Brain and Cognition*, 56, 279-285.

Church, D. (2006). *The Genie in Your Genes: Epigenetic Medicine and the New Biology of Intention.* Santa Rosa, CA: Elite Books.

Clayton, V. & Birren, J.E. (1980). "The Development of Wisdom Across the Lifespan: A Reexamination of an Ancient Topic" in Baltes, P.B. & Brim, O.G.J. (Eds), *Life Spa Development and Behavior.* Academic Press, 104-135.

Clynes, M. (Ed.) (1982). *Music, Mind and Brain.* New York: Plenum Press.

Coch, D., Fischer, K.W. & Dawson, G. (2007). *Human Behavior, Learning, and the Developing Brain: Typical Development.* New York: The Guilford Press.

Cohen, D. Granot, R., Pratt, H. & Barneah, A. (1993). "Cognitive Meanings of Musical Elements as Disclosed by Event-Related Potential (ERP) and Verbal Experiments" in *Music Perception, V*, 11, 153-184.

Costa, J.D. (1995). *Working Wisdom: The Ultimate Value in the New Economy.* Stoddart, Toronto, Canada.

Cowan, W. M., & Kandel, E. R. (2001). "A Brief History of Synapses and Synaptic Transmission" in W. C. Cowan, T. C. Sudhof, & C. F. Stevens (Eds.), *Synapses.* Baltimore: Johns Hopkins Press.

Cowley, M. (ed.) (1958). *Writers at Work: The Paris Review Interviews.* New York: The Paris Review.

Cozolino, L., & Sprokay, S. (2006). "Neuroscience and Adult Learning" in S. Johnson & T. Taylor (Eds.), *The Neuroscience of Adult Learning.* San Francisco: Jossey-Bass, 11-19.

Cozolino, L. J. (2002). *The Neuroscience of Psychotherapy: Building and Rebuilding the Human Brain.* New York: Norton.

Cozolino, L. J. (2006). *The Neuroscience of Human Relationships: Attachment and the Developing Social Brain.* New York: W.W. Norton.

Cozolino, L. (2013). *The Social Neuroscience of Education: Optimizing Attachment and Learning in the Classroom.* New York, NY: W.W. Norton & Co.

Crandall, B., Klein, G., & Hoffman, R. R. (2006). *Working Minds: A Practitioner's Guide to Cognitive Task Analysis.* Cambridge, MA: The MIT Press.

Crowley, V. (1999). *Jung: A Journey of Transformation.* Wheaton, IL: Quest Books.

Csikszentmihalyi, M. (1990). *Flow: The Psychology of Optimal Experience.* New York: Harper Perennial.

Csikszentmihalyi, M. & Nakamura, J. (2005). "The Role of Emotions in the Development of Wisdom" in Sternberg, R.J. and Jordan, J., *A Handbook of Wisdom: Psychological Perspectives.* New York: Cambridge University Press.

Csikszentmihalyi, M. & Rathunde, K. (1990). "The Psychology of Wisdom: An Evolutionary Interpretation" in Sternberg, R.J. (Ed.), *Wisdom: Its Nature, Origins, and Development.* Cambridge: Cambridge University Press.

Daloz, L. (1986). Effective teaching and mentoring. San Francisco: Jossey-Bass.

Daloz, L. (1999). *Mentor: Guiding the Journey of Adult Learners.* San Francisco: Jossey-Bass.

Damasio, A. R. (1994). *Descartes' Error: Emotion, Reason, and the Human Brain.* New York: G.P. Putnam's Sons.

Damasio, A. R. (1999). *The Feeling of What Happens: Body and Emotion in the Making of Consciousness.* New York: Harcourt Brace & Company.
Damasio, A. R. (2007). "How the Brain Creates the Mind" in F. E. Bloom (Ed.), *Best of the Brain from Scientific American: Mind, Matter, and Tomorrow's Brain.* New York: Dana Press, 58-67.
Damasio, A.R. (2010). *Self Comes to Mind: Constructing the Conscious Brain.* New York: Vintage Books.
Damon, W. (2000). "Setting the Stage for the Development of Wisdom: Self-Understanding and Moral Identity During Adolescence" in Brown, W.S. (Ed.), *Understanding Wisdom: Sources, Science and Society.* Philadelphia, PA: Templeton Foundation Press.
Danielson, C. (2008). "Final Report: The Benefits of Long-Term Participation in The Monroe Institute Programs", Faber, VA: The Monroe Institute. See www.monroeinstitute.com
Darwin, C. (1998). *The Descent of Man.* Amherst, NY: Prometheus Books.
Davis, J. (1997). *Alternate Realities: How Science Shapes Our Vision of the World.* New York: Plenum Trade.
de Chardin, T. (1966). *The Vision of the Past.* Collected Works of Teilhard de Chardin in English translation (Collins). UK: Harper and Row.
Delmonte, M. M. (1984). "Electrocortical Activity and Related Phenomena Associated with Meditation Practice: A Literature Review" in *International Journal of Neuroscience, 24*, 217-231.
Denning, S. (2001). *The Springboard: How Storytelling Ignites Action in Knowledge-Era Organizations.* Boston: Butterworth Heinemann.
de Waal, R. (2009). *The Age of Empathy: Nature's Lessons for a Kinder Society.* New York: Crown Publishing Group.
Dewey, J. (1938/1997). *Experience and Education.* New York: Simon & Schuster.
Dewey, J. (1958). *Experience and Nature.* New York: Dover Publications.
Diamond, M. (2001). *Successful Aging of the Healthy Brain.* Article originally presented at the conference on the American Society on Aging, March 10, 2001, New Orleans. Retrieved April 12, 2006, from http://www.newhorizons.org/neuro/diamond_aging.htm
Diekman, A. (1971). "Biomodal Consciousness" in *Archives of General Psychiatry, 25,* 481-89.
Dittmann-Kohli, F. & Baltes, P.B. (1990). "Toward a Neofunctionalist Conception of Adult Intellectual Development: Wisdom as a Prototypical Case of Intellectual Growth" in Alexander, C. & Langer, E. (Eds.), *Beyond Formal Operations: Alternative Endpoints to Human Development.* New York: Oxford University Press.
Dobbs, D. (2007). "Turning Off Depression" in F. E. Bloom (Ed.), *Best of the Brain from Scientific American: Mind, Matter, and Tomorrow's Brain.* New York: Dana Press, 169-178.
Dorfman, J., Shames, V. A., & Kihlstrom, J. F. (1996). "Intuition, Incubation, and Insight: Implicit Cognition in Problem-Solving" in G. Underwood (Ed.), *Implicit Cognition.* Oxford, UK: Oxford University Press.
Dunning, J. (2014). Discussion of Consciousness via the Internet on December 13.
Eagleman, D. (2011). *Incognito: The Secret Lives of the Brain.* New York, NY: Pantheon Books.
Edelman, G. M. (1992). *Bright Air, Brilliant Fire: On the Matter of the Mind.* New York: Basic Books.
Edelman, G. (1989). *The Remembered Present: A Biological Theory of Consciousness.* New York: Basic Books.
Edelman, G., & Tononi, G. (2000). *A Universe of Consciousness: How Matter Becomes Imagination.* New York: Basic Books.
Edrington, D. (1983). "Hypermnesia Experiment" in *Breakthrough.* Faber, VA: The Monroe Institute, Faber, VA.
Eich, E., Kihlstrom, J. F., Bower, G. H., Forgas, J. P., & Niedenthal, P. M. (2000). *Cognition and Emotion.* New York: Oxford University Press.
Eilan, N.(1995). "Consciousness and the Self" in Bermudez, J.L., Marcel, A. & Eilan, N., *The Body and the Self.* Cambridge, MA: MIT Press.

Eilan, N., Marcel, A. & Bermudez, J.L. (1995). "Self-Consciousness and the Body: An Interdisciplinary Introduction" in Bermudez, J.L., Marcel, A. & Eilan, N., *The Body and the Self*. Cambridge, MA: MIT Press.

Einstein, A., & Infeld, L. (1950). *The Evolution of Physics*. New York: Simon & Schuster.

Emig, J. (1983). *The Web of Meaning: Essays on Writing, Teaching, Learning, and Thinking*. New Jersey: Boynton/Cook Publishers, Inc.

Encarta World English Dictionary (1999). New York: St. Martin's Press.

Ericsson, K. A., Charness, N., Feltovich, P. J., & Hoffman, R. R. (Eds.) (2006). *The Cambridge Handbook of Expertise and Expert Performance*. Cambridge, NY: Cambridge University Press.

Erikson, J.M. (1988), *Wisdom and the Senses: The Way of Creativity*. New York: Norton.

Fagan, J., Prigot, J., Carroll, M., Pioli, L., Stein, A., & Franco, A. (1997). "Auditory Context and Memory Retrieval in Young Infants" in *Child Development, 68*, 1057-1066.

Feigl, H. (1958). "The Mental and the Physical" in *Concepts, Theories and the Mind-Body Problem*. Minneapolis: University of Minnesota Press, 370-497.

Feldman, A. (1996). "Enhancing the Practice of Physics Teachers" in *Journal of Research in Science Teaching*, 33(5), 513-540.

Feldman, S. (1965). *The Storytelling Stone*. New York: Delta Trade Paperbacks.

Felix, U. (1993). "The Contribution of Background Music to the Enhancement of Learning in Suggestopedia: A Critical Review of the Literature" in *Journal of the Society for Accelerative Learning and Teaching*, 18.3-4, 277-303.

Fine, G. (2003). Introduction in Plato on *Knowledge and forms: Selected essays*, Oxford University Press, New York.

Fischer, R. (1971). "A Cartography of Ecstatic and Meditative States" in *Science*, 174 (12), 897-904.

Flohr, J., Miller, D. & DeBeus, R. (2000). "EEG studies with young children" in *Music Educators Journal*, 87(2), 28-32.

Freud, S. (1901/1989). *The Psychopathology of Everyday Life*. (J. Strachey, Trans.). New York: W.W. Norton.

Friedman, T. L. (2005). *The World is Flat: A Brief History of the Twenty-First Century*. New York: Farrar, Straus & Giroux.

Frijda, N. H. (2000)."The Psychologists' Point of View" in M. Lewis & J. M. Haviland-Jones (Eds.), *Handbook of Emotions*. New York: The Guilford Press.

Frith, C., & Wolpert, D. (2003). *The Neuroscience of Social Interaction: Decoding, Imitating, and Influencing the Actions of Others*. New York: Oxford University Press.

Frusec, J. (1992). "Social Learning Theory and Developmental Psychology: The Legacies of Robert Sears and Albert Bandura" in *Developmental Psychology* 28 (5).

Gardner, H. (2006). *Five Minds for the Future*. Boston: Harvard Business School Press.

Gardner, J. N. (2003). *Biocosm: The New Scientific Theory of Evolution: Intelligent Life is the Architect of the Universe*. Makawao, Maui, HI: Inner Ocean.

Gazzaniga, M.S. (2008). *Human: The Science Behind What Makes Us Unique*. New York: HarperCollins.

Gediman, C. (2005). *Brainfit: 10 Minutes a Day for a Sharper Mind and Memory*. Nashville, TN: Rutledge Hill Press.

Gell-Mann, M. (1994). *The Quark and the Jaguar: Adventures in the Simple and the Complex*. New York: Abacus.

George, M. S. (2007). "Stimulating the Brain" in F. E. Bloom (Ed.), *Best of the Brain from Scientific American: Mind, Matter, and Tomorrow's Brain*. New York: The Dana Foundation, 20-34.

Gettier, E. L. (1963). "Is Justified True Belief Knowledge?" in *Oxford Journals*, Oxford University Press. Retrieved June 4, 2014 from http://rintintin.colorado.edu/~vancecd/phil1000/Gettier.pdf

Gibson, J.J. (1979). *The Ecological Approach to Visual Perception*. Boston: Houghton Mifflin.

Gigerenzer, G. (2007). *Gut Feelings: The Intelligence of the Unconscious*. New York: Penguin Books.

Gladwell, M. (2000). *The Tipping Point: How Little Things Can Make a Big Difference.* Boston: Little, Brown.
Gladwell, M. (2005). *Blink: The Power of Thinking without Thinking.* New York: Little, Brown.
Godden, D.R. & Baddeley, A.D. (1975). "Context-Dependent Memory in Two Natural Environments: On Land and Underwater" in *British Journal of Psychology* 66, pp. 325-331.
Goldberg, E. (2001). *The Executive Brain: Frontal Lobes and the Civilized Mind.* New York: Oxford University Press.
Goldberg, E. (2005). *The Wisdom Paradox: How Your Mind Can Grow Stronger as Your Brain Grows Older,* Gotham Books, New York, NY.
Goldberg, E. (2009). The New Executive Brain: Frontal Lobes in a Complex World. New York, NY: Oxford University Press.
Goldman, D. (2006). *Social Intelligence: The New Science of Human Relations.* New York, NY: Bantam Dell.
Goldman, D. (2011). *Leadership: The Power of Emotional Intelligence.* Amazon Digital Services, Inc.
Goleman (2000). "Leadership That Gets Results" in *Harvard Business Review,* March-April, 78-90.
Goleman, G.M. (1988). *Meditative Mind: The Varieties of Meditative Experience.* New York: G.P. Putnam.
Gordon, E. (Ed.) (2000). *Integrative Neuroscience: Bringing Together Biological, Psychological and Clinical Models of the Human Brain.* Singapore: Harwood Academic Publishers.
Graziano, A.B., Peterson, M. & Shaw, G.L. (1999). "Enhanced Learning of Proportional Math through Music Training and Spatial-Temporal Training" in *Neurological Research, 21,* 139-152.
Greenfield, S. (2000). *The Private Life of the Brain: Emotions, Consciousness, and the Secret of the Self.* New York: John Wiley & Sons.
Grusec, J.E. & Lytton, H. (1992). *Social Development: History, Theory, and Research.* New York: Springer-Verlag.
Gusnard, D. A., & Raichle, M. E. (2004). "Functional Imaging, Neurophysiology, and the Resting State of the Human Brain" in *The Cognitive Neurosciences III*. Cambridge, MA: MIT Press, 1267-1280.
Haberlandt, K. (1998). *Human Memory: Exploration and Application.* Boston: Allyn & Bacon.
Hallom, S. (2002). "The Effects of Background Music on Studying" in Deasy, R.J. (Ed.), *Critical Links: Learning in the Arts and Student Academic and Social Development, Arts Education Partnership,* Washington, D.C., 74-75.
Hannon, E.E. & Johnson, S.P. (2005). "Infants Use Meter to Categorize Rhythms and Melodies: Implications for Musical Structure Learning" in *Cognitive Psychology, 50,* 354-377.
Hawkins, J., with Blakeslee, S. (2004). *On Intelligence: How a New Understanding of the Brain will Lead to the Creation of Truly Intelligent Machines.* New York: Times Books.
HBR (2015). *Human Brain Project Mediation Report.* Juelich, Germany: Human Brain Project.
Heisenbert, W. (1949). Eckart, C. & Hoyt, F.C. (Trans.). *The Physical Principles of the Quantum Theory.* Chicago: Dover Publications, Inc.
Hetland, L. (2000). "Listening to Music Enhances Spatial-Temporal Reasoning: Evidence for the 'Mozart Effect' in *Journal of Aesthetic Education, 34,* 105-148.
Hiew, C.C. (1995). "Hemi-Sync® Into Creativity" in *Hemi-Sync® Journal, XIII*(1), 35-50.
Hink, R. F., Kodera, K., Yamada, O., Kaga, K., & Suzuki, J. (1980). "Binaural Interaction of a Beating Frequency Following Responses" in *Audiology, 19,* 36-43.
Ho, Y-C., Cheung, M-C., & Chan, A.S. (2003). "Music Training Improves Verbal but Not Visual Memory: Cross-Sectional and Longitudinal Explorations in Children" in *Neuropsychology, 17,* 439-450.
Hobson, J. A. (1999). *Consciousness.* New York: Scientific American Library.
Hodges, D. (2000). "Implications of Music and Brain Research" in *Music Educators Journal, 87*(2), 17-22.
Hodgkin (1991). "Michael Polanyi—Profit of life, the universe, and everything" in *Times Higher Educational Supplement*, September 27, p.15.

Holman, D., Pavlica, K., & Thorpe, R. (1997). "Rethinking Kolb's Theory of Experiential Learning: The Contribution of Social Constructivism and Activity Theory" in *Management Learning, 28*, 135-148.

Holliday, S.G. & Chandler, M.J. (1986). *Wisdom: Explorations in Adult Competence: Contributions to Human Development*, Vol. 17, Karger, Basel.

Hopkins, R. (1993). "David Kolb's Learning Machine" in *Journal of Phenomenological Psychology, 24*, 46-62.

Horstman, J. (2010). *The Scientific American Brave New Brain: How Neuroscience, Brain-Machine Interfaces, Neuroimaging, Psychopharmacology, Epigenetics, the Internet, and Our Minds are Stimulating and Enhancing the Future of Mental Power*. San Francisco: CA: John Wiley & Sons, Inc. and Scientific American.

Houston, J. (1982). *The Possible Human: A Course in Enhancing Your Physical, Mental and Creative Abilities*. Los Angeles: Jeremy Tarcher.

Huberman, A. M. & Miles, M. B. (2002). *The Qualitative Researcher's Companion*. New York: Sage Publications.

Hughes, J.R., Fino, J.J. & Melyn, M.A. (1999). "Is There a Chronic Change of the 'Mozart Effect' on Epileptiform Activity? A Case Study" in *Clinical Electroenceph. 30*, 44-45.

Hyman, S. E. (2007). "Diagnosing Disorders" in F. E. Bloom (Ed.), *Best of the Brain from Scientific American: Mind, Matter, and Tomorrow's Brain.* (pp. 132-141). 132-141.

Iacoboni, M. (2008). *The New Science of How We Connect with Others: Mirroring People*. New York: Farrar, Straus & Giroux.

Illeris, K. (2004). *Three Dimensions of Learning*. Roskilde, Denmark: Roskilde UniversityPress.

Jablonka. E. & Lamb, M. (1995). *Epigenetic Inheritance and Evolution: The Lamarckian Dimension.* Oxford, UK: Oxford University Press.

Jackson, P.L., Meltzoff, A.N. & Decety, J. (2005). "How Do We Perceive the Pain of Others? A window into the Neural Processes Involved in Empathy" in *NeuroImage, 24*, 771-779.

James, W. (1890/1980). *The Principles of Psychology*, (Vol. I.). New York: Holt, Rinehar & Winston.

Jarvis, P. (2004). *Adult Education and Lifelong Learning: Theory and Practice*. New York: RoutledgeFalmer.

Jarvis, P. (1987). *Adult Learning in the Social Context*. New York: Croom Helm.

Jarvis, P. (1992). *Paradoxes of Learning: On Becoming an Individual in Society*. San Francisco: Jossey-Bass.

Jensen, E. (1998). *Teaching with the Brain in Mind*. Alexandria, VA: Association for Supervision and Curriculum Development.

Jensen, E. (2000a). *Music with the Brain in Mind*. San Diego, CA: The Brain Store.

Jensen, E. (2000b). *Brain Based Learning: The New Science of Teaching and Training*. San Diego, CA: The Brain Store.

Jensen, E. (2005). *Teaching with the Brain in Mind*. Alexandria, VA: Association for Supervision and Curriculum Development.

Jensen, E. (2006). *Enriching the Brain: How to Maximize Every Learners Potential*. San Francisco: Jossey-Bass.

Jevning, R., Wallace, R.K. & Beidenbach, M. (1992). "The Physiology of Meditation: A Review" in *Neuroscience and Behavioral Reviews, 16*, 415-424.

Johnson, J.D.; Cotman, C.W.; Tasaki, C.S. & Shaw, G.L. (1998). "Enhancement of Spatial-Temporal Reasoning after a Mozart Listening Condition in Alzheimer's Disease: A Case Study" in *Neurology Research 20*, 666-672.

Johnson, J.K., Petsche, H., Richter, P., Von Stein, A., & Filz, O. (1996). "The Dependence of Coherence Estimates of Spontaneous EEG on Gender and Music Training" in *Music Perception, 13*, 563-582.

Johnson, S. (2001). *Emergence*. New York: Scribner.

Johnson, S. (2006). "The Neuroscience of the Mentor-Learner Relationship" in S. Johnson & K. Taylor (Eds.), *The Neuroscience of Adult Learning: New Directions for Adult and Continuing Education*. San Francisco: Jossey-Bass, 63-70.

Johnson, S., & Taylor, K. (2006). *The Neuroscience of Adult Learning: New Directions for Adult and Continuing Education*. San Francisco: Jossey-Bass.

Jonassen, D.H. (2004). *Handbook of Research for Educational Communication and Technology*. Mawah, NJ: Lawrence Erlbaum associates, 785-812.

Jung, C. G. (1990). *The Undiscovered Self with Symbols and the Interpretation of Dreams*. (R. F. Hull, Trans.) Princeton NJ: Princeton University Press.

Kahneman, D., P. Slovic & A. Tversky (1982). *Judgment Under Uncertainty: Heuristics and Biases*. New York: Cambridge University Press.

Kandel, E. R. (2006). *In Search of Memory: The Emergence of a New Science of Mind*. New York: W.W. Norton & Company.

Kandel, E. R. (2007). "The New Science of Mind" in F. E. Bloom (Ed.), *Best of the Brain from Scientific American: Mind, Matter, and Tomorrow's Brain*. New York: Dana Press, 68-78.

Kawashima, R., Sugiura, M., Kato, T., Nakamura, A., Hatano, K., Ito, K, et al. (1999). "The Human Amygdala Plays an Important Role in Gaze Monitoring: A PET Study" in *Brain, 122*, 779-783.

Kay, A. (2000). "Effective Music Education" in *Teaching Music, 7*(8), 51-53.

Kayes, D. C. (2002). "Experiential Learning and Its Critics: Preserving the Role of Experience in Management Learning and Education" in *Academy of Management Learning and Education 1* (2), 137-149.

Kegan, R. (1982). *The Evolving Self*. Boston, MA: Harvard University Press.

Kempermann, G., Kuhn, H. G., & Gage, F. H. (1997). "More Hippocampal Neurons in Adult Mice Living in an Enriched Environment" in *Nature, 386*, 493-95.

Kennerly, R.C. (1994). Downloaded June 20, 2008, at http:/www.MonroeInstitute.org/research/human-memory-ennerly.html

Kihlstrom, J. F. (1987). "The Cognitive Unconscious" in *Science, 237*, 1445-1452.

Kihlstrom, J. F., Shames, V. A., & Dorfman, J. (1996). "Imitations of Memory and Thought" in Reber, L. (Ed.), *Implicit Memory and Metacognition*. Mahwah, NJ: Erlbaum.

King, J. (1991). "Comparing Alpha Induction Differences between Two Music Samples", abstract from the Center for Research on Learning and Cognition, University of North Texas, TX.

Kirsner, K., Speelman, C., Maybetry, M. O'Brien-Malone, A., Anderson, M. & MacLeod, C. (Eds.) (1998). *Implicit and Expicit Mental Processes*. Mahwah, NJ: Lawrence Erlbaum Associates.

Klein, G. (2003). *Intuition at Work: Why Developing Your Gut Instincts will Make You Better at What You Do*. New York: Doubleday.

Kluwe, R. H., Luer, G., & Rosler, F. (Eds.) (2003). *Principles of Learning and Memory*. Basel, Switzerland: Birkhauser Verlag.

Knowles, M. S., Holton, E. F., & Swanson, R. A. (1998). *The Adult Learner: The Definitive Classic in Adult Education and Human Resource Development*. Houston, TX: Gulf.

Kohut, H. (1984). *How Does Analysis Cure?* Chicago: University of Chicago Press.

Kolb, D. A. (1984). *Experiential Learning: Experience as the Source of Learning and Development*. New Jersey: Prentice-Hall.

Kramer, D.A. & Bacelar, W.T. (1994). "The Educated Adult in Today's World: Wisdom and the Mature Learner" in Sinnott, J.D. (Ed.), *Interdisciplinary Handbook of Adult Lifespan Learning*. Westport, CN: Greenwood Press.

Kropotkin, P. (1902). *Mutual Aid: A Factor of Evolution*, downloaded on 01/26/15 from http://libcom.org/files/Peter%20Kropotkin-%20Mutual%20Aid;%20A%20Factor%20of%20Evolution.pdf

Kumar, G. P. & Khanum, F. (2012). "Neuroprotective Potential of Phytochemicals" in *Pharmacogn Rev*. Jul-Dec. 6(12), 81-90.

Kuntz, P. G. (1968). *The Concept of Order*. Seattle: University of Washington Press.

Kurzweil, R. (2005). *The Singularity is Near: When Humans Transcend Biology*. New York: Viking.

Kurzweil, R. (2012). *How to Create a Mind: The Secret of Human Thought Revealed*. New York, NY: Penguin Group.

Lakoff, G. & R. E. Nunez (2000). *Where Mathematics Comes From*. New York: Basic Books.

Lakoff, G., & Johnson, M. (1999). *Philosophy in the Flesh: The Embodied Mind and Its Challenge to Western Thought*. New York: Basic Books.

Laughlin, S. B. (2004). "The Implications of Metabolic Energy Requirements for the Representation of Information in Neurons" in M. S. Gazzaniga (Ed.), *The Cognitive Neuroscience III*. Cambridge, MA: The MIT Press, 187-196.

LeDoux, J. (1996). *The Emotional Brain: The Mysterious Underpinnings of Emotional Life*. New York: Touchstone.

LeDoux, J. (2002). *Synaptic Self: How Our Brains Become Who We Are*. New York: Viking.

Leotta, J. (1997). "Tongue or Pen: Which is the Way for Folklore?" in *Storytelling Magazine*. Special Edition/September.

Levine, S., & Ursin, H. (1991). "What is stress?" in M. R. Brown, G. F. Koob, C. Rivier (Eds.), *Stress: Neurobiology and Neuroendocrinology*. New York: Marcel Dekker, Inc., 3-21.

Levitt, H.M. (1999). "The Development of Wisdom: An Analysis of Tibetan Buddhist Experience" in *Journal of Humanistic Psychology*, 39(2), pp. 86-105.

Levy, J. (1985). "Right Brain, Left Brain: Fact or Fiction" in *Psychology Today*, May 1985, p. 43.

Lewicki, P., Hill, T., & Bizot, E. (1988). "Acquisition of Procedural Knowledge about a Pattern of Stimuli that Cannot be Articulated" in *Cognitive Psychology, 20*, 24-37.

Lewicki, P., Hill, T., & Czyzewska, M. (1992). "Nonconscious Acquisition of Information" in *American Psychologist, 47*, 796-801.

Liggan, D. Y., & Kay, J. (1999). "Some Neurobiological Aspects of Psychotherapy: A Review" in *Journal of Psychotherapy Practice and Research, 8*, 103-114.

Lindeman, E. C. (1961). *The Meaning of Adult Education in the United States*. New York: Harvest House.

Lipton, B. (2005). *The Biology of Belief: Unleashing the Power of Consciousness, Matter & Miracles*. Santa Rosa, CA: Mountain of Love/Elite Books.

Llinas, R. R. (2001). *I of the Vortex: From Neurons to Self*. Cambridge, MA: The MIT Press.

Loewenstein, W.R. (2013). *Physics in Mind: A Quantum View of the Brain*. New York, NY: Basic Books.

Long, T. A. (1986). "Narrative Unity and Clinical Judgment" in *Theoretical Medicine 7*: pp. 75-92.

Lozanov, G. (1991). "On Some Problems of the Anatomy, Physiology and Biochemistry of Cerebral Activities in the Global-Artistic Approach in Modern Sugestopedagogic Training" in *The Journal of the Society for Accelerative Learning and Teaching 16*.2, 101-16.

Lynch, Z. & Laursen B. (2009). *The Neuro Revolution: How Brain Science is Changing Our World*. New York, NY: St. Martin's Press.

Macdonald, C. (1996). *Toward Wisdom: Finding Our Way to Inner Peace, Love, and Happiness*. Hampton Roads, Charlottesville, VA.

MacFlouer, N. (1999). *Life's Hidden Meaning*. Tempe, AZ: Ageless Wisdom Publishers.

MacGregor, R. J. (2006). *On the Contexts of Things Human: An Integrative View of Brain, Consciousness, and Freedom of Will*. Hackensack, NJ: World Scientific.

Macguire, J. (1998). *The Power of Personal Storytelling: Spinning Tales to Connect with Others*. New York: Putnam.

MacIntyre, A. (1981). *After Virtue*. Notre Dame, IND: University of Notre Dame Press.

Mahoney, D. & Restak, R. (1998). *The Longevity Strategy: How to Live to 100 Using the Brain-Body Connection*. New York: John Wiley & Sons, Inc.

Mandel, M. (2007, August 20). "Which Way to the Future?" in *BusinessWeek*, 46.

Maples, M. F. & Webster, J. M. (1980). "Thorndike's Connectionism" in G. B. Gazda & R. J. Corsini (Eds.), *Theories of Learning*. Itasca, IL: Peacock, 1-280.

Marchese, T. J. (1998). "The New Conversations about Learning: Insights from Neuroscience and Anthropology, Cognitive Science and Workplace Studies" in *New Horizons for Learning*. Retrieved January 19, 2008, from http://www.newhorizons.org/lifelong/higher_ed/marchese.htm

Markowitsch, H. (1999). "Functional Neuroimaging Correlates of Functional Amnesia" in *Memory, 7*, 561-583.

Markowitsch, H. (2000). "The Anatomical Basis of Memory" in M. S. Gazzaniga (Ed.), *The New Cognitive Neurosciences*. Cambridge, MA: MIT Press.

Marquardt, M. J. (1999). *Action Learning in Action: Transforming Problems and People for World-Class Organizational Learning*. Palo Alto, CA: Davies-Black.

Marrow, A. J. (1969). *The Practical Theorist*. New York: Basic Books.

Marsh, J. T., Brown, W. S., & Smith, J. C. (1975). "Far-Field Recorded Frequency-Following Responses: Correlates of Low Pitch Auditory Perception in Humans" in *Electroencephalography and Clinical Neurophysiology, 38*, 113-119.

Marshall, S. P. (2005 September-November). "A Decidedly Different Mind" in *Shift: At the Frontiers of Consciousness*.

Marsick, V. J., & Watkins, K. E. (2001). "Informal and Incidental Learning" in S. B. Merriam (Ed.), *The New Update on Adult Learning Theory*. San Francisco: Jossey-Bass.

Marton, F., & Booth, S. (1997). *Learning and Awareness*. Mahwah, NJ: Erlbaum.

Mason, R. (2004). "The Sound Medicine of Brian Dailey, M.D." in *Alternative & Complementary Therapies*, June (reprint).

Masserman, J., Wechkin, S. & Terris, W. (1964). "'Altruistic' Behavior in Fhesus Monkeys" in *American Journal of Psychiatry* Vol. 121 (December), 584-585.

Matthews, R.C. (1991). "The Forgetting Algorithm: How Fragmentary Knowledge of Exemplars Can Yield Abstract Knowledge" in *Journal of Experimental Psychology: General, 120*, 117-119.

Maturana, H. R., & Varela, F. J. (1987). *The Tree of Knowledge: The Biological Roots of Human Understanding*. Boston: Shambhala.

Mavromatis, A. (1991). *Hypnagogia*. Routledge, New York, NY.

Mayer-Schönberger, V. & Cukier, K. (2013). *Big Data*. Great Britain: John Murray.

McDermott, J.J. (1977). *The Writings of William James*. Chicago, IL: University of Chicago Press.

McMaster, M.D. (1996). *The Intelligence Advantage: Organizing for Complexity*. Boston: Butterworth-Heinemann.

Meacham, J. A. (1995). "The Loss of Wisdom" in R. J. Sternberg (Ed.), *Wisdom, Its Nature, Origins, and Development*. New York: Cambridge University Press.

Medina, J. (2008, 2014). *Brain Rules: 12 Principles for Surviving and Thriving at Work, Home, and School*. Seattle, WA: Pear Press.

Mellon, N. (1992). *Storytelling and the Imagination*. Rockport, MA: Element Books.

Meltzoff, A. N., & Decety, J. (2002). "What Imitation Tells us About Social Cognition: A Rapproachement between Developmental Psychology and Cognitive Neuroscience" in *Philosophical Transactions of the Royal Society of London—Series B: Biological Sciences, 358*, 491-500.

"Mental illness in America: More than a quarter of adults are afflicted." (2008, February/March 15). *Scientific American Mind*.

Merriam, S. B., Caffarella, A. S., & Baumgartner, L. M. (2007). *Learning in Adulthood: A Comprehensive Guide*. San Francisco: Jossey-Bass.

Merriam, S.B. and Caffarella, R.S. (1999). *Learning in Adulthood: A Comprehensive Guide* (2nd Ed.). San Francisco: Jossey-Bass.

Merry, U. (1995). *Coping with Uncertainty: Insights from the New Sciences of Chaos, Self-Organization and Complexity*. London: Praeger.

Mezirow, J. (1991). *Transformative Dimensions of Adult Learning*. San Francisco: Jossey-Bass.

Mezirow, J. & Associates. (2000). *Learning at Transformation: Critical Perspectives on a Theory in Progress*. San Francisco: Jossey-Bass.

Miettinen, R. (1998). "About the Legacy of Experiential Learning" in *Lifelong Learning in Europe, 3*, 165-171.

Miles, M.B. & Huberman, A.M. (1994). *Qualitative Data Analysis*. Thousand Oaks, CA: SAGE Publications.

Miller, G. A. (1956). "The Magical Number Seven, Plus or Minus Two: Some Limits on Our Capacity for Processing Information" in *Psychological Review, 63*, 81-96.

Miller, J. G. (1978). *Living Systems*. New York: McGraw-Hill Book Company.

Miller, N. (2000). "Learning from Experience in Adult Education" in A. L. Wilson & E. R. Hayes (Eds.), *Handbook of Adult and Continuing Education*. San Francisco: Jossey-Bass.

Moon, J. A. (2004). *A Handbook of Reflective and Experiential Learning: Theory and Practice*. New York: Routledge-Falmer.

Monroe, R. (2007). Quote in *The Catalog*. Faber, VA: Monroe Products.

The Monroe Institute (1985). "Achieving Optimal Learning States" in *Breakthrough*, March. Faber, VA: The Monroe Institute.

Morowitz, H. J., & Singer, J. L. (Eds.). (1995) *The Mind, the Brain, and Complex Adaptive Systems*. Reading, MA: Addison-Wesley.

Morris, S.E. (1990). "Hemi-Sync® and the Facilitation of Sensory Interaction" in *Hemi-Sync® Journal, VIII*(4), 5-6.

Muftuler, L.T., Bodner, M., Shaw, G.L & Nalcioglu, O. (1999). "fMRI of Mozart Effect Using Auditory Stimuli", abstract presented at the 87th meeting of the International Society for Magnetic Resonance in Medicine, Philadelphia.

Mulvihill, M. K. (2003). "The Catholic Church in Crisis: Will Transformative Learning Lead to Social Change through the Uncovering of Emotion?" in C.A. Weissner, S. R. Meyers, N. L. Pfhal & P. J. Neaman (Eds.), *Proceedings for the 5th International Conference on Transformative Learning*. New York: Teachers College, Columbia University, 320-325.

Murphy, N. (2000). "Introduction: A Hierarchical Framework for Understanding Wisdom" in Brown, W.S. (Ed.), *Understanding Wisdom: Sources, Science and Society*. Philadelphia, PA: Templeton Foundation Press.

Naidu, A.S. (2013). *Redox LIFE*. Pomona, CA: Bio-Rep Network.

Nakamura, S., Sadato, N., Oohashi, T., Nishina, E., Fuwamoto, Y. & Yonekura, Y. (1999). "Analysis of Music-Brain Interaction with Simultaneous Measurement of Regional Cerebral Blood Flow and Electroencephalogram Beta Rhythm in Human Subjects" in *Neuroscience Letters, 275*, 222-226.

National Institutes of Health (2014). "Brain Research through Advancing Innovative Neurotechnologies (BRAIN)", Working Group Report to the Advisory Committee to the Director, NIH. Downloaded 09/19/2015 from www.braininitiative.nih.gov/pdf/BRAIN2025_508C.pdf

National Institutes of Health (2015). Downloaded 09/19/2015 from www.braininitiative.nih.gov/about.htm

National Research Council. (1994). *Learning, Remembering, Believing: Enhancing Human Performance*. Washington, DC: National Academy Press.

National Research Council. (2000). *How People Learn: Brain, Mind, Experience, and School*. Washington, DC: National Academy Press.

Neal, A., & Hesketh, B. (1997). "Episodic Knowledge and Implicit Learning" in *Psychonomic Bulletin & Review, 4*, 24-37.

Nelson, A. (2004). "Sophia: Transformation of Human Consciousness to Wisdom", unpublished paper, Fielding Graduate University, Santa Barbara, CA.

Nelson, C. A., deHaan, M., & Thomas, K. M. (2006). *Neuroscience of Cognitive Development: The Role of Experience and the Developing Brain*. Hoboken, NJ: John Wiley & Sons.

Nevis, E.C. (1987). *Organizational Consulting: A Gestalt Approach*. New York: Gardner Press, Inc.

Nicolelis, M. A. L., & Chapin, J. K. (2007). "Controlling Robots with the Mind" i F. E. Bloom (Ed.), *Best of the Brain from Scientific American: Mind, Matter, and Tomorrow's Brain*. New York: Dana Press, 197-212.

Norton, A., Winner, E., Cronin, K., Overy, K., Lee, D.J., & Schlaug, G. (2005). "Are There Pre-Existing Neural, Cognitive, or Motoric Markers for Musical Ability?" in *Brain and Cognition*.

Novak, J.D. (1998). *Learning, Creating and Using Knowledge: Concept Maps as Facilitative Tools in Schools and Corporations*. Mahwah: Lawrence Erlbaum Associates.

Novak, J.D. & Gowin, D.B. (1996). *Learning How to Learn*. New York: Cambridge University Press.

Nussbaum, S.W. (2000). "Profundity with Panache: the Unappreciated Proverbial Wisdom of Sub-Saharan Africa" in Brown, W.S. (Ed.), *Understanding Wisdom: Sources, Science and Society*. Philadelphia, PA: Templeton Foundation Press.

Oakshott, M. (1933). *Experience and Its Modes*. Cambridge, UK: Cambridge University Press.

O'Halloran, S. (2000). "Compassionate Action through Storytelling" in *Storytelling magazine*, Vol. 4, Issue 4, July/August.

Orwoll, L. & Perlmutter, M. (1990). "The Study of a Wise Person: Integrating a Personality Perspective" in Sternberg, R.J. (Ed.), *Wisdom: Its Nature, Origins and Development*. Cambridge, MA: Cambridge University Press.

Oster, G. (1973). "Auditory Beats in the Brain" in *Scientific American, 229*, 94-102.

Patterson, K., Grenny, J., McMillan, R. & Switzler, A. (2012). *Crucial Conversations: Tools for Talking When Stakes Are High* (2nd Ed.). New York: McGraw Hill.

Perkins, M. (1971). "Matter, Sensation and Understanding" in *American Philosophical Quarterly, 8*, 1-12.

Perry, W. G. (1970/1988). *Forms of Ethical and Intellectual Development in the College Years*. San Francisco: Jossey-Bass.

Pert, C. B. (1997). *Molecules of Emotion: A Science Behind Mind-Body Medicine*. New York: Touchstone.

Petsche, H. (1993). "Brainwave Coherence" in *Music Perception, V.* 11, 117-151.

Phelps, E. A. (2004). "The Human Amygdala and Awareness: Interactions of the Amygdale and Hippocampal Complex" in *Current Opinion in Neurobiology, 14*, 198-202.

Phelps, E. A., O'Connor, K. J., Gatenby, J. C., Grillon, C., Gore, J.C., & Davis, M. (2001). "Activation of the Left Amygdala to a Cognitive Representation of Fear" in *Natural Neuroscience, 4*, 437-441.

Piaget, J. (1951). *Play, Dreams and Imitation in Childhood*. New York: W.W. Norton.

Piaget, J. (1968). *Structuralism*. New York: Harper Torchbooks.

Piaget, J. (1971). *Psychology and Epistemology*. Middlesex, UK: Penguin Books.

Pickles, T. (2007). "Experiential Learning"... On the web. Retrieved December 11, 2007, from http://www.reviewing.co.uk/research/experiential.learning.htm

Pinker, S. (2007). *The Stuff of Thought: Language as Window into Human Nature*. New York: Viking.

Planck, M. (2015) (Reprint). *The Origin and Development of the Quantum Theory*. London: Forgotten Books.

Plotkin, H. (1994). *Darwin Machines and the Nature of Knowledge*. Cambridge, MA: Harvard University Press.

Pogue, D. (2015). Downloaded from https://twitter.com/intent/follow?original_referer=https%3A%2F%2Fwww.yahoo.com%2Ftech%2Fapples-researchkit-takes-medical-research-years117781601479.html&ref_src=twsrc^tfw&screen_name=Pogue&tw_p=followbutton

Polanyi, M. (1958). *Personal Knowledge: Towards a Post-Critical Philosophy*. Chicago: The University of Chicago Press.

Polanyi, M. (1967). *The Tacit Dimension*. New York, NY: Anchor Books.

Polster, E. & Polster, M. (1973). *Gestalt Therapy Integrated*. New York: Random House.

Porter, D., Bennet, A., Turner, R. & Wennergren, D. (2002). *The Power of Team: The Making of a CIO*. U.S. Department of the Navy, Washington, D.C.

Purves, D., Augustine, G. J., Fitzpatrick, D., Hall, W.C., LaMantia, A., McNamara, J.O., & White, L.E. (Eds.) (2008). *Neuroscience*, 4th Ed. Sunderland, MA: Sinauer Associates, Inc.

Race, P. (2005). *Making Learning Happen: A Guide for Post-Compulsory Education*. London: SAGE Publications.

Ramon, S. (1997). *Earthly Cycles. How Past Lives and Soul Patterns Shape Your Life*. Ojai, CA: Pepperwood Press.

Rao, R.P.N., Stocco, A., Bryan, M., Sarma, D. Youngquist, T.M., Wu, J. et al. (2014). "A Direct Brain-to-Brain Interface in Humans". PLOS ONE 9(11): e111332. doi: 10.1371/journal.pone.0111332 . Downloaded 09/21/2015 from http://journals.plos.org/plosone/article?id=10.1371/journal.pone.0111332

Ratey, J. J. (2001). *A User's Guide to the Brain: Perceptions, Attention, and the Four Theaters of the Brain*. New York: Pantheon Books.

Rauscher, F.H., Shaw, G.L., & Ky, K.N. (1993). "Music and Spatial Task Performance" in *Nature, 365*, 611.

Rauscher, F.H., Shaw, G.L., Levine, L.J., Wright, E.L., Dennis, W.R., & Newcomb, R.L. (1997). "Preschool Keyboarding Practice Enhances Long-Term Spatial Temporal Reasoning" in *Neurological Research*, Feb, Vol 19.

Reber, A. S. (1993). Implicit *Learning and Tacit Knowledge: An Essay on the Cognitive Unconscious*. New York: Oxford University Press.

Reik, W., & Walter, J. (2001). "Genomic Imprinting: Parental Influence on the Genome" in *Nature Reviews Genetics, 2*, 21+.

Restack, R.M. (2003). *The New Brain: How the Modern Age is Rewiring Your Mind*. New York: Rodale.

Revans, R. W. (1980). *Action Learning*. London: Frederick Muller.

Reynolds, M. (1999). "Critical Reflection and Management Education: Rehabilitating Less Hierarchical Approaches" in *Journal of Management Education, 23*, 537-553.

Rideout, B.E. & Laubach, C.M. (1996). "EEG Correlates of Enhanced Spatial Performance Following Exposure to Music" in *Perceptual & Motor Skills, 2*, 427-432.

Rideout, B.E. & Taylor, J. (1997). "Enhanced Spatial Performance Following 10 Minutes Exposure to Music: A Replication" in *Perceptual & Motor Skills, 85*, pp. 112-114.

Rideout, B.E., Dougherty, S. & Wernert, L. (1998). "Effect of Music on Spatial Performance: A Test of Generality" in *Perceptual & Motor Skills, 86*, 512-514.

Ritchey, D. (2003). *The H.I.S.S. of the A.S.P.: Understanding the Anomalously Sensitive Person*. Terra Alta, WV: Headline Books.

Rizzolatti, G. (2006, November). "Mirrors in the Mind" in *Scientific American*.

Roberts, J. (1994). *The Nature of Personal Reality*. New Jersey: Amber-Allen Publishing.

Rock, A. (2004). *The Mind at Night: The New Science of How and Why We Dream*. New York: Perseus Books Group.

Rose, S. (2005). *The Future of the Brain: The Promise and Perils of Tomorrow's Neuroscience*. New York: Oxford University Press.

Rosenfield, I. (1988). *The Invention of Memory*. New York: Basic Books.

Ross, C. A. (2006). "Brain Self-Repair in Psychotherapy: Implications for Education" in S. Johnson & K. Taylor (Eds.), *The Neuroscience of Adult Learning: New Directions for Adult and Continuing Education*. San Francisco: Jossey-Bass, 29-34.

Ross, P. E. (2006, August). "The Expert Mind" in *Scientific American*, 64-71.

Russell, P. (2007). *What is Wisdom?* downloaded 1/14/2008 from http://www.peterrussell.com/SP/Wisdom.php

Russell, P. (1995). *The Global Brain Awakens*. Saline, MI: McNaughton & Gunn.

Ryle, G. (1949). *The Concept of Mind*. London, England: Hutchinson.

Sapolsky, R. M. (1999). "Glucocorticoids, Stress, and Their Adverse Neurological Effects: Relevance to Aging" in *Experimental Gerontology, 34*, 721-732.

Schacter, D. L. (1996). *Searching for Memory: The Brain, the Mind, and the Past*. New York: Basic Books.

Schacter, D. L. (2001). *The Seven Sins of Memory: How the Mind Forgets and Remembers*. New York: Houghton Mifflin.
Schank, R.E. (1995). *Tell me a Story: Narrative and Intelligence*. Evanston, IL: Northwestern University Press.
Schlaug, G., Jancke, L., Huang, Y., Staiger, J. & Steinmetz, H. (1995). "Increased Corpus Callosum Size in Musicians" in *Neuropsychologia 33*, 1047-1055.
Schloss, J.P. (2000). "Wisdom Traditions as Mechanisms for Organismal Integration: Evolutionary Perspectives on Homeostatic 'Laws of Life'" in Brown, W.S. (Ed.), *Understanding Wisdom: Sources, Science and Society*. Philadelphia, PA: Templeton Foundation Press.
Schmithhorst, V.J. & Holland, S.K. (2004). "The Effect of Musical Training on the Neural Correlates of Math Processing: A Functional Magnetic Resonance Imaging Study in Humans" in *Neuroscience Letters, 354*, 193-196.
Scholey, A., Moss, M., Naeve, N., & Wesnes, K. (1999). "Cognitive Performance, Hyperoxia, and Heart Rate Following Oxygen Administration in Healthy Young Adults" in *Physiological Behavior, 67*, 783-789.
Schon, D. (1983). *The Reflective Practitioner: How Professionals Think in Action*. New York: Basic books.
Schore, A. N. (1994). *Affect Regulation and the Origin of the Self: The Neurobiology of Emotional Development*. Hillsdale, NJ: Erlbaum.
Schore, A. N. (2002). "Dysregulation of the Right Brain: A Fundamental Mechanism of Traumatic Attachment and the Psychopathogenesis of Posttraumatic Stress Disorder" in *Australian and New Zealand Journal of Psychiatry, 36*, 9-30.
Schwartz, P. (2003). *Inevitable Surprises: Thinking Ahead in a Time of Turbulence*. New York: Penguin Group.
Seashore, C.N., Shawver, M.N., Thompson, G., & Mattare, M. (2004). "Doing Good by Knowing Who You Are: The Instrumental Self as an Agent of Change" in *OD Practitioner, Vol. 36*, No. 3., pp. 42-46.
Seashore, C.N., Seashore, E.W., & Weinberg, G.M. (2001). *What Did You Say? The Art of Giving and Receiving Feedback*. Columbia, MD: Bingham House Books.
Senge, P. (1990). *The Fifth Discipline*. New York: Doubleday.
Shedlock, D.J. & Cornelius, S.W. (2000). "Wisdom: Perceptions and Performance", paper presented at the Cognitive Aging Conference, Atlanta, GA.
Sherman, N. (2000). "Wise Emotions" in Brown, W.S. (Ed.), *Understanding Wisdom: Sources, Science and Society*. Philadelphia, PA: Templeton Foundation Press.
Shorter Oxford English Dictionary (5th Ed.) (2002). Oxford, England: Oxford University Press.
Siegel, D. J. (2007). *The Mindful Brain: Reflection and Attunement in the Cultivation of Well-Being*. New York: W. W. Norton & Company.
Silberman, M. (2007). *The Handbook of Experiential Learning*. San Francisco: Pfeiffer.
Silverman, D. P. (ed.) (1997). *Ancient Egypt*. New York: Oxford University Press.
Simmons, A. (2001). *The Story Factor: Inspiration, Influence, and Persuasion Through the Art of Storytelling*. New York: Perseus Publishing.
Singer, T., Seymour, B., O'Doherty, J., Kaube, H., Dolan, R.J. & Frith, C.D. (2004). "Empathy for Pain Involves the Affective but Not Sensory Components of Pain" in *Science, 303*, 1157-1162.
Skoyles, J. R., & Sagan, D. (2002). *Up from Dragons: The Evolution of Human Intelligence*. New York: McGraw-Hill.
Smith, J., Dixon, R.A. & Baltes, P.B. (1987). "Age Differences in Response to Life Planning Problems: A Research Analog for the Study of Wisdom, Related Knowledge", unpublished manuscript.
Smith, J.C., Marsh, J.T., Greenberg, S. & Brown, W.S. (1978). "Human Auditory Frequency-Following Responses to a Missing Fundamental" in *Science, 201*, 639-641.
Smith, M.K. (2003). "Michael Polanyi and Tacit Knowledge" in *The Encyclopedia of Informal Education*, p. 2, www.infed.org/thinkers/Polanyi.htm

Smith, C. A., & Ellsworth, P. C. (1985). "Patterns of Cognitive Appraisal in Emotion" in *Journal of Personality and Social Psychology, 56*, 339-53.

Smith, J. C., Marsh, J. T., Greebnerg, S., & Brown, W. S. (1978). "Human Auditory Frequency-Following Responses to a Missing Fundamental" in *Science, 201*, 639-641.

Soundlab. Downloaded, May 26, 2008, from http://soundlab.cs.princeton.edu/learning/tutorials/SoundVoice/sndvoic2.htm

Sousa, D. A. (2006). *How the Brain Learns*. Thousand Oaks CA: Corwin Press.

Sousa, D.A (Ed) (2010). *Mind, Brain, & Education: Neuroscience Implications for the Classroom*. Bloomington, IN: Solution Tree Press.

Sousa, D. A. (2011). *How the Brain Learns*, 4th Ed. Thousand Oaks CA: Corwin Press.

Springer, S.P. & Deutsch, G. (1997). *Left Brain/Right Brain: Perspectives from Cognitive Neuroscience*. New York: W.H. Freemand and Company.

Squire, L. R., & Knowlton, B. (1995). "Memory, Hippocampus, and Brain Systems" in M. S. Gazzaniga (Ed.), *The cognitive neurosciences*. Cambridge, MA: The MIT Press.

Stacy, R. D. (1996). *Complexity and Creativity in Organizations*. San Francisco: Berrett-Koehler Publishers.

Stacy, R. D., Griffin, D., & Shaw, P. (2000). *Complexity and Management: Fad or Radical Challenge to Systems Thinking?* New York: Routledge.

Steele, K.M., Brown, J.D. & Stoecker, J.A. (1999). "Failure to Confirm the Raushcer and Shaw Description of Recovery of the Mozart Effect" in *Perceptual & Motor Skills 88*, 843-849.

Stern, D. N. (2004). *The Present Moment in Psychotherapy and Everyday Life*. New York: Norton.

Sternberg, R.J. (Ed.) (1998). *Wisdom: Its Nature, Origins, and Development*. Cambridge, MA: Cambridge University Press.

Stevens, K. (2000). "Wisdom as an Organizational Construct: Reality or Rhetoric?", unpublished dissertation, Fielding Institute, Santa Barbara, CA.

Stonier, T. (1990). *Information and the Internal Structure of the Universe*. London: Springer-Verlag.

Stonier, T. (1992). *Beyond Information: The Natural History of Intelligence*. London: Springer-Verlag.

Stonier, T. (1997). *Information and Meaning: An Evolutionary Perspective*. London: Springer-Verlag.

Surani, M.A. (2001). "Reprogramming of Genome Function through Epigenetic Inheritance" in *Nature, 414*, 122-128.

Swain, J. (1997). *Musical Languages*. New York: W.W. Norton.

Swann, R., Bosanko, S., Cohen, R., Midgley, R., & Seed, K. M. (1982). *The Brain—A User's Manual*. New York: G.P. Putnam & Sons.

Sweeney, M.S. (2009). *Brain: The Complete Mind*. Washington, DC: National Geographic Society.

Swomley, J. (2000). "Violence: Competition or cooperation" in *Christian Ethics Today* 26, Vol. 6, No. 1.

Tallis, F. (2002). *Hidden Minds: A History of the Unconscious*. New York: Arcade.

Tan, O. (Ed.). (2004). *Enhancing Thinking through Problem-Based Learning Approaches: International Perspectives*. Singapore: Thompson Learning.

Tapscott, D. (2009). *Grown up Digital*. New York: McGraw Hill.

Tatsuya, I., Mitsuo, H., & Tadao, H. (1997). "Changes in Alpha Band EEG Activity in the Frontal Area after Stimulation with Music of Different Affective Content" in *Perceptual & Motor Skills, 84*, 515-526.

Taylor, D. (1996). *The Healing Power of Stories: Creating Yourself through the Stories of Your Life*. New York: Doubleday.

Taylor, K. (2006). "Brain Function and Adult Learning: Implications for Practice" in S. Johnson & K. Taylor (Eds.), The *The Neuroscience of Adult Learning: New Directions for Adult and Continuing Education*. San Francisco: Jossey-Bass, 71-86.

Teasdale, W. & the Dali Lama (1999). *The Mystic Heart: Discovering a Universal Spirituality in the World's Religions*. Novato,CA: New World Library.

Tennant, M. (1997). *Psychology and Adult Learning*. London: Routledge.
Thompson, J.D. (2008), "Acoustic Brainwave Entrainment with Binaural Beats", downloaded June 16, 2008, from http://www.neuroacoustic.com/entrainment.html
Thompson, R. F. (2000). *The Brain: A Neuroscience Primer*. New York: Worth.
Tomatis, A. (1983). "Brain/Mind Bulletin Collections" in *New Sense Bulletin Vol. 8*, Los Angeles, CA, Jan 24, #4A.
Tooby, J., & Cosmides, L. (1990). "The Past Explains the Present: Emotional Adaptations and the Structure of Ancestral Environments" in *Ethological Sociobiology 11*, 375-424.
Torbert, W.R. & Rogers, M.P. (1972). *Being for the Most Part Puppets: Interactions Among Men's Labor, Leisure and Politics*. Cambridge, MA: Schenkman Publishing.
Trumpa, C. (1991). *The Heart of the Buddha*, Shambhala, Boston, MA.
Uleman, J. (2005). "Becoming Aware of the New Unconscious" in R. R. Hassin, J. S. Uleman & J. A. Bargh (Eds.), *The New Unconscious*. New York: Oxford University Press.
Vaughn, K. (2000). "Music and Mathematics: Modest Support for the Oft-Claimed Relationships" in *Journal of Aesthetic Education, 34*, 149-166.
Vedantam, S. (2010). *The Hidden Brain: How Our Unconscious Minds Elect Presidents, Control Markets, Wage Wars, and Save Our Lives*. New York, NY: Spiegel & Grau.
Vince, R. (1998). "Behind and Beyond Kolb's Learning Cycle" in *Journal of Management Education, 22*, 304-319.
von Krogh, G., & Roos, J. (1995). *Organizational Epistemology*. New York: St. Martin's Press.
Vygotsky, L. S. (1978). *Mind in Society: The Development of Higher Psychological Processes*. Cambridge, MA: Harvard University Press.
Waldkoetter, R. (1982). "Executive Summary", unpublished manuscript, The Monroe Institute, Professional Division, Faber, VA.
Wang, X., Merzenich, M. M., Sameshima, K., & Jenkins, W. M. (1995). "Remodeling of Hand Representation in Adult Cortex Determined by Timing of Tactile Stimulation" in *Nature, 378*, 71-75.
Ward, J. (2006). *The Student's Guide to Cognitive Neuroscience*. New York: Psychology Press.
Webb, D. & Webb, T. (1990). Accelerated Learning with Music, Accelerated Learning Systems, Norcross, GA.
Weinberger, N.M. (2004). "Music and the brain", Scientific American, 291, pp. 89-95.
Weinberger, N. M. (1999). "Can Music Really Improve the Mind? The Question of Transfer Effects", MuSICA Research Notes: V VI, 12, Spring 1999.
Weinberger, N. M. (1995). "Non Musical Outcomes of Music Education" in *Musical Journal, Fall: II*(2), 6.
West, M.A. (1980). "Meditation and the EEG" in *Psychological Medicine, 10*, 69-375.
Wiig, K. (1993). *Knowledge Management Methods—Practical Approaches to Managing Knowledge*. Arlington, TX: Schema Press.
Wikipedia (2015). Downloaded 10/07/15 from https://en.wikipedia.org/wiki/Quantified_Self
Wild, B., Rodden, F. A., Grodd, W., & Ruch, W. (2003). "Neural Correlates of Laughter and Humor" in *Brain, 126*, 2121-2138.
Wilson, A. L., & Hayes, E. R. (Eds.) (2000). *Handbook of Adult and Continuing Education*. San Francisco: Jossey-Bass.
Wilson, E. O. (1998). *Consilience: The Unity of Knowledge*. New York: Alfred A. Knopf.
Wilson, F. (1991). "Music and the Neurology of Time" in *Music Educators Journal* 77(5), 26-30.
Wilson, T.L. & Brown, T.L. (1997). "Reexamination of the Effect of Mozart's Music on Spatial-Task Performance" in *Journal of Psychology, 13*, 365-370.
Wolfe, P. (2006). "The Role of Meaning and Emotion in Learning" in S. Johnson & K. Taylor (Eds.), *The Neuroscience of Adult Learning: New Directions for Adult and Continuing Education*. San Francisco: Jossey-Bass, 35-42.
Wolff, J. (1999). "Digital Storytelling: Wave of the Future?" in *Storytelling magazine, Vol. 11*, Issue 3, May/June.

Woodman, M. & Dickson, E. (1996). *Dancing in the Flames: The Dark Goddess in the Transformation of Consciousness*. Boston, MA: Shambhala, Boston, MA.

Writing: The Nature, Development and Teaching of Written Communication (Vol. II) (1982). Lawrence Erlbaum Associates.

Wong, C. Y. L., Choi, C. J., & Millar, C. C. J. M. (2006). "The Case of Singapore as a Knowledge-Based City" in F. J. Carrillo. (Ed.) *Knowledge Cities: Approaches, Experiences, and Perspectives*. New York: Elsevier, 87-96.

Zatorre, R. (1997). "Hemispheric Specialization of Human Auditory Processing: Perception of Speech and Musical Sounds" in *Advances in Psychology, 123*, 299.

Zhu, X. O., & Waite, P. M. E. (1998). "Cholinergic Depletion Reduces Plasticity of Barrel Field Cortex" in *Cerebral Cortex, 8*, 63-72.

Zigmond, M. J., Bloom, F. E., Landis, S. C., Roberts, J. L., & Squire, L. R. (Eds.) (1999). *Fundamental Neuroscience*. San Diego, CA: Academic Press.

Zimmer, C. (2007). "The Neurobiology of the Self" in F. E. Bloom (Ed.), *Best of the Brain from Scientific American: Mind, Matter, and Tomorrow's Brain*. New York: Dana Press, 47-57.

Zull, J.E. (2011). *From Brain to Mind: Using Neuroscience to Guide Change in Education*. Sterling, VA: Stylus.

Zull, J. E. (2002). *The Art of Changing the Brain: Enriching the Practice of Teaching by Exploring the Biology of Learning*. Sterling, VA: Stylus.

Subject Index

adaptation (def) 162
adult learning
   history 2
aging 57-59
   neuroscience findings 144-146
   personal addendum 213-214
   wisdom of 280
anticipating the future 64-67
   neuroscience findings 129-131
anxiety 212-213
   ubiquitous 5
associative patterning 88, 196
   description 12
   picture 14
   process 12-14
   sensemaking 13
assumptions vii-ix
attention
   brain, in 68
   stress 123
autotelic work 33
body/mind
   emotions 120
   information network 11
brain
   (see mind/brain)
   age 57-59
   Decade of the 8
   description 61
   exercise 55-57
   health 205
   Initiative 9-10
   modification of chemistry 141, 188
   music in 227-240
   plasticity 59-60
      neuroscience findings 140-142
   research 10
   storing information 62-63
   structure 188, 203
   thoughts, relationship 141
change
   increasing 5
cognitive mimicry
   (see mirror neurons)
complex adaptive system
   (def) 27, 162-163
   properties 28
   ways to influence 28
complexity

lifelong learning 6
   limits of theory 6
   shortcomings 8
   (def) 26, 162
   growing 5
   optimum 28
concept mapping
   examples 106, 107
   process 104-108
consciousness 73
   extraordinary 272-274
   ordinary 272-274
consilience 3, 42
constructivism 42
creativity 21, 86-89, 186-187
   enriched environment 125, 142, 222-226
   extraordinary 87, 126
   neuroscience findings 124-126
   ordinary 87
CUCA 5, 6
data (def) 19
emotions 69-77, 204
   cognition, relationship with 72, 75
   (def) 70
   emotional intelligence 253-254
   fear 122-123
   feelings, as 70
   guidance system, as a 76-77
   memory, relationship with 83-84
   neuroscience findings 117-120
   passion 76
   priority of 75, 204
   tags 115, 119, 204, 264
empathy 251-252
environment 95-102
   brain co-evolution with 95, 215-217
   enriched 222-226
   external 98-99
   genes as operating options 139
   influence of 277-278
   internal 95-97
   neuroscience findings 155-156
epigenetics 95-97
   beliefs, relationship to 139
   genes as destiny 139
   neuroscience findings 138-140
exercise, 144
   mental 55-57, 146, 211-212
   neuroscience findings 142-144

physical 55-57, 146, 211-212
   stimulation, as 137
experience (def) 25
   mediated 33
   practical 33
   way people learn 32
experiential learning
   complex adaptive learning system, as 165
   (def) 25
   Dewey, John 33-36
   history 33
   Kolb model 4, 32-33, 37-40
   Kolb/Zull model 40-41
   Lewin, Kurt 34-36
   modes 43-44, 105
   Piaget, Jean 34-36
forces
   alignment of 18
Golden Age 2
health
   brain 205-211
   learning and 55
   neuroscience findings 142-144
hemispheric synchronization 88-89, 236-238
   Monroe Institute 237-239
ICALS
   assessing the items 147-153
   BrainKnow Toolkit, 208
   characteristics 45-48
   complex adaptive system, as a 165
      model 165
   enhancement, areas of
      effectiveness 104
      efficiency 104
      meta-learning 104
      sustainable learning 104
   expanded Kolb/Zull/Bennet model 153-155
   living a new frame of reference 294-296
   model 43-44, 166-169
   modes 43-44, 45, 105, 170-185
   self-organizing 42-43, 48
   Introduction 42-43
idea resonance 260-261
information
   (def) 19
   non-random patterns, as 19
   property of Universe 19
intelligence
   communication 200
   comprehension 200

   (def) 162-163
   data finding 200
   data manipulation 200
   dimensions 200-202
   emotional 15, 253-254
   explanation 200
   integration 200
   measuring 199
   planning 200-201
   spiritual 15
intelligent activity (def) 199
intention
   definition 17-18
   power of 17-
intuition 21
judgment 5, 15
knowing 282-293
   cognitive capabilities 290-291
   cognitive processes 291
   critical areas 287-288
   framework 290-293
   kn and knowing loop (model) 284
   principles 289-290
   self as agent of change 292-293
   spiritual characteristics 287
   superconscious 286
   unconscious connection 283-287
knowledge
   consciousness and 274
   context sensitive & situation dependent 24, 131
   creation 14
   deep 23-24
   (def) 20
   demands on 4
   growth of knowledge and sharing 269
   incomplete and imperfect 24
   justified true belief, as 20, 22-23
   kn (informing) 21, 22, 23
   kn (proceeding) 22, 23
   knowing and 282-293
   levels of 23
   responsibility of 278
   shallow 23
   surface 20, 23
   tacit 192-196
      affective 195
      embodied 195
      intuitive 195
      spiritual 195
   transfer 128

328 | Expanding the Self

understanding, as 20
workers 6
law of requisite variety 28
learning
    (see adult learning)
    action 6
    beliefs, power of 277
    (def) 24
    guidelines for 275-281
    meta-learning 104
    music 227-240
    process, as a 45-46, 47
    self-organized 163-164
    social 241-254
    spiritual 286-287
    sustainable 104
    transformation theory of 6
    voluntary 123, 144, 187
    wisdom of 267-282
learning-knowledge loop 25-26
learning modes 43-44, 45, 105, 170-185
    action 181-183
    comprehension 178-181
    experience 172-173
    reflection 174-177
    social engagement 183-185
meaning 14, 20, 115, 119
meditation 88, 126, 144
memory 81-84
    binding problem 83
    emotions, relationship with 84
    invariant forms, as 65, 82, 131
    long term 63
    memory traces 83-84
    neuroscience findings 113-117
    recreated 116
    systems 62
    working 116
mind
    biology of 2
    infinite potential 276
mind/brain
    analogy 61
    anticipating the future 64-67, 129-131
    appresentation 66
    attention 68
    (def) 10
    hierarchal structure 67
    incoming signals 62
    learning, and 62
    as patterns 11
    storing information 62-63
mind/brain/body 52-53

exercise 55-57
health 54-55
nature of 54
mirror neurons 85-86, 186
    cognitive memory, form of 128
    imitation 252-253
    neuroscience findings 126-129
music in the brain 227-240
    (see hemispheric synchronization)
    Mozart Effect 229-231
    musical instrument, impact of 233-236
    transfer effects 231-233
neurons
    description 12
    picture 11
    relationship to experience 13
    throughout body 12
neuroplasticity 59-60
neuroscience
    measurement techniques 2, 8, 9, 53
neuroscience findings
    aging 144-146
    assessing the items 147-153
    anticipating the future 129-131
    creativity 124-126
    emotions 117-120
    epigenetics 138-140
    exercise and health 142-144
    memory 113-117
    mirror neurons 126-129
    plasticity 140-142
    social interaction 135-137
    social support 132-134
    stress 121-124
    unconscious 109-112
observer effect 17
planning 200-201
point of singularity 5
prediction 21
    basis for intelligence 64
Quantum
    frame of reference 3
relationship network management 254
Self 190-202
    autobiographical self 17, 93
    awareness and beyond 261-265
    change, locus of 255-265
    co-creating reality 216-222
    co-evolving with environment 21-226
    conscious, use of 197
    core self 17
    (def) 190
    foundation for model, as 44

learned pattern 11
model from unconscious 112
neuroscience findings 156-158
protoself 17
Seashore Model 196-197
story of 198-202
social learner, as 241-254
subject and object 15-17
substantive self-consciousness thesis 15
unconscious impact 192
social
affective attunement 101-102, 133, 134, 137
brain, relationship with 100
learner 241-254
social interaction 99-100, 244-245
collaborative entanglement 260
context 246-247
conversation 246-247
figure 245
idea resonance 260-261
neuroscience findings 135-137
physical mechanisms 136
relationship network management 254
social support 100-102
bonding 248-251
empathy 251-252
neuroscience findings 132-134
social bonding 137
story 116
living a new frame of reference 294-296
native American tradition 257-258
Self, of 198-202
telling 255-259

stress 77-80, 212-213
arousal, relationship with 77-79, 212-213
figure 213
flight and fight 79
neuroscience findings 121-124
optimal level 123
psychological component 78
synaptic connections (see neurons)
systems 26-29
(see complex adaptive system)
(def) 26, 162
systems thinking 26
theory (def) 29
thought
(see neuroplasticity)
creates reality 14
uncertainty
rising 5, 6
unconscious
brain 89-94
communication 100
connection 283-287
(def) 89
imitation 252-253
insight 125
manipulating inputs 92
neuroscience findings 109-112
power of 279
Weizmann Institute of Science 17
wisdom 267-281
definitions and descriptions 268-270
learning and 274-275
patterns, as 270-271

About Mountain Quest Institute

MQI is a research, retreat and learning center dedicated to helping individuals achieve personal and professional growth, and helping organizations create and sustain high performance in a rapidly changing, uncertain, and increasingly complex world.

Current research is focused on Human and Organizational Development, Knowledge, Knowledge Capacities, Adult Learning, Values, Complexity, Consciousness and Spirituality. MQI has three questions: The Quest for Knowledge, The Quest for Consciousness, and The Quest for Meaning. **MQI is scientific, humanistic and spiritual and finds no contradiction in this combination**. See www.mountainquestinstitute.com

MQI is the birthplace of Organizational Survival in the New World: The Intelligent Complex Adaptive System (Elsevier, 2004), a new theory of the firm that turns the living system metaphor into a reality for organizations. Based on research in complexity and neuroscience—and incorporating networking theory and knowledge management—this book is filled with new ideas married to practical advice, all embedded within a thorough description of the new organization in terms of structure, culture, strategy, leadership, knowledge workers and integrative competencies.

Mountain Quest Institute, situated four hours from Washington, D.C. in the Monongahela Forest of the Allegheny Mountains, is part of the Mountain Quest complex which includes a Retreat Center, Inn, and the old Farm House, Outbuildings and mountain trails and farmland. See www.mountainquestinn.com The Retreat Center is designed to provide full learning experiences, including hosting training, workshops, retreats and business meetings for professional and executive groups of 25 people or less. The Center includes a 26,000 volume research library, a conference room, community center, computer room, 12 themed bedrooms, a workout and hot tub area, and a four-story tower with a glass ceiling for enjoying the magnificent view of the valley during the day and the stars at night. Situated on a 430 acres farm, there is a labyrinth, creeks, four miles of mountain trails, and horses, Longhorn cattle, Llamas and a myriad of wild neighbors. Other neighbors include the Snowshoe Ski Resort, the National Radio Astronomy Observatory and the CASS Railroad.

About the Authors

Drs. Alex and David Bennet are co-founders of the Mountain Quest Institute. They may be contacted at alex@mountainquestinstitute.com

Alex Bennet, a Professor at the Bangkok University Institute for Knowledge and Innovation Management, is internationally recognized as an expert in knowledge management and an agent for organizational change. Prior to founding the Mountain Quest Institute, she served as the Chief Knowledge Officer and Deputy Chief Information Officer for Enterprise Integration for the U.S. Department of the Navy, and was co-chair of the Federal Knowledge Management Working Group. Dr. Bennet is the recipient of the Distinguished and Superior Public Service Awards from the U.S. government for her work in the Federal Sector. She is a Delta Epsilon Sigma and Golden Key National Honor Society graduate with a Ph.D. in Human and Organizational Systems; degrees in Management for Organizational Effectiveness, Human Development, English and Marketing; and certificates in Total Quality Management, System Dynamics and Defense Acquisition Management. Alex believes in the **multidimensionality and interconnectedness of humanity as we move out of infancy into full consciousness**.

David Bennet's experience spans many years of service in the Military, Civil Service and Private Industry, including fundamental research in underwater acoustics and nuclear physics, frequent design and facilitation of organizational interventions, and serving as technical director of two major DoD Acquisition programs. Prior to founding the Mountain Quest Institute, Dr. Bennet was CEO, then Chairman of the Board and Chief Knowledge Officer of a professional services firm located in Alexandria, Virginia. He is a Phi Beta Kappa, Sigma Pi Sigma, and Suma Cum Laude graduate of the University of Texas, and holds degrees in Mathematics, Physics, Nuclear Physics, Liberal Arts, Human and Organizational Development, and a Ph.D. in Human Development focused on Neuroscience and adult learning. He is currently researching the nexus of Science, the Humanities and Spirituality.

Robert Turner served in the military in Army Intelligence and Organizational Development, where he co-developed the U.S. Army Fusion Center, an advanced decision support center. He subsequently directed the Federal Aviation Administration Team Technology Center and managed programs in support of FAA leadership development. His work at the FAA included representing the FAA at the Institute for the Future and at the IBM Institute for Knowledge Management. He served for four years as the Chairman of the government-wide Federal KM Network. In 2003, he received the first government-wide award for service in KM. In 2006, as co-developer of the FAA Knowledge Services Network (KSN), he received an acclaimed government-wide award for innovation excellence. He is a member of Phi Kappa Phi whose motto is "*Let the love of learning rule humanity.*" He graduated magna cum laude and received a special academic achievement medal from the University of Maryland in psychology and business. He completed his master's degree in education with Boston University. He recently co-led with his wife Jane a one year cohort in the joint BYU-Idaho Pathway & LDS Institute Program, an innovative global university endeavor. His research interests include individual and organizational high performance and accelerated learning of genealogical research tools.

We hope you have enjoyed this book.

MQIPress is a wholly-owned subsidiary of Mountain Quest Institute, LLC, located at 303 Mountain Quest Lane, Marlinton, West Virginia 24954, USA.

Possibilities that are YOU!

These little **Conscious Look Books** are focused on sharing 22 large concepts from *The Profundity and Bifurcation of Change*. Conversational in nature, each with seven ideas offered for the student of life experience. Available in soft cover from Amazon.

eBooks available in PDF format from MQIPress (US 304-799-7267 or alex@mountainquestinstitute.com) and Kindle format from Amazon.

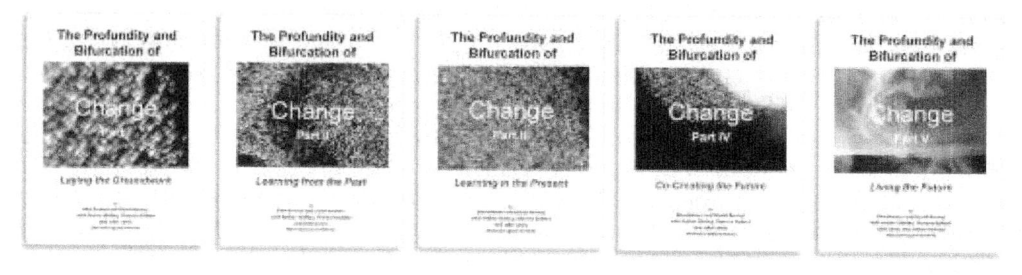

Five in-depth eBooks, *The Profundity and Bifurcation of Change*, heavily referenced and resourced. These books lay the groundwork for the **Intelligent Social Change Journey** (ISCJ), a developmental journey of the body, mind and heart, moving from the heaviness of cause-and-effect linear extrapolations, to the fluidity of co-evolving with our environment, to the lightness of breathing our thought and feelings into reality. Grounded in development of our mental faculties, these are phase changes, each building on and expanding previous learning in our movement toward intelligent activity. Available as eBooks from Amazon.

eBooks available NOW
(Available in soft back copy from Amazon end of 2018)

The Course of Knowledge: A 21st Century Theory

by Alex Bennet and David Bennet with Joyce Avedisian (2015)

Knowledge is at the core of what it is to be human, the substance which informs our thoughts and determines the course of our actions. Our growing focus on, and understanding of, knowledge and its consequent actions is changing our relationship with the world. Because **knowledge determines the quality of every single decision we make**, it is critical to learn about and understand what knowledge is. **From a 21st century viewpoint,** we explore a theory of knowledge that is both pragmatic and biological. Pragmatic in that it is based on taking effective action, and biological because it is created by humans via patterns of neuronal connections in the mind/brain.

In this book we explore *the course of knowledge*. Just as a winding stream in the bowls of the mountains curves and dips through ravines and high valleys, so, too, with knowledge. In a continuous journey towards intelligent activity, context sensitive and situation dependent knowledge, imperfect and incomplete, experientially engages a changing landscape in a continuous cycle of learning and expanding. *We are in a continuous cycle of knowledge creation such that every moment offers the opportunity for the emergence of new and exciting ideas, all waiting to be put in service to an interconnected world.* Learn more about this **exciting human capacity**!

Leading with the Future in Mind: Knowledge and Emergent Leadership

by David Bennet and Alex Bennet with John Lewis (2015)

We exist in a new reality, a global world where the individuated power of the mind/brain offers possibilities beyond our imagination. It is within this framework that thought leading emerges, and when married to our collaborative nature, makes the impossible an everyday occurrence. Leading with the Future in Mind, building on profound insights unleashed by recent findings in neuroscience, provides a new view that converges leadership, knowledge and learning for individual and organizational advancement.

This book provides a research-based tour de force for the future of leadership. Moving from the leadership of the past, for the few at the top, using authority as the explanation, we now find leadership emerging from all levels of the organization, with knowledge as the explanation. The future will be owned by the organizations that understand and can master the relationships between knowledge and leadership. Being familiar with the role of a knowledge worker is not the same as understanding the role of a knowledge leader. As the key ingredient, collaboration is much more than "getting along"; it embraces and engages.

The nature of the organization has moved beyond the factory and process metaphor, and is now understood as an intelligent complex adaptive system (ICAS). Leading with the Future in Mind covers the essentials of working, learning, and leading in an ICAS, covering knowledge and complexity, but also passion and spiritual energy. As social creatures living in an entangled world, our brains are linked together. We are in continuous interaction with those around us, and the brain is continuously changing in response. Wrapped in the mantle of collaborative leadership and engaging our full resources—physical, mental, emotional and spiritual—we open the door to possibilities. We are dreaming the future together.

Decision-Making in The New Reality: Complexity, Knowledge and Knowing

by Alex Bennet and David Bennet (2013)

We live in a world that offers many possible futures. The ever-expanding complexity of information and knowledge provide many choices for decision-makers, and we are all making decisions every single day! As the problems and messes of the world become more complex, our decision consequences are more and more difficult to anticipate, and our decision-making processes must change to keep up with this world complexification. This book takes a consilience approach to explore decision-making in The New Reality, fully engaging systems and complexity theory, knowledge research, and recent neuroscience findings. It also presents methodologies for decision-makers to tap into their unconscious, accessing tacit knowledge resources and increasingly relying on the sense of knowing that is available to each of us.

Almost every day new energies are erupting around the world: new thoughts, new feelings, new knowing, all contributing to new situations that require new decisions and actions from each and every one of us. Indeed, with the rise of the Net Generation and social media, a global consciousness may well be emerging. As individuals and organizations we are realizing that there are larger resources available to us, and that, as complex adaptive systems linked to a flowing fount of knowing, we can bring these resources to bear to achieve our ever-expanding vision of the future. Are we up to the challenge?

Other books available from the authors and on Amazon..

Organizational Survival in the New World: the Intelligent Complex Adaptive System

by Alex and David Bennet (Elsevier, 2004), available in hard and soft formats from Amazon.

In this book David and Alex Bennet propose a new model for organizations that enables them to react more quickly and fluidly to today's fast-changing, dynamic business environment: the Intelligent Complex Adaptive System (ICAS). ICAS is a new organic model of the firm based on recent research in complexity and neuroscience, and incorporating networking theory and knowledge management, and turns the living system metaphor into a reality for organizations. This book synthesizes new thinking about organizational structure from the fields listed above into ICAS, a new systems model for the successful organization of the future designed to help leaders and managers of knowledge organizations succeed in a non-linear, complex, fast-changing and turbulent environment. Technology enables connectivity, and the ICAS model takes advantage of that connectivity by fostering the development of dynamic, effective and trusting relationships in a new organizational structure. AVAILABLE as a hardback and as an eBook FROM AMAZON.

Knowledge Mobilization in the Social Sciences and Humanities: Moving from Research to Action

by Alex Bennet and David Bennet (2007), available in hard and soft formats from Amazon.

This book takes the reader from the University lab to the playgrounds of communities. It shows how to integrate, move and use knowledge, an action journey within an identified action space that is called knowledge mobilization. Whether knowledge is mobilized through an individual, organization, community or nation, it becomes a powerful asset creating a synergy and focus that brings forth the best of action and values. Individuals and teams who can envision, feel, create and apply this power are the true leaders of tomorrow. When we can mobilize knowledge for the greater good humanity will have left the information age and entered the age of knowledge, ultimately leading to compassion and—hopefully—wisdom. AVAILABLE as an eBook FROM AMAZON

Also available in PDF format from MQIPress (US 304-799-7267 or alex@mountainquestinstitute.com) and Kindle format from Amazon.

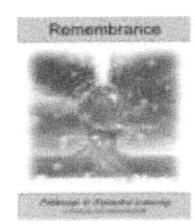

REMEMBRANCE: Pathways to Expanded Learning with Music and Metamusic®

by Barbara Bullard and Alex Bennet (2013)

Take a journey of discovery into the last great frontier—the human mind/brain, an instrument of amazing flexibility and plasticity. This eBook is written for brain users who are intent on mining more of the golden possibilities that lie inherent in each of our unique brains. Begin by discovering the role positive attitudes play in learning, and the power of self affirmations and visualizations. Then explore the use of brain wave entrainment mixed with designer music called Metamusic® to achieve enhanced learning states. Join students of all ages who are creating magical learning outcomes using music and Metamusic.® AVAILABLE as an eBook FROM AMAZON

The Journey into the Myst (Vol 1 of The Myst Series)

by Alex Bennet and David Bennet (2012)

What we are about to tell you would have been quite unbelievable to me before this journey began. It is not a story of the reality either of us has known for well over our 60 and 70 years of age, but rather, the reality of dreams and fairytales." This is the true story of a sequence of events that happened at Mountain Quest Institute, situated in a high valley of the Allegheny Mountains of West Virginia. The story begins with a miracle, expanding into the capture and cataloging of thousands of pictures of electromagnetic spheres widely known as "orbs." This joyous experience became an exploration into the unknown with the emergence of what the authors fondly call the *Myst*, the forming and shaping of non-random patterns such as human faces, angels and animals. As this phenomenon unfolds, you will discover how Drs. Alex and David Bennet began to observe and interact with the *Myst*. This book shares the beginning of an extraordinary *Journey into the Myst*. AVAILABLE as an eBook FROM AMAZON

Patterns in the Myst (Vol 2 of The Myst Series)

by Alex Bennet and David Bennet (2013)

The Journey into the Myst was just the beginning for Drs. Alex and David Bennet. Volume II of the *Myst* Series brings Science into the Spiritual experience, bringing to bear what the Bennets have learned through their research and educational experiences in physics, neuroscience, human systems, knowledge management and human development. Embracing the paralogical, patterns in the Myst are observed, felt, interpreted, analyzed and compared in terms of their physical make-up, non-randomness, intelligent sources and potential implications. Along the way, the Bennets were provided amazing pictures reflecting the forming of the *Myst*. The Bennets shift to introspection in the third volume of the series to explore the continuing impact of the *Myst* experience on the human psyche. AVAILABLE as an eBook FROM AMAZON

Made in the USA
Columbia, SC
18 January 2020